Parliament today

MANCHESTER
1824

Manchester University Press

Politics Today

Series editor: Bill Jones

Ideology and politics in Britain today
  Ian Adams
Political ideology today, 2nd edition
  Ian Adams
Scandinavian politics today   David Arter
American society today   Edward Ashbee
US politics today, 2nd edition
  Edward Ashbee
French politics today, new edition
  David S. Bell
Local government today, 3rd edition
  J. A. Chandler
Irish politics today, 4th edition
  Neil Collins and Terry Cradden
Political issues in Ireland today,
  3rd edition   Neil Collins and
  Terry Cradden (editors)
US elections today (Elections USA,
  2nd edition)   Philip John Davies
Political issues in America today
  Philip John Davies and Fredric A.
  Waldstein (editors)
British political parties today,
  2nd edition
  Robert Garner and Richard Kelly
Spanish politics today   John Gibbons
The Politics Today companion to American
  government
  Alan Grant and Edward Ashbee

European politics today, 2nd edition
  Patricia Hogwood and
  Geoffrey K. Roberts
Political issues in Britain today,
  5th edition   Bill Jones (editor)
British politics today, 7th edition
  Bill Jones and Dennis Kavanagh
Political issues in the world today
  Don MacIver
Italian politics today   Hilary Partridge
Britain in the European Union today,
  2nd edition   Colin Pilkington
The Civil Service in Britain today
  Colin Pilkington
Devolution in Britain today
  Colin Pilkington
The Politics Today companion to the British
  Constitution   Colin Pilkington
German politics today   Geoffrey Roberts
The Politics Today companion to West
  European politics   Geoffrey K. Roberts
  and Patricia Hogwood
Debates in British politics today   Lynton
  Robins and Bill Jones (editors)
Government and the economy today
  Graham P. Thomas
Russian politics today   Michael Waller
Political communication today
  Duncan Watts

Parliament today

Michael Rush

Manchester University Press
Manchester and New York

distributed exclusively in the USA by Palgrave

Published by Manchester University Press
Oxford Road, Manchester M13 9NR, UK
and Room 400, 175 Fifth Avenue, New York, NY 10010, USA
www.manchesteruniversitypress.co.uk

Distributed exclusively in the USA by
Palgrave, 175 Fifth Avenue, New York,
NY 10010, USA

Distributed exclusively in Canada by
UBC Press, University of British Columbia, 2029 West Mall,
Vancouver, BC, Canada V6T 1Z2

British Library Cataloguing-in-Publication Data
A catalogue record for this book is available from the British Library

Library of Congress Cataloging-in-Publication Data applied for

ISBN   0 7190 5794 9   *hardback*
EAN   978 0 7190 5794 6
ISBN   0 7190 5795 7   *paperback*
EAN   978 0 7190 5795 3

First published 2005

14 13 12 11 10 09 08 07 06 05   10 9 8 7 6 5 4 3 2 1

Typeset in 10/12pt Photina
by Graphiraft Limited, Hong Kong
Printed in Great Britain
by CPI, Bath

For Alex,
who prefers Thomas the Tank Engine to Parliament

Contents

List of figures, boxes and tables		*page* viii
Foreword		xiii
Acknowledgements		xiv

1	Parliament in context	1
2	The origins and development of Parliament	26
3	The functions of Parliament	57
4	Parliament and democracy	71
5	The personnel of Parliament	96
6	The professionalisation of Parliament	113
7	The organisation of business	137
8	The legislative role	166
9	The scrutiny role	202
10	Parliament and the people	241
11	Parliament and the government	268
12	Reforming Parliament	288

Sources and further reading	315
Index	328

Figures, boxes and tables

Figures

7.1	A simplified plan of the Chamber of the House of Commons	*page* 139
7.2	A simplified plan of the Chamber of the House of Lords	140
7.3	A simplified layout of a standing committee room	142
7.4	A simplified layout of a select committee room	143
7.5	A simplified layout of Westminster Hall sittings	144
7.6	'The whip': three-line, two-line and one-line whips	147
7.7	'The usual channels' in the House of Commons	153
7.8	'The usual channels' in the House of Lords	155

Boxes

1.1	The separation of powers in the United States	5
1.2	Extract from the American Declaration of Independence, 4 July 1776	7
1.3	The principal conventions of the constitution	16
2.1	The principal provisions of the Declaration of Right, 1689	38
3.1	The particular functions of the House of Lords	68
8.1	The technical scrutiny of statutory instruments (SIs)	194
8.2	Parliamentary approval of SIs	196
9.1	Opposition Day debates, 1999–2000	220
9.2	The core tasks of departmental Select Committees	234
11.1	Ministers and Parliament	271
11.2	Defining ministerial responsibility	272

Tables

1.1	Civil rights in France, the United States, Germany, the former USSR, Spain and Europe	9
1.2	Libertarian and collectivist values	10
1.3	The subject matter of written constitutions	11
1.4	The elements of the UK constitution	13
1.5	Examples of constitutional statutes	14
1.6	The privileges claimed by the House of Commons	19
1.7	Examples of authoritative constitutional texts	20
2.1	The development of Parliament: origins and early growth	28
2.2	Magna Carta: clauses 39 and 40	30
2.3	The development of Parliament: growth and challenge	35
2.4	The development of Parliament: shifting power from the monarch to the politicians	38
2.5	The development of Parliament: the growth of the party system, democratisation and executive dominance	41
2.6	The growth of government	51
2.7	Party composition of the House of Lords, 1999 and 2003	55
3.1	The functions of Parliament	59
3.2	MPs' views on the functions of Parliament	66
3.3	MPs' views on their roles	66
3.4	The three roles of the MP	67
3.5	The growth of House of Lords' activity, 1950–2000	69
4.1	Democracy: consent and control mechanisms	72
4.2	Electoral systems used in the United Kingdom	80
4.3	The relationship between seats and votes in the Scottish Parliament, the National Assembly for Wales, Northern Ireland Assembly, and UK Parliament	84
4.4	The distribution of votes and seats at general elections between 1945 and 2001	85
4.5	Two-party domination, 1945–2001	89
4.6	Party support, 1945–2001	93
5.1	The number and proportion of women MPs, 1922–2001 (selected elections)	100
5.2	The representation of economic interests in the House of Commons, 1832, 1868 and 1900	101
5.3	The educational background of MPs, 1945–97	102
5.4	The educational background of MPs, 2001	102
5.5	The occupational background of MPs, 1945–97	104
5.6	The occupational background of MPs, 2001	104
5.7	The membership of the House of Lords before and after the House of Lords Act, 1999	107

5.8	Occupational experience of life peers, 1981	109
6.1	MPs' salaries, 1912–2004 (selected years)	115
6.2	Salaries of ministers and other office-holders, 2004	117
6.3	Average hours per week spent by MPs (backbenchers and opposition frontbenchers) on parliamentary work during the parliamentary session, 1971–96	118
6.4	Age at which MPs entered and left the House of Commons and length of service, 1945–97, and 1997–2001	120
6.5	Participation in parliamentary activity, 1871–1995 (selected sessions)	122
6.6	Parliamentary activity by frontbenchers and backbenchers, 1994–95	123
6.7	Proportions of MPs and peers serving as ministers, 1900–2001	124
6.8	Attendance in the House of Lords, 1950–2002 (selected sessions)	127
6.9	MPs' allowances, 2004	130
6.10	Peers' allowances and services, 2004	133
6.11	Cost of the House of Commons and the House of Lords	134
7.1	Distribution of time and initiative of business on the floor of the House of Commons and House of Lords	138
7.2	The party whips, 2004	148
7.3	Sitting days per session, 1955–2001	157
7.4	The 1999–2000 parliamentary session	158
7.5	The distribution of business in the House of Commons and House of Lords, 1999–2000	159
7.6	The weekly and daily timetable of the House of Commons	161
7.7	Westminster Hall sittings	162
7.8	The weekly and daily timetable of the House of Lords	163
8.1	Types of legislation	168
8.2	The legislative process: the stages of a public bill	170
8.3	The success rate of government bills, 1992–2001	171
8.4	Draft bills presented to Parliament, 1997–2002	176
8.5	Government bills, 1999–2000	178
8.6	Number of amendments to government bills, 1968–69 and 1970–71	183
8.7	Number of amendments to the Broadcasting Bill, 1990	184
8.8	Amendments to government bills made in the House of Lords, 1999–2000	185
8.9	The formal timetabling of bills, 1945–2001	185
8.10	Types of Private Members' Bills	188
8.11	The success rate of Private Members' bills, 1992–2001	189
8.12	Examples of successful Private Members' bills	192
8.13	Number of statutory instruments, 1995–2002	193

8.14	Examples of statutory instruments	193
8.15	Reasons for drawing attention to SIs, 1992–2000	195
8.16	Consideration of statutory instruments by the House of Commons, 1999–2000	196
8.17	The parliamentary scrutiny of European Union documents	199
9.1	The parliamentary financial cycle: expenditure	205
9.2	The parliamentary financial cycle: taxation	209
9.3	Non-legislative scrutiny mechanisms	212
9.4	Number of parliamentary Questions answered in the House of Commons and House of Lords, 1999–2000	213
9.5	The use of parliamentary Questions by MPs, 2001–02 (%)	215
9.6	The initiative in non-legislative debates	217
9.7	Westminster Hall debates, 1999–2000	222
9.8	The growth of investigatory committees in the House of Commons (selected sessions)	226
9.9	Investigatory committees in the House of Commons, 2003	228
9.10	Investigatory committees in the House of Lords, 2003	229
9.11	The number and type of witnesses appearing before investigatory committees, 1999–2000	232
9.12	Number of meetings held and reports published by departmental committees, 1979–2000	234
9.13	Examples of select committee reports critical of government policy and administration, 1999–2002	236
9.14	How effective is Parliament in scrutinising government activity in the following areas?	237
9.15	How effective are the following mechanisms in securing information and explanations from government?	238
10.1	MPs with e-mail addresses and websites accessible to the public, 2003	246
10.2	Time spent by backbenchers on constituency and non-constituency work, 1982 and 1996 (hours per week (%))	247
10.3	Proportion of backbench MPs raising constituency issues in Parliament, 1871–1995	248
10.4	The constituency role of the Member of Parliament	252
10.5	The growth of pressure groups	256
10.6	Pressure group contacts with Parliament	258
10.7	The value of contacts with Parliament	259
10.8	Sponsored Labour MPs (selected years)	261
10.9	Backbench MPs acting as parliamentary consultants or advisers, 1975–2004	262
10.10	Agreement with the statement that 'Parliament does not have sufficient control over the executive' (selected years)	265

10.11   How much power do people want between elections
         and how much power do you think they have? (2000)   265
11.1   Ministerial resignations on the grounds of individual
         ministerial responsibility, 1945–2004   273
11.2   Individual ministerial responsibility: the absence of
         resignations   276
11.3   The suspension of collective responsibility   282
11.4   Resignations on the grounds of collective ministerial
         responsibility, 1945–2004   283
11.5   Number of rebellions by government MPs, 1945–2001   284
11.6   Number of government defeats in the House of
         Commons, 1945–2001   285
12.1   The Labour Party's manifesto commitments on
         constitutional reform, 1979–2001   289
12.2   Reforming Parliament: internal reform – a checklist   293
12.3   Reforming Parliament: external reform – a checklist   302
12.4   Public support for the use of referendums, 1995   308

Foreword

Parliament today

Parliament lies at the heart of British politics. This new edition seeks to place Parliament in wider social, historical and political context, as well as looking at its operation, taking account of the widespread changes that have taken place since the general election of 1997 and, where appropriate, drawing on the experience of other countries. It uses a wide range of academic and non-academic sources, including those published by Parliament itself. Rather than treating the House of Commons and House of Lords separately, it examines them as part of a single political institution, similar in many respects, different in others. The concluding chapter explores the question of the reform of Parliament, not only internally but in the context of wider political reform. I am grateful to Bill Jones and others who have made valuable suggestions and pointed out typographical and other errors, but I, of course, remain responsible for any that remain.

Acknowledgements

Tony Benn once remarked that politics is simple, but academics make it complicated: it isn't and they don't. Politics is a complex phenomenon, and political institutions like Parliament are complicated organisations. This complexity is seen by examining not only the internal working of Parliament but also its societal, historical and political context, which is what this new edition of *Parliament today* seeks to do. The resulting book inevitably places me in the debt of many people: to my departmental colleagues, especially Victor Wiseman, first holder of the Chair of Politics at the University of Exeter, who strongly encouraged my interest in Parliament; to the many students who took my course on Parliament, who provided much food for thought; and to my fellow-members of the Study of Parliament Group, who have greatly enriched my knowledge and understanding of Parliament. Particular debts are owed to Bill Jones, who persuaded me to write this book, to Tony Mason, the editor at MUP, without whose unfailing patience it would never have seen the light of day and to Graeme Leonard for his excellent copy-editing; above all, to Jean, my wife, who continues to tolerate me and my computer, even during retirement.

1

Parliament in context

Politics, power and parliamentary government

Politics: Who Gets What, When, How?[1]

The title of Harold Lasswell's book offers a succinct definition of politics, whether it is politics within a particular society or between societies, whether it is within the confines of a particular state or between states. Put another way, politics is about how societies seek to resolve conflicts, including conflicts with other societies. Conflicts and attempts to resolve them may involve violence or the threat of violence, but for the most part politics is conducted peacefully through mechanisms and processes developed to contain conflict and avoid or minimise any resort to violence. Indeed, for most people in most societies politics is something that other people do, not just politicians (who are often held in varying degrees of contempt), but those who belong to a political party or some other political organisation or who engage in some form of political activity, such as demonstrations, marches or sit-ins. Elections, of course, are the exception that prove the general rule and many societies hold elections, regardless of whether they see themselves or are seen as 'democratic' societies. But most people have little or no interest in politics: in richer societies they have more appealing things to do, whether at work or leisure; in poorer societies they are more concerned with the physical survival of themselves and their families.

Yet politics affects everyone, whether it does much or nothing for them. The decisions made and policies pursued by governments, regardless of type or ideological hue, have an impact on people's lives, sustaining and shaping them over time, often changing them and the society in which they live. To expand Laswell's formula: some people get more than others; some get none; some get it sooner than others, some later; how they get it varies, some fairly, some unfairly, because of who they are or who they know, or what they already have. Implicit in all this is the ultimate question for students of politics: it is not just who gets what, when, how, but also why? Two sorts of answer emerge. The first relates to the ideas and values that permeate a particular society – ideas about the nature of the human condition, about identity and status, about social relations, about the very nature of society, or even whether there is such a thing as society. In short, politics needs to be understood within the context of the society in which it operates, a matter taken up later in the chapter.

The second type of answer relates to the concept of power. Indeed, it is sometimes argued that ultimately politics is about the exercise of power. The German sociologist, Max Weber (1864–1921), defined power as 'the probability that one actor within a social relationship will be in a position to carry out his own will despite resistance, regardless of the basis on which this probability exists'.[2] For Weber, power, like politics, operates within a social context, but it can be based on a variety of resources – obviously upon force (or other forms of coercion), but also upon wealth, status, knowledge, charisma and, crucially, authority. Thus Jean-Jacques Rousseau (1712–78), argued, 'The strongest man is never strong enough to be always master unless he transfers his power into right and obedience into duty'.[3] Weber believed that power was most effective and at its most stable when it was combined with authority, the willing acceptance of the exercise of power. As with power, the basis for that authority could vary: it might, as in the divine right of kings, be god-given, or it might be conferred by hereditary tradition; it might rest on the effectiveness of a particular leader – what Weber called charisma; it might rest on the consent of the governed; it might rest on the acceptance of a set of rational-legal rules. In practice, Weber argued, authority invariably depends on a mixture, both temporally and spatially.

Authority is often regarded as synonymous with another term – legitimacy, but there is an analytical advantage in using authority to describe the basis of a particular government's use of power and legitimacy as a wider concept – the extent to which social and political norms in a given society are accepted, so that authority operates within the parameters of legitimacy. Crucially, however, both terms imply a limiting of power and one of the concerns of many political philosophers and others is how to channel or limit the use of power and, above all, how to prevent its abuse. Contract theorists, such as Thomas Hobbes (1588–1679) and John Locke (1632–1704) argued that power was exercised in return for providing protection, but whereas Hobbes argued that this was the only way to avoid anarchy and chaos, Locke argued consent was necessary, as did Rousseau, the most famous contract theorist.

Parliamentary government represents one solution to this problem. It is not the only solution available, but it is an important one, partly because it is the solution adopted in the UK and partly because it has been adopted and adapted by many other countries, notably in Europe and the former British Empire. Thus, most Western European countries and a number of those in

Central and Eastern Europe, which were formerly part of the Soviet Communist bloc, have developed or adopted some form of parliamentary government. Similarly, but not surprisingly, it is the most common form of government in the Commonwealth, not just in the obvious cases of Australia, Canada and New Zealand and, more recently, South Africa, but in many former British colonies.

In essence, parliamentary government seeks to limit and control the exercise of power by making those who hold power – the executive – directly and constitutionally responsible to the legislature. More precisely, parliamentary government is that form of government in which the executive is drawn from and constitutionally responsible to the legislature. It rests on two pillars or devices: first, the executive (or government) derives its authority or right to govern from initially securing and subsequently retaining the support or confidence of a majority of the members of the legislature; second, members of the government are accountable to the legislature for the exercise of the authority conferred upon them. In principle, therefore, the legislature may change the government in whole or part by withholding or threatening to withhold its support and it may similarly reject or modify government policy. Power is thus limited by making those who exercise it dependent upon and answerable to those from whom they derive their power. This arrangement is commonly called a fusion of powers, because, on the one hand, members of the executive are also members of the legislature and, on the other, the executive exercises its power to make laws through the legislature. In short, parliamentary government does not mean government by parliament, but government through parliament.

The idea of drawing an analytical distinction between the different areas or branches of government or the exercise of different powers – in modern terms, the executive, the legislative and the judicial – can be traced back to Aristotle, but the concept of the separation of powers – limiting the exercise of power by seeking to ensure that no one person or body of persons holds power in more than sphere – is of later origin. In the late seventeenth century John Locke, the ex post facto philosopher of the English Revolution, argued in his *Second Treatise on Government* (1689) that executive and legislative power should be separated, but the most famous exposition of the separation of powers was that of the French philosopher, the Baron de Montesquieu (1689–1755). In his most well-known work, *L'esprit des loix* (1748, translated into English 1750), Montesquieu advocated a strict separation of powers, basing his argument on his understanding of early eighteenth-century British political practice. There is, however, a double irony in Montesquieu's interpretation of the latter: on the one hand, the Act of Settlement of 1701 introduced a partial separation of powers by stipulating that ministers – the holders of executive office – could not be members of the House of Commons, but ministers and MPs quickly came to the view that this would be an inconvenient arrangement and the relevant section of the Act was repealed before it was even implemented; on the other hand, the continued combination of an executive in the form of ministers appointed by the monarch, a different institution in the form of Parliament that passed laws, and a largely independent judiciary led Montesquieu to believe that a genuine separation of powers existed in Britain. Montesquieu's importance, in fact, is the influence he, and for that matter Locke, had on the Founding Fathers of the United States, particularly James Madison (1752–1836) and Alexander Hamilton (1755–1804), the principal authors of the *Federalist Papers* (1787–88).

Britain's relations with the thirteen American colonies deteriorated after the military threat to them had been removed by the defeat of France in the Seven Years' War (1756–63). Such a deterioration was probably inevitable, as the economic interests of Britain and the colonies diverged and matters were brought to a head as Britain sought to impose taxes on the colonists, leading to the cry, 'no taxation without representation'. What began as a rebellion swiftly developed into a full-blown struggle for independence, with the American Declaration of Independence in 1776 and Britain being forced to recognise the United States in 1783. Initially, the thirteen states formed a loose confederation, but this proved unsatisfactory and a closer union was agreed with the adoption of the Constitution of the United States in 1789.

The framers of the American Constitution were much influenced by what they thought was wrong with British political arrangements at the time. Quite apart from their particular grievances over a range of policies and representation, the Founding Fathers believed that too much power was concentrated in the hands of the king, George III. They were not alone in this belief: in 1780 the House of Commons passed what became known as Dunning's motion, 'That the influence of the Crown has increased, is increasing and ought to be diminished'.[4] However, whereas Dunning and his supporters were concerned about the influence that the king and his ministers were able to exert over the House of Commons, for the Americans the ultimate problem was not the king but the policies being pursued and, at the time, those policies had the support of a majority in the Commons. Nonetheless, the Founding Fathers had a point: the concentration of power in the hands of the few could and, in their view, had, led to the abuse of power. Their solution was to disperse power by dividing it between the three branches of government, as shown in Box 1.1.

Not only were the three powers separated but so were the personnel: members of the Congress could not simultaneously hold executive or judicial posts; the President and all members of the President's Cabinet were excluded from the Congress; and members of the judiciary were similarly restricted. However, the Constitution did not provide for a complete separation of powers, since it also established a series of 'checks and balances'. Thus, the President may veto legislation passed by the Congress, although the Congress may override the presidential veto by a two-thirds majority; various presidential appointments, including members of the Cabinet, the heads of various

---

Box 1.1   The separation of powers in the United States

Constitution of the United States, 1789

Article I: All legislative Powers herein granted shall be vested in a Congress
of the United States, which shall consist of a Senate and a House of
Representatives.

Article II: The executive power shall be vested in a President of the United
States.

Article III: The judicial Power of the United States shall be vested in one
Supreme Court, and in such inferior Courts as the Congress may
from time to time ordain and establish.

Source: S. E. Finer (ed.), *Five Constitutions*, London, Penguin, 1979, pp. 91, 97, 100.

---

government agencies, and ambassadors are subject to approval by the Senate;
the President also appoints justices to the Supreme Court, but again subject to
the approval of the Senate; the Senate must also ratify any treaties concluded
by the President with foreign states; and only the Congress may declare
war. Moreover, the President, Senate and House of Representatives are elected
separately and for fixed terms of office. In addition, there are no circumstances
in which constitutionally the President can get rid of either or both Houses
of Congress in order to secure the election of a more amenable legislature and
it is only in exceptional circumstances that the Congress can get rid of the
President – by the process known as impeachment. In that process the House
of Representatives acts as prosecutor by voting on articles of impeachment
and the Senate tries the case. In fact, the House of Representatives has voted
to impeach only three Presidents, Andrew Johnson in 1868, Richard Nixon
in 1974 and Bill Clinton in 1998. Johnson survived trial in the Senate by a
single vote – two-thirds of the full Senate must vote in favour to secure a
conviction; Nixon resigned before the matter reached the Senate, but would
almost certainly have been convicted; and early in 1999 Clinton was found
not guilty on one charge and survived a second, with fifty Senators in favour
and fifty against, well short of the 67 needed. The fact that two Presidents
have faced impeachment within a period of twenty-five years suggests that it
is more likely to be used and all three cases were marked by strong partisan
views in Congress. Nevertheless, the circumstances still need to be exceptional
and impeachment remains a political weapon of last resort, hardly comparable to the ability of the House of Commons to withdraw its confidence from a
prime minister and a government, uncommon as it is in practice.

Some countries have adopted other devices to limit the use of power. A
number of Latin American states, for example, have constitutional provisions
that prevent the immediate re-election of an incumbent president, while no

Mexican president may *ever* be re-elected. France provides yet another variation: having had a parliamentary system similar to that of the UK between
1870 and 1958, in the latter year a new, hybrid parliamentary-presidential
system was adopted. On the one hand, the Prime Minister and the Cabinet
are constitutionally responsible to the National Assembly but may not be
members of it, though they may take part in debates. On the other hand,
there is also a separately elected President, who serves for a fixed term of
office, appoints the Prime Minister and shares executive powers with the Prime
Minister and Cabinet.

Politics and power go hand in hand. Individuals may seek power for a
variety of reasons – status, ego satisfaction, to accumulate wealth, advance or
defend their personal interests or those with whom they are closely associated,
but also for more altruistic reasons – to improve people's lives, to create fairer
and more just societies, to protect the weak against the strong, the poor against
the rich, and so on. Whatever their motives, people seek power to implement
whatever policies they believe will achieve their ends. There are others, however, also for a variety of reasons, often some of the same reasons, who seek
to curb and limit the exercise of power and parliamentary government,
presidential-congressional systems, and similar sets of political arrangements
are essentially devices to limit the exercise of power. But much depends on theory and practice and how these sets of political arrangements actually operate.

Theory and practice

Theory and practice are crucial to any understanding of politics. They are
crucial because politics does not operate in a vacuum but within the context
of a particular society, reflecting and responding to the prevailing ideas
and values of that society and, as ideas and values change, so does politics.
The most obvious manifestation of ideas and values is found in the form of a
state's constitution, usually written, that establishes the institutional framework within which politics operate. However, one of the most dramatic and
well-known proclamations of the values underpinning a political system
is the American Declaration of Independence (see Box 1.2), which preceded
the adoption of the United States Constitution by thirteen years.

The Declaration not only claims particular rights, which it says are 'inalienable', but also speaks of governments deriving their powers from 'the consent
of the governed' and that, in the event of the government failing to protect
them, the people have a right to change the government. Couched in these
terms these were seventeenth- and eighteenth-century ideas, influenced by
philosophers such as Locke, but in more specific terms some of them can be
traced back to medieval England – trial by jury and no deprivation of life, liberty
or property except by due process of law. Others emanated from the clash
between king and Parliament in the seventeenth century, notably that of no

---

Box 1.2   Extract from the American Declaration of Independence, 4 July 1776

We hold these truths to be self-evident, that all men are created equal, that they are endowed by their Creator with certain inalienable Rights, that among these are Life, Liberty and the pursuit of Happiness. That to secure these rights, Governments are instituted among Men, deriving their just powers from the consent of the governed. That whenever any Form of Government becomes destructive of these ends, it is the Right of the People to alter or abolish it, and to institute new Government, laying its foundations on such principles and organising its powers in such forms, as to them shall seem most likely to effect their Safety and Happiness.

Source: *Encyclopaedia Britannica CD 2000.*

---

taxation without representation. All these and more could be found in the 'Body of Liberties' adopted by the English colonists in Massachusetts in 1641. In the same year as the Declaration of Independence, Virginia adopted a Declaration of Rights. However, these ideas and such declarations were not peculiar to English jurists and philosophers or American colonists: in 1789 the French National Assembly passed the Declaration of the Rights of Man, claiming 'natural, inalienable and sacred rights' and that 'legislation is the expression of the general will', the collective view of the people, a concept developed by Rousseau. Exactly how the general will was to be elicited was not clear, but it implied popular consent and, arguably and ultimately, popular control. Among the rights claimed were those of liberty, freedom from arbitrary arrest, equality before the law, freedom of expression, and freedom of religion. Liberty was defined negatively and broadly as 'the capacity to do anything that does no harm to others. However, the only limitation on the individual's exercise of his natural rights are those which ensure the enjoyment of those same rights to all other individuals'.[5] Such statements and the specific rights claimed reflect the values of the society concerned, or, perhaps more realistically, to which it aspires. Most constitutions include a statement of values, declaration or bill of rights, although the original United States Constitution did not. However, a bill of rights was discussed during the drafting of the constitution and while it was being ratified by the various states. Furthermore, George Washington urged the adoption of a bill of rights during his inaugural address as the first President of the United States in 1789. Thus the first ten amendments to the constitution are known as the Bill of Rights and came into effect in 1791.

Precisely because constitutions in general and rights in particular reflect the prevailing values or aspirations of a society, they change over time. Some are inevitably anachronistic, resulting from particular concerns at the time the constitution or rights were promulgated. For instance, the second amendment to the American Constitution reflected the fear of a standing army and therefore sought to establish 'a well-regulated militia' by proclaiming the right of the people 'to keep and bear arms'. This did not prevent the establishment of permanent American forces and now forms the basis of resistance to efforts to strengthen gun control laws. Similarly, the third amendment forbids the billeting of troops except 'in manner to be prescribed by law' – an issue of particular concern during the American War of Independence. Again, it was not until the thirteenth Amendment, passed towards the end of the Civil War in 1865, that slavery was abolished in the United States. All illustrate the significance of changing social values. Thus, as attitudes towards rights have broadened, so the range of rights claimed has become more and more extensive. Neither the American Bill of Rights nor the Declaration of the Rights of Man addresses the rights of women. Indeed, the very title 'Declaration of Rights of Man' reflects the inferior social position of women. Both documents claimed what may be termed traditional rights, such as freedom of expression, freedom of religion, and equality before the law, but increasingly various social rights – to education, work, housing, health, and freedom from racial and sexual discrimination – were claimed. Such rights are embodied, for example, in the constitutions of the former Soviet Union, post-war Germany, Spain, and the People's Republic of China (PRC), and in the European Convention on Human Rights, as shown in Table 1.1. Furthermore, unlike its predecessor of 1936, the 1977 Soviet Constitution proclaimed rights of cultural protection, education and marriage and the family.

Some constitutions and declarations of rights not only proclaim rights but impose duties on citizens. For instance, the preamble of the Constitution of the Fourth French Republic in 1946 states that the citizen has a *duty* to work, as well as a right to employment. Similarly, the Spanish Constitution of 1978 says that citizens have a *duty* to defend Spain, pay taxes and to work (Articles 30, 31 and 35). However, much the most extensive range of duties are found in the two Soviet Constitutions (Articles 130–3, 1936 and Articles 59–69) and the Constitution of the People's Republic of China (Articles 42, 55 and 56). These reflect a self-proclaimed fundamental difference in values between 'liberal democracies' and 'socialist' societies. The former place a much greater emphasis on the importance of the individual or libertarian values, the latter on the importance of society or collectivist values (see Table 1.2).

In stressing the paramountcy of the individual, libertarianism argues that inequalities of ability and wealth are natural phenomena and should therefore be accepted, that freedom of the individual maximises their development and that rights should be concerned solely with limiting the concentration and abuse of power. Thus, economically, libertarians favour the free market and minimising the role of government. Ideally, the latter should concentrate exclusively on the maintenance of law and order and political stability. In contrast, collectivists place the welfare of society or the community before that of the individual, even if this results in some individuals suffering. Thus, power should be used to whatever extent may be necessary for the benefit of

Table 1.1   *Civil rights in France, the United States, Germany, the former USSR, Spain and Europe*

Rights	France 1789	US 1791	France 1946	Germany 1949	ECHR 1950	USSR 1977	Spain 1978	China 1982
Traditional rights								
Equality before the law	+	+	+	+	+	+	+	+
Freedom from arbitrary arrest	+	+	+	+	+	+	+	+
Freedom of association		+		+	+	+	+	+
Freedom of expression	+	+	+	+	+	+	+	+
Freedom of religion	+	+	+	+	+	+	+	+
Right to liberty	+			+	+		+	+
Prohibition of torture		+			+		+	
Right to petition		+		+		+	+	
Social rights								
Cultural protection						+		+
Right to education		+		+	+	+	+	+
Freedom of movement				+			+	
Gender discrimination		+*	+	+	+	+	+	+
Racial discrimination		+†	+	+	+	+	+	+
Right to health			+		+	+		+
Right to housing					+			
Right to life				+	+		+	
Right to marriage and a family			+	+	+	+	+	+
Right to privacy				+‡	+	+	+	+§
Right to property or protection of home				+		+		+
Right to leisure						+		+
Right to work/ occupation			+	+		+	+	+

Source: France, US, Germany and USSR: S. E. Finer (ed.), *Five Constitutions*, London, Penguin, 1979; Spain, People's Republic of China: www.uni-wuerzburg.de/law/ch00000; ECHR: Human Rights Act 1998, Schedule 1.

Notes: * Voting only (1919). † Amendments 1868, 1870 and 1964. ‡ Germany – post and telephones. § China – correspondence.

all, intervening extensively in the economy to secure the redistribution of wealth and improving everyone's quality of life, thereby justifying an active, even pervasive role for government. These values constitute the extremes of a continuum on which can be ranged various political systems according to their values. The closest to the libertarian model is the United States; the closest to the collectivist model are the People's Republic of China and the former Soviet Union. In the American case it is reflected in the claim to inalienable individual rights, the adoption of the separation of powers, and the incorporation of a series of checks and balances in the constitution. In the Chinese case it is clearly reflected in Article 51 of the Constitution: 'The

Table 1.2   *Libertarian and collectivist values*

Libertarianism	Collectivism
Importance of the individual	Importance of the community
Accepting inequality	Equality
Limiting the concentration of power	Using power for collective ends
Free market economy	Economic interventionism
Limiting the role of government	Active role of government

Source: Adapted from W. H. Greenleaf, *The British Political Tradition: Vol. 1 – The Rise of Collectivism*, London, Routledge, 1983, pp. 14–28.

exercise by citizens ... of these freedoms and rights may not infringe upon the interests of the state, of society, and of the collective'. In practice, most political systems have libertarian and collectivist strands, found in Britain in the ideological positions of the two major parties, with the Conservatives leaning towards libertarianism and Labour towards collectivism, but with both having important elements of the other strand.

How much theory accords with practice is, of course, a matter for observation and judgement. In the midst of the purges of the 1930s Stalin had a new constitution promulgated, significant sections of which were totally at odds with the reality of Soviet politics and society under his rule. On the other hand, Article 126 of that same constitution spelt out unequivocally the role of the Communist Party of the Soviet Union as 'the vanguard of the working people in their struggle to build a communist society and ... the leading core of all organisations of the people, both governmental and non-governmental'.[6] Furthermore, both the 1936 and 1977 Soviet Constitutions set out in considerable detail the institutional structures of the Soviet political system through which Stalin and his successors exercised power. Constitutions therefore matter, since they provide the institutional framework for a society's politics, setting the parameters within which the politicians operate and providing the means through which policy is determined and implemented.

Constitutions and political institutions

As already noted, most countries have written constitutions, a document setting out the basic rules of the political game and establishing the institutional framework of politics.

Table 1.3 comprises the basic provisions of six constitutions, the earliest being that of the United States, the most recent those of Spain and the People's Republic of China (itself replacing an earlier version). Although they differ significantly in the values on which they are based and the institutional framework each establishes, they also have a good deal in common. Each

Table 1.3   *The subject matter of written constitutions*

Subject matter	US (1789)	USSR (1977)	Germany (1949)	France (1958)	Spain (1978)	China (1982)
Legislature: membership	X	X	X	X	X	X
Legislature: powers	X	X	X	X	X	X
Executive: head of state	X		X	X	X	X
Executive: powers	X	X	X	X	X	X
Executive: removal	X		X	X	X	X
Exec-legis relations	X	X	X	X	X	X
Judiciary	X	X	X	X	X	X
Citizenship and rights	X	X	X	X	X	X
Amendment	X	X	X	X	X	X
Division of powers	X	X	X		X†	
Local govt	X	Extensive	Limited	Limited	Limited	Extensive
Elections*		X*	X*	X*	X*	X*
Parties		X	Limited	Limited	Limited	X

Source: France, US, Germany and USSR: S. E. Finer (ed.), *Five Constitutions*, London, Penguin, 1979; Spain, People's Republic of China: www.uni-wuerzburg.de/law/ch00000.

Notes: * Excluding electoral systems. † Spain is a quasi- or asymmetric federal system, with some regions (autonomous communities) opting for a greater powers than others e.g. Catalonia, the Basque Country.

deals explicitly with the role of the legislative, executive and judicial branches of government: the membership and powers of the legislature are defined; the choice, powers and, if necessary, removal of the executive and the relationship between the legislature and the executive are set out; and the system of courts and their jurisdiction laid down. In addition, each sets out the rights of citizens and the means by which the constitution can be amended, a process which is deliberately made more difficult than changing the normal law, thus setting the constitution above normal law. In four of the six cases, the constitution also includes details of the division of powers between national and regional governments, since three – the United States, the USSR and Germany – are federal systems and one, Spain, a quasi-federal system in which some regions have greater autonomy than others, notably Catalonia and the Basque Country. With the exception of the USSR and the PRC, the constitutions have less to say about local government, elections and, interestingly, political parties. In the Soviet and Chinese cases the crucial role of the Communist Party is written into the constitution, but the limited constitutional attention paid to parties in other cases illustrates the important fact that not all political institutions are directly the subject of constitutional law, even though they are expected to work within the political framework established by the constitution. Similarly, the details of elections, as distinct from the elective principle, are usually left to normal rather than constitutional law.

Constitutions have also become more complex over time, reflecting the growing complexity of modern societies and an ideological shift on the libertarian-collectivist scale leading to greater governmental intervention. The United States Constitution, for example, originally consisted of a mere 33 sections or articles, including the first 10 amendments comprising the Bill of Rights, totalling some 16 pages. Even including all 27 amendments, the total number of pages is only 25. The German Constitution of 1949 has 141 articles covering 70 pages, the Soviet Constitution 174 articles and 48 pages, and the Spanish 169 articles and 48 pages. The French and Chinese unitary constitutions consist of 125 articles and 30 pages and 138 articles and 32 pages respectively. Technological developments account for some of the greater length and complexity of constitutions, developments such as aviation and broadcasting, but the expansion is primarily due to governments intervening more in the affairs of society and the extension of rights from the traditional to the social.

The Constitution of the United Kingdom

Unlike most other states, the United Kingdom does not have a written or codified constitution in the sense that the rules setting up and regulating the institutional framework within which politics operates can be found in a single document, a document having a higher legal status than all other laws. The UK is not alone in this respect – neither New Zealand nor Israel have written constitutions, although it has been suggested that, with passing of the Constitution Act in 1986 and a Bill of Rights in 1990, New Zealand now has a written constitution. However, while the Constitution Act placed within a single Act of the New Zealand Parliament the provisions of various other statutes and incorporated a number of principles, it has no higher status than other laws, and significant aspects of constitutional practice in New Zealand remain the subject of constitutional conventions, which do not have the force of law. In fact, it can be argued that both Canada and Australia are closer to having written constitutions than New Zealand in that the Constitution Act, 1982 (incorporating the British North America Act, 1867 and all subsequent amending acts), and the Commonwealth of Australia Act, 1900, are subject to special amending processes, are open to legal interpretation by their respective Supreme Courts and cannot be altered at will by the Canadian or Australian Parliaments respectively. However, in both Canada and Australia, as in New Zealand, convention again plays a major and crucial part in the operation of government. Israel is a different case: at its founding in 1948 a lack of agreement about the status of religion led Israel to eschew a written constitution. Instead, a number of 'Basic Laws' setting out an institutional framework were adopted and constitutional rules were passed, but none of these laws or rules have special legal status.

Table 1.4   *The elements of the UK constitution*

Subject matter	Statute	Conven.	Custom	Royal prerog.	Auth. texts	Courts
Legislature: membership	X	X	X	X	X	X
Legislature: powers	X	X	X		X	X
Executive: head of state	X	X	X		X	
Executive: membership	X	X	X	X	X	
Executive: powers	X	X	X	X	X	X
Executive: removal		X		X	X	
Judiciary	X		X	X	X	
Citizenship and rights	X				X	X
Amendment	X	X			X	X
Division of powers	X					X
Local govt	X					
Elections	X			X		X
Parties	X	X				X

The elements of the constitution

The UK may lack a formal constitution, but it does have a discernible set of political arrangements and an institutional framework within which politics normally operates, comparable to those found in most other states (see Table 1.4). Whether it is accurate to say that Britain has no constitution can be argued semantically or substantively, but lawyers in the UK recognise constitutional law as a distinct branch of the law in the same way as they recognise criminal law, contract law, tort, administrative law, company law, employment law, competition law and so on. In practice, the constitution of the UK comprises six different elements or sources – statute law, constitutional conventions, custom, the royal prerogative, authoritative texts and the courts. To take each of these in turn.

Constitutional statutes

Over time statute law has become an increasingly important feature of the constitution. This means that substantial parts of the latter are written in the form of statutes or Acts of Parliament dealing with various aspects of matters normally included in a formal, written constitution (see Table 1.5). However, as already noted, these statutes have no special status in law: they are passed by Parliament in the same way as all other statutes, requiring only simple majority for their approval, subsequent repeal or amendment. This means that a government with an overall majority in the House of Commons can make significant changes to the constitution against strong

Table 1.5   *Examples of constitutional statutes*

Subject matter	Statutes
Legislature: membership	*House of Lords*: Life Peerages Act, 1958; Peerages Act, 1963; House of Lords Act, 1999 *House of Commons*: House of Commons Disqualification Act, 1975; House of Commons Disqualification (Removal of Clergy Disqualification), 2001
Legislature: powers	Parliament Acts, 1911 and 1949; European Communities Act, 1972
Executive: head of state	Act of Settlement, 1700; Royal Marriages Act, 1772; Regency Acts, 1937–53; Royal Titles Act, 1953
Executive: membership	Ministers of the Crown Act, 1937; House of Commons Disqualification Act, 1975; Ministerial and Other Salaries Act, 1975; Ministerial Salaries Act 1997
Executive: powers	Many Acts of Parliament conferring on ministers the power to implement particular policies
Judiciary	Appellate Jurisdiction Act, 1876; Superior Court of Judicature (Consolidation) Act, 1925
Citizenship and rights	Habeas Corpus Act, 1679; British Nationality Act, 1981; Data Protection Act, 1998; Human Rights Act, 1998; Freedom of Information Act, 2000
Division of powers	Scotland Act, 1998; Wales Act, 1998, Northern Ireland Act, 1998
Local government	Local Government Act, 1972; Local Government Finance Act 1991; Regional Development Agencies Act, 1998; Greater London Authority Act, 1999; Local Government Act, 2000
Elections	Successive Representation of the People Acts since 1832; European Elections Act, 1999
Parties	Political Parties, Elections and Referendums Act, 2000

opposition from other parties. The introduction of life peerages by a Conservative government in 1958, for instance, was opposed by Labour. Similarly, devolution for Scotland and Wales was opposed by the Conservatives in 1998. Moreover, by using the Parliament Acts of 1911 and 1949, a government can overcome the opposition of the House of Lords, as the Labour government did in 1999 with the European Elections Act. Indeed, the 1949 Act was itself passed using the 1911 Parliament Act to outflank opposition in the Lords. That said, what can be changed easily procedurally, may be less easy, even impossible, to change politically. This is clearly illustrated by the example of devolution: what Parliament has given, it may take away, as was shown by the suspension of the devolved arrangements for Northern Ireland and the imposition of direct rule from Westminster and Whitehall in 1972, but it took extreme circumstances to bring this about. Politically, the revocation of devolution for Scotland and Wales is likely only if either or both of these parts of the UK were to request it, an eventuality that does not seem very likely.

Conventions of the constitution

Constitutional conventions are the second and crucial element of the constitution (see Box 1.3). They are rules of political practice which have no legal force but which are regarded as binding by those engaged in political activity. They are the informal rules of the political game, without which the political system could not operate effectively. It is, however, misleading to assume that they are a peculiarly British phenomenon; most political systems have conventions or informal rules because they are necessary. In the United States, for example, technically the President is not directly elected but indirectly elected by an electoral college consisting of delegates from each state. The original intention was the states would send sensible and experienced delegates who would choose the most 'suitable' person to be President and the next most 'suitable' person to be Vice-President. However, with the rapid development of political parties, it became the convention that delegates normally cast their votes in accordance with the majority popular vote in their state. Similarly, George Washington set a precedent by refusing to serve more than two terms as President, a precedent that became a convention, until it was broken by Franklin D. Roosevelt in 1940, when he was elected for a third term as President (and again upon his re-election in 1944). This led to the passing of a constitutional amendment in 1952, limiting a President to two full terms in office in his or her own right. What makes the UK different, and to a significant degree countries like Canada, Australia, India and New Zealand – all based on the Westminster model, of course, is that conventions play a much more important role in their political arrangements. However, because they are not matters of law but of practice, conventions can be broken or at very least become a matter of dispute. For example, it is a convention that, if the governing party is defeated in a general election and the opposition party wins a majority of seats in the House of Commons, the Prime Minister should resign and the Queen should invite the leader of the new majority party to for a government. This is precisely what happened in 1945 and 1964, when Conservative governments were defeated and Labour won parliamentary majorities, and in 1951 and 1970, when Labour governments were defeated and the Conservatives won majorities. In February 1974, however, the Conservative Prime Minister, Edward Heath, was defeated at the polls in the sense that the Conservative

Box 1.3   The principal conventions of the constitution

Conventions are rules of political practice that have no legal force but are widely accepted as binding by those engaged in political activity.

1   The Queen must invite the leader of the political party with an absolute majority of seats in the House of Commons to accept the office of Prime Minister and form a government. In the event of no party having an overall majority, the leader of the party most likely to be able to form a coalition government or a minority government must be invited to take office as Prime Minister.

2   The government continues in office only so long as it retains the confidence of a majority of the members of the House of Commons. If the government is defeated on a vote of confidence or a major issue of government policy, the Prime Minister must resign or advise the Queen to dissolve Parliament to allow a general election to take place.

3   The Queen must normally agree to the Prime Minister's request for a dissolution of Parliament.

4   The Queen must accept the advice of the Prime Minister in appointing members of the government.

5   The twenty or so leading members of the government constitute the Cabinet, which is in effect the active committee of the Queen's Privy Council.

6   The Queen must exercise her legal powers in accordance with the advice of the Prime Minister and the Cabinet, whose advice is expected to be unanimous.

7   The Queen must give her assent to any bill passed by the two Houses of Parliament or by the House of Commons under the terms of the Parliament Acts 1911 and 1949.

8   All members of the government must normally be members of either the House of Commons or the House of Lords, any exceptions being either temporary or exceptional. The Prime Minister and the Chancellor of the Exchequer must be members of the House of Commons.

9   Parliament must meet annually to authorise public expenditure and to approve the raising of additional taxes to meet such expenditure.

10   Proposals for public expenditure or the raising of revenue may only be made by a minister in and must be approved by the House of Commons.

11   Ministers are bound by the decisions of the Cabinet and are collectively responsible to Parliament for the conduct of affairs.

12   Ministers are individually responsible to Parliament for the formulation and implementation of policy.

13   Parliamentary business in each of the two Houses and between the Houses is arranged informally by representatives of the government and the opposition through what are euphemistically known as 'the usual channels'.

14   The Speaker should act impartially in presiding over the House of Commons and protect the rights of minorities in the House.

15   Political parties are represented on parliamentary committees in proportion to their numbers in each House.

Party lost the majority it had held since 1970, but no other party had an overall majority, although Labour had four more seats than the Conservatives. Heath did not resign immediately but discussed with the then Liberal Leader, Jeremy Thorpe, the possibility of continuing in office as a minority government or forming a coalition government with the Liberals. In the event, no agreement was reached: Heath resigned and the Labour Leader, Harold Wilson, formed a minority Labour government. Some constitutional commentators took the view that Heath should have resigned as soon as it became clear that he had lost the election, that his appeal for a renewed mandate had failed, even though no other party had an overall majority. In short, they argued that he was constitutionally obliged to resign, but they could do no more than express their opinion. No legal remedy was available to them or anyone else, although the Queen could have dismissed Heath, but that would almost certainly have led to arguments that she had acted unconstitutionally. In fact, constitutional opinion was divided; others argued that Heath was entitled to seek an accommodation with the Liberals and that the convention only required him to resign once it was clear that such an accommodation was not forthcoming.

It is for similar reasons that it is difficult to say exactly when a precedent or series of precedents becomes a convention. It is now clearly a convention that the Prime Minister must be a member of the House of Commons rather than the House of Lords. The last member of the upper house to be Prime Minister was Lord Salisbury who retired from office in 1902. However, in 1923 and 1940 peers were again serious contenders for the office, although in 1940 Lord Halifax, the peer in question, took the view that not being a member of the Commons would make his position as premier difficult. Even then, his view was much influenced by the fact that Britain was at war with Germany and his view might have been different had it been peacetime. The attitude of the Labour Party played an important part in 1940, since many of its members favoured the abolition of the House of Lords and, in any case, felt strongly that the Prime Minister should be directly answerable to the popularly elected lower house. A much stronger factor, however, was the presence of a formidable rival to Halifax in the person of Winston Churchill. Yet by 1957, when Harold Macmillan succeeded Sir Anthony Eden as Prime Minister, no peer was seriously considered and, in 1963, when Macmillan himself resigned, it was taken for granted that two of the contenders, Lord Hailsham and Lord Hume, would need to disclaim their peerages in order to be eligible, a course of action open to them but not to Halifax in 1940.

The principal conventions listed in Box 1.3 make it abundantly clear just how significant conventions are to the functioning of the British political system. No doubt many, even most of them, could be written down and incorporated in a formal constitution. In practice, however, the application of formal rules would still be open to interpretation, but that interpretation would ultimately be the task of the courts under the process of judicial review. Not only would the courts play a much more important role in the operation of the constitution, but they would have the power to declare actions (or, indeed, failure to act) unconstitutional, a concept with no meaning in British law. A written or codified constitution would thus mean that constitutional law would have a higher status than other law and could normally be changed only by a special process deliberately designed to make amendment of the constitution more difficult than changing any other laws by, for example, requiring amendments to be approved by a national referendum or by a specified majority in the legislature.

Custom and the royal prerogative

Custom and the royal prerogative are the oldest elements of the constitution and both are closely connected with constitutional conventions and the role of the courts. Early English law developed largely on the basis of precedents set by judgements in the courts, so that judges take into account the decisions made in earlier, comparable cases. This is the basis of the English common law tradition, but over time many common law matters have been incorporated into statute law or become the subject of conventions. However, the royal prerogative, that is, the formal powers of the monarch, is regarded as part of the common law, but it too is subject to constitutional convention, whether in the summoning or dissolution of Parliament, the appointment or dismissal of ministers, or the giving of the royal assent to bills. In practice, in most cases the royal prerogative is exercised by ministers, which illustrates how the monarchy has been transformed over time from an active executive to a largely ceremonial head of state and from a feudal monarchy to a constitutional monarchy, with power passing from the monarch and a few close advisers to mostly elected politicians. This process was largely complete by the end of the eighteenth century and enabled Walter Bagehot, a prominent writer and commentator in the mid-nineteenth century, to describe the role of the monarchy as 'a dignified part' of the constitution. Even though most ministerial powers are now derived from Acts of Parliament, so that the royal prerogative is limited in scope, some of the areas it covers remain crucially important. Furthermore, areas in which ministers exercise the royal prerogative are not subject to parliamentary approval, notably in foreign affairs (including the declaration of war), the granting of honours, the granting of pardons, and the appointment of bishops of the Church of England, though this does not mean that they cannot be subject to parliamentary scrutiny. The symbiotic relationship between the monarchy and Parliament is encapsulated in the opening words of most Acts of Parliament: 'Be it enacted by the Queen's Most Excellent Majesty, by and with the consent of the Lords Spiritual and Temporal, and Commons, in this present Parliament assembled, and by the authority of the same, as follows'.

Custom is now less important than the royal prerogative, but it retains some significance, particularly in relation to Parliament. This is illustrated by the authority accorded to Erskine May's *Treatise on the Law, Privileges, Proceedings and Usage of Parliament*, first published in 1844. Sir Thomas Erskine May was Clerk of the House of Commons from 1871 to 1886, but had already established himself as an authority on Parliament long before becoming Clerk. His *Treatise* has been updated and revised at regular intervals by his successors as Clerk and has become 'the parliamentary Bible'. Another important example of custom is the House of Commons' claim to a number of privileges, dating from medieval and Tudor times (see Table 1.6):

Table 1.6   *The privileges claimed by the House of Commons*

Privilege	Comment
1 The right to regulate its own proceedings	Remains crucial in controlling the operation of the House and in devising appropriate procedures and practices
2 The right to punish Members and 'strangers' (non-Members) for breach of privilege and contempt	Remains important in ensuring that MPs and others observe the rules of the House, including securing evidence for its committees
3 The right to control finance and initiate financial legislation	Historically crucial and remains important as a basis of parliamentary scrutiny
4 The right of the Commons to regulate its own composition	Historically important to prevent the 'packing' of Parliament, but remains important in setting the dates of by-elections and disciplining MPs, including expulsion
5 The right of impeachment	Historically important in dealing with ministers and others who defied the House, but not used since 1805
6 The Crown will place the best construction on the deliberations of the Commons	Historically important, but no longer significant
7 Freedom of speech and debate	Historically crucial, but still important in enabling MPs to express views and make comments during parliamentary proceedings without fear of being sued
8 Freedom from arrest	Protected MPs against civil arrest (e.g. for debt), but no longer significant
9 Access of the Commons to the monarch through the Speaker	Historically important, but no longer significant

Source: Thomas Erskine May, *Treatise on the Law, Privileges, Proceedings and Usage of Parliament*, ed. Sir William McKay, London, LexisNexis, 23rd edn, 2004, chs 5–7.

Historically, these privileges played a major part in the development of the Commons, reflecting, on the one hand, a determination to secure some control over the exercise of power and, on the other, the need to protect its members from control by the executive. Their contemporary importance, however, centres on the extent to which the House of Commons continues to exert control over its membership and operation.

Authoritative texts

Custom is also linked to the penultimate element of the constitution – authoritative texts (see Table 1.7). Some of these date from medieval times, but some are as recent as the nineteenth century. As already noted, the most important is Erskine May, but to this could be added the House of Lords' *Companion to the Standing Orders*, a guide to the procedure and practices of the upper house. On the one hand, such texts are important in providing guidance in the application of constitutional conventions and, on the other, play a vital but more mundane role in the day-to-day operation of Parliament.

The courts

The courts not only played a crucial role in the development of the common law but continue to play an important part through the process of judicial

Table 1.7   *Examples of authoritative constitutional texts*

Author	Title	Date
Henry de Bracton	On the Laws and Customs of England	1250
Sir Anthony Fitzherbert (lawyer and judge)	The Great Abridgement (a digest of legal cases)	1514
Sir Edward Coke (lawyer and judge)	Institutes of the Laws of England	1628–44
Sir William Blackstone (lawyer and jurist)	Commentaries on the Laws of England	1765
John Hatsell (Clerk of the House of Commons, 1768–1820)	Precedents of Proceedings in the House of Commons	1781
Sir Thomas Erskine May (Clerk of the House of Commons, 1871–86)	Treatise on the Law, Privileges, Proceedings and Usage of Parliament	Successive editions since 1844
A. V. Dicey (jurist)	An Introduction to the Law of the Constitution	1885 (1st edn)

review – interpreting statutes in the light of the actions of ministers and others in authority. The role of the courts in this respect has grown considerably since the 1960s, when the number of cases of judicial review numbered less than a thousand, but by 2000 the number had risen to over four thousand. Moreover, the significance of judicial review has increased further with the incorporation of the European Convention on Human Rights into British law by the Human Rights Act, 1998. Before then, the Convention had no force in law, but the courts recognised any rulings involving UK citizens made by the European Court of Human Rights in Strasbourg and there was a judicial assumption that, as the UK was a signatory to the Convention, Parliament would not knowingly legislate in contravention of it.

Parliamentary supremacy

The absence of a written constitution also means that Parliament in the form of Queen, Lords and Commons is constitutionally supreme or sovereign. Put simply, this means that constitutionally and legally Parliament can pass any law it likes and cannot be overruled. More starkly, it means that a government with majority support in the House of Commons can pass any legislation it chooses, subject only to the agreement of the House of Lords and even the latter's opposition can be overcome by using the Parliament Acts of 1911 and 1949. In practice, of course, the supremacy of Parliament is subject to the realities of politics. The Bill of Rights, 1689, for example, claims jurisdiction over France, even though English control of France had not been a reality since the middle of the fifteenth century. The signing of many treaties involves a limitation on sovereignty, none more than the Treaty of Rome, whose signing preceded Britain's accession to the European Economic Communities – now the European Union (EU). Here again the courts come into play, because the European Communities Act, 1972, gives precedence to EU law over UK law. Yet in a legal sense Parliament's sovereignty remains intact, in that the European Communities Act could be repealed, just like any other act, as some opponents of British membership of the EU strongly desire. That this is within Parliament's constitutional capacity cannot be doubted; how likely it is to happen is another matter entirely. By joining the EU the UK accepted a limit on what Parliament could do in practice and the same could be said about the legislation passed by Parliament devolving power and authority to Scotland, Wales and Northern Ireland. As actually happened in the case of Northern Ireland, what Parliament can legally give, it can legally take away, but only in circumstances that make it politically feasible to do so – parliamentary supremacy is ever tempered by political reality.

   What parliamentary supremacy illustrates most crucially is the importance of attitudes, particularly those of the politicians. The overwhelming majority of politicians operate within the institutional framework established by the constitution; they accept the rules of the political game. They may, of course, seek to alter those rules – membership of the EU and devolution both involved significant changes in the political system, but they were brought about within and using the rules of the game, even though they did amend them in the process. There are others, however, who wish not only to change the political system but are prepared to do so by means that lie outside the normal rules, in particular by resorting to violence. Violence itself, while usually illegal, has from time to time been used by those objecting to particular policies or situations, sometimes in combination with other illegal but peaceful activities, such as sit-ins, obstruction, trespass and so on. The long struggle for women's suffrage is a case in point, but once their particular objective has been achieved the normal rules of the game are again accepted, whereas those who use violence to bring about fundamental change to the political system tend to be seen in a different light. A political system can only survive so long as most of those living under that system accept or tolerate it, at worst believing that opposition is useless, and parliamentary government is no exception.

Parliament and the constitution

Whatever limitations, self-imposed by membership of the EU, devolution or the acceptance of the rules of the game, a British Prime Minister is a particularly powerful figure within the context of the UK Constitution. The absence of a written or codified constitution and the supremacy of Parliament make a Prime Minister with majority support in the House of Commons more powerful within the context of the British political system than is the President of the United States within the context of the American political system. Of course, this is partly due to the fact that the United States is a federal system, so that some matters are the responsibility of the states rather than the government in Washington. However, the President is also limited in his exercise of power by the Congress and the system of checks and balances. Thus, Prime Ministers in parliamentary systems, even those which are also federal systems, such as Australia, Canada and Germany, are more powerful within their own political systems than American presidents, however different the situation may be on the world stage. Even a Prime Minister lacking a parliamentary majority has greater powers of legislative initiative and control than the President.

Parliament, parties and the adversary system

Much of the power of presidents and prime ministers rests, however, on the nature of the party system. As it happens, the United States, like many parliamentary systems, has a two-party system in the sense that national politics is dominated by two large political parties, even though there may be other, smaller parties represented in the legislature. But parties in parliamentary systems tend to be more cohesive, with members of the legislature almost always voting with their parties, whereas the two major parties in the United States, the Democrats and the Republicans, are less cohesive and cross-voting is more common than in parliamentary systems. This places the President at a further disadvantage: even when the same party controls the Congress as well as the Presidency, there is no guarantee that the President's legislative programme will be approved by the Congress, a situation applying as much to the budget as to any other legislation, if not more so. Were American parties much more cohesive, the situation might be different, in spite of the separation of powers, as has been the case in a number of countries that have US-style presidential-congressional systems. The Philippines under the regime of Ferdinand Marcos illustrates this only too well, as does the experience of several Latin American countries.

Parties matter; they form a crucial part of the context within which the constitution operates. In the UK the two major parties – Conservative and Liberal and then Conservative and Labour – form the basis of what has been called the adversary system. This is the institutionalisation of parliamentary government into government and opposition. Parliament operates on the basis that not only is the government drawn from and responsible to Parliament, but that it is confronted in Parliament by a formally constituted opposition which offers itself as an alternative government. Parliament is organised almost entirely on this dichotomy between government and opposition: apart from a small amount of time made available to backbench MPs and peers, all parliamentary time is at the disposal of either the government or the opposition. The business of Parliament is informally arranged between government and opposition through what are euphemistically known as 'the usual channels'. Physically the two houses are divided into government and opposition benches, with ministers facing and confronting the opposition's 'shadow ministers'. The leader of the principal opposition party in the Commons is known as the Leader of Her Majesty's Opposition and, along with the opposition chief whip and two colleagues, is paid an official salary. Similar arrangements operate in the Lords.

Parliamentary business is conducted on the adversary basis of government versus opposition: the government present its proposals, the opposition criticises them; the government and its supporters defend them, the opposition and its supporters offer further criticism; and so on. Sometimes the initiative is in the hands of the opposition, but debate is conducted in the same fashion. Speakers are called from alternate sides, although some allowance is made for the views of parties other than those forming the government and the official opposition.

The institutionalisation of government and opposition in the form of the adversary system is not peculiar to the UK; it can be found in Australia, Canada and New Zealand – all based on the Westminster model. It is less common in other European countries, however: governmental control of the agenda is comparable and the main opposition party has a considerable input, but is not necessarily institutionalised to the same extent and smaller parties generally have a proportionate share of parliamentary time. To varying degrees this reflects different party systems, resulting in coalition rather than single-party governments being the norm in many cases. In the UK the adversary system operates within the context of a strongly cohesive party system, in which the two major parties seek parliamentary majorities in their own right, accept minority governments only when circumstances dictate, and abhor coalitions. Since 1868 elections have mostly produced single-party majorities and both major parties normally have had a reasonable expectation of winning office at the next general election. Neither party therefore regards itself or is generally regarded as 'the party of government' or 'the party of opposition'. Both therefore have a vested interest in the adversary system, in the prevailing constitutional arrangements, and in the way in which parliamentary government operates in the UK.

Parliament, power and authority

Politics is ultimately about the exercise of power, but most politics is about the exercise of power with authority and Parliament lies at the centre of authority in the UK, but that does not mean that Parliament lies at the centre of power. Governments collectively and ministers individually derive their authority from Parliament, an authority centred primarily on the House of Commons rather than the House of Lords. Power, however, is mostly exercised by the government and Parliament has the dual role, on the one hand, of granting authority to the government and legitimising its policies and, on the other, of scrutinising the exercise of that authority. The government's power rests on its ability to control the Commons through party, but to conclude that it is the majority party that normally wields power is to misunderstand the nature of party politics. Just as the government largely controls Parliament, so the party leadership normally controls its party, whether in government or opposition. Neither parties nor Parliament govern: party government means government by the leader of the majority party and his or her principal supporters; parliamentary government means government through, not by, Parliament.

Notes

1   Harold Lasswell, *Politics: Who Gets What, When, How?*, Chicago, McGraw-Hill, 1936.
2   Max Weber, *The Theory of Social and Economic Organisation* (trans. A. M. Henderson, ed. T. Parsons), New York, The Free Press, 1947, p. 152.

3 Jean Jacques Rouseau, *The Social Contract*, London, J. M. Dent, 1913 (trans. with an introduction by G. D. H. Cole), p. 6 (originally published 1762).
4 *Parliamentary History*, London, T. C. Hansard, 21 April 1780, cc. 340–74.
5 *Declaration of the Rights of Man*, Article 4, cited in S. E. Finer (ed.), *Five Constitutions*, London, Penguin, 1979, pp. 269–70.
6 Cited in Finer, *Five Constitutions*, p. 139.

2

The origins and development of Parliament[1]

Introduction

Parliamentary government in Britain is the product of a long and complex historical process. It has no clearly defined origins and its development was not continuous, or regular, or inevitable. The political system could have developed differently: absolute rather than constitutional monarchies, tyrannies rather than republics and authoritarian rather than libertarian regimes are more typical of the European historical experience. The English Parliament was the exception rather than the rule in surviving the vicissitudes of medieval Europe to become a major force in the state and to challenge successfully the power of the monarchy. Elsewhere in Europe the fate of similar institutions was more commonly swift demise or lingering impotence.

As political institutions, Parliament, the Cabinet and the Prime Minister nowadays have such an aura of permanence that their existence and continuance are taken for granted. Members of Parliament, Cabinets and Prime Ministers come and go, but the institutions live on and it is easy to extend this aura of permanence backwards and forwards in time. The history of parliamentary government, however, is not one of steady growth or progression from feudal origins to democracy: such a view is more than misleading; it is a distortion of history. The development of parliamentary government was neither steady nor uncheckered. There can be no certainty that parliamentary government would have been the same, or in some cases, even survived, if a number of medieval kings had not found themselves in conflict with their feudal inferiors, or if: Richard III had won the Battle of Bosworth; Henry VIII had not embarked on the English Reformation; Charles I had won the Civil War; James II's army had not deserted him in 1688; the first two Georges had been more interested in British affairs; the Thirteen Colonies had lost the

American War of Independence; the Reform Bill of 1832 and subsequent extensions of the franchise had not been passed; the first Home Rule Bill had been passed in 1886; the Liberal Party had not concluded an electoral pact with the Labour Representation Committee in 1903; the Liberals had not split in 1916, or if the alternative vote had been adopted in 1931. It is too early to say with certainty what the longer-term impact of setting up the Scottish Parliament and the National Assembly for Wales in 1999 will be, but already their impact on Scottish and Welsh politics has been significant and may well be the first step to a federal United Kingdom. At very least, devolution has created two mini-parliamentary systems, one in Scotland and one in Northern Ireland, and a quasi-parliamentary system in Wales.

The history of parliamentary government in the UK has been one of the adaptation and re-adaptation of existing institutions rather than the creation of new ones. There were constitutional experiments between 1649 and 1660. However, these were not attempts to make a total break with the past, but rather to build on what were regarded as the desirable features of the political system and eradicate its undesirable features; in short, to build on the past, not to abandon it. Similarly, devolution involves adapting existing institutions to regional government, not creating entirely new ones.

The modern picture of parliamentary government also gives it a unity which it lacks historically. The very concept of responsible government rests on the constitutional dependency of the executive on the legislature, and ministers are not only responsible to Parliament, but drawn from it. Historically, however, the executive, legislature and judiciary operated separately in many respects and responsible government is a relatively modern concept. Similarly, although early parliaments clearly involved the idea of representative government, it is misleading to equate representation with democracy. Quite apart from arguments about the meaning of democracy, early parliamentarians did not regard themselves as democrats, nor did they think in democratic terms.

None of this should be taken to mean that, like Topsy, parliamentary government 'just growed': no period has been without its political philosophers, whether they sought to vindicate the existing state of affairs, prescribe remedies for the ills of society, justify the need for fundamental change, or posit utopian ideals. Neither have kings, statesmen, politicians and others active in politics been devoid of opinions, whether based on prejudice or principle. It is commonly said that British history and politics are characterised by a strong tendency to pragmatism, but even pragmatism is a response to opinions and ideas, right or wrong, wise or foolish. Social and political institutions are products of the ideas and values of those who create the institutions. The extent to which those same ideas and values are accepted by others in society and by subsequent generations and therefore the extent to which institutions are accepted is something that varies over space and time.

Origins and early development

It is not difficult to trace back various executive, legislative and judicial elements of the modern system of parliamentary government in the UK to Norman times and, in some cases, to Anglo-Saxon England (see Table 2.1). The significance of this is twofold: first, some offices or institutions can be traced back quite specifically to a particular period and, second, and much more important, it is possible to trace back ideas which were of vital importance to the development of parliamentary government. Thus the title of chancellor can be traced back to the reign of Edward the Confessor (1042–66) and the office of Chancellor of the Exchequer to the reign of Henry I (1100–35), while many parts of the modern judicial system go back to the time of Henry II (1154–89) and earlier. Similarly, Parliament itself is commonly traced back to Simon de Montfort's Parliament of 1265, but the use of some sort of representative body or national assembly goes back to the Anglo-Saxon *Witanagemot*.

Table 2.1   *The development of Parliament: origins and early growth*

Date/period	Development
Pre-1066	Witanagemot
Post-1066	Curia Regis
1213	John summoned territorial representatives to attend Councils at St Albans and Oxford
1215	Magna Carta
1254	Council at Westminster to advise Henry III on finance: two knights summoned from each shire
1264	De Montfort's first Parliament: four knights summoned from each shire
1265	De Montfort's second Parliament: two knights from each shire, two citizens from each city and two burgesses from each borough.
1275	Edward I's first parliament
1295	The 'Model Parliament'
1297	Confirmation of the Charters (i.e. Magna Carta and the Charter of the Forests (1217)) by Edward I and that the consent of Parliament was necessary for additional taxation presented to a Parliament for that purpose
1341	Separation of Lords and Commons
1348	Commons claims redress of grievances before supply
1362	Established by statute that Commons must assent to lay taxation
1376	First use of impeachment
1407	Henry IV acknowledges that taxation is subject to the assent of the Commons

Such historical threads, though sometimes tortuous, are of great import-ance. However, the ideas that lay behind these offices or institutions are of much greater importance. In general, they reflect, on the one hand, a desire to establish and maintain effective government and, on the other, to impose limits on the exercise of political power. The creation of an efficient system for the administration of justice contributed to both these aims, but a judicial system alone was not regarded as a sufficient guarantee that power would not be abused.

Anglo-Saxon and Norman societies both recognised a relationship of mutual obligation between rulers and ruled. In the Anglo-Saxon case this was through the practice of *commendation* – the submission of a freeman to a lord in return for the lord's protection – and the similar relationship between thegns and other ranks of nobility and the king. The systematic extension of feudalism in England under the Normans made this relationship much more complex and formalised. Feudal society was rooted in land tenure and all land was held as a fief from a superior lord to whom the landholder owed allegiance, thus creating a clearly defined societal hierarchy, at the head of which was the king. The earlier concepts of protection and service remained, but the relationship between rulers and ruled was governed by more detailed and specific rules.

The existence of such rules is no guarantee against arbitrary government, but it does make attempts to resist arbitrary government easier, especially if institutions designed to enforce the rules and to settle matters of dispute have been established. The power of early monarchs was considerable, sometimes exercised in an arbtitary manner, but far from absolute. Beginning in the reign of William I (1066–87), the first of the Norman kings, the *Curia Regis* – originally a feudal assembly of the king's tenants-in-chief or vassals – met three times a year, partly though not exclusively, for the purpose of acting as a court of law. In addition, William I (in 1086) and Henry I (in 1116) held great assemblies of all tenants-in-chief at Salisbury, confirming the feudal relationship.

The meetings of the *Curia Regis* or the Moots of Salisbury should not be regarded in any sense as early parliaments, but they can quite properly be seen as precedents for the *possible* development of Parliament. Moreover, though not directly descended from the Anglo-Saxon *Witanagemot* – in theory the national assembly of freemen, but in practice a more restricted body – these meetings amounted to a continuation of an earlier tradition. It was also during the reign of the Norman kings and their Angevin successors that the foundations of the English judicial system were laid. Together with the creation of machinery to enforce the rules governing the relationship between rulers and ruled and to settle disputes, the significance of these early events lies in the credence they gave to what later became known as the *rule of law*. Thus, in the words of Bracton, a thirteenth-century lawyer, 'the king himself ought not to be subject to man but subject to God and to the law, because the law makes him king'.

The nature of feudalism, the creation of some socio-political machinery and the concept of the rule of law, however, were not sufficient conditions for the development of parliamentary government, even in the most rudimentary form. The meeting of the king with his feudal inferiors and the executive and judicial institutions established at the time served, and were intended to serve, essentially *feudal* purposes. Even Magna Carta, hailed in later times as a cornerstone, even the very foundation of English liberty, was and is essentially feudal document concerned with the detailed working of feudalism, a reassertion of the contractual relationship between the king and his vassals. This is not to say that Magna Carta has no wider constitutional significance, but merely that in the context of its time its purpose was feudal not libertarian. Nonetheless, it is possible to discern the seeds of parliamentary government in these developments, not so much in terms of clearly defined precedents, as in a number of avenues that might be explored if and when serious conflict between rulers and ruled developed.

From time to time such conflicts occurred, but the most serious occurred in the reign of John (1199–1216) culminating in the signing of Magna Carta in 1215. Apart from its immediate feudal significance, Magna Carta surpasses earlier charters issued by monarchs on their coronation in that it was an unequivocal declaration of opposition to arbitrary monarchy and sought to devise machinery to control the king through the appointment of twenty-five barons to supervise his actions. In the context of the time these were developments of great importance, especially as an assertion of the rule of law, but Magna Carta is revered above all else as a symbol of English liberty, notably as a result of the provisions contained in clauses 39 and 40 (see Table 2.2).

These two clauses illustrate the nature of Magna Carta: their immediate intention was feudal, but their historical and constitutional significance is both symbolic and particular – symbolic as a basis for liberty and particular as a basis (accurate or otherwise) for such devices as habeas corpus and trial by jury. Perhaps of even greater interest from a political point of view, and a further illustration of the substantially pragmatic nature of the charter, is the provision that in determining what action they should take at any

Table 2.2   *Magna Carta: clauses 39 and 40*

Cl. no.	Text
39	No free man shall be taken or imprisoned or disseised, or outlawed, or exiled, or anyways destroyed; nor will we go upon him, unless by the lawful judgement of his peers, or by the law of the land
40	To none will we sell, to none will we deny or delay, right or justice

Source: *Taswell-Langmead's English Constitutional History*, ed. T. F. T. Plucknett, London, Sweet & Maxwell, 11th edn, 1960, p. 80.

future date, the twenty-five barons should follow the opinion of a majority of those present – an early English assertion of the concept of majority rule. Yet it was only an idea, a practical response to the immediate problem of curbing the arbitrary actions of the king and not an assertion of a great principle, that the right and proper way to determine a course of action was to follow the view of the majority. Thus, to trace back unerringly the concept of majority rule to Magna Carta, especially linking it to ideas about democracy is inaccurate and obscures the real significance of its presence in the charter. Quite apart from the fact that majority rule has more ancient antecedents than Magna Carta, the significance of its presence is that it was in the minds of those who framed the charter and constituted yet another seed which might or might not germinate into something of constitutional and political importance.

Similarly, important as it was in breaking new ground, Magna Carta was far from unique: the issuing of charters was a common practice stretching back to the reign of William I and earlier; many towns found charters a useful means of establishing and extending their rights; while foreign precedents for Magna Carta can be found in Germany and north-western Spain and Magna Carta itself predates a similar Hungarian charter by only a few years. It is perhaps ironical that it was originally called the 'Great Charter' because of its size rather than its importance, since long before its feudal significance had disappeared and before it assumed its major role as a symbol of English liberty, Magna Carta had become a symbol of legitimacy.

Legitimacy in medieval England illustrates Weber's three 'ideal types' of tradition, charisma and rational-legal authority:[2] the very existence of the monarchy rested heavily on tradition; a number of medieval kings undoubtedly possessed charisma; and the feudal system was a very obvious manifestation of rational-legal authority. Tradition, of course, remains important today, not merely in the ceremonial sense, but as a meaningful explanation of why present-day institutions and practices are as they are. For instance, it may be interesting to know that the reason why MPs bow in the direction of the Speaker when entering and leaving the House of Commons is because between about 1400 and 1834 the Commons met in St Stephen's Chapel and always bowed to where the altar had formerly stood and the place where the Speaker sat, but it is of no great consequence for the operation of the Commons today, other than to illustrate how much is remains bound by tradition. On the other hand, the fact that the Commons' chamber is rectangular and the tradition developed that the government and its supporters sat on one side of the House and the opposition and its supporters on the other, greatly facilitated the development of the adversary system – the confrontation between government and opposition.

Similarly, charismatic leaders are by no means a thing of the past, although by it very nature charismatic authority is a more intermittent and variable factor. It is hardly necessary to delve back as far as Henry V or Henry VIII, the

Elder or Younger Pitts, Disraeli or Gladstone to find charismatic leaders – Lloyd George and Winston Churchill, Margaret Thatcher and Tony Blair have all been described as having charisma.

Tradition and charisma alone, however, could not ensure the development of parliamentary government: this could come about only through the growth of rational-legal authority, which itself could take many forms, parliamentary government being only one. Thus it was that successive monarchs after John sought to legitimate their rule by confirming Magna Carta. Between the death of John in 1216 and 1422, the second year of the reign of Henry VI, Magna Carta was confirmed no fewer than thirty-seven times. These were not their sole claim to rule legitimately, not even their most important, but they were rational-legal claims. Furthermore, the confirmation of Magna Carta was an acceptance of the rule of law and was not itself a specific move towards the creation of parliamentary institutions; for this it is necessary to look elsewhere, but still within the realms of legitimacy.

It is common to regard Simon de Montfort's Parliament of 1265 as the first English Parliament, yet it was not entirely without precedent. In 1213 John called two Councils, one at St Albans and one at Oxford, to which territorial representatives were summoned; and later, in 1254, Henry III summoned two knights from each shire to attend a Council at Westminster. Similarly, in 1261 the barons in dispute with the king summoned three knights from each shire to a Council at St Albans and de Montfort himself summoned four knights from each shire to attend his first parliament in 1264. The significance of the Parliament of 1265, however, is twofold: it provided the basis for future representation in what was to become the House of Commons and it was the model for the Parliaments of Edward I (1272–1307). Even though de Montfort's Parliament of 1265 consisted mainly of his supporters, it was the most systematically representative Parliament that had ever been summoned – two knights from each shire, two citizens from each city and two burgesses from each borough. It is because of this that Simon de Montfort is widely regarded as the founder of the House of Commons.

Nonetheless, the precedents set by de Montfort could have died with him in 1265 at the Battle of Evesham, but ironically it was the man who defeated him who, later, as Edward I, firmly established Parliament as an accepted part of English constitutional machinery. In 1275 Edward summoned his first Parliament consisting of representatives of the aristocracy, the higher clergy and the rural and urban 'middle classes' and between 1275 and 1286 Edward summoned no fewer than eighteen Parliaments. Between 1290 and the end of his reign Edward called a further twenty-seven Parliaments, including the famous 'Model Parliament' of 1295, which was long thought to be the first fully 'representative' Parliament but which has since been superseded by the Parliament of 1275 in that respect.

The situation, however, remained fluid and the nature and role of Parliament in the middle ages is better understood if Parliament is regarded as an occasion or a meeting, rather than a fully fledged institution. Thus it is more meaningful to speak of Parliaments than Parliament. Moreover, such occasions or meetings invariably had a major legitimising function – legitimising royal or baronial policies, legitimising taxation and, eventually, legitimising the possession of the Crown itself.

The frequency and composition of early Parliaments varied considerably. Edward I, for instance, called Parliaments more regularly in the earlier than in the later part of his reign, while the Commons were represented in only about a third of the Parliaments summoned in the reigns of Henry III and Edward I. However, the Commons were present in all but two of the Parliaments of Edward II (1307–27) and usually present after 1377. In due course, the Lords and Commons began to meet separately and the clergy operated through their own assembly, Convocation, although the higher clergy retained their membership of the House of Lords.

It was also during the middle ages that Parliament established its claims to control taxation and to share in the legislative and executive functions of the state. In medieval times, and long after, a king was expected to 'live of his own' – that is, support himself from his own resources (various traditional taxes and revenue from the royal estates), but kings frequently needed extra money, especially to fight wars, thus providing Parliament with a basis for bargaining. In practice, the king had to negotiate the granting of any additional taxes and in 1348 the Commons stipulated that the redress of grievances should precede the granting of supply. From 1400 until the advent of the Stuart kings, attempts by the monarch to raise taxes without parliamentary consent were rare. In the meantime, the Commons began to play a legislative role by presenting petitions to the king and, after 1500, the House began to draft its own bills. During this period the Commons also acquired the right to audit the accounts of the Exchequer and first made use of the weapon of impeachment – formally indicting individuals – as a means of controlling the king's ministers. Finally, it is important to note that Parliament 'deposed' two kings – Edward II and Richard II – and that the title of every king from Henry IV onwards was 'confirmed' by Parliament.

There is, of course, a danger of over-estimating the power of Parliaments: certainly, there were occasions when kings desperately needed money and Parliament was able to exact concessions in return for granting supply, when Parliament was consulted and able to influence affairs, when some control was exerted over the king's ministers and Henry IV and his successors probably felt that parliamentary confirmation of their positions made them more secure. However, medieval Parliaments were often 'packed' with supporters of the king or, on occasion, the barons and constituted utterly subservient assemblies. Parliament therefore primarily served the role of legitimation, but it was nonetheless during the middle ages that the foundations of Parliament as an *institution* were laid, providing the structure and powers with which we are familiar today.

Growth and challenge

Henry VII (1485–1509), the first of the Tudors, inherited a constitutional device which could have become a curb on royal power or could have withered and died. In fact, neither happened: Henry VII summoned only seven Parliaments and then only to raise additional revenue. It was left to his son, Henry VIII (1509–47) to give Parliament a more central role in the political system, for he chose to use Parliament as an instrument to legitimise the Reformation in England. As a result, statute law – law made by the king, Lords and Commons in Parliament – was recognised as supreme, reversing the medieval doctrine of the supremacy of the common law and establishing the foundation of parliamentary sovereignty.

Moreover, Tudor Parliaments were not 'packed' in the medieval sense, as may be seen from the fact that it was during this period that parliamentary privilege developed: at the beginning of each Parliament the Speaker claimed the privilges of freedom of speech in debate, freedom from arrest, freedom of access to the monarch through the Speaker, and that the monarch should place the most favourable construction on proceedings in the Commons. It is this last privilege that illustrates the nature of Tudor Parliaments: they were willing to question and, on occasion, to show resistance to the royal will, but they normally acquiesced in royal policies and were distinctly wary of falling foul of the royal temper. During the reign of Elizabeth I (1558–1603) in particular, the Commons showed increasing signs of restiveness and independence, which grew apace in the reign of James I (1603–25) and developed into a struggle over 'who governs?' (see Table 2.3).

Quite apart from James' adherence to the divine right of kings to rule, clashes developed between the king and the Commons over the levying of taxes without parliamentary consent, over foreign policy and over religion. After a series of clashes between 1603 and 1611, James ruled most of the time without summoning any Parliaments. Charles I (1625–49) produced no change: faced with strong opposition over the same issues, added to which was bitter resentment over his arbitrary imprisonment of opponents, he too resorted to rule without Parliament between 1629 and 1640, but financial necessity forced Charles to summon two Parliaments in 1640, the latter of which, the Long Parliament, passed a series of acts designed to curb royal power. Under the Triennial Act, Parliament had to be summoned at least every three years; parliamentary consent was necessary for all taxes; arbitrary courts, such as the Star Chamber, were abolished; and Parliament could not be dissolved without its own consent. Action was taken against two of the king's leading advisers, with the impeachment of the Earl of Strafford and Archbishop Laud, although Strafford's impeachment failed and his execution was secured by means of a bill of attainder.

However, Parliament was itself split over religion and over the extent to which royal authority should be curbed, but Charles exacerbated the situation

Table 2.3 *The development of Parliament: growth and challenge*

Date/period	Development
1529–36	Beginning of English Reformation: Reformation Parliament 1529–36
1536	Wales represented in the Commons
1558–1601	Periodic clashes between Elizabeth I and the Commons
1621	Commons' protestation against royal policy
1629–40	Charles I ruled without summoning Parliament
1640	Short Parliament: summoned to raise additional taxes; dissolved when Parliament insisted on the redress of grievances before granting supply
1640–60	Long Parliament: summoned because the king needed money; used to curb the king's power
1642–52	English Civil War
1648–53	The Rump Parliament: MPs favouring negotiations with king expelled; rule by remaining MPs; expelled by Cromwell 1653
1649	Trial and execution of Charles I. Abolition of the monarchy and the House of Lords. England declared a 'Free Commonwealth'
1649–60	The Interregnum: rule first by Parliament, then by Cromwell (Protector 1654–58)
1654	Cromwell's first Parliament
1655–56	Military rule – the Major-Generals
1656	Cromwell's second Parliament
1660	Restoration of the monarchy and the House of Lords
1679	Habeas Corpus Act
1688–89	Glorious Revolution: the establishment of constitutional monarchy

by attempting to arrest five of his leading opponents in the House of Commons. This virtually precipitated the Civil War, which, with brief intermissions, lasted from 1642 to 1652, when Charles II was defeated at Worcester. The main struggle ended with Charles I's defeat and his execution in 1649 and resulted in the only period in which England could literally be said to have had *parliamentary* government (1649–53), but the military success of Charles' opponents did not produce a satisfactory solution to the problems which had preceded the Civil War. In particular, there were disputes within Parliament and between Parliament and the army, which culminated in the Protectorate (1653–59), a period dominated by Oliver Cromwell. It was a period of constitutional experiment, though not one of constitutional innovation, other than the negative innovation of abolishing the House of Lords. This period effectively ended with the death of Cromwell in 1658 and amply demonstrated that there was no easy solution to the problems of establishing and maintaining effective government and imposing limits on the exercise of power.

The restoration of the monarchy in 1660 was, in a sense, the restoration of Parliament, not least with the reinstitution of the House of Lords. However, it would be wrong to assume that the protagonists had, like the Bourbon supporters in exile after the French Revolution, 'learnt nothing and forgotten nothing'. Not only did Charles II not wish to 'go on his travels again', but few wished to return to the many harsh policies of the republican period, least of all to military rule. England therefore began to edge towards a constitutional monarchy. Charles II (1660–85) and James II (1685–88) facilitated this process, the one by his political astuteness, the other by his obduracy.

Charles II had no more wish than his father to see his power curbed, but he was infinitely more realistic. He was helped by the fact that his first Parliament (1661–79) was, as the historian Macaulay later wrote, more royalist than the king and possessed of more Anglican zeal than the bishops. The House of Commons in particular exercised considerable influence over national affairs and the restoration of the monarchy did not result in a reversion to the pre-Civil War situation, although the king retained a wide degree of initiative and, by skilful manoeuvring, Charles often managed to pursue polices he favoured, sometimes from a position of weakness.

The constitutional significance of the reign of Charles II was that he had to share power with his ministers and with Parliament, but this sharing of power resulted from a recognition of the political realities of the time and not from any fundamental constitutional change. It is often said that Charles' reign was also important for marking the beginnings of the party system and of the Cabinet. This is true in the sense that signs of such developments can be detected, but their significance can be exaggerated.

Although the broad issues that divided the parliamentary factions of Tories and Whigs can be traced back to the growth of puritanism in Elizabethan parliaments, neither Tories nor Whigs were parties in the modern sense: they had no party organisation; they did not fight elections as clearly defined groups; they possessed no party discipline; and they did not seek to implement detailed policy programmes. It was more meaningful then and later to speak of 'ins' and 'outs' – those in power and those who were not, a situation which is epitomised in the contemporary terms of 'court party' and 'country party'. 'Court' and 'country' were shifting groups, however, and in spite of the use of the term party, they too were not parties in the modern sense, but factions. That said, the names Tory and Whig and the broad divisions between them continued into the eighteenth century and beyond, and ministries were generally built around either prominent Tories or Whigs.

Similarly, the beginning of the Cabinet can be detected, since Charles tended to rely on the advice of a small group of trusted and confidential advisers, but the existence of such a group owed much to Charles' political manoeuvres and was a means of seeking to evade the limits that the wider Privy Council sought to impose on him. Technically, these advisers were usually members of the king's Privy Council; in practice, they were, as now, usually the active leaders of the government and became known as the Cabinet Council, although in a celebrated instance they were dubbed the 'Cabal', after the initials of the ministers concerned. It is important to reiterate, however, that Charles' Cabinet had its origins in attempts to evade any responsibility to Parliament, political or constitutional, and in no sense developed as a means of establishing parliamentary control of the executive.

Charles II's reign ended, in fact, with Parliament again under threat: from 1681 until his death in 1685, Charles, like his father and grandfather before him, ruled without Parliament – a situation made possible largely because of the payment to Charles of considerable subsidies by Louis XIV of France. Parliament faced a much greater threat, however, with the accession of Charles' brother, James II. James lacked his brother's political acumen, over-estimated the strength of his position and refused all compromise. Although his first Parliament was largely subservient and granted him a substantial revenue for life, James, a fervent Catholic, sought to evade anti-Catholic laws and appeared to be taking steps to avoid all constitutional limitation on his power. His actions action constituted a direct challenge to the system of government established as a result of the Civil War and the Restoration and, although the Tories had their specific origins in their opposition in 1679 to the Exclusion Bill, which sought to bar James from the succession to the throne, they joined with the Whigs – the exclusionists – to invite William of Orange, the husband of James' elder daughter, Mary, both Protestants, to accept the English Crown. James fled the country and was deemed to have abdicated: the 'Glorious Revolution' of 1688 had been accomplished.

The Revolution Settlement of 1689 was a major landmark in English constitutional history, but, like so many other developments, it was an essentially pragmatic response to a particular situation. Moreover, it was characterised more by a reassertion of the traditional rights and liberties of Parliament and the individual than by constitutional innovation.

In 1689 a Convention Parliament – a Parliament summoned by an assembly rather than the Crown – passed the Bill of Rights, which included a Declaration of Right (see Box 2.1), which, in addition to reasserting traditional rights and liberties, declared that the royal powers to suspend laws and to exempt certain individuals from the application of particular laws were illegal and that the existence of a standing army – one of the grievances against James – was subject to parliamentary consent.

Shifting power from the monarch to the politicians

The process of consolidation marked by the Glorious Revolution proceeded further after 1689 (see Table 2.4). More than ever the monarch had to share power with his ministers and with Parliament, but this too was reinforced by circumstances, particularly William III's need to finance the struggle with France in Europe. Parliament further strengthened its position in 1694 by passing a Triennial Act, which sought to prevent the monarch from prolonging

> ### Box 2.1   The principal provisions of the Declaration of Right, 1689
>
> #### *The Declaration of Right, 1689*
>
> 1 The suspending of laws by the king without the consent of Parliament is illegal.
> 2 The dispensing power (i.e. excluding particular individuals or actions from the application of the law) without the consent of Parliament in illegal.
> 3 The levying of taxes without the consent of Parliament is illegal.
> 4 The creation of commissions and courts for dealing with ecclesiastical cases without the consent of Parliament is illegal.
> 5 Subjects have a right to petition the monarch.
> 6 The raising and maintaining of a standing army without the consent of Parliament is illegal.
> 7 Protestants have the right to bear arms for their own defence.
> 8 The election of Members of Parliament ought to be free.
> 9 Freedom of speech and debate in Parliament and parliamentary proceedings may not be questioned.
> 10 Excessive bail ought not to be required, nor excessive fines or cruel and unusual punishments inflicted.
> 11 Parliament should meet frequently.

Table 2.4   *The development of Parliament: shifting power from the monarch to the politicians*

Date/period	Development
1694	Triennial Act: Parliament must be summoned at least every 3 years; maximum lifespan of 3 years
1701	Act of Settlement: the Protestant succession
1707	Union of England and Scotland: abolition of the Scottish Parliament
1707	Last occasion the royal assent refused: Scottish Militia Bill
1716	Septennial Act: lifespan of Parliament extended to 7 years
1721–42	Sir Robert Walpole first 'Prime Minister'
1760–83	George III as an 'interventionist' king
1783–	Supremacy of the politicians
1801	Union with Ireland: abolition of the Irish Parliament

the life of a subservient Parliament by stipulating that no Parliament could last longer than three years, and further secured annual meetings of Parliament by limiting the duration of financial support for the army and of the Mutiny Act, on which military discipline depended, to a year.

However, consolidation began to shift to innovation when the succession to the throne again became a matter of concern. William and Mary had no children and Mary's sister, Anne, had no surviving children. The Act of Settlement, 1701 settled the succession on the Electress of Hanover and her heirs, which was later to have a considerable political and constitutional impact, but it also established the principle of a constitutional monarchy much more firmly in the political system. Although the right of Parliament to settle the succession had a number of precedents, it was now firmly established and the monarch was required to act in accordance with the advice of the Privy Council. This last provision, however, was not to come into operation until after the deaths of William and Anne (Mary having died in 1694) and was therefore intended as a restriction on the future Hanoverian kings. Like many previous constitutional changes, the Act of Settlement was primarily a reaction to immediate and specific problems. Thus it also contained a provision that the monarch must be an Anglican and, mindful of William III's connection with the Netherlands and in anticipation of the Hanoverian succession, a provision that parliamentary consent was necessary before English forces were committed to the defence of lands that did not belong to the English Crown.

The reign of Anne (1702–14) was notable for two other important changes. First, there was the clearer emergence of a Cabinet requiring not only the confidence of the monarch but also of the House of Commons, although needing the confidence of the Commons fell far short of being responsible to it in the modern sense of the term – this was a much later development. Second, the union with Scotland in 1707, which abolished the separate Scottish Parliament, was a major step towards establishing a unitary system of government, in which a single Parliament and administration governed the whole of the United Kingdom – a situation which prevailed until 1999, with the devolution of power to Scotland and Wales, although Northern Ireland had been a partial exception to that for most of the time since 1920. In terms of the distribution of power, however, more important changes were to occur after the accession of George I (1714–27).

George I was somewhat indifferent to British affairs and spent a good deal of his time in Hanover. More importantly, he was sufficiently astute not to attempt exerting too great an influence in his new kingdom, with the result that the practice of the Cabinet meeting in the absence of the king developed. This situation continued under George II (1727–60). The first two Georges found in Sir Robert Walpole an able and trustworthy chief minister, whose long period of office from 1721 to 1742 did much to establish the Cabinet as a permanent part of the political system and, more importantly, resulted in power being concentrated in the hands of the politicians. Thus, when George III (1760–1820) sought to play a more active political role in the earlier part of his reign, he was not promoting a radical constitutional innovation, but trying to revert to an earlier situation. George III, however, was a poor judge of men (and therefore often chose poor ministers), a poor tactician (and therefore made serious errors) and politically inexperienced (and therefore made errors early in his reign). In particular, in spite of having an able Prime Minister in Lord North (a much-maligned politician), his handling of the American colonies and war with France was disastrous and led eventually to the appointment as Prime Minister of William Pitt the Younger, who re-established the supremacy of the politicians.

Walpole is commonly regarded as the first 'Prime Minister' – indeed, his portrait hangs in No. 10 Downing Street as the first of a long line, but this is a somewhat simplistic view. In the first place, the term 'Prime Minister', much disliked by Lord North, like many others, such as 'Cabal', 'Cabinet', 'Tory' and 'Whig', was initially one of abuse and, while it is true that Walpole secured a dominance over his fellow-ministers which had not been achieved before, it was not enjoyed by most of his eighteenth-century successors as First Lord of the Treasury. In fact, for most of the eighteenth century not all ministers resigned when the First Lord resigned, some continuing in office under a succession of First Lords. Furthermore, Walpole was not the leader of a party or a group with a clear majority in the House of Commons: he owed his continuance in office to what became known as the 'system'. This involved, on the one hand, the management of elections and, on the other, the management of the House of Commons itself. In both cases the 'system' depended on the effective use of bribery, corruption and influence through the distribution of honours, offices, contracts and pensions and, if necessary, straightforward bribery and, especially in elections, of treating. With its control over honours, offices, contracts and pensions, the government was obviously in a very powerful position to secure the return at elections of a substantial number of supporters, but seldom enough to control the Commons, whose members had to be managed by a similar means. Nonetheless, Walpole did secure a dominance similar in many ways to that associated with modern Prime Ministers and, though they may not have achieved his degree of dominance, there is no difficulty in identifying the leading politician in most succeeding eighteenth-century governments. Certainly, by the time of the Younger Pitt the position of Prime Minister had been accepted and Pitt himself expressed the view that a Prime Minister was necessary for the effective working of the political system. However, it is typical of British constitutional practice that, strictly speaking, then and now, the term 'Prime Minister' remains a title rather than a formal office and its holder continues to be First Lord of the Treasury.

The growth of the party system, democratisation and executive dominance

The system of electoral and parliamentary management which characterised eighteenth-century politics was bound to lead to demands for the reform of

Table 2.5   *The development of Parliament: the growth of the party system, democratisation and executive dominance*

Date/period	Development
1832	First Reform Act: enfranchising the middle classes
1838–39	Chartist agitation for reform
1846–68	Party realignment: development of Conservative-Liberal dominance
1848	Brief revival of Chartism
1867	Second Reform Act: enfranchising urban working class males
1872	Ballot Act: introduction of the secret ballot
1881	First use of closure in the House of Commons
1883	Corrupt and Illegal Practices Act
1884	Third Reform Act: enfranchising rural working-class males
1887	Closure and the 'guillotine' adopted as regular procedures in the House of Commons
1902	'Mr Balfour's parliamentary railway timetable'
1906–11	Conflict between Lords and Commons
1911	Parliament Act: removal of the Lords' veto; lifespan of Parliament reduced to five years
1912	Payment of MPs
1918	Representation of the People Act: enfranchising women of 30 and over
1918	Parliamentary (Qualification of Women) Act
1919	First woman MP takes her seat
1920	Government of Ireland Act: partition of Ireland and creation of Stormont Parliament
1928	Representation of the People Act: universal adult suffrage introduced
1945–70	Zenith of the two-party system
1949	Parliament Act: reduction of the Lords' veto from 2 years to 1

representation and of the right to vote (see Table 2.5). The eighteenth-century concept of representation differs from its modern counterpart in that it involved the representation of interests and property rather than people. Thus, the fact that representation in the House of Commons bore little resemblance to the distribution of the population, especially as the agricultural and industrial revolutions were generating extensive population movement, did not strike many eighteenth-century politicians as incongruous, least of all undemocratic, since in no sense was representation equated with democracy. Indeed, democracy was more commonly equated with the rule of the mob and therefore to be feared rather than applauded.

Elections in some constituencies, mainly counties, had, in the context of the times, a fairly wide franchise, but in others, mainly boroughs, the franchise was restricted. There was a widespread system of 'rotten' boroughs, in which elections were determined by corruption, and 'pocket' boroughs, in which the nomination was in the hands of one person or of a very few. Electorates varied enormously in size, from the uninhabited constituencies of Old Sarum, near Salisbury, and Dunwich, which lay submerged beneath the North Sea, to the 9,000 voters of Westminster, but the vast majority of constituencies had fewer than two hundred voters. In addition, the growing industrial towns in the midlands and the north of England were mostly without representation.

Various attempts to eliminate corruption and reform representation were made in the latter part of the eighteenth century, but it was not until 1832 that major changes occurred. The Reform Act, 1832 disenfranchised 183 'rotten' and 'pocket' boroughs and reduced the representation of a further 31 boroughs which returned two MPs. These seats were redistributed to the industrial towns of the midlands and the north and to the more populous counties. The franchise was extended so that whereas 1 male in 50 had the vote before 1832, it was now 1 in 25. The effect of the 1832 reform was to enfranchise the emerging middle classes.

It is very easy to see the Reform Act of 1832 as the first of a series of electoral reforms which ushered in the era of modern democracy. Historically, it is possible to argue this, but that would not only ignore the views of those who dispute the existence of democracy in modern Britain, but also make unjustified assumptions about the views of many of the reformers of 1832. If democracy is equated with the extension of the franchise, then it certainly came in instalments, but the prevailing view in 1832 was that the Reform Act was a final settlement based on the eighteenth-century concept of representation, not the first instalment of democracy. The franchise was still firmly based on property qualifications and was to remain so for nearly another century. The fact that within a few years the Chartists were to demand one man–one vote or that somewhat later the eminent political philosopher, John Stuart Mill, argued in favour of universal adult suffrage serves only to emphasise the point. Nevertheless, 1832 and the later extensions of the franchise in 1867 and 1884 were the first steps on the road to democratisation, whatever contemporary views may have been – a process which may have been inevitable, but was not regarded so by many at the time.

The widening of the franchise in 1832 was significant for two other reasons: first, regardless of the prevailing view, it was a precedent for further extensions of the right to vote; and, second, the increase in the size of the electorate made electoral management much more difficult, facilitating the growth of parties more firmly based on principle than beholden to patronage.

Thus, by 1832 the office of Prime Minister had become firmly established, the Cabinet had become a permanent part of the machinery of government, the franchise had been significantly widened and Parliament was a more representative body in relation to the distribution of the population, and the role of patronage and corruption in the political system had been considerably reduced, though far from eliminated. For some later observers, the changes emanating from the Reform Act of 1832 ushered in 'the golden age of Parliament'.

'The golden age of Parliament'?

In 1867 Walter Bagehot, editor of *The Economist* and a political and social observer of some note, published his book, *The English Constitution*,[3] in which he argued not only that Britain had a political system superior to that of the United States, but that the efficacy of the constitution rested on an 'efficient secret'. That 'efficient secret' was that the various institutions of the political system could be divided into two elements, the 'dignified' and the 'efficient', and that the crucial 'efficient' institution was the Cabinet, which he described as 'a hyphen which joins – a buckle which fastens' the executive to the legislature. The monarchy and the various ceremonial trappings of state were the 'dignified' elements of the constitution and conferred legitimacy upon the 'efficient' parts of the system – principally the House of Commons and the Cabinet – allowing them to work quietly and effectively in exercising the reality of political power.

It was precisely because the cardinal principle of the American Constitution was the separation of powers that Bagehot regarded the British system as superior. His concept of Cabinet government envisages a body of individuals drawn from Parliament and constitutionally responsible to it – the cardinal principle of parliamentary government. Constitutionally, of course, this is the situation that prevails today, but ironically Bagehot's description was out of date almost as soon as he had written it, for he did not envisage the emergence of two strongly disciplined political parties, one or other of which would normally enjoy the support of a majority in the House of Commons. Armed with such a majority reinforced by party cohesion, the Prime Minister and the Cabinet could enjoy the benefits of parliamentary sovereignty to the full. Provided the government retained the support of its party and did not run into serious opposition from the Conservative-dominated House of Lords, as Liberal governments did from time to time, there was little difficulty in securing the passage of any legislation, and it is this situation that has generally existed in British politics since 1868. Bagehot contrasted this with the position of an American President, who could be faced with a Congress controlled by his political opponents, but, even where the President's party had a majority in both Houses of Congress, party cohesion in the United States was much lower so that presidential control of Congress could not be guaranteed.

After 1832, there was a gradual realignment in British politics so that between 1846 and 1868 no single party secured a majority in the House of Commons, resulting in coalition governments of two or more groups or parties in Parliament. Inevitably, this enhanced the extent to which the Prime Minister and the Cabinet were dependent on Parliament and Parliament's influence was correspondingly greater. In particular, the Commons had the power to make or break governments to an extent that was not to occur again until after the First World War and, more recently, between 1974 and 1979. Even when the government enjoyed majority support in the Commons, as Palmerston did for most of his two terms of office as Prime Minister (1855–58 and 1859–65), it was a majority not based on a single party but on the willingness of several groups regularly to sustain the government in power. The government had to beware of losing support over particular issues or generally losing the confidence of sufficient supporters to undermine its majority. Thus Palmerston did lose his majority in 1858 when he sought the passage of a Conspiracy to Murder Bill, a measure widely interpreted as having been introduced at the behest of the French government.

Similarly, in 1857 *The Times* divided MPs into 'Ministerialists' and 'Opposition', rather than assigning party or group labels. Before 1868, and to some extent afterwards, a variety of labels were used in addition to the traditional ones of 'Tory' and 'Whig'. In the 1830s the names 'Conservative and 'Liberal' came into use. However, it was not just a simple substitute of Conservative for Tory and Liberal for Whig: both Tories and Whigs were split into conservative and radical groups and these divisions were a major factor in the realignment that took place between 1846 and 1868. Some labels, such as 'Peelite Free Traders' reflected issues involved in the realignment, others, such as 'Liberal-Conservative' or 'Radicals', reflected the process of realignment itself. By 1868, however, it is reasonable to speak of the Conservative and Liberal Parties, although the other labels lingered on into the twentieth century – the term 'Tory' has never disappeared and is still widely used by supporters and opponents alike as a synonym for Conservative.

An equally momentous change was also taking place at this time, justifying the use of the term 'party' to the two major political groupings that emerged from the realignment: this was the development of party organisation. Spasmodic party organisation existed earlier in the nineteenth century, notably at election times when some central fund-raising occurred, but the main impetus in the formation of party organisation came from successive extensions of the franchise during the nineteenth century. The Reform Act, 1832, required, for the first time, the drawing up of registers of electors. As a consequence, local registration societies were formed and many of these later formed the basis of local Conservative and Liberal associations. In 1861 the Liberals created a national Liberal Registration Association, followed in 1877 by the formation of the National Liberal Federation. Similarly, the Conservatives formed the National Union of Conservative and Constitutional Associations in 1867 and both parties established central offices in London headed by full-time organisers. The Reform Act, 1867, was a major factor in the development of party organisation, because it brought about such a vast increase in the size of the electorate that organising electoral support could no longer be sensibly left to ad hoc means. This trend received a further impetus with the virtual elimination of electoral bribery and corruption by the introduction of the secret ballot in 1872 and the passing of the Corrupt and Illegal Practices Act in 1883, as well the further extension of the franchise in the Reform Act, 1884. Thus, what had begun as intra-parliamentary groupings had developed extra-parliamentary organisations and laid the foundations of the party system that was to prevail until the First World War.

There can be little doubt that after 1832, and throughout the rest of the nineteenth century, Parliament, in particular the House of Commons, was the principal focus of political activity and attention and this was not a situation confined to the period 1846–68. Of course, this period of realignment was a major reason why Parliament occupied this position, but even before 1846 governments did not control the House of Commons in the modern sense of the term, even when they had majority support. Furthermore, after 1868, when governments were normally based on a single-party majority and had much greater control over the Commons, the tradition of Parliament as the centre of attention lived on, epitomised by the clashes between Disraeli and Gladstone, but owing far more to the fact that governmental control was seldom absolute. Party discipline certainly existed and no MP lightly courted the approbation of his party's whips. Indeed, during the 1850s and 1860s the whips made strenuous efforts to secure the maximum turnout of their supporters. In one session, for instance, the Conservative with the best record was rewarded with a silver salver and his colleague with the poorest record, a wooden spoon. Later observers, such as Richard Crossman, a former Oxford don and prominent Labour MP from 1945 to 1970, described the period 1846 to 1868 as 'the golden age of Parliament', suggesting that there existed in the Commons 'a solid centre, composed of the majority of solid, sensible independent MPs, collectively able to make and unmake ministries, to defy when necessary their own whips and above all to frustrate the growth of "constituency government" outside'.[4] 'Constituency government' was Bagehot's term for 'immoderate' or extremist forces outside Parliament. But Crossman and others who thought of 1848–68 as 'the classic age of parliamentary government' were wrong: it was principally the frontbenches of the two main parties who were the moderates and significant minorities of their backbenchers, especially in the Liberal Party, who were the extremists. The idea that most MPs actively participated in Parliament in this period, that backbenchers, truly independent of party, assiduously subjected ministers to parliamentary scrutiny, that governments constantly failed to get bills through the Commons, and that governments frequently fell as a result of losing votes of confidence does not bear historical examination: the 'golden age' is a myth.

After 1868, the outcome of the majority of votes or divisions in the Commons was predictable, and MPs voted increasingly with their parties, but on a minority of issues, sometimes major, the outcome was uncertain. In the particular instance of Home Rule for Ireland the result in 1886 was a major split in the Liberal Party and a partial realignment of political and electoral forces. However, the two-party system survived to face what was to prove a more serious challenge in the form of the Labour Party, but before that challenge fully materialised the characteristics of the modern political system had been firmly established. The position of the Prime Minister and the Cabinet had been consolidated, but during the nineteenth century, as Bagehot had rightly pointed out, the executive had clearly become constitutionally responsible to the legislature: the doctrine of ministerial responsibility had taken root in both its individual and collective forms.

Thus, when the political system was faced with the rise of a party which did not owe its origins to the groupings within Parliament, but developed from extra-parliamentary forces, it was the party – the Labour Party – which adapted to the system, rather than the system to the party. In a more fluid situation the Labour Party might have had a profound institutional impact on the British political system; as it was, the impact of the Labour Party was much greater in electoral and policy terms.

'Mr Balfour's parliamentary railway timetable'

As governments acquired greater control over the House of Commons through normally having a majority and through the growth of party cohesion, so they also acquired greater procedural control over the House. In part this arose out of Irish Nationalist obstruction between 1877 and 1888, but Irish attempts to secure Home Rule by preventing the Commons from carrying out its business were the immediate rather than the underlying cause of the extension of the government's procedural control. In the middle of the nine-teenth century most legislation was private legislation; that is, bills promoted by individuals and organisations outside Parliament for limited purposes, such as the construction of canals, railways and harbours. This was the era of *laissez-faire* not only in the limited economic sense, but in the wider context of governmental intervention. Gradually, public legislation; that is, bills having a general application to the whole population, superseded private legislation in importance. Thus, between 1800 and 1884 there were 18,497 private bills, compared with 9,556 public acts, whereas nowadays public normally outnumber private acts by six or seven to one. Moreover, most of the public bills completing their passage through Parliament were introduced by the government of the day and the government increasingly assumed the respons-ibility for taking the initiative in most matters of public policy.

This increase in governmental initiative meant that governments demanded and secured an increasing share of parliamentary time. At the beginning of the nineteenth century, government business had precedence on only one day a week; by 1832 this had increased to two days, in 1852 to three; but by 1902 government business had precedence on all days except Fridays and parts of Tuesdays and Wednesdays. In addition, six years earlier, in 1896, a limit of twenty days (then known as supply days) had been placed on the discussion of the annual estimates of government or public expenditure, thus further enhancing the governmental control of business.

In addition, Irish obstruction resulted in the introduction of a number of procedural devices which increased governmental control, most notably the introduction of closure, by which a debate could be brought to and end by the will of the majority – usually the government majority. The procedures for controlling the business of the Commons were gradually extended and refined, so that not only could the government effectively terminate a debate, but also limit the amount of time spent on any particular item of business. Naturally, then as now, the opposition would greet such limitations with howls of anguish and denounce them as a negation of democracy, but as an alternative government no opposition has sought the significant curtailment of such powers nor hesitated to use them when next in office.

The way in which the House of Commons conducted its business was thoroughly reorganised in 1902 by changes introduced by the then Prime Minister, Arthur Balfour, and the new system was quickly dubbed 'Mr Balfour's parliamentary railway timetable'. Other changes have occurred since, but these did not depart markedly from Balfour's basic scheme – for the most part, they have strengthened the government's grip on the House of Commons.

Paralleling this extension of governmental control was the development of a formally constituted opposition, normally led by the leaders of the second-largest party in the Commons. This sometimes presented problems in designating a particular individual leader, since none of the parties chose their leaders by election. In some cases a former Prime Minister was clearly acknowledged as leader and putative Prime Minister, in others a generally accepted leader emerged. Following the death of Disraeli in 1881, however, and on more than one occasion when Gladstone announced his retirement, no clear successor emerged. Furthermore, since a Prime Minister sitting in the House of lords was still acceptable, it was not uncommon to designate a leader in each of the two Houses without it being clear who would become Prime Minister in the event of the party forming a government. This was the case, for instance, among the Conservatives for most of Gladstone's Second Ministry (1880–85), when Lord Salisbury led the party in the Lords and Sir Stafford Northcote in the Commons. This particular problem became less important as the prospect of a Prime Minister being drawn from the Lords became less acceptable, as the tactical disadvantages of not having a clearly designated leader became apparent, and as the politicians felt it less necessary to pay more than lip-service to the royal prerogative of appointing the Prime Minister. Above all, the growth of a disciplined two-party system made a virtue out of party loyalty and unity, so that the main opposition party increasingly presented itself as an alternative government and its leader as an alternative Prime Minister.

This dual process of increasing government control over the House of Commons and the establishment of a formally constituted opposition – the adversary system – was undoubted facilitated by the two major twentieth-century extensions of the franchise in 1918 and 1928, which gave women the vote and established universal adult suffrage, although a residue of double-voting remained until their abolition in 1948. The overwhelming majority of voters, then as now, supported parties rather than candidates and this provided a major underpinning of party discipline, since few candidates could hope to be elected unless they possessed the backing of one of the major parties – other forces, notably the electoral system, saw to it that only a handful of minor party or independent candidates were elected. Ironically, it has long been the case that local parties are largely autonomous in the selection of parliamentary candidates, but most local parties could be relied upon to choose candidates loyal to the party leadership and, more often than not, discipline the MP whose loyalty wavered.

None of this prevents splits occurring in parties from time to time, but these factors militated against party fissures. The split in the Liberal Party in 1916 between supporters of Asquith and Lloyd George was ultimately disastrous and Labour's split in 1931 resulted in the party spending long years in opposition, but these splits transcended the normal processes of party discipline and cohesion.

Governmental control is far from absolute, even though the government usually has a majority in the Commons, since most parliamentary time not directly in the hands of the government is in the hands of the official opposition. The opposition, however, is effectively circumscribed in its use of time by several factors. First, although the opposition decides what subjects will be debated on Opposition Days, it cannot allocate its time to any parliamentary business of its choosing; second, although the government must find time from its own allocation for a censure motion tabled by the opposition, the latter risks devaluing such motions if used too often; third, in practice the allocation of time is negotiated between the government and the opposition through 'the usual channels' – the respective party managers on the two sides of the House; and, most important of all, the initiative in parliamentary business lies primarily in the hands of the government. It is the government which draws up most of the parliamentary agenda, annually in the form of the Queen's Speech outlining the government's programme for the ensuing session, weekly through its announcement of the business for the following two weeks, and daily in that most major items of business are introduced in the House of Commons by ministers.

The official opposition normally co-operates in this process because it lives in the hope (though not always the belief) that it will be the government after the next election. From time to time co-operation breaks down, usually over a particular matter, more rarely on a wider basis, but sooner or later it is resumed and behind the bluster and rhetoric the parliamentary machine continues to operate. Co-operation is undoubtedly encouraged by the fact that neither of the two major parties is so dominant that one party is condemned to more or less permanent opposition and between most general elections both parties usually have reasonable expectations of victory at the next election, whatever may ultimately transpire. This in turn is a major bulwark of the adversary system and, many would argue, a major obstacle to the reform of Parliament. Whether, in the light of Conservative Party fortunes since 1992, the party system and therefore this situation is in the process of changing, remains a matter for conjecture and later discussion, but there are some signs that it is. However, a further change did take place and that was a growing feeling that the balance had swung too far in favour of the executive and it was time to 'shift the balance'.

Changes in the relationship between Lords and Commons also strengthened the position of the executive. Although individual members of the House of Lords remained prominent in politics during the nineteenth century – six of the eleven holders of the office of Prime Minister, as well as many members of the Cabinet were members of the Lords rather than the Commons, the political supremacy of the latter had long been acknowledged. There were periodic clashes between the two Houses, notably over the abolition of paper duty in 1861 and Irish Home Rule; Liberal governments in particular had to bear in mind that the Conservatives had a very substantial majority in the Lords. It was, however, the Liberal government elected in 1906 that encountered the most serious opposition from the upper house, culminating in the rejection by the Lords of Lloyd George's 'People's Budget' – a direct challenge to the financial supremacy of the Commons. The ensuing constitutional crisis led to two general elections in 1910 being fought on the issue of limiting the power of the Lords. The Liberals lost their overall majority, but remained in office through Labour and Irish Nationalist support. Under the threat of the creation of sufficient Liberal peers[5] to ensure the passage of a bill to curb the powers of the upper house, the Lords gave way, resulting in the Parliament Act, 1911. This removed the power of the House of Lords to amend financial legislation and limited its veto power over other legislation. Under the act, the Commons could override the Lords' rejection of a bill by passing it again in two successive sessions – effectively a two-year delay. To offset what some regarded as unduly strengthening the position of the government with a Commons majority, two other changes were made – the maximum period between general elections was reduced from seven years to five and the Lords were given an absolute veto over any bill seeking to extend the life of Parliament. In both world wars, in fact, the life of Parliament was extended with the agreement of the House of Lords; on no other occasion has a government sought to extend the life of a Parliament. However, the preamble to the Parliament Act makes it clear that this was to be the first instalment of a more thorough-going reform: 'it is intended to substitute for the House of Lords as it at present exists a Second Chamber constituted on a popular instead of hereditary basis, but such substitution cannot immediately be brought into operation'. Action was further delayed by the First World War, although towards the end of the war a commission on reform of the second chamber was appointed, reporting in 1918. Its recommendations, however, were not implemented: the Liberals were never in government again, the Conservatives had little or no interest in further reform, and the first two Labour governments (1924 and 1929–31) were pre-occupied with other, more pressing, matters.

Reform of the Lords did not appear on the political agenda again until 1948, when the first majority Labour government became concerned that the Conservative-dominated House of Lords might obstruct legislation nationalising the iron and steel industry as the next election (due in 1950 at the latest) drew nearer. The government initiated all-party talks, which led to an agreement on a number of principles for the composition of a reformed house, but foundered over reducing the Lords' delaying power. Unable to proceed on an all-party basis, the Attlee government introduced a new Parliament Bill to reduce the delaying power from two parliamentary sessions to one, using the 1911 Parliament Act to overcome Conservative opposition in the Lords.

In practice, after 1911 conflict between Lords and Commons became 'normalised'. The Lords engaged in an initial flurry of using the delaying power by rejecting bills on Irish Home Rule, the disestablishment of the Church of Wales, and a plural voting bill. The Liberal government overrode the Lords' veto on the first two and both became law (although Irish Home Rule was suspended on the outbreak of the First World War), but withdrew the plural voting bill. Another bill, the Temperance (Scotland) Bill, was passed after amendments acceptable to the Lords were agreed. Apart from the 1949 Parliament Bill, the delaying power remained unused until the 1990s, although its use was threatened by the 1974–79 Labour government over the its Trade Union and Labour Relations Bill in 1975–76 and its Aircraft Shipbuilding Bill in 1976–77 but proved unnecessary when amendments were agreed. In the meantime, the Lords reserved the right to amend government bills, usually giving way in the face of resistance by the Commons. It was, of course, Labour rather than Conservative governments that encountered more problems in the Lords, but 'normalisation' received an added boost with the adoption of the 'Salisbury doctrine' after 1945, by which the Conservative opposition in the Lords refrained from opposing the second reading of bills contained in Labour's election manifestos. Executive dominance was therefore not only little affected by changes in the behaviour of the House of Lords but, if anything, enhanced by them.

'Shifting the balance'

'Shifting the Balance' was the title of a House of Commons' committee report presented in 2000.[6] It echoed a widely held view that governments had become too powerful and that Parliament's ability to scrutinise the executive needed strengthening. It was to be followed by two further reports, one from

Table 2.6 *The growth of government*

Indicator	Early to mid-nineteenth century		Late twentieth century	
Legislative output*	237	(1831–32)	2,732	(1992–97)
No. of non-industrial civil servants	21,000	(1832)	430,000	(1998)
No. of ministers	47	(1830)	112	(1997)
House of Commons: no. of sitting days per year	125	(mean 1832–68)	164	(mean 1945–97)
House of Commons: no. of standing orders on public business†	7	(1830)	146	(1990)
House of Commons: participation in divisions‡	26.5%	(1871)	75.4%	(1994–95)

Notes: * Number of pages of public acts per year. The number of statutory instruments (delegated legislation) increased from 995 in 1900 to 3,327 in 1994. † I.e. rules dealing with matters affecting the public or the country generally, rather than private individuals or named and limited geographical areas. ‡ I.e. number divisions in which 300 or more MPs voted.

the Conservative Party[7] and one by the Hansard Society for Parliamentary Government,[8] arguing in even stronger terms that parliamentary scrutiny had not kept pace with executive power. The government's initial reaction to the Liaison Committee's report was dismissive, yet early in 2002 the government itself brought forward proposals that owed much to this and the other two reports. The immediate cause was a government reshuffle, which produced a new Leader of the House of Commons (the minister in charge of dealing with the government's business in the House), Robin Cook, who was much more sympathetic towards proposals for change than his predecessor had been. However, this gives a misleading view of what had been happening in Parliament, implying an unremitting growth in governmental control in no way offset by any improvement in Parliament's ability to keep a check on the executive (see Table 2.6). This is an accurate enough picture from the Reform Act of 1832 to the 1960s, but it obscures the stirrings of parliamentary reform and developments in parliamentary scrutiny and behaviour.

Increased governmental control of Parliament, particularly of the House of Commons, was a necessary response to changes in British society, especially those brought about by the industrial revolution. Ironically, in legislative terms Parliament had played a major part in the industrial revolution by passing thousands of private Acts of Parliament to facilitate the creation of an infrastructure of roads, canals and railways that were vital to industrial development. Private legislation – applying to a named and limited geographical area – was necessary in an era of limited government, which placed great emphasis on private property and eschewed the idea of systematic state intervention through public or general legislation to facilitate such development. As already noted, private acts outnumbered public acts by a ratio of 2 to 1 between 1800 and 1884. This was reinforced in the first half of the nineteenth century by the widespread acceptance of the economic doctrine of *laissez-faire* – allowing market forces a free rein and minimising state intervention in the economy, epitomised by the repeal of the Corn Laws in 1846 and the adoption of free trade. In practice, governments did intervene, particularly in the spheres of public health, provision for the poor, factory conditions, education, banking and rail safety. Such intervention was widely seen as complementary, not contradictory, with improvements in health, working conditions and education as conducive to industrial efficiency. In the second half of the nineteenth century there was an ideological shift, however, with collectivist ideas finding more favour, not just in the nascent socialist movement but in the two major parties as well, especially the Liberal Party. Put another way, this meant that parties claimed that governments could and should do more. The rise of the Labour Party gave collectivist policies even greater impetus and government intervention was at its greatest between 1945 and 1951, with the Attlee government's creation of the welfare state, especially the National Health Service, and the taking into public ownership of industries such as coal, gas, electricity, and iron and steel and services such as the railways and water. The Conservative governments of 1951–64 and 1970–74, while less interventionist, maintained the welfare state and engaged in only limited denationalisation. As a consequence, people not only became used to government intervention and involvement but increasingly came to expect governments to do something about the many problems facing modern society, inevitably arousing great expectations.

Growing post-Second World War prosperity largely justified the claim by Harold Macmillan (Conservative Prime Minister 1957–63) that 'many of our people have never had it so good', but the economy began to falter in the early 1960s and Britain's first attempt to join the European Economic Community (now the European Union) in 1963 failed. Growing criticism of Britain's social and political institutions developed, manifesting itself in a number of ways: in the satire of TV programmes like *That Was the Week That Was* and publications like *Private Eye*; in a series of books published by Penguin between 1961 and 1964 – *What's Wrong with the Unions?*, *What's Wrong with British Industry?*, *What's Wrong with the Church?*, *What's Wrong with Hospitals?*, and *What's Wrong with Parliament?*; in academic writing, such as Brian Chapman's *British Government Observed* (1963)[9] and Bernard Crick's *The Reform of Parliament* (1964);[10] and in a growing discussion of the need to reform local government, the civil service and Parliament. In part this criticism was assuaged by the election of a Labour government in 1964, which pledged 'to get Britain moving', apparently imbued with a reforming zeal and as yet untarnished by economic difficulties or having any wider doubts about the political system. However, Harold Wilson's government (1964–70) encountered considerable economic difficulties, as did its Conservative successor under Edward Heath (1970–74), resulting in the Conservatives, now led by Margaret Thatcher, shifting to the right and subsequently Labour, particularly under the leadership of Michael Foot (1980–83), shifting to the left. The Thatcher government of 1979–90 espoused free market economic policies, embarked on a massive programme of denationalising or privatising most publicly owned industries and major changes in the structure and operation of the civil service. Her successor as Prime Minister, John Major, continued with these policies, with more privatisation and the introduction of private sector managerial practices in local government and the Health Service, but never recovered from the forced withdrawal from the EU's Exchange Rate Mechanism (ERM) in September 1992 and experienced increasing difficulty with Euro-sceptic members of his party. Meanwhile, Labour under the leadership of, first, Neil Kinnock (1983–92), then John Smith (1992–94) and finally Tony Blair (1994–) gradually moved back to the ideological centre-ground of politics, reformed the party's organisation and structure, and swept to power with a 179-seat majority in 1997.

What has been happening to Parliament in this time, particularly since 1945? The period 1945–70 is widely regarded as the apogee of two-party politics in the UK. Conservative and Labour dominance of British politics was marked by the inability of any other party to secure more than 10 per cent of the votes cast (the Liberals' 11.2 per cent in 1964 being the only exception) and a consequent failure to win more than a handful of parliamentary seats. It was even more marked by the levels of party cohesion in the Commons: backbench rebellions were infrequent and the few defeats governments suffered on the floor of the House were more the result of miscalculation than intent. Yet the disquiet expressed in the early 1960s was reflected in Parliament. The pseudonymous *What's Wrong with Parliament?* (1964) had been written by two House of Commons clerks; Bernard Crick's *Reform of Parliament* (1964) had been preceded by a Fabian Society pamphlet in 1959; other academics were proposing parliamentary reform and in 1964 came together with parliamentary officials to form the Study of Parliament Group. Crucially, other changes were taking place within the House of Commons itself: a subtle but important shift in the types of people being elected to Parliament was taking place – MPs elected in 1959 and later were less willing to play a largely passive role and demanded more involvement and better pay and resources; the Wilson government began a cautious experiment with investigatory select committees; and by the later 1960s there had been a marked growth in backbench dissidence, so that while party cohesion remained the norm, rebellions became a more normal part of parliamentary life. These three developments gathered pace in the last three decades of the twentieth century: the role of the Member of Parliament was professionalised, MPs became full-time with appropriate salaries and resources; the setting up of departmental select committees in 1979 systematised and widened the scope of parliamentary scrutiny across the whole range of governmental activity; and backbench dissidence achieved its own norm alongside that of party cohesion. Moreover, changes made by the Blair government since 1997 – programming most bills, producing more bills in draft, increasing select committee resources, changing the hours of sitting – have simply reinforced this trend. Thus, change there has been, but it has been piecemeal and incremental, rather than wholesale and sudden and through which an immensely strong thread of continuity had continued to run. Gladstone and Disraeli and their contemporaries would still recognise the Parliament of the twenty-first century, obviously enough in that the two chambers have changed little physically – the Commons deliberately decided to rebuild the chamber with the same layout and dimensions afters its destruction in 1941 – the presence of women Members would be the most obvious change, followed by that of microphones and cameras. But they would recognise it procedurally, not least because the House of Commons of the later nineteenth century is much closer procedurally to that of 2004 than it is that of 1800.

In the meantime, further changes have also taken place in the House of Lords, with the introduction of life peers in 1958, a development that rejuvenated the upper house in terms of activity, though not age – life peers often being older than hereditary peers. The House of Lords greatly expanded its activity and carved out a positive but subordinate role for itself, largely complementing the work of the Commons. However, the election of a Labour government in 1964 and its re-election in 1966 with a substantial Commons' majority, brought the question of Lords' reform back onto the political agenda. The Conservative opposition in the Lords became more active and in 1968 all-party talks on reform took place. The Conservative and Labour leaderships actually agreed on proposals for reform of both composition and powers and the government introduced a bill to implement the proposals. Fierce backbench opposition, however, and what was dubbed 'an unholy alliance' between the Conservative right and the Labour left, the former against any reform, the latter in favour of abolition of the upper house, resulted in the government withdrawing the bill.

The House of Lords continued to play an active role, not only amending government legislation but extending its scrutiny role through the use of select committees, particularly after Britain's accession to Europe in 1973. The Labour governments of 1974–79 inevitably clashed with the upper house, but the post-1979 Conservative governments were far from immune and in 1990 the Lords rejected the government's War Crimes Bill on the grounds that it was retrospective in claiming jurisdiction over people and territory not subject to British rule or control at the time the alleged crimes were committed. For the first time since 1949 the government – a Conservative government at that – resorted to the use of the Parliament Acts, although Labour had twice threatened it in 1975–77.

Table 2.7   *Party composition of the House of Lords, 1999 and 2003*

Party	1999	2003
Conservative	39.9	31.6
Labour	16.0	27.6
Liberal Democrat	6.0	9.6
Crossbenchers	29.2	26.5
No affiliation	8.8	4.7
Total	99.9	100.0

Source: www.parliament.uk.

Labour's experience of 1968 and 1974–79 resulted in a hardening of its position towards the upper house and its 1983 election manifesto pledged the party to abolition, but Labour shifted back to reform in 1992 and in 1997 the manifesto promised 'to make the House of Lords more democratic and representative'. This set the scene for the most dramatic change since 1911. Lords' reform was to be in two stages: first, the removal of the hereditary peers and, second, the creation of 'a more democratic and representative' second chamber. The House of Lords Act, 1999 removed all but 92 of the hereditary peers (the result of a compromise to secure the bill's passage through the Lords) and the government set up a royal commission to bring forward proposals for further reform. This left the House of Lords dominated by life peers, whose numbers were substantially increased by Tony Blair after 1997, resulting in the balance between Conservative and Labour peers becoming much more even, once most of the hereditary peers had been removed (see Table 2.7).

The removal of the hereditaries and the shift in party balance made the upper house feel more legitimate and it not only continued to amend government legislation but rejected two bills – the European Elections Bill and the Sexual Offences (Amendment) Bill, leading the government to invoke the Parliament Acts in order to secure their passage. The royal commission, chaired by Lord Wakeham, a former Conservative Chief Whip in the Commons, took widespread evidence and produced a report that proposed alternative proportions of elected and appointed members of the Lords, but no fundamental change in the role of the upper house. A joint committee of the two houses was then appointed and set seven options for the future composition of the upper house, ranging from 100 per cent appointed to 100 per cent elected, with various mixtures of appointed and elected in between. In February 2003 the House of Lords voted clearly for an all-appointed house, but the House of Commons rejected all seven options, leaving the government to bring forward its own preference for the removal of the remaining 92 hereditary peers and creation by default of an all-appointed House of Lords.

Like the House of Commons, the Lords is procedurally similar to its predecessor of 1900, with the important exception of the loss of its legislative veto, but in terms of its composition it has changed dramatically and its relationship with the Commons is essentially complementary rather than confrontational. It has also enhanced its ability to scrutinise the executive, particularly since the introduction of life peers, but hardly to the extent that it seriously distorts the executive dominance of Parliament.

Has the balance shifted? Compared with the situation in the 1940s and 1950s, the answer is yes, but for many observers it has not shifted nearly enough: executive dominance remains the norm. Harking back to a mythical 'golden age of Parliament' serves no useful purpose. What is needed is a sober consideration of the appropriate balance between the ability of governments to govern and the need for governments to be accountable. In the context of parliamentary government that means examining the relationship between Parliament and the executive.

Notes

1   This chapter is a substantially revised and updated version of Chapter 3 in Michael Rush, *Parliamentary Government in Britain*, Pitman, London, 1981.
2   Max Weber, *The Theory of Social and Economic Organisation* (trans. A. M. Henderson, ed. T. Parsons), New York, The Free Press, 1947, p. 328.
3   Walter Bagehot, *The English Constitution*, London, C. A. Watts, 1964 (originally published between 1865 and 1867).
4   R. H. S. Crossman, 'Introduction' to Bagehot, *The English Constitution*, p. 40.
5   Such threat had actually been carried out in 1712, when twelve Tory peers were created to ensure the passage of the Treaty of Utrecht. It was a more substantial threat in 1911, since a large number of Liberal peers would have had to be created in order to overwhelm the considerable Conservative majority.
6   Liaison Committee, First Report: Shifting the Balance: Select Committees and the Executive, HC 300, 1999–2000.
7   *Report of the Commission to Strengthen Parliament: Strengthening Parliament*, London, Conservative Party, 2000.
8   Hansard Society, *Report of the Hansard Society Commission on Parliamentary Scrutiny: The Challenge for Parliament*, London, Vacher Dod, 2001.
9   Brian Chapman, *British Government Observed*, London, Allen & Unwin, 1963.
10 Bernard Crick, *The Reform of Parliament*, London, Weidenfeld and Nicolson, 1963 (2nd edn, 1968).

3

The functions of Parliament

Instead of the function of governing, for which it is radically unfit, the proper office of a representative assembly is to watch and control the government: to throw the light of publicity on its acts; to compel a full exposition and justification of all of them which anyone considers questionable; to censure them if found condemnable, and, if the men who compose the government abuse their trust, or fulfil it in a manner which conflicts with the deliberate sense of the nation, to expel them from office, and either expressly or virtually appoint their successors.[1]

The concept of parliamentary control

In discussing the functions of Parliament it is as well to begin by saying what Parliament does not do – it does not govern. Parliamentary government does not mean government by Parliament but government through Parliament. For John Stuart Mill, the role of a representative body or assembly was that of control. Thus, although he enumerated several functions of an assembly – financial, deliberative, legislative, the monitoring of personnel, and the redressing of grievances, they were not to be performed in a detailed way but as ultimate oversight or accountability. Indeed, Mill is very clear on what Parliament should not do: it should not propose taxation or expenditure; it should not administer policy; and it should not examine or approve legislative proposals in detail. To become involved in such matters was not only inappropriate but inefficient and counter-productive. 'There is', Mill argued, 'a radical distinction between controlling the business of government and actually doing it'.[2]

Mill was writing at a time – 1861 – when the party system was in a state of flux: the old Tory–Whig dichotomy was breaking down and the new

Conservative–Liberal dichotomy was emerging, but it was not clearly discernible until the general election of 1868. Mill's ideal of representation is

> that the whole people, or some numerous portion of them, exercise through
> deputies periodically elected by themselves the ultimate controlling power, which,
> in every constitution, must reside somewhere. This ultimate power they must
> possess in all its completeness. They must be masters, when they please, of all
> the operations of government.[3]

However, Mill, like other contemporary observers, did not envisage the emergence of the monolithic parties that were soon to dominate British politics. Between the defeat of Sir Robert Peel's Conservative government in 1846 and the election of Gladstone's Liberals in 1868 governments could not be certain of retaining majority support in the House of Commons – the Commons did exercise ultimate control. Of the seven governments that held office between 1846 and 1868, five fell because of adverse votes in the Commons – those of Russell in 1852, Aberdeen in 1855, Palmerston in 1858, Derby in 1859 and Russell again in 1866. Since 1868 only three governments have lost office following adverse votes in the Commons – Rosebery in 1895, Macdonald in 1924 and Callaghan in 1979. After 1868 the ultimate authority passed from the House of Commons to the electorate and changes of government normally resulted from defeats at the polls rather than defeats in the Commons. Moreover, after 1868 governments normally had majority support in the Commons and the growth of party cohesion reduced and then minimised the likelihood of parliamentary defeats. Nonetheless, Mill's view of the essential role or function of Parliament was one that was recognised by contemporary politicians. In fact, some six years before the publication of *Representative Government*, Gladstone told the House of Commons: 'Your business is not to govern the country, but it is, if you think fit, to call to account those who do govern it.'[4]

Gladstone was speaking in a debate which ended in defeat for the government and its resignation. Does the fact that governments are now rarely forced to resign or forced into an election as a result of a defeat in the Commons mean that the concept of parliamentary control has become a fiction? One answer is a resounding yes, reflecting the view that it is not Parliament which controls the executive but the executive which controls Parliament. Governments rarely lose a vote of confidence in the Commons; most government legislation is passed; governments suffer few defeats on either the floor of the Commons or in legislative committees. In short, most of the time governments not only survive, but get their way. And yet there is a more complex, subtle answer: there is more give and take by governments than the formal record suggests; governments listen to backbenchers, particularly their own supporters, and try to head off or reduce the size of rebellions; and, however much control they may have over the Commons, governments do not control the House of Lords, even Conservative governments before the removal of almost all the hereditary peers. Parliamentary control, it is argued, is not an absolute but a relative concept. This view is aptly summarised by Crick: 'Control means influence, not direct power; advice, not command; criticism, not obstruction; scrutiny, not initiation; and publicity, not secrecy.'[5]

An ideal view, perhaps, but not one that is necessarily totally at odds with reality. Arguably, it is a view that seeks to balance reality with what is achievable, rather than seeking a return to a mythical 'golden age' of Parliament. It is also a view that needs to be borne very much in mind when considering the functions of Parliament in more detail.

A multi-functional view of Parliament

Parliament is a multi-functional institution (see Table 3.1). With the important exception of the judicial function, which is carried out by the twelve Lords of Appeal, the Law Lords, all parliamentary functions are performed by both Houses, but in each case the House of Commons is the more important of the two. In addition, all these functions are carried out collectively by the two Houses, that is by the House as a whole or through its committees, but a number are also carried out individually by the members of each House. Analytically, they are separate functions, but in practice there is significant overlap between them.

Table 3.1   *The functions of Parliament*

Function*	Performed by			
	House of Commons	House of Lords	Collectively	Individually
Legitimising	X	x	X	
Representative	X	x	X	X
Financial	X	x	X	
Redressing grievances	X	x	X	X
Legislative	X	x	X	x
Recruitment of ministers	X	x	X	
Scrutinising and informing	X	x	X	x
Judicial		X	x†	

Source: Michael Rush, *Parliament and the Public*, London, Longman, 2nd edn, 1986, p. 25.

Notes: * X indicates the more important of the two Houses in performing a particular function, x the less important. † Performed exclusively by the Law Lords (the 12 Lords of Appeal), the Lord Chancellor and former Lord Chancellors.

The legitimacy function

Early Parliaments and their pre-parliamentary predecessors were first and foremost legitimising bodies, giving authority to the actions and proposals of monarchs and sometimes their opponents, such as de Montfort, who would summon a Parliament as a basis for support in seeking to curb the monarch. The fact that Parliaments were sometimes 'packed' with the supporters of the monarch or one faction or another is beside the point: Parliaments were a means of formally justifying the prevailing political reality. The legitimacy of modern governments rests on Parliament, from whom they derive their authority. In medieval times Parliament as a whole conferred such legitimacy, but increasingly it was the House of Commons that was the true fount of legitimacy – the elected representatives of the people. That these representatives were elected on a variable and often narrow franchise, that later elections were determined by bribery, corruption and patronage, that nowadays they would not be regarded as democratically elected is also beside the point. The House of Commons eventually became and remains the linchpin of political legitimacy, the essential foundation of the political system. Of course, constitutionally important aspects of governmental authority stem from the royal prerogative, but the right to exercise the royal prerogative rests on the ability of the government to retain the confidence of the House of Commons. It is now common to argue that the government's legitimacy comes ultimately from the people – the electorate, but that legitimacy is channelled through the Commons.

There is a further, more mundane, aspect of legitimacy: with the 'advice and consent' of Parliament the monarch proclaims Acts of Parliament. Statute law now constitutes the huge bulk of law in the UK – some of it now devolved to other bodies but based on the same ultimate authority. The courts can and do interpret the law but it is principally the law passed by Parliament. Put another way, Parliament legitimises the government's policies by passing the laws necessary for their implementation and by approving the necessary expenditure and taxation. Although the Lords has no power over financial business, this involves both Houses, since the Commons can act alone only if it chooses to invoke the Parliament Acts to override the Lords' veto. Parliament's ability to confer legitimacy, however, rests on its status as a representative institution.

The representative function

From its inception the House of Commons has been seen as a representative body in that its members have always been chosen to represent those living in clearly defined territorial areas or constituencies. The means of choosing such representatives may have been imperfect, and for some observers remain so, but they were and are representatives of those who sent them to Parliament, charged with the task of protecting and advancing the interests of their constituents and, it came to be argued, of the people or the nation as a whole. It was Edmund Burke (1729–97) who articulated this view most eloquently in 1774 his Letter to the Electors of Bristol:

> it ought to be the happiness and glory of a representative to live in the strictest union, the closest correspondence, and most unreserved communication with his constituents. Their wishes ought to have great weight with him, their opinion high respect, their business his unremitted attention. It is his duty to sacrifice his repose, his pleasures, his satisfaction, to theirs, and, above all, even, and in all cases, to prefer their interest to his own. But, his unbiased opinion, his mature judgement, his enlightened conscience, he ought not to sacrifice to you, to any man, to any set of men living ... Your representative owes you, not his industry only, but his judgement; and he betrays, instead of serving you, if he sacrifices it to your opinion ...
>
> Parliament is not a Congress of ambassadors from different and hostile interests; which interests each must maintain, as an agent, and advocate, against other agents and advocates; but Parliament is a deliberative assembly of one nation, with one interest, that of the whole; where, not local purposes, not local prejudices, ought to guide, but the general good, resulting from the general reason of the whole. You choose a Member indeed: but when you have chosen him, he is not the Member for Bristol, but he is a Member of Parliament.[6]

In short, Burke argued that MPs were representatives, not delegates bound by instructions and that, while having a duty to protect and advance the interests of their constituents, also have a duty to protect and advance the interests of the nation – the population as whole.

The representative function inevitably falls principally on the House of Commons, though historically the House of Lords represented the landed aristocracy and, to a lesser extent, the established church. Nonetheless, in a more amorphous way Parliament also claims to represent public opinion, acting as a conduit for the people's views, whether as individuals or collectively, organised or unorganised. In this aspect of representation the House of Lords also plays a part, even though most of its present members represent no one but themselves. However, just as individuals may (and many do) contact their Members of Parliament, so they may also contact members of the Lords (even if in not particularly large numbers) and pressure groups certainly see the upper house as useful means of securing a hearing for their views. Should an elected element be introduced into the House of Lords, its representative role would expand considerably.

The financial function

Constitutionally and formally since 1911, but by convention long before then, the financial function has been exclusively that of the House of Commons. It can be linked directly to the legitimacy and representative functions in that a number of early Parliaments were summoned specifically to approve the raising of additional taxation and, as a representative body, the Commons in particular was seen as an appropriate legitimising body. More crucially, the authorisation of taxation and expenditure was used, historically, by the Commons as a means of extracting concessions from the monarch and generally seeking to exert control over the executive. Although for many years the Commons has been regarded as largely ineffective in exerting financial control, the financial function remains the basis on which government is obliged to present annually to Parliament its proposals for expenditure and taxation, and this provides important opportunities for the Commons in particular to fulfil its scrutiny and informing function.

The redress of grievances function

The right of consent to taxation also gave Parliament its most important and powerful weapon historically: the demand that the redress of grievances should precede the granting of supply or authority to raise money. Initially, this took the form of demands for the redress by the monarch of particular and limited grievances. However, it gradually expanded to looking after the collective interests of the constituencies, especially economic interests, and in due course to dealing more broadly with the problems of individual constituents to the extent that the constituency role has become a major function of the individual MP. Seeking remedies for particular grievances or problems, however, opened the way to a further function – the legislative function.

The legislative function

Parliament is a legislature or, more precisely, is a crucial part of the legislative machinery and therefore of the legislative process. Dealing with particular problems led the way to broader initiatives in the form of proposing and approving legislation. At first, this was in the form of a petition to the monarch, but it was not long before the Commons also claimed the right to approve proposals made by the monarch. Legislation fell into two categories – private and public. Private legislation applied to named persons or specified localities and was therefore of limited application, whereas public legislation applied to everyone and to the country as a whole and therefore had general application. These distinctions remain, although private Acts of Parliament are now few in number. They are used mainly to enable local authorities and similar statutory bodies to undertake particular tasks, such as the development of a harbour or marina, tramway or light railway. These are known as local acts. There is a further category – personal acts, necessary before 1857, for example, to obtain a divorce, but also to deal with particular problems relating to legacies and estates or to permit marriage between persons not eligible to marry under existing law. These are even fewer in number. Historically, however, private acts were of considerable importance: they were the origin of Parliament's legislative function and later played a vital part in facilitating the industrial revolution, since the building of canals, roads and railways and, later, municipal utilities, such as the supply of gas and water, required parliamentary approval. Thus during the nineteenth century the number of private acts considerably exceeded the number of public acts.

Both houses are closely involved in the legislative function, although the financial supremacy of the Commons means that bills concerning taxation and expenditure must be first introduced in the lower house. Private legislation is dealt with separately and by a quasi-judicial procedure that allows those promoting a particular bill and any opposed to it to be formally represented.

As the level of governmental intervention grew, an additional type of legislation was developed – rules and regulations issued by those in authority, mainly ministers, under powers granted by an Act of Parliament. The principal form of such legislation is the statutory instrument (SI), with a limited number being issued under the royal prerogative, called Orders in Council. Together these are generically known as delegated, subordinate or secondary legislation, primary legislation being the Acts of Parliament authorising them. They too are dealt with by both houses, partly separately, partly through a joint committee. At the beginning of the twentieth century there were less than 1,000 SIs a year; by the end of the century SIs were running at more than 3,000 a year. This area of delegated legislation was further expanded by the UK's accession to the EU in 1973 and Parliament has devised similar but separate procedures for dealing with the considerable amount of legislation emanating from Brussels.

The responsibility for initiating most legislation passed by Parliament is, of course, that of the executive. Although the number of bills tabled by backbenchers in the Commons (though not the Lords), exceeds the number initiated by the government, the success rate of Private Members' bills only occasionally exceeds 20 per cent and is often less than 10 per cent, whereas that of government bills invariably exceeds 95 per cent, sometimes reaching 100 per cent. This does not mean that government bills are unchanged, some are subject to a significant and extensive amendment, but here too the initiative lies mainly with the government. Ministers are therefore key actors in the legislative process and it is through Parliament, again the Commons in particular, that ministers are almost exclusively recruited.

The recruitment of ministers

By convention ministers are expected not only to be accountable to Parliament, principally the Commons, but to be members of one or other of the two houses in order to facilitate such accountability. Increasingly, this means being a member of the Commons rather than the Lords: in 1830 just under half (48.9 per cent) of the government were MPs; in 1900 it was 55.0 per cent; in 1920 71.6 per cent; and the norm since then has been four-fifths. In 1997, no fewer than 78.6 per cent of the 112 members of the Blair government were MPs. Furthermore, as already noted, the Prime Minister, the Chancellor of the Exchequer and most other leading member of the government are also expected to be MPs. Of course, the government needs ministers in the House of Lords to see its business through the upper house, but most are middle-ranking or junior ministers, although at least two members of the Lords, the Lord Chancellor and the Leader of the Government in the Lords, are always members of the Cabinet.

Nonetheless, the path to ministerial office is through Parliament in general and the Commons in particular, so that by the time they become ministers, most will have served a 'parliamentary apprenticeship' through several years' membership of the Lords or Commons. Those appointed to more senior offices will normally have also served a 'ministerial apprenticeship' lower down the ministerial hierarchy, although the Blair government of 1997 was a significant exception. Parliament, however, is where most ministers 'learn their trade' and even members of the first Blair Cabinet had spent an average of 18 years in Parliament, with none fewer than 10. Ministers are also at the heart of what is arguably Parliament's most important role, its scrutinising and informing function.

The scrutinising and informing function

The scrutinising and informing function consists, on the one hand, of seeking to render the executive accountable by examining government policy and administration and, on the other, of providing the public with information about what the government is doing and why. Parliament exercises its scrutinising and informing function through most of its other functions – by representing the interests and opinions of constituents and the nation as a whole, by seeking to exert financial accountability, by the redressing of grievances, and by examining and approving legislation. It does so through a variety of settings and procedures. The chambers of the two houses provide the most public setting, particularly since the introduction of the broadcasting of Parliament, but much parliamentary work is done less publicly in committees. On rare occasions secret sessions are held and the public is excluded, as happened on a number of occasions during the Second World War. Since November 1999 there have been additional debates – known as Westminster Hall sittings because they are held in the former grand committee room off Westminster Hall. Apart from a relatively small number of committee meetings, the public is normally admitted to all parliamentary proceedings, but neither the public nor the media pay a great deal of attention to Parliament outside the proceedings in the two chambers. In addition, most parliamentary proceedings are published either in the Official Report, commonly known as *Hansard*, or in reports issued by select committees. However, as far as the public and the media are concerned, once again far more attention is focused on what happens in the two chambers than elsewhere. Nonetheless, what Parliament does is there for all who wish to see or read it.

Both houses also have at their disposal a range of procedures for scrutinising the executive, including a variety of debates – some directed at specific types of business, such as bills or financial matters, others to discuss policy proposals or matters the opposition wish debated, the asking of parliamentary Questions for oral answer in the chamber or written answer printed in *Hansard*. Members of either house may table bills and motions for debate. Committees deal with much of the detailed consideration of legislation, both primary and secondary, and also conduct investigations into government policy and its administration, usually by taking oral and written evidence from ministers, civil servants, pressure groups and experts in the fields concerned. Procedurally, there is no shortage of means by which Parliament can seek to fulfil its scrutiny and informing function, but two major constraints exist – party and time. This is true more of the Commons than the Lords, since party is much more important in the former and the government, through its majority, largely controls the agenda. In the House of Lords, however, the absence of an assured majority, much less control over the agenda and the presence of a significant non-party or crossbench element sometimes makes the upper house a more fruitful source of scrutiny. The ultimate question, of course, is how effective is parliamentary scrutiny? That, however, is a question for later and more extensive discussion.

The MP's view of Parliament

Theoretical constructs of the functions of Parliament are all very well, but what is the MP's view? A survey conducted on behalf of the Hansard Society in 2000 provides one answer. It is clear from the data in Table 3.2 that the scrutiny function is overwhelmingly accepted by MPs with more than nine out of ten regarding scrutinising legislation and government departments as 'very important' or 'quite important'. The survey similarly shows that more than four-fifths regard dealing with constituents' problems in the same light. Further questions elicited very strong support for the representative function, with 94.8 per cent seeing representing their geographical constituency as 'very important' or 'quite important' and 91.4 per cent 'the nation as a whole', 82.9 per cent individual constituents, and 73.1 per cent their political party. Asked which of these various functions is the most important, however, far more said scrutinising legislation or government departments than solving constituents' problems or supporting their party. In short, the survey suggests that there is a strong correlation between the

Table 3.2　MPs' views on the functions of Parliament

Function	Very important	Quite important	Total	Most important
Scrutinising legislation	85.4	10.1	95.5	47.8
Scrutinising government depts	74.6	20.9	95.5	20.3
Debating issues of national importance	65.5	24.3	89.8	8.0
Solving constituents' problems	57.1	26.5	83.6	15.2
Supporting party policy	25.3	37.3	62.6	2.2

Source: Hansard Society, *Report of the Hansard Society Commission on Parliamentary Scrutiny: The Challenge for Parliament – Making Government Accountable*, London, Vacher Dod Publishing, 2001, Appendix 4, Table 2.1.

Note: N = 179.

Table 3.3　MPs' views on their roles

Role	Very important	Quite important	Total	Most important
Protecting the interests of the constituency	67.4	26.3	93.7	21.4
Dealing with constituents' grievances	54.3	36.6	90.9	17.5
Holding the government to account	53.1	30.3	83.4	38.3
Examining legislation	41.1	30.9	72.0	14.9
Voting with my party	24.0	44.6	68.6	2.6
Informing constituents about government activity	20.0	42.9	62.9	0.6
Working on a departmental committee	24.7	30.5	55.2	2.6
Speaking in the Chamber	19.3	31.3	50.6	0.6
Writing/giving speeches	12.6	36.2	48.8	0.6
Appearing on radio/TV	10.3	31.6	41.9	0.6
Writing articles for newspapers/ magazines	6.3	22.0	28.3	0.6

Source: Hansard Society, *Report of the Hansard Society Commission on Parliamentary Scrutiny: The Challenge for Parliament – Making Government Accountable*, London, Vacher Dod Publishing, 2001, Appendix 4, Table 3.2.

Note: N = 179.

functions delineated in Table 3.1 and what MPs regard as the functions of Parliament.

It is also important to look at what MPs think their role is: the Hansard survey again provides a detailed picture (see Table 3.3). A more complex

Table 3.4 *The three roles of the MP*

Role	Description
The partisan role	Supporting the party in debates, the asking of parliamentary Questions and signing of motions, committee work and, above all, in the division lobbies
The constituency role	Helping constituents with individual problems, e.g. access to welfare, housing and other local council issues, and immigration cases. Dealing with the collective interests of the constituency, e.g. promoting local business, seeking funds for the constituency, environmental issues
The scrutiny role	Assessing government policy proposals; examining primary and secondary legislation; evaluating expenditure and taxation; checking on the implementation and administration of government policy

picture emerges: the constituency role heads the list in rating roles as 'very important' or 'quite important', but 'holding the government to account' is seen as the 'most important', with the constituency role and that of examining legislation some way behind and all others as insignificant when ranked by importance. From this data it is possible to delineate three principal roles of the MP (see Table 3.4).

With the exception of the occasional Member elected as an Independent, all MPs perform these three roles: MPs are elected as members of parties and normally support their parties in the House, in committees and in the division lobbies; MPs are seen and see themselves as constituency representatives and therefore look after the individual and collective interests of their constituents; and through debates, the asking of parliamentary Questions, the tabling and signing of motions, various types of committee activity MPs scrutinise the government and its policies. The extent to which they perform them, the balance between them and the effectiveness with which they do so are matters of choice and judgement, the choice of MPs and the judgement of others. If MPs have roles, however, so also do members of the House of Lords.

The particular functions of the House of Lords

The two Houses of Parliament largely operate separately, co-ordinating their activities where necessary. Even though they have a great deal in common, they differ organisationally and procedurally and have separate staffs. Relations between the two houses have altered over time: the Commons quickly established its financial supremacy and later its general superiority in that the

Box 3.1   The particular functions of the House of Lords

The Bryce functions

1 Causing sufficient delay to legislation to enable the government or the public, or both, to reconsider legislation passed by the House of Commons.
2 Examining and revising bills passed by the House of Commons.
3 Initiating non-controversial legislation, so that less time is needed for it in
   the House of Commons.
4 Holding debates on major issues and policies in a less partisan atmosphere
   than the House of Commons

The post-1958 functions

5 The consolidation of existing legislation and saving time in the House of
   Commons.
6 Dealing with private legislation and saving time in the House of Commons.
7 Dealing with delegated legislation, including European Union legislation.
8 Scrutinising government policy and administration

Source: *Report of the Conference on the Reform of the Second Chamber* (Bryce Commission),
Cd. 9038, 1918; Bernard Crick, *The Reform of Parliament*, London, Weidenfeld and Nicolson,
2nd edn, 1968, pp. 111–21; and Donald Shell, *The House of Lords*, London, Harvester-
Wheatsheaf, 2nd edn, 1992, pp. 20–8.

survival of the government depended on retaining majority support in the
lower house and that the Lords would normally give way to the Commons
on disagreements over legislation. Since the latter was and is a matter of
convention, not law, there were periodic clashes between the two houses,
culminating in the passage of the Parliament Act, 1911, which gave the Commons the power to override the Lords' veto, as well as enshrining its financial
supremacy in statute.

As the subordinate of the two houses, the Lords has carved out a role for
itself based partly on the report of a commission, which, though delayed by
the First World War, was set up after the Parliament Act to further reform,
and partly since the passing of the Life Peerages Act, 1958, which boosted its
membership (see Box 3.1).

The preamble of the 1911 Act anticipated further reform of the Lords and
in 1917 a commission chaired by Lord Bryce, a constitutional lawyer and
Liberal politician, was appointed to draw up proposals. In the event, no action
was taken on the Bryce proposals on the composition of the Lords, nor were
the functions suggested as appropriate to a second chamber formally adopted,
but in practice they became the basis of what the House of Lords actually did.

Bryce argued that, with majority-based governments in the Commons normally able to pass whatever legislation they wished, from time to time there were likely to be bills which, in whole or part, aroused considerable controversy, justifying a delay or pause for thought, possibly leading to compromise. If, however, the Commons persisted, the Lords would normally give way or leave the government to invoke the Parliament Act. The revising function was largely uncontroversial, although from time to time the Lords found itself in conflict with the Commons. Initiating non-controversial legislation, proposals on which the government and opposition were largely agreed, had the advantage of saving the Commons time – most of the donkey-work had been done on such bills, allowing the Commons to devote less time to them. By its very composition the Commons was more partisan than the Lords and there had long been a crossbench element in the upper house, which was given a significant boost by the introduction of life peerages from 1958. Moreover, the range of expertise in the House of Lords is considerable. All these factors combine to facilitate less confrontational and more wide-ranging debates in the upper house.

It would be misleading to suggest that the 'post-1958 functions' date from the 1958 Life Peerages Act, let alone are the product of it. With the important exception of EU legislation, each existed before, but each has taken on a greater importance as the introduction of life peers extended the composition of the Lords and made it an increasingly active house, as is clearly shown in Table 3.5.

In effect, the House of Lords has carved out for itself a more active role by extending these functions, mostly mundane but important tasks. Over time the statute book gets increasingly complex as act after act is passed. Some acts extend the law in a particular policy area, others supersede earlier legislation and, periodically, the law in a particular field is brought together in a single act, a process known as consolidation. Much of the detailed work on these consolidation bills is done by the Lords, again saving the Commons time. Similarly, the upper house shares the burden of private legislation. However,

Table 3.5 *The growth of House of Lords' activity, 1950–2000*

Activity	1950	1959–60	1997	2000
Average daily attendance	86	136	394	346
Sitting days	100	113	125	169
Sitting hrs.	294	450	817	1,261
Length of sitting(h/m)	2.57	4.00	6.32	7.28
Sittings after 10 p.m.	1	1	47	80+

Source: Donald Shell, *The House of Lords*, London, Harvester-Wheatsheaf, 1st edn, 1988 and 2nd edn 1992, Table 4.2 and *House of Lords, Annual Report and Accounts*, 2000–01.

it is in the area of delegated legislation and the scrutiny of policy and administration that the House of Lords has most significantly extended its role. Here, partly jointly with the Commons but more importantly through setting up a Delegated Powers and Deregulation Committee, the upper house makes a major contribution to the scrutiny of delegated legislation. Furthermore, since the UK's accession to the EU in 1973, the House of Lords has played a very active role in the scrutiny of EU legislation. More generally, by its use of committees, through parliamentary Questions and debates the Lords extends the parliamentary scrutiny of policy and administration beyond that provided by the Commons.

In a similar fashion to MPs, therefore, peers perform a number of roles, but they differ from MPs in not having constituency responsibilities and about a quarter have no party affiliation. Of course, if further reform of the composition of the upper house were to take place and an elected element were introduced, then those peers would have constituents to represent, unless they were elected on a nation-wide rather than a regional or constituency basis. It is also highly likely that most would also represent parties and possibly create a more partisan atmosphere in the second chamber.

Conclusion

Parliament is thus a complex multi-functional institution, with two houses that operate largely separately and in different ways to a significant degree. The House of Commons is the more important of the two in theory and practice, but the House of Lords performs a number of mostly mundane but important functions. In practice, Parliament's performance of its functions depends on party, especially in the Commons. Parties are the engines of Parliament and the fact that most general elections result in one party having an absolute majority of seats in the Commons profoundly affects the way in which Parliament operates and, therefore, how effectively it performs its functions. However, these are also affected by the personnel of Parliament and by the resources made available to sustain them in their roles as MPs and peers.

Notes

1 J. S. Mill, *Representative Government*, London, J. M. Dent, 1910, p. 239.
2 *Ibid.*, p. 230.
3 *Ibid.*, p. 228.
4 HC Debs, 3rd series, 136, 29 June 1855, c. 1202.
5 Bernard Crick, *The Reform of Parliament*, London, Weidenfeld and Nicolson, 2nd edn, 1968, p. 80.
6 Edmund Burke, *Works*, London, George Bell, 1883, Vol. I, pp. 446–7.

4

Parliament and democracy

Defining democracy

Democracy is that form of government based on the principle of popular consent and control. The difficulty in defining it more precisely is that, while there is no shortage of means and devices by which attempts to elicit consent and exert control can be made, there is a lack of agreement about the effectiveness of these means and devices. Whether a political system or a particular political institution or practice is democratic is therefore a matter of opinion.

Democracy is widely regarded today as a desirable form of government, even the most desirable, but it has not always been so. It can be traced back historically to the Greeks, in particular to the Greek city-states such as Athens, but the two most famous Greek political philosophers, Plato and Aristotle, did not look favourably on democracy. Both feared that people could be swayed by unscrupulous demagogues and Aristotle regarded democracy as a perverted form of the rule of the many. However, Aristotle's beliefs on a desirable form of the rule of the many, involving a well-informed and responsible citizenry, have much in common with modern ideas about democracy. The practices of those in power seeking the consent of the governed for particular purposes and of the governed seeking to control those holding power are closely linked to the origins of the development of Parliament, as already noted. However, contemporaries did not see such practices as manifestations of democracy, but rather as pragmatic responses to particular needs and situations. In any case, as late as the latter part of the eighteenth century, democracy tended to be equated with the rule of the mob, something to be feared rather than admired. Political philosophers, such as Locke, and practising politicians, such as the Founding Fathers of the United States or members of the House of Commons, did not see themselves as democrats, even though they believed in the importance of securing the consent of the governed. The Founding Father feared what Alexis de Tocqueville (1835–40) and John Stuart

Table 4.1   *Democracy: consent and control mechanisms*

Consent	Control
Direct	
Elections	Elections
Referendums	Referendums
Initiatives	Initiatives
Recalls	Recalls
Opinion polls	Opinion polls
E-democracy	E-democracy
Indirect	
Legislative representation	The rule of law
Pressure politics	Pressure politics
	Judicial review
	Legislative scrutiny
	Ombudsman systems

Source: Michael Rush, *Politics and Society: An Introduction to Political Sociology*, London, Prentice-Hall, 1992, p. 81.

Mill referred to as 'the tyranny of the majority' – that the many, particularly the ill-informed or ignorant many, could and would impose their will on the few. In order to counter this the framers of the US Constitution created a number of checks and balances, not only separating powers but providing for the President to check the power of the Congress and the Congress to check the power of the President. Because of these mechanisms, designed to give some built-in protection to minorities, the American Constitution is described as anti-majoritarian. Thus, to equate democracy with the rule of the majority is simplistic: for a majority to use its numerical superiority to oppress a minority is regarded as profoundly anti-democratic. Consent and control mechanisms have to be much more sophisticated than just counting heads (see Table 4.1).

Democratic consent and control mechanisms can be divided into the direct and the indirect, direct in that people can participate directly in deciding something, indirect in that consent and control operate through intermediate institutions, individuals, processes or principles. Elections are the mechanism most commonly associated with democracy, but whether they are considered democratic depends on a number of factors. Who are the electorate? What are they deciding? How frequently should elections be held? Who decides when to hold an election? What type of electoral system should be used? Should decisions be based on a simple or relative majority (largest number) or an absolute majority (more than 50 per cent)? Are some matters so important that they should be decided by an even higher proportion, such as two-thirds or four-fifths? Does it matter what proportion of the electorate actually votes? If it is a system of representative democracy, what should be the basis of representation – people, territory, interests? There is no definitive answer to each of these questions, although wider agreement can be secured on some more than others.

Specific answers can be provided in the British case. The electorate consists of all persons of 18 years and over who are citizens of the UK or of other members of the EU or a Commonwealth country, who are not members of the House of Lords, serving a prison sentence of longer than 12 months, or certified insane, resident in the UK on the annual qualifying date of 10 October or has a right of residence in the UK and whose names appear on the electoral register. Thus, someone who fulfils all the appropriate criteria but is not on the electoral register is not a member of the electorate. On this basis, the UK claims to have universal adult suffrage; in practice, it is somewhat short of this. On a UK-wide basis elections are used to choose Members of Parliament, but indirectly they are used to choose which party will form the government, or more precisely, which party's leader will become Prime Minister. Only rarely nowadays is this not the case, when no party wins a majority of seats in the Commons and the Queen must decide whom to invite to form a government. Even then, the Queen's choice is circumscribed by what is politically and practically feasible. Under the terms of the Parliament Act 1911, elections must be held at least every five years, although the Prime Minister may in practice call an election before the full five years have expired, as happened, for instance, in 1983, 1987 and 2001 and, very occasionally, a Prime Minister is forced into an election, as happened in 1979. The electoral system used in general elections is the simple plurality, commonly known as the first-past-the-post system (FPTP) because the candidate with the largest number of votes in each constituency is elected MP for that constituency. MPs therefore need only a relative majority to be elected, so that, while some do win more than 50 per cent of the votes cast in their constituency, others have the support of less than 50 per cent. This means that general elections are not conducted on the basis of proportional representation, so that parties do not normally win a number of seats commensurate with number of votes they have received. Elections are valid regardless of the proportion of the electorate actually casting their votes, either in a particular constituency or in the country generally. The UK's claim to be a representative democracy rests on the fact that in each of, currently, 659 constituencies the electorate choose a single MP.

Elections in the UK also allow the electorate to exert some control indirectly over the government between elections through the holding of by-elections to fill casual vacancies in particular constituencies and through elections held for other purposes. These can be used to send 'messages' to the government of the day. Of course, by-elections take place only in the constituency in which there is a vacancy caused by the death, resignation, appointment to various posts outside Parliament, elevation to the House of Lords, or, on rare occasions, the disqualification of the sitting MP. However, a number of by-elections in different parts of the country over a period of time can give the governing party and its opponents a clear message about how the public feels about various matters and the government's performance generally. In the period since the Second World War this was especially true of the time between 1945 and 1970, when the average number of by-elections per year between general elections was 11.2. Governments, however, became increasingly wary of creating by-election vacancies by appointing MPs to positions incompatible with continued membership of the Commons, since they too often lost the ensuing by-election. This led to a marked decrease in the number of MPs appointed, for example, to judicial posts and chairs of various public bodies – all 'unnecessary' appointments because they did not have to be filled by MPs and therefore to a fall in the number of by-elections. Between 1970 and 1997 they averaged 5.7 a year. Even so, by-elections can still convey a powerful message and, indeed, had a significant impact of on John Major's Conservative government between 1992 and 1997. Not only did the government fail to win a single by-election but its original majority of 21 in 1992 was gradually whittled away, helped to a degree by the defection of two MPs to the Liberal Democrats and one to Labour, but resulting mainly from by-election losses.

Other elections – notably local government elections in England since devolution, but local elections generally before, and elections to the European Parliament – have also been used by the electorate to send messages to the government about its performance, although this is not, of course, the only factor affecting or explaining local electoral behaviour. The fact that turnout in both local and European elections is significantly lower than in general elections is beside the point, since failure to vote may be an expression of opinion too. Whether elections to the Scottish Parliament and the National Assembly for Wales should be interpreted as expressions of opinion in whole or part on Westminster politics, however, is doubtful – to some degree, perhaps, but it likely that here electoral opinion is much more focused on the performance of the Scottish and Welsh executives, especially as the electorates of Scotland and Wales become more familiar with devolution.

Some of the other devices shown in Table 4.1 by which attempts can be made to elicit consent or exert control are either not available in the UK or available on a limited basis. Referendums, initiatives and recalls are variations on a theme: they are devices enabling the electorate to vote on a particular proposal. A referendum is a vote on a particular proposal or set or proposals; an initiative allows a specified proportion of the electorate to secure a referendum on a particular issue; and a recall similarly enables the electorate to demand that the holders of a public office submit themselves for re-election before the expiry of their normal term of office. All are used in a number of states in the United States – the recall of the Democratic Governor of California and election in his place of Arnold Schwarzenegger in 2003 being a dramatic example of the recall. There is, however, no provision for the use of the recall in the UK and only limited provision for the use of referendums or initiatives. In fact, the only nation-wide referendum in the UK took place in 1975 on Britain's continued membership of the European Economic Community (now the EU), although the Labour government elected in 1997 made two manifesto pledges to hold referendums – one on electoral reform and one on the adoption of the European single currency, the euro. Although a commission on the electoral system was appointed in 1997 and reported in 1998, no referendum on its recommendations has been held, but a referendum on the euro is likely to be held sooner or later and in 2004 Tony Blair committed the government to a referendum on the proposed European Constitution. Referendums have been more widely used at the sub-national level. A referendum was held in 1973 on whether Northern Ireland should remain part of the UK or join the Republic of Ireland and in 1998 on the provisions of the Good Friday Agreement, which set up the present power-sharing arrangements. Referendums have also been used to seek approval for devolution in Scotland and Wales, first in 1979 and then again in 1997. Those held in 1979 are of particular interest because the terms of the referendums set by Parliament included a threshold requirement that, in order to secure approval, the devolution proposals had to be supported by a minimum of 40 per cent of the electorate, not just of those actually voting. In the event, this was of no consequence in Wales, since only 11.9 per cent of the electorate voted in favour. In Scotland, however, the situation was more complex: a small majority, 32.8 per cent compared with 30.8 per cent, voted in favour, but this was well short of the 40 per cent threshold and so devolution was not introduced. There were no threshold provisions in the 1997 referendums in Scotland and Wales, although it is interesting to compare the results with those of 1979. In Wales, 50.3 of those voting supported the government's devolution proposals, but the turnout was only 50.1 per cent so that the proportion of the electorate voting in favour was only 25.2 per cent. In Scotland, 74.3 per cent voted in favour, but the turnout of 60.2 per cent meant that less than half the electorate – 44.7 per cent actually voted for devolution. A referendum was also used to secure approval of the Labour government's proposals for an elected mayor for London and a Greater London Assembly in 1998. In this case the proposals were approved by 72 to 28 per cent but on a turnout of only 34 per cent.

Referendums have also been used to test public opinion on local issues, most commonly to decide whether alcohol should be sold on Sundays in areas of Wales. In the latter case, the referendum has been combined with the initiative and the initiative has been used much more recently in particular local government areas on whether or not to have directly elected mayors as the chief executive of the local authority. By April 2002, when local authorities were required to respond to government proposals to reorganise their political management structures, including the possibility of having a directly elected mayor, twenty-two local authorities had held referendums, following initiatives, in which seven endorsed directly elected mayor proposals.

Referendums, initiatives and recalls are formal mechanisms of consent and control, but it can be argued that opinion polls perform a similar role as less formal or informal mechanisms. Governments in Britain have increasingly come to use surveys of public opinion as a means of eliciting people's views on various matters, dating back at least to the Mass Observation surveys conducted immediately before and during the Second World War. Royal commissions and other government inquiries have also had surveys conducted on their behalf and the National Centre for Social Research, an independent body, has been conducting surveys for government departments and others since 1983. Private polling organisations have operated in Britain since the mid-1930s but did not become widespread until after 1945. The media regularly publish their findings on a wide range of issues, as well as the standing of the government and each of the political parties. For many years the parties themselves commissioned private polls to help them gauge public opinion, especially in the run-up to general elections, although the Labour Party was initially reluctant to use such polls, feeling that it was the job of politicians to know what people felt. More recently, however, Labour has made extensive use of focus groups – small, carefully selected cross-sections of the electorate – to test opinion on party and government policy. Following quickly on this last development has been e-democracy, the use of the internet as a mean of communication between rulers and ruled. The simplest and most commonly used for of internet communication is the e-mail and at the end of 2003 81.8 per cent of MPs had publicly available e-mail addresses. Rather fewer – 60.8 per cent had websites, many of which were interactive, mostly in the form of e-mail reply boxes. In both cases, Labour MPs were more likely than Conservatives to have public e-mail addresses and websites, with Liberal Democrats exceeding both. Interactive websites and the growing use of the internet by polling organisations such as YouGov enable governments and political parties and the public to communicate directly with each other, exchanging information and views to an extent and with an ease and frequency unknown before. Such communication is becoming increasingly sophisticated and is likely in future to play an increasingly important part in eliciting public opinion and eventually to forms of direct democracy of the sort already used by television programmes like *Big Brother*, *Pop Idol* and *Fame Academy*.

The mechanisms of surveys, opinion polls e-democracy do not constitute formal consent in the sense that electoral mechanisms do, but they add significantly to the ability of the power-holders to know about and understand public opinion. Indeed, with increasing technological sophistication, it is not difficult to envisage e-democracy becoming a consent and control mechanism of increasing, even overwhelming importance. Already experiments in voting via the internet have taken place in local elections, though with mixed results as measured by turnout.

The indirect mechanisms shown in Table 4.1 can all be found operating in the UK. Legislative representation enables people, including those not eligible to be or actually registered as voters, to express their views to and through MPs and, indeed, members of the House of Lords. Of course, MPs, still less peers, are not obliged to give voice let alone follows the views of those who contact them, but it is a foolish MP who totally ignores all constituency opinion or, for that matter, opinion from beyond the constituency. Both MPs and peers are mindful of public opinion however it may be expressed, whether by direct contact, public demonstrations, opinion polls, media contacts and reporting, and so on. Few, if any, MPs see themselves as delegates, but public opinion can and does find an expression through and in Parliament. These mechanisms have also long been available at local level through elected local authorities, with whom most MPs have close contact, but more recently they have been extended through the creation of the devolved bodies in Scotland and Wales, as well as the longer-standing devolution arrangements in Northern Ireland.

Pressure groups provide another avenue for consent and, arguably, to some extent, control. People are free to organise opinion not only for the purposes of ad hoc demonstrations and other expressions of opinion, but also on a more systematic basis by setting up organisations to defend and advance their interests. Much of pressure politics is directed specifically at the power-holders – ministers and senior civil servants, but Parliament provides a means of influencing the power-holders, especially over the details of government policy and legislation. Moreover, on legislative proposals brought forward by backbenchers, as distinct from the government, it is Parliament that makes the final decision and here pressure politics often becomes closely involved in the legislative process.

Legislative scrutiny generally, by both Commons and Lords, also provides an important means of control. Government policy and administration is subject to legislative approval and oversight. The government needs to retain the support of its party in the Commons and no government totally ignores parliamentary opinion. Of course, the more ideological a view the government adopts on a particular matter, the less likely it is to take notice of opinion beyond the confines of party, but even here the details of policy are invariably influence by non-ideological considerations, even though the main thrust of the policy remains ideologically intact.

There are also other extra-parliamentary control mechanisms, the principle of the rule of law, judicial review and, in the latter part of the twentieth century, the development of ombudsmen systems. The principle of the rule of law can be traced back to at least feudal times – the idea that no one is above the law is deeply rooted in English history and reflected in the American phrase 'by due process of law'. Indeed, the rule of law predates modern ideas about democratic politics, but democratic politics is seen as politics that operate within and through the law. If laws need changing or new laws are thought necessary, then the rule of law argues that such changes should be made through and within the existing constitutional and legal framework to the point that, if the constitutional and legal framework is thought to be in need of change, it too should be changed by a recognised and accepted process. Part of that process is judicial review, the use of the courts to challenge the use of power by those in authority. The absence of a written constitution means that it is not possible, as it is in most political systems, to mount a legal challenge to the exercise of power on constitutional grounds, but judicial review has become increasingly important as a means of challenging the actions of ministers and others in authority in their use of power.

Ombudsmen systems are a more recent development. Originating in Sweden and spreading to other Scandinavian countries, ombudsmen – officials empowered to investigate complaints from individual citizens against those in authority – are now a common feature of democratic political systems. In the British case, the first ombudsman, the Parliamentary Commissioner for Administration (now known as the Parliamentary Ombudsman) was appointed in 1967, the Northern Ireland Parliamentary Commissioner for Administration and Northern Ireland Commissioner for Complaints in 1969, the Health Ombudsman (originally the Health Service Commissioner) and the Director-General of Fair Trading in 1973, and the Local Commission for Administration in England and Wales in 1974 and for Scotland in 1975. This ombudsmen system has since expanded yet further to cover most public services and, indeed, a number of services provided by the private sector, some of which have been set up by statute, such as the Building Societies Ombudsman, the Legal Service Ombudsman, and the Pensions Ombudsman, others on a voluntary basis by the private sector, such as the Banking Ombudsman, the Estate Agents Ombudsman and the Press Complaints Commission. Various other complaints mechanisms also exist and, along with the ombudsmen system, provide a means not only of dealing with complaints from the public – redressing particular grievances, but by doing so exerting a degree of democratic control, specifically by focusing on 'where the shoe pinches' and more generally by drawing attention to the effectiveness or otherwise of services provided to the public.

It remains and will always remain a matter of opinion how effective consent and control mechanisms are and, therefore, ultimately whether or not the UK is a democracy, but to judge in absolute rather than relative terms is to distort the reality of politics. There is, however, a further dimension: most modern democracies claim to be and are widely seen as *liberal*-democratic systems, involving not only popular consent and control but also the existence of a range of rights without which, it is argued, popular consent and control are not possible.

The rights discussed in Chapter 1 were divided into traditional and social rights and, the Greek experience of democracy aside, traditional rights – freedom of expression, freedom of association and freedom from arbitrary arrest and, of course, the right to vote – are pre-democratic. Yet they are regarded as essential to democracy: eliciting popular consent and exerting popular control are at best difficult, at worst impossible if people are unable freely to express their views, gather together to do so and, if they so wish, organise themselves to act upon their views, or are subject to restrictions on their movements or imprisonment with little or no legal redress. These rights are, it is argued, fundamental to the existence of democracy. However, claims to social rights – to housing, education, employment, equality of gender and ethnicity, and so on – have taken the argument a crucial stage further. If people are suffering from significant social and economic deprivation, the existence of traditional rights may be overshadowed, even irrelevant to their struggle for day-to-day survival. Nonetheless, even the existence of social as well as traditional rights should be seen as a necessary but not sufficient condition for the existence of democracy. Democracy is, in the end, a matter of perception and is bound up in the concepts of power, authority and legitimacy. The legitimacy of a democratic system rests on the claim that the means of eliciting consent and exerting control are effective: democracy is therefore as much a matter of perception as it is of fact.

Democracy, the electoral system and electoral behaviour

Electoral systems

For most observers it is not just a question of whether the UK is a democracy, but how democratic it is and, as far as Parliament is concerned, two major factors are the electoral system and electoral behaviour.

A variety of electoral systems are used in the UK (see Table 4.2), but this is a recent phenomenon. Until 1921, all elections used the simple plurality or first-past-the-post (FPTP) system, but it was only in elections to the Northern Ireland Parliament in 1921 and 1925 that a form of proportional representation (PR) – the single transferable vote (STV) was used. Thereafter FPTP was used until the Northern Ireland Assembly was elected by STV in 1973, which had also been used for local elections in Northern Ireland earlier that year.

John Stuart Mill favoured PR, although he wished to see a complex system devised by Thomas Hare introduced, which would have enabled an elector not liking the choice in his particular constituency to vote for a candidate in another constituency.[1] Proposals for the introduction of PR by STV were included in the Representation of the People Bill 1918 but rejected on a free vote. The same bill also contained proposals for the use of the alternative vote (AV) in certain constituencies. This is a device designed to prevent a candidate being elected on a minority vote by allowing the redistribution of second preferences of those who came bottom of the poll until one candidate has received more than 50 per cent of the votes cast. This too was rejected on a

Table 4.2 *Electoral systems used in the United Kingdom*

Representative body/post	Electoral system	Term of office
House of Commons	*First-past-the-post (FPTP)*: 659 MPs elected for single-member constits; candidate with a simple plurality (majority) of votes in each constituency elected	Variable – maximum of 5 years
Scottish Parliament	*PR Added Member System (AMS)*: 129 MSPs, 73 directly elected for single-member constits by FPTP; 56 in 8 regional constits. using regional party list PR system to achieve overall proportionality	Fixed term 4 years
National Assembly for Wales	*PR (AMS)*: 60 AMs, 40 directly-elected for single-member constits by FPTP; 20 in 4 regional constits. using regional party list PR system to achieve overall proportionality	Fixed term 4 years
Northern Ireland Assembly	*Single Transferable Vote (STV) (PR system)*: 108 AMs	Fixed term 4 years
Mayor of London	*Supplementary vote (SV) (preferential system)*: a candidate receiving more than 50% of the votes cast is elected; failing that the preferences of the third and other candidates are redistributed between top two candidates	Fixed term 4 years
Greater London Assembly	*PR (AMS)*: 25 AMs, 14 directly-elected for single-member constits by FPTP; 11 using party list PR system to achieve overall proportionality	Fixed term 4 years
Other local authorities/mayors	*FPTP*: for councils. *SV*: for mayors	Fixed term 3 or 4 years, some staggered
European Parliament	*PR systems*: 75 for England, Scotland and Wales using closed regional party list system; 3 for N. Ireland by STV	Fixed term of 5 years

free vote. Another bill, which would have introduced the AV for all parliamentary elections was actually passed by the House of Commons in 1931 but rejected by the House of Lords. The then Labour government said that it intended to ensure the passage of the bill by using the 1911 Parliament Act, but before it could do so the government resigned. Much more recently, a Labour working party – the Plant Commission in 1993 – recommended the adoption of the supplementary vote (SV), a variation of the AV in which the third and lower candidates on first preferences are eliminated and their second preferences redistributed between the top two candidates.

PR, however, remained on the fringes of the political agenda, kept there partly by a Liberal Party pushed into third place by the Labour Party and partly by campaigners and organisations like the Electoral Reform Society. It did not begin to move up the political agenda until the 1960s and 1970s, when Labour began seriously to consider proposals for the devolution of power to Scotland and Wales and failed to implement them in 1979. The commitment to devolution was repeated in the election manifestos of 1983 and 1987, but the 1992 manifesto promised that the devolved legislatures would be elected by a PR system known as the added-member system (AMS), by which some members were elected by FPTP and others by PR to make the overall result more proportional. Once in power in 1997, Labour was able to fulfil this promise and then, in 2000, extended the use of PR to the Greater London Assembly. However, the newly created Mayor of London in 2000 and mayors in seven other town and cities in 2002 were elected by SV. In addition, the post-Good Friday Agreement Northern Ireland Assembly, like its predecessor, was elected by STV and, following an EU directive that all member states must use PR to elect its members of the European Parliament, PR was introduced for the 1999 European elections. But here, Labour opted for a closed regional party-list system of PR, which, for the first time, meant that electors could vote only for parties and not for individual candidates. The 1997 manifesto also included a promise to set up a commission 'to recommend a proportional alternative to the first-past-the-post system' followed by a referendum. The Jenkins Commission was duly appointed in 1997 and reported in 1998, but no referendum has taken place and the 2001 manifesto made a less firm commitment, promising that the government would 'review the experience of the new systems and the Jenkins Commission and assess whether changes might be made to the electoral system for the House of Commons. A referendum remains the right way to agree any change for Westminster'.

Only the House of Commons and most local authorities continue to use FPTP, but the House of Commons is out of step in another respect: all other elected bodies and offices in the UK have fixed terms of office, mostly of four years. Parliaments, however, have a maximum life of five years, but the Prime Minister may advise the monarch to dissolve Parliament and a call an election at any time, advice that by convention the monarch must normally follow. This practice, however, is common in parliamentary systems based on the Westminster model, such as those in Australia, Canada, India and New Zealand, and in many European parliamentary systems. However, in the case of Germany, the constitution restricts the circumstances in which the Bundestag can be dissolved before the end of its normal term. Similarly, there were considerable restrictions on the dissolution of Parliament in the French Fourth Republic (1946–58). The power to dissolve Parliament stems from its origins: Parliaments were summoned by monarchs when needed and dissolved when no longer needed. Thus, in the later struggle between king and Parliament in the seventeenth century, Parliament sought to prevent the king ruling without Parliament for more than a few years by passing a Triennial Act stipulating that Parliament must be called at least every three years. Later in the seventeenth century Parliament ensured that it must meet annually in order to renew legislation regulating the army, but it also passed another Triennial Act laying down that no Parliament should last longer than three years, a reversal of its earlier concern. In 1715, after power had passed from the monarch to the politicians, the maximum length of a Parliament was extended to seven years and then, in 1911, reduced to five, but the power dissolve Parliament within the maximum period remains. Dissolving Parliament and the calling of a general election can be used in an attempt to resolve a crisis (as happened with the two elections of 1910 during the clash between Lords and Commons) or break an impasse when a government lacks a majority in the Commons (as happened in October 1974). However, these are exceptions to the general rule that the power of dissolution is used mainly to call an election at a time the Prime Minister believes his or her party will win. It is therefore a power of considerable attraction to Prime Ministers and would-be Prime Ministers, but it can also be seen as giving the governing party an unfair advantage and for that reason undemocratic. In its 1992 election manifesto, Labour pledged itself to introduce fixed-term elections for the Westminster Parliament, but no such pledge was given in 1997 or 2001. Of course, it is perfectly possible, as in the case of the German Bundestag, to make provision for the dissolution of the legislature in crisis or other special circumstances. In contrast, all offices in the United States at federal and state levels (with the limited exception of some states where is a provision for invoking a recall) are subject to fixed terms and this is the norm in presidential-congressional systems based on the American model.

Just as the dissolution of Parliament in order to call an election gives Prime Ministers a potential and often considerable advantage over their opponents, so also do electoral systems have an impact that goes far beyond exercising the democratic right to vote.[2] Electoral systems are not neutral; they benefit some candidates and some parties at the expense of others. Although, by definition, the principal objective of a proportional representation system is to distribute seats in a representative body in proportion to the votes cast for parties (or take account of the preferences of all those voting in electing a candidate to a single office), in practice some PR systems favour larger parties at the expense of smaller, others smaller parties at the expense of larger. Moreover, the use of constituencies will have an effect on the extent to which proportionality is achieved. Thus, in countries such as Israel and the Netherlands, in which the whole country is treated as a single constituency, the degree of proportionality achieved is very high. In the Israeli election of 1999, for instance, the largest deviation from absolute proportionality for a particular party was 1.7 per cent and in the Dutch election of 2002 0.8 per cent. However, PR systems using constituencies produce a less proportional outcome: in the 2002 election in the Irish Republic, using the STV, the largest deviation was 7.0 per cent; in the German federal election of 1998, using the AMS, it was 3.5 per cent. The degree of proportionality is also affected by the number of seats in the legislature, so that the larger the number the higher the degree of proportionality, within, of course, the parameters of particular PR systems. It is not therefore surprising (see Table 4.3) that the degree of proportionality in the devolved legislatures of the UK is lower than that achieved in the Bundestag, which had 666 members in 1998, though not in comparison with the Irish Dail of 165 members.

The greatest contrast, however, is not between legislatures elected by different PR systems, but between those using PR and those using non-proportional systems, notably the FPTP. In the general election of 2001 Labour won more than three-fifths of the seats with only two-fifths of the votes, whereas the Conservatives had 6.5 per cent fewer seats than their proportional entitlement, the Liberal Democrats 10.4 per cent fewer and other parties 4.9 per cent. The reason is simple: candidates are elected by a simple plurality – more votes than any other single candidate – in single-member constituencies, so that it is possible and not uncommon for a successful candidate to have considerably fewer votes than the combined votes of his or her opponents. For example, the winning candidate may have 40 per cent of the votes cast – more than any other candidate, with the other 60 per cent of the votes shared among the other candidates; indeed, one vote more is enough. The winning candidate is therefore elected on a minority of the votes. If a party wins a significant number of seats on a minority of votes, the relationship between seats and votes is distorted and, the more this happens, the greater the likely distortion. This is most common when there is greater support for third parties, as has been the case since 1974. Between 1945 and 1970 the mean proportion of votes for third parties was 8.7 per cent, but from 1974 to 2001 it was 25.4 per cent, as support for the Liberals and their Liberal Democrat successors and the nationalist parties in Scotland and Wales grew. The FPTP system can result in the 'wrong' party winning the election. In 1951, Labour won 0.8 per cent more votes but 26 fewer seats than the Conservatives, leaving the latter with an overall majority. However, in February 1974, the Conservatives won 0.7 per cent more votes than Labour but far fewer seats, although Labour fell short of an overall majority. However, the

Table 4.3   *The relationship between seats and votes in the Scottish Parliament,
the National Assembly for Wales, Northern Ireland Assembly, and UK
Parliament*

Scottish Parliament 1999

	Cons.	Lab.	LD	SNP	Other	Total	Largest deviation	No. of seats
Direct votes	15.6	38.8	14.2	28.7	2.7	100.0		
Seats	14.0	43.4	13.2	27.1	2.3	100.0	4.6	129

National Assembly for Wales 1999

	Cons.	Lab.	LD	Plaid Cymru	Other	Total
Direct votes	15.9	37.6	13.4	28.4	4.7	100.0		
Seats	15.0	46.7	10.0	28.3	0.0	100.0	9.1	60

NI Assembly 1998

	Unionist bloc	Nationalist bloc	Other	Total		
Votes	47.7	39.6	12.7	100.0		
Seats	53.7	38.9	7.4	100.0	4.6	108

House of Commons 2001

	Cons.	Lab.	LD	Others	Total		
Votes	31.7	40.7	18.3	9.3	100.0		
Seats	25.2	62.5	7.9	4.4	100.0	21.8	659

Source: Official election returns.

most important impact of FPTP is that it is more likely to produce single-party
majority government, as Table 4.4 shows.

Only once since 1945 has a general election not resulted in either the
Conservative or Labour Parties winning a majority of the seats in the House
of Commons, enabling one or the other to form a government without needing the support of any other party, either as a coalition partner or as a minority government. Only in February 1974 did neither party win a majority,
although after Labour had won a small majority in October 1974 by-election
losses reduced the government to a minority position by April 1976 and John

Table 4.4   *The distribution of votes and seats at general elections between 1945 and 2001*

	Cons.		Lab.		Lib/LD		Others		No. of
Election	Votes	Seats	Votes	Seats	Votes	Seats	Votes	Seats	seats
1945	39.6	32.8	48.0	**61.4**	9.0	1.9	3.4	3.9	640
1950	43.5	47.7	46.1	**50.4**	9.1	1.4	1.3	0.5	625
1951	48.0	**51.3**	48.8	47.2	2.6	1.0	0.6	0.5	625
1955	49.7	**53.8**	46.4	44.0	2.7	0.9	1.2	0.3	630
1959	49.3	**57.9**	43.9	41.0	5.9	0.9	0.9	0.2	630
1964	43.4	48.3	44.1	**50.3**	11.2	1.4	1.3	0.0	630
1966	41.9	40.1	48.1	**57.8**	8.5	1.9	1.5	0.2	630
1970	46.4	**52.3**	43.1	45.7	7.5	1.0	3.0	1.0	630
1974 (F)	37.9	46.8	37.2	47.4	19.3	2.2	5.6	3.6	635
1974 (O)	35.8	43.6	39.2	*50.2**	18.3	2.1	6.7	4.1	635
1979	43.9	**53.4**	36.9	42.2	13.8	1.7	5.4	2.6	635
1983	42.4	**61.1**	27.6	32.2	25.4†	3.5	4.6	3.2	650
1987	42.2	**57.1**	30.8	35.2	22.5†	3.4	4.4	3.6	650
1992	41.9	**51.6**	34.4	41.6	17.8	3.1	5.8	3.7	651
1997	30.7	25.0	43.2	**63.4**	16.8	7.0	9.3	4.6	659
2001	31.7	25.2	40.7	**62.5**	18.3	7.9	9.3	4.4	659

Source: David Butler and Gareth Butler, *Twentieth Century British Political Facts, 1900–2000*, London, Macmillan, 8th edn, pp. 236–9.

Notes: * The October 1974–1979 Labour Government became a minority government in April 1976. † Liberal-SDP Alliance. (F: February). (O: October). Bold text = majority government; italic text = minority government.

Major's Conservative government also found its majority gradually whittled away by by-election losses and defections. What is striking about the figures in Table 4.4 is that, in spite of the inroads made by third parties, majority government remains the norm, but it is necessary to go back to 1935 to find the governing party winning more than 50 per cent of the votes cast and before that to 1900. Another measure of the distorting effect of FPTP is that since 1979 the electoral support for the majority party has ranged from 43.9 per cent (1979) to 40.7 per cent (2001) – a mere 3.2 per cent, whereas the proportion of seats won has ranged from 51.6 per cent (1992) to 63.4 per cent (1997) – a massive 11.8 per cent. An even greater distortion of votes–seats relationship would have occurred in 1997 (and again in 2001) had the AV system been used: researchers at Democratic Audit calculated that Labour's number of seats would have increased from 419 to 452, the Liberal Democrats from 46 to 82, but the Conservatives would have suffered a dramatic fall from 165 to 96, giving Labour an overall majority of 246. It is misleading, however, to assume that had PR operated in Britain since 1945 that minority or coalition government would have been the norm. That would probably have been the case for most of the time from 1974, but not for most of time between 1945 and February 1974. Much would have depended on the type of PR used – the purer the form of PR the more difficult it would have been for a single party to win a majority, but it is worth noting that in the 2002 Irish election Fianna Fail came within three seats of an overall majority with only 41.5 per cent of the vote and the Republic uses the STV. On the other hand, no party has succeeded in winning an overall majority in the Dail since 1977, so that coalition governments have become the norm. Similarly, coalitions are the norm in Germany, where a single party has only once secured an absolute majority in the Bundestag since the establishment of the Federal Republic in 1949 and only then by winning just over 50 per cent of the vote.

Electoral systems therefore have an impact on the outcome of elections and play a part in shaping the party system, but it is misleading to see the relationship between electoral systems and party systems as one of simple cause and effect. FPTP systems are commonly associated with two-party systems, PR systems with multi-party systems. However, the characteristics of party systems relate less to the number of parties represented in the legislature and more to how many parties are likely to be involved in the formation of a government. Thus, while the 1999 Israeli and 2002 Dutch elections resulted in fifteen and ten parties respectively winning seats in the legislature, as many as nine parties won seats in the House of Commons in 2001. But electors in the UK are used to single-party majority government, with coalitions reserved for national emergencies and therefore a rare occurrence. Electors in most countries using PR are used to coalitions, but the nature of the coalition varies: in Germany, for example, governments have always been coalitions of one of the two major parties, the Christian Democrats or the Social Democrats, and a much smaller party, except between 1966 and 1969 when the two major parties formed a grand coalition. Between 1949 and 1998 that smaller party was the Free Democrats; since 1998 it has been the Greens. It is not unreasonable therefore to say that essentially Germany has a two-party system. In contrast, governments in Israel, the Netherlands and Belgium are multi-party coalitions. Opponents of PR invariably argue that coalitions are inherently unstable, but in practice this varies considerably from country to country and sometimes over time. Until the rise of Likud in the early 1970s, coalitions in Israel were stable, dominated by the Labour Party, but the growth in support for religious parties in particular has made Israeli politics much less stable. Germany under the Weimar Republic became increasingly unstable, especially with the rise of the Nazis, but post-1949 Germany is seen as an exemplar of electoral and political stability. Similarly, PR did not prevent the Social Democrats in Sweden remaining in power for 44 years between 1932 and 1976, from the 1950s the dominant partner in a coalition. Even Italy between 1946 and 1994, when it adopted a less proportional system, always cited as evidence of the instability inherent in proportional systems, had its own peculiar form of stability – the Christian Democrats always being a member of the coalition, the Communist Party always excluded.

Ultimately, party systems reflect cleavages in a particular society and electoral systems affect how those cleavages are reflected in the legislature. Changing the electoral system, however, will normally affect, even significantly change, the party system, but not the basic cleavages in society. In 1994 both Italy and New Zealand changed their electoral systems – Italy from a highly proportional to a less proportional system, New Zealand from FPTP to AMS. Following the collapse of the Communist Party in the aftermath of the Cold War and of the Christian Democrats amid allegations of corruption, the party system in Italy was refashioned. New parties emerged and older parties reformulated themselves, but the basic left–right ideological divide remained and the new electoral system encouraged the formation of left- and right-wing alliances to secure an overall majority, with some success, but the underlying instability remained and the number of parties represented in the Chamber of Deputies was only marginally reduced. New Zealand provides a different story: single party majority government was the norm before 1996, but the outcome with a mixed member, proportional system of multi-member constituencies and regional lists, increased the number of parties in the New Zealand Parliament, preventing either the National Party or the Labour Party from achieving an absolute majority and necessitating the formation of coalition or minority governments. Precisely because electoral systems are not neutral in their impact, political parties may not only advocate a change in the electoral system but make such a change when in power. In 1958, for example, the Gaullist framers of the constitution of the Fifth French Republic abandoned PR and introduced a second ballot system, which disadvantaged the socialists and communists because of divisions between them. In 1985, the socialist government of President Mitterrand reintroduced PR, only to switch back to the second ballot in 1993, following the decline of the Communist Party.

In spite of the introduction of PR systems for the devolved legislatures in the UK and for elections to the European Parliament, FPTP remains firmly entrenched for Westminster elections and for local elections in England and Wales (Scotland is in the process of adopting the STV for its local elections, following a post-election deal between the members of the ruling coalition, Labour and the Liberal Democrats). Those in favour of the retention of FPTP argue that it provides 'strong government' in that it normally produces a single party with an overall majority in the Commons, enabling the party concerned to claim a clear mandate from the electorate for its policies and at least five years in which to put those policies to the test. FPTP, so the argument runs, also provides stability and avoids the need for coalitions, often formed after an election and no consultation of the electorate. That FPTP is more likely to produce single-party, majority government is clear enough, but such governments are only as strong as their personnel, internal cohesion and circumstances beyond their control allow them. In addition, the doctrine of the mandate is inherently flawed by the fact that the winning party seldom has the support of more than 50 per cent of the electorate and elections themselves provide no obvious way of knowing which of the winning party's policies the electorate favoured and which it did not.

A further argument advanced in support of FPTP is that it preserves the single-member constituency, allowing a direct link between Members of Parliament and those they are elected to represent. This link is particularly valued in British politics, probably more so than in most other European countries, though certainly not more than in the United States. The multi-member constituencies necessary under the STV and the larger single-member constituencies used by the AMS weaken the MP–constituency link. That link, however, needs to judged against the electoral distortion that FPTP produces – the greater the distortion, the less defensible FPTP becomes.

By encouraging and sustaining two-party systems in the sense of politics dominated by two major parties, FPTP also contributes significantly to the adversary system – the confrontation of government versus opposition, which forms the basis of the operation of parliamentary business and therefore of the operation of Parliament.

Electoral behaviour

If the electoral system plays a part in shaping the party system, electoral behaviour plays a much more important role. Electoral behaviour reflects both short-term and long-term opinion, but it is changes in the latter which are most likely to change the party system, as the experience of the UK between 1945 and the present demonstrates. Although 1970 could be said to be the watershed election in post-war electoral behaviour, there were already signs of change before then and this change accelerated after 1970.

The period 1945 to 1970 marked the zenith of the two-party system, as the figures in Table 4.5 show: three-quarters of the candidates, nine out of ten of the votes cast, and virtually all the MPs elected were either Conservative or Labour. Two-partyism was at it most dominant between 1950 and 1959, when the mean proportions of candidates was 86.4 per cent, of votes 95.4 per cent and of MPs 98.7 per cent. The proportion of MPs drawn from the Conservative and Labour Parties remained at a similarly high level until 1970, but there had already been an increase in the proportions of third party candidates and votes in 1959 and these grew in the 1960s, so that in 1970 third parties accounted for nearly one in three candidates and secured more than one in ten votes. However, there were also other signs of electoral change, particularly in the growth of electoral volatility. This showed itself in two ways – the loss of government seats in by-elections and larger electoral swings in general elections. Governments have always been potentially vulnerable at by-elections (used to fill casual vacancies between general elections) and adverse by-election results were commonplace in the nineteenth century and

Table 4.5   *Two-party domination, 1945–2001*

Election period	Two major parties: % of candidates	Two major parties: % of votes cast	Two major parties: % of MPs elected	Governing party: years
1945–70	76.4	91.3	97.9	13 Cons. 12 Lab.
1974–2001	49.3	74.6	92.3	18 Cons. 9 Lab.
1992	54.6	76.3	93.2	5 Cons.
1997	34.4	73.9	88.4	4 Lab.
2001	39.8	72.4	87.7	4/5 Lab.

before 1945. However, between 1945 and 1955 neither Labour (1945–51) nor the Conservatives (1951–55) lost any by-elections, but thereafter by-election losses mounted, culminating in Labour losing no fewer than fifteen seats between 1966 and 1970. Government by-election losses actually fell after 1974, but that was because governments created fewer by-election vacancies by appointing MPs to positions incompatible with continued membership of the Commons. Losses rose again in the 1987–92 and 1992–97 Parliaments, but most of these by-elections were caused by the death of the sitting Members and the unpopularity of the Conservative government, especially between 1992 and 1997. Similarly, not only did large electoral swings – the net movement of votes between the two major parties from one election to the next – occur at by-elections, but increased at general elections. The mean swing at general elections between 1950 and 1959 was 1.7 per cent, but between 1964 and 1970 it was 3.5 per cent. Put another way, it took the two general elections of 1950 and 1951 to turn Labour's 147-seat majority of 1945 into a 16-seat Conservative majority and the two general elections of 1964 and 1966 to turn a Conservative majority of 99 in 1959 to a Labour majority of 97, but the size of Labour's 1966 majority is itself clear evidence of increased volatility. These changes in electoral behaviour and the party system are clearly seen in the figures for the period 1974–2001 in Table 4.5. The mean proportion of candidates for the two majority parties is less than half and has continued to fall in succeeding elections; the two-party vote has fallen to three-quarters; and there has been an increase in the number and proportion of MPs elected for third parties.

Electoral behaviour between 1945 and 1970 was characterised by another feature – its homogeneity. The movement of electoral support between Conservative and Labour was notable both in direction and magnitude throughout the country. That is, any movement of support from Conservative to Labour or vice versa would take place in the overwhelming majority of constituencies and the magnitude or size of the electoral swing would be within a narrow range in the overwhelming majority of constituencies. The mean swing between 1950 and 1959 was 2.0 per cent and between 1964 and 1974 2.8 per cent, but from 1974 to 2001 it was 4.4 per cent, ranging from a swing to the Conservatives of 5.2 per cent in 1979 and no less than 10.0 per cent to Labour in 1997. Moreover, regional variations in electoral behaviour began to appear: in six of the seven general elections from 1950 to 1970 England, Scotland and Wales moved in the same direction – the only exception was 1955; but from 1974 significant regional variations began to occur, so that even in elections like 1979, when all regions moved in the same direction, the variations ranged from a 6.9 per swing to the Conservatives in the South to a 0.7 per cent swing in Scotland. Even Labour's massive landslide of 1997 produced significant regional variations, with a swing of 13.3 per cent in the South and 7.4 per cent in the Northern Region and even greater variations among constituencies.

Various explanations have been put forward for these changes in electoral behaviour. In 1967 Peter Pulzer baldly stated that 'class is the basis of British party politics; all else is embellishment and detail'[3] and the evidence in support of this statement was strong. Put simply, Pulzer argued that electoral behaviour could be explained largely in terms of class in that the middle-class or non-manual voters were more likely to vote Conservative and working-class or manual voters to vote Labour. Of course, given the distribution of the population between manual and non-manual workers, especially during the twenty or so years after 1945, there is no suggestion that class voting was absolute. Indeed, the Conservatives could not have won any elections without significant working-class support. Nonetheless, the class connection was very strong and more detailed analysis merely serves to reinforce the relationship between class and voting. From the 1970s onwards class voting shows a clear and marked decline: an index of class voting, based on the combined percentage of manual workers voting Labour and non-manual workers voting Conservative, shows that the mean figure for elections from 1945 to 1970 was 63 per cent, compared with 44 per cent from February 1974 to 2001. The highest levels of class voting were recorded in 1951 (67 per cent), 1955 (65 per cent) and 1966 (66 per cent); the lowest levels were in 1983 (47 per cent), 1997 (45 per cent) and 2001 (44 per cent). This decline in class voting was paralleled by a decline in partisan identification, the extent to which voters were regular supporters of or strongly identified with a particular party.

This weakening of the relationship between class and party gave rise to two related explanations – class dealignment and partisan dealignment. The former argued that there had been a decline in the proportion of voters who saw one or other of the two major parties as representing their socioeconomic interests; the latter argued that there had been a decline among voters in party loyalty, that they were less willing to support the same party election after election. These two explanations are not, of course, incompatible and together offer a credible explanation of for the growth of electoral volatility. A third explanation also emerged – rational-choice theory, the idea that electoral behaviour is a reflection of perceived self-interest. This too is compatible with a decline in class voting and party identification, in that some electors may perceive that Labour is most likely to protect the interests of working-class voters and others that the Conservatives are most likely to protect the interests of middle-class voters. However, experience might undermine such perceptions and that, arguably, is what began to happen from the late 1960s onwards, leading to a loosening of party ties and a weakening of the relationship between class and party.

Yet a further explanation came to the fore in the early 1980s, that of partisan realignment. The growth in support for third parties, initially the Liberals after 1955 and then the nationalist parties in Scotland and Wales from 1966, reduced two-party hegemony in terms of candidates and votes, but only had a marginal impact on membership of the Commons before the general election of February 1974, when the proportion of third party MPs rose from 1.9 per cent (12) in 1970 to 5.8 per cent (39) in February 1974. However, 13 of the 39 were from the various Unionist parties in Northern Ireland, most of which had taken the Conservative whip before direct rule was imposed in 1972. The most significant change, and the one that led to the theory of partisan realignment, was the formation of the Social Democratic Party (SDP) in 1981 and to its subsequent electoral alliance with the Liberals. The SDP was formed by four former Labour Cabinet ministers (Roy Jenkins, David Owen, Bill Rodgers and Shirley Williams) and they were joined by 26 Labour MPs (Owen and Rodgers were already MPs, Jenkins and Williams were ex-MPs). They had become disillusioned by Labour's ideological shift to the left after its defeat in 1979. The SDP sought to 'break the mould' of British politics by bringing about a party realignment, occupying the centre ground between the Conservatives, who had moved to the right under Margaret Thatcher, and Labour. Its alliance with the Liberals brought significant success in the general election of 1983 – 25.3 per cent of the vote and 23 MPs (17 Liberal, 6 SDP), but the electoral system worked against the Alliance in that Labour won no fewer than 209 seats with only 2.2 per cent more of the vote (27.6 per cent). In 1987 the Alliance vote fell by 2.9 per cent to 22.5 for the net loss of one seat, but disputes between the SDP and the Liberals led to a merger of the two parties, leaving a small rump of SDP MPs who finally disappeared in 1992. Clearly, the SDP did not manage to bring about a partisan realignment by replacing one of the two major parties, as Labour had done in the inter-war period, nor had it, in alliance with the Liberals, succeeded in creating a tripartite system, with three more or less equal parties. However, since the Liberal–SDP merger, the Liberal Democrats have prospered, particularly in 1997 and 2001, due largely to the practice of tactical voting. By-elections have always offered a particular form of tactical voting – supporters of the governing party can vote for the main opposition party or a third party as a means of expressing their dissatisfaction with their government; alternatively, they can simply not vote. In either case, they may well intend to support the governing party at the next election. Similarly, the Liberals/Liberal-Democrats became adept at persuading Labour supporters in particular constituencies to vote for them as the party most likely to defeat the Conservative candidate. This form of tactical voting was used to considerable effect in the general elections of 1997 and 2001, helping the Liberal Democrats double their number of seats in 1997 and secure a modest increase in 2001. In turn, this helped Labour win a larger majority in 1997 than would have been the case and help preserve it virtually intact in 2001.

The crucial impact of the SDP in alliance with the Liberals was to contribute to Labour's massive defeat in 1983, resulting in a gradual ideological shift by Labour to the centre ground, culminating in Labour's landslide victory in 1997 and its re-election in 2001. Arguably, therefore, there has been a partisan realignment but it has been within the confines of the existing party system, rather than through the creation of a new party or the displacement of an existing one. What remains to be seen is whether Labour will continue to occupy the centre ground or shift leftwards to any significant extent. Were the latter to happen, then any party realignment would have been tactical rather than strategic.

There is one further feature of electoral behaviour which has potential implications for the party system and therefore for Parliament. This is shown in Table 4.6 based on the mean support for the three main parties between 1945 and 2001. Two features stand out for the figures covering the period 1945 to 1992: first, Conservative and Labour support is evenly balanced, although it reflects the decline in two-party support after 1970; second, the main opposition party frequently held an opinion poll lead (even though it did not necessarily win the following general election) and at other times the government led. In other words, the opposition had a reasonable expectation for significant periods between general elections that it would win the next election, even if in the event it did not. Contrast this with the position of the Conservatives in two recent Parliaments: in only one month in each did the Conservatives lead. In 1992–97 that one month was before 'Black Wednesday' of September 1992, when the UK was forced to withdraw from the European Monetary System; from that point, the Conservatives never held the lead again. The one month in the 1997–2001 Parliament was during the fuel blockade of September 2000. If this situation were to continue beyond the next general election, the Conservatives would have undergone what Labour has twice experienced in the post-war period – the loss of three or more general elections in succession, but with a crucial difference. However much hindsight might suggest that Labour's defeats in 1951, 1955 and 1959 and again in 1979, 1983, 1987 and 1992 were inevitable, Labour held opinion poll leads for periods during each of the Parliaments concerned and had the elections

Table 4.6 *Party support, 1945–2001*

Period	Con.	Lab.	Lib/LD*	Con. lead†	Lab. lead†	All. lead†	Equal†
1945–50	43	42	11	24	8		3
1950–51	47	42	9	9	9		
1951–55	44	46	8	9	23		5
1955–59	43	46	10	12	32		3
1959–64	40	44	14	21	36		2
1964–66	43	47	9	4	11		1
1966–70	47	38	11	38	9		2
1970–74	39	46	12	5	37		1
1974	35	41	18	1	5		
1974–79	45	41	10	33	14		7
1979–83	38	36	23	21	20	6	1
1983–87	36	35	26	23	18	2	4
1987–92	40	40	14	32	23		2
1992–97	27	52	16	1	57		1
1997–2001	29	52	14	1	46		

Source: Gallup Poll.

Notes: * Includes SDP 1981–89; SDP-Liberal Alliance 1983–87. † Number of months.

been held at other times, as, for example, fixed-term Parliaments would have ensured, then the outcome might have been different. That cannot be said for the Conservatives from September 1992 to June 2001, apart from a single month, with Labour quickly regaining its lead. In order to win an overall majority at the next election the Conservatives would need a lead of 11.5 per cent,[4] requiring a swing greater than Labour achieved in 1997. However, it is not the loss of three successive elections that is crucial; it is the Conservatives' failure to make any significant inroad into Labour's lead between elections. If this were to lead the Conservative Party to see itself as in more or less permanent or indefinite opposition, it could change the relationship between government and opposition. The adversary system emphasises the confrontation between government and opposition, but it is tempered by the belief on both sides that sooner or later their roles will be reversed. On this belief rests the co-operation that makes the parliamentary machine work. Were perceptions to change – Labour seeing itself as more or less permanently in government and the Conservatives seeing themselves more or less permanently in opposition – the adversary system would remain intact, but the incentive to co-operate would be much reduced. Such a situation is not unprecedented: after the 1959 and 1979 elections Labour's future was widely seen as one of indefinite opposition, yet in both cases signs of recovery came before an opposition mentality prevailed. Electoral volatility may come to the Conservatives' rescue, but if it does not the impact on Parliament could be considerable.

Parliament and democracy

Is Parliament a democratic institution? One of Parliament's functions is that of representation and historically both Lords and Commons had their origins as representative bodies, but not as democratically representative institutions. The House of Lords represented the landed nobility, but peers were not elected but summoned to attend Parliament by the monarch. The House of Commons represented cities, towns and counties and, although elected from an early stage, the franchise varied from place to place, totally excluded women and was very limited among men. The idea of universal adult suffrage is of much more recent origin and was much contested during the nineteenth and early twentieth centuries when the right to vote was gradually extended. The House of Lords is patently not a democratic institution and would not be seen as such unless it were wholly elected. A partly elected upper house would probably gain in legitimacy, but legitimacy and democracy are not synonymous. It is possible to argue that a nominated legislative chamber has legitimacy if the means by which its members are chosen are widely regarded as appropriate.

The House of Commons is a different case. By contemporary standards it did not become a democratic institution until at least 1928, when women became eligible to vote on the same terms as men. Indeed, for some the date would be 1948, when plural voting – additional votes for university graduates and owners of business premises – was abolished. Other criteria are also commonly applied, notably that elections must be conducted freely and not subject to fraud, intimidation, corruption or any other form of manipulation. The Ballot Act 1972 introduced secret voting and the Corrupt and Illegal Practices Act 1883 virtually eliminated intimidation and corruption from British elections. A degree of electoral fraud or manipulation still occurs, most commonly in Northern Ireland, where personation – fraudulently voting in place of another person – still takes place. To counter this, stricter rules over voting have been adopted in Northern Ireland, principally the use of voter identity cards. More recently, there have been allegations of the fraudulent use of postal votes, although these have been more common in relation to local rather than national elections. The 1883 Act introduced strict limits on the amount candidates may spend in each constituency and the 1998 Political Parties and Referendums Act sets limits on national election expenditure. Apart from elections, it can also be pointed out that between elections members of the public have access to their Members of Parliament, both at Westminster and in their constituencies, something that is invariably welcomed by the Member.

It is not therefore difficult to argue that the House of Commons is now a democratic institution, but there remains the question of whether it needs to be socio-economically representative to claim to be truly democratic. That, however, is a question to be addressed in the next chapter. On the other hand, the distortions produced by FPTP can be seen as undermining the Commons' democratic credentials, even to deny them. This can be judged as a matter of principle, that some form of PR is a necessary condition for democracy; or pragmatically, that it is a matter of degree (the distortion must not be too great) or that the advantage of 'strong government' (single-party, majority government) outweighs the distortion of electoral opinion. As with much about politics, it is ultimately a matter of opinion, aptly summarised by Burke: 'If any ask me what free government is, I answer, that for any practical purpose, it is what people think so'.[5]

Notes

1 J. S. Mill, *Representative Government*, London, J. M. Dent, 1910, pp. 260–75.
2 See Douglas Rae, *The Political Consequences of Electoral Laws*, New Haven, Conn., Yale University Press, 1967, and Robert Blackburn, *The Electoral System in Britain*, London, Macmillan, 1995.
3 Peter Pulzer, *Political representation and Elections in Britain*, London, Allen & Unwin, 1967, p. 88.
4 David Butler and Denis Kavanagh, *The British General Election of 2001*, London, MacMillan, 2002, p. 254.
5 *The Works of Edmund Burke*, London, George Bell, Vol. II, p. 29.

The personnel of Parliament

Introduction

It matters who the members of the House of Commons and the House of Lords are. It matters because it is by electing Members of Parliament that the electorate decides who governs; it matters because MPs are widely regarded as representatives, a means by which public opinion can be expressed, formally or informally, to ministers and the government; it matters because almost all ministers are chosen by the Prime Minister from those in Parliament, mainly from the Commons but also from the Lords; and it matters because the government is constitutionally responsible to Parliament and MPs and peers are expected to scrutinise the actions and policies of ministers. Even if Parliament is judged to be ineffective, generally or specifically, it matters because that might be as much a failure of personnel as of organisation and procedure.

The House of Commons

The role of the 'selectorate'

Who determines the composition of the House of Commons? The obvious answer is the electorate, but most voters have long voted for parties rather than candidates, so that only rarely are independent or non-party candidates elected. The electorate determines which candidates become Members of Parliament and therefore how many MPs each party has in the House of Commons, but the parties select the candidates. The composition of the Commons is thus decided by a combination of the electorate and what may be termed the 'selectorate'. However, a significant proportion of constituencies – at least two-thirds – are 'safe' seats, seats which the incumbent party normally holds regardless of how well or badly it does in the election as a whole. In these constituencies the candidate chosen by the incumbent party is virtually guaranteed election; selection is tantamount to election. Moreover, even in 'marginal' constituencies, where the balance between two or more of the parties is such that the outcome is in doubt, it is invariably a party candidate who wins.

The selectorate is therefore crucial, but in spite of powerful national party organisations, it operates locally rather than nationally. Local autonomy in the selection of candidates was largely the norm before 1832, although widespread patronage and corruption, especially in borough constituencies complicated the situation. Nearly half the members of the Commons owed their seats to patronage, but in most of these cases patronage was locally based, leaving most other seats in the hands of small electorates open to various forms of influence and corruption. The Reform Act of 1832 substantially reduced the number of so-called 'pocket' or nomination boroughs and increased the size of electorates by extending the franchise, but, crucially, reinforced local autonomy in selection by requiring the introduction of electoral registers. This led rapidly to the setting up of local registration societies in many constituencies, forming the basis for local party organisation. Hitherto, reasonably clearly defined parties had existed in Parliament, with a modicum of organisation, but reducing patronage and increasing the size of the electorate created the need for extra-parliamentary organisation, a need reinforced by further extensions of the franchise in 1867 and 1884. National party organisation followed in due course, with the first annual Conservative Party Conference in 1867 and the formation of the National Liberal Federation in 1877. The setting up of the Labour Representation Committee in 1900 rested partly on the existing organisation, national and local, of the Independent Labour Party (ILP), but local Constituency Labour Parties (CLPs) were quickly established in a number of constituencies. Even though the Labour Party Constitution concentrated authority in the Annual Conference and the National Executive Committee (NEC), CLPs retained substantial local autonomy in selection.

The national party organisation and the party leadership in all the political parties in the UK play a role in the selection of candidates, but it is a limited and largely supervisory role. Essentially, it has three elements – setting out the rules governing the selection of candidates by local party organisations; maintaining lists of would-be candidates from which the latter normally choose candidates; and retaining a veto over the local choice of candidates. In practice, this gives the national party an important but subordinate role: common rules of selection establish an important degree of equity in the selection process; national candidate lists provide a limited form of 'quality control'; and the national veto allows the party leadership to disown candidates to whom it objects but not to impose a particular individual of its choice on the local party. There have, however, been some changes in recent years, particularly in the Labour Party, which have allowed the national party to play a more dirigiste role.

The Labour Party's NEC has long had the power to intervene in the choice of candidates for by-elections and used this power in the earlier history of the party to secure the re-election of leading members of the party who had been defeated in a general election. However, this practice fell into abeyance but was revived in the 1980s and 1990s to ensure the selection of 'suitable' by-election candidates. In addition, under the leadership of Tony Blair, the Labour Party has used last-minute pre-general election vacancies to 'parachute' in candidates it particularly wishes to see chosen. The actual choice remains that of the CLP, but inclusion on the shortlist of an 'impressive' and favoured individual can have its impact, as was the case with Alan Howarth at Newport East in 1997, Shaun Woodward at St Helens and David Miliband at South Shields in 2001. In the Conservative and Liberal Democratic Parties the ability to impose candidates favoured by the party leadership does not exist, but both are particularly sensitive to the choice of candidates for by-elections, when the media spotlight on candidates is much stronger. However, this tends to be a largely negative power – avoiding the selection of an 'unsuitable' candidate, rather than imposing a particular individual on the local party. Indeed, in both parties (and to a lesser extent in the Labour Party), local autonomy is jealously guarded and any suggestion of national party support, let alone pressure, can be fatal to the favoured would-be candidate. This is true even in unfavourable circumstances, illustrated by Tatton Conservative Association's refusal to bow to national party pressure and deselect Neil Hamilton, who was humiliatingly defeated by Martin Bell, standing as an anti-sleaze candidate in the 1997 general election.

In the longer term, other developments may lead to a yet more centrally directed or dirigiste role for national parties. The adoption of proportional representation for all three devolved bodies in the UK, using added-member systems, necessitated the use of party lists. In addition, party lists were used for all UK candidates for the 1999 European Parliament elections. The national party organisations – and their Scottish and Welsh counterparts in the case of the Conservatives and Liberal Democrats – played a much more proactive role in the selection of candidates, although regional party organisations were involved too. Were PR to be introduced for Westminster elections, a similar process would probably ensue.

The selection of candidates has been described as the 'secret garden' of British politics, a process carried on behind closed doors by people who were largely anonymous. To a significant degree that remains true, but the process has become more open and democratic in recent years, notably by allowing the final choice of candidates to be made by the local party members. In some cases, this has been by allowing the latter to make a choice from a shortlist at a general meeting, in others by a postal ballot of all local party members. However, one factor fundamentally affecting the selection of candidates is that of *supply* – *who* makes themselves available to be chosen in the first place. The national party organisations in compiling lists of suitable would-be candidates and the local selectorate in drawing up a shortlist and making the final choice, apply a range of criteria as to what constitutes a 'suitable' candidate.

These criteria are a combination of the individual's personality, age, gender, ethnicity, educational and occupational background, and political experience and, of course, ideological views, but the ability to fulfil these criteria does not lie entirely in their hands. These are *demand* criteria, but demand is much influenced by supply. This interplay between supply and demand is most clearly seen in the efforts of national party organisations to secure more women candidates and MPs and more drawn from the UK's ethnic minorities. Norris and Lovenduski found that the supply-side factors played an important part in explaining the socio-economic composition of the Commons, but that demand factors were no less important and that, in general, selection was a complex mixture of the two. They concluded that the House of Commons 'includes a social bias towards the younger, better-educated and those in brokerage occupations [lawyers, teachers and journalists] in large part because this reflects the pool of applicants [i.e. those on the party lists]'.[1] However, when they compared those on the party lists with party membership supply-side factors reflected occupation, age and, in the case of the Conservatives, gender. Moreover, when comparisons with those who vote for each of the parties and those who become party members were made, much greater supply-side discrepancies emerged, particularly in relation to education and female candidates. Assessing the position of ethnic minority candidates is more difficult, given the small numbers involved, but the supply side is a major factor in the Conservative Party, whereas in the Labour case there is some evidence of a demand factor working against such would-be candidates, in spite of the party's success in securing the election of greater number of black and Asian MPs than ever before.[2] Norris and Lovenduski do not, however, take the electoral status of constituencies into account, especially the incumbent party factor (who holds the seat) and their relative safeness, hopelessness or marginality. There is evidence to suggest that candidates chosen by the local selectorate in seats held by their party, particularly marginal ones, have more in common in terms of experience and background with those chosen in marginal seats held by their opponents than with candidates in 'hopeless' seats.[3] And there is also evidence to suggest that the failure to select more women and ethnic minority candidates, especially but not only in the Conservative Party, stems from a relative unwillingness of local parties in constituencies held by their party to select such candidates. This has led parties, notably Labour, to take both affirmative action and also engage in positive discrimination, at least in the case of women. For example, Labour introduced all-women shortlists for Westminster selections, although these were declared illegal in 1996, and the device of 'twinning' constituencies in Scotland and Wales, so that of a pair of constituencies had to choose a male, the other a female candidate. Both devices contributed to a significant number of women candidates being elected – 18.2 per cent to Westminster in 1997 (24.2 per cent of Labour MPs) and two-fifths of those elected to the Scottish Parliament and the National Assembly for Wales. All-women shortlists have now been made legal and all parties continue to seek ways of increasing the number of women and ethnic minority MPs. In the short term, and possibly in the longer term as well, this is likely to be achieved only by greater intervention by the national party organisations, intervention which is likely to be resisted by local parties, ironically on the grounds of democracy.

The House of Commons and socio-economic change

There were originally few legal restrictions on who could be elected to the House of Commons, other than the most obvious, the ineligibility of women. Gradually, however, various restrictions were introduced, such as the exclusion of various office-holders, religious tests, oaths of allegiance, and property qualifications. Subsequently, but also gradually, most of these were removed, but members of the House of Lords, civil servants, judges, and serving members of the armed services and police forces remain ineligible, as do those certified insane, convicted prisoners serving sentences of a year or more, and persons found guilty of corrupt or illegal electoral practices. Women remained ineligible until 1918, when the first woman, Countess Markievicz, was elected, but like all other Sinn Fein candidates she refused to take her seat, so that the first women MP was Lady Astor elected at a by-election in 1919.

The figures in Table 5.1 illustrate a more general feature of the way in which the socio-economic composition of the Commons changes. Removing legal barriers or widening the legal opportunity structures seldom has a dramatic effect. Thus, it was not until 1987 that the proportion of women MPs exceeded 5 per cent and it was only as the result of positive discrimination in the selection of Labour candidates that proportion rose to nearly one in five in 1997. Similarly, socio-economic changes in society generally only gradually permeate through to the Commons, as the impact of the industrial revolution illustrates:

Table 5.1   *The number and proportion of women MPs, 1922–2001 (selected elections)*

Election	No.	% of MPs	Election	No.	% of MPs
1922	2	0.3	1959	25	4.0
1923	8	1.3	1964	29	4.6
1929	14	2.3	1987	41	6.3
1931	15	2.4	1992	60	9.2
1945	24	3.8	1997	120	18.2
1951	17	2.7	2001	118	17.9
1955	24	3.8			

Source: 1922–97: David Butler and Gareth Butler, *Twentieth Century British Political Facts, 1900–2000*, London, Macmillan, 8th edn, 2000, p. 261; *Dod's Guide to the General Election June 2001*, London, Vacher-Dod, 2001, pp. 322–3.

Table 5.2　*The representation of economic interests in the House of Commons, 1832, 1868 and 1900 (%)*

Economic interest	1832	1868	1900
Landed interests	52.4	34.0	15.5
Industrial, comm. and finan. interests	27.3	43.1	52.2
Professional interests	20.3	22.9	29.4
Workers' representatives	0.0	0.0	0.9
Miscellaneous	0.0	0.0	1.9
Total	100.0	100.0	99.9
Number	934	1,224	1,319

Source: J. A. Thomas, *The House of Commons, 1832–1901: A Study of its Economic and Functional Character*, University of Wales Press, Cardiff, 1939, Section 1, Tables 1–5 and Section 2, Tables 1–6.

Note: The totals exceed the membership of the House of Commons since many MPs represented more than one interest. The ratios of interests to MPs were 1:1.4 in 1832, 1:1.9 in 1868, and 1:2.0 in 1900.

As Table 5.2 shows, one in three MPs still represented landed interests in the middle of the nineteenth century and they still remained a significant proportion in 1900, although a sharp decline occurred during the agricultural depression in the 1880s. Conversely, although industrial, commercial and financial interests grew markedly between 1832 and 1868, it was not until 1900 that more than half of all MPs represented such interests, and significant workers' representation had to wait until the arrival of a party established for the purpose – the Labour Party. In fact, it is precisely because they represent different interests in society, though not necessarily exclusively, that parties have such a profound effect on the socio-economic composition of the Commons. This is made all the more important because since 1945 only two independent candidates have been elected to Parliament – Martin Bell for Tatton in 1997 and Richard Taylor for Wyre Forest in 2001 – and only a handful of others have managed to defy the party machines, usually fighting under labels such as 'Independent Conservative' or 'Independent Labour'. It is therefore electoral movement between the parties that tends to have the most dramatic effect on the socio-economic make-up of the House. A victory for one party normally brings in more MPs similar to those already sitting for the party concerned.

Just as societal changes brought about by the industrial revolution gradually permeated Parliament during the nineteenth century, so have changes since then. For example, in 1868 no less than 44.9 per cent of Conservative MPs had aristocratic connections, but by 1918 it had fallen to 17 per cent. Even so, it was still as high as 8 per cent in 1974, though falling yet further to

1.8 per cent by 2001. Similarly, nearly a third of Conservative and fifth of Liberal MPs elected between 1868 and 1895 had no particular occupations but relied on private income; between 1918 and 1935 they constituted less than 5 per cent of Conservatives and Liberals. On the other hand, from its foundation in 1900 to when it first became the official opposition in 1918, the Labour Party reflected its purpose – the representation of working men, with nine out of ten Labour MPs being working class. However, the decline of the Liberal Party and the consequent party realignment resulted in an increasing number of middle-class Labour MPs being elected from 1922 and a slow decline in working-class representation. Similarly, all the parties reflected increasing educational opportunities, especially in higher education, although majorities of Conservative and Liberal MPs have long been graduates. However, each party has a distinct profile, as Tables 5.3 and 5.4 show.

Table 5.3   *The educational background of MPs, 1945–97*

Education	Cons.	Lab.	Lib/LD
Elementary	–	16.2	–
All public schools	70.1	17.5	42.9
Clarendon schools*	30.6	3.6	8.3
All graduates	72.6	50.3	75.0
Oxford graduates	26.2	11.1	21.4
Cambridge graduates	21.0	5.7	14.3
All 'Oxbridge'	47.2	16.8	35.7
Other universities	25.4	33.5	39.3

Source: Michael Rush, *The Role of the Member of Parliament Since 1868*, Oxford, Oxford University Press, 2001, Tables 4.6, 4.8 and 4.10.

Note: * I.e. Eton, Harrow, Winchester, Charterhouse, Shrewsbury, Rugby, St Paul's, Westminster, and Merchant Taylors'.

Table 5.4   *The educational background of MPs, 2001*

Education	Cons.	Lab.	LD	Other*	Total
All public schools	62.6	14.3	34.6	6.9	27.8
Clarendon schools	15.7	1.5	5.8	0.0	5.3
All graduates	87.3	72.6	84.6	58.6	76.6
Oxford graduates	26.5	11.2	17.3	0.0	15.0
Cambridge graduates	22.9	5.6	9.6	6.9	10.3
All 'Oxbridge'	49.4	16.8	26.9	6.9	25.3
Other universities	37.9	55.8	57.7	51.7	51.3

Note: * Including the Speaker.

The educational profiles of the parties represented in the House of Commons differ not only from each other but from the population generally. The great majority of the population is educated in state schools – between 5 and 6 per cent are educated privately, mainly in independent or public schools. In contrast, more than a quarter of the MPs elected in 2001 had attended public schools, including three-fifths of Conservatives and more than a third of the Liberal Democrats, but even among Labour MPs as many as one in seven. In addition, a significant minority of MPs attended the prestigious 'Clarendon' schools, although these are mainly Conservatives. The proportion of MPs educated at public schools still considerably exceeds the national figure.

A similar picture emerges with the proportions of graduates. In 1902 only 1 per cent of the population was receiving full-time education at the age of 19 and it was still only 7 per cent by 1962, shortly before the first major post-war expansion of higher education. In 1990 18 per cent of 19 and 20 year-olds were in full-time education, shortly before the second and larger post-war expansion. By 1996–97 the number of students in full-time higher education, including teacher training, had exceeded two million – some 3.5 per cent of the population. In spite of the expansion of educational opportunities, especially in higher education, these pale beside the proportion of MPs who are graduates – three-quarters in 2001, the highest ever. Again, party differences emerge: nearly nine out of ten Conservatives, more than eight out of ten Liberal Democrats, and nearly three out of four Labour MPs are graduates, but the 'elitist' picture found in schooling is again apparent. In 2001, a quarter of all MPs were graduates of Oxford or Cambridge; this included half the Conservatives and a quarter of Liberal Democrats, but only one in six Labour MPs. Moreover, not only were Labour MPs more likely to be non-Oxbridge graduates but more came from the former polytechnics than was the case with other parties.

That MPs are in most cases better-qualified educationally than those they represent should come as no surprise. Indeed, but again not surprisingly, MPs are also better-qualified than those who actually vote for them and those who are party members. British society has long had a significant meritocratic element and the expansion of educational opportunities has increased that element considerably. Education opens up what political recruitment theorists call the opportunity structures, widening the pool of those interested in and available for a career in politics. However, only a minority of those with similar educational qualifications to MPs actually aspire to such a career and other factors, not least ambition and motivation, play a crucial part.

Tables 5.5 and 5.6 extend and reinforce the educational profile of MPs: they are no more typical of those they represent in occupational background than educationally and this is similarly the case in comparison with party voters and members. In 2001, nearly two-fifths of MPs were drawn from the professions, another fifth from business, nearly a third from various other occupations and well below 10 per cent were manual or non-manual workers.

Table 5.5   *The occupational background of MPs, 1945–97 (%)*

Occupation	Cons.	Lab.	Lib/LD
Professional	33.7	33.9	39.3
Business	52.4	9.7	39.3
Workers	0.7	30.5	0.0
Miscellaneous	10.9	25.5	20.2
Private means	2.1	0.2	1.2
Not known	0.2	0.2	0.0
Total	100.0	100.0	100.0

Source: Michael Rush, *The Role of the Member of Parliament Since 1868*, Oxford, Oxford University Press, 2001, Tables 4.5, 4.7 and 4.9.

Table 5.6   *The occupational background of MPs, 2001 (%)*

Occupation	Cons.	Lab.	LD	Other	All
Professional	32.5	38.3	36.5	51.7	37.3
Business	53.6	7.8	38.5	20.7	22.3
Workers	0.6	11.6	0.0	3.4	7.6
Miscellaneous	13.3	42.2	25.0	24.1	32.8
Total	100.0	99.9	100.0	99.9	100.0

As would be expected, three-fifths of those with a business background were Conservatives, but so were nearly two-fifths of Liberal Democrats and a significant minority of Labour MPs. What is most marked, however, is the small proportion of workers, almost all of whom are Labour but still constituting little more than one in ten. As already noted, the number and proportion of manual and non-manual workers among Labour MPs began to decline from 1922, but as recently as 1945 they comprised two-fifths. The miscellaneous category conceals an interesting development. Originally a residuary grouping to accommodate a minority of MPs who did not fall into one of the main three categories, it included journalists, welfare workers, and those who worked for parties and pressure groups. In 1945, the miscellaneous category accounted for 12.1 per cent of MPs but by 2001 it had risen to nearly a third. Although a variety of factors have contributed to this growth, such as increases in pressure group activity and the number of individuals employed by groups, a substantial part of it arises from the increased number of party officials and workers becoming MPs. From its inception the Labour Party's strong links with the trade unions resulted in a substantial proportion of Labour MPs having served as full-time union officials and this remains an important recruitment path, accounting for 8 per cent of Labour MPs in 2001. There was also a more limited tradition in all parties of local, regional or national officials seeking and securing election, but Labour party rules actually restricted such recruitment and it was a more important source for the Conservatives. Thus, in the post-war period a small but steady stream of individuals who had worked at Conservative Central Office or the Conservative Research Department became MPs. However, a similar but different career path opened up with the increasing appointment of policy advisers, mostly in government but increasingly in opposition too, and the growing number of MPs employing research assistants. Again, this has affected all parties, but has been of particular importance in the Labour Party. Although, in 2001, the proportions of Conservative and Labour MPs drawn from such backgrounds was the same – 10.8 per cent, this accounted for eighteen Conservatives compared with no fewer than 44 Labour MPs.

In educational and occupational terms the House of Commons has become increasingly middle class. Compared with the nineteenth-century House it is a less aristocratic body, representing a wider range of occupations and better educated, but there has been a marked decline in working-class representation. The Labour Party continues to be the almost exclusive vehicle for such representation, but the Parliamentary Party has become increasingly middle class to the point that the parliamentary profiles of the two major parties appear similar. However, this is misleading: Conservative and Labour MPs may have become more middle class, but they are drawn largely from different sectors of it. Conservative MPs are more likely to have been educated at independent schools and be Oxbridge graduates. Occupationally, they are more likely to come from the professions, especially the law, and from business. In contrast, Labour MPs are more likely to have been state educated, to have attended 'redbrick' universities or former polytechnics, with relatively few from a business background and many more from public-sector occupations, especially teaching. Even though similar numbers of lawyers are found among Conservative and Labour in 2001, Conservatives are more likely to be barristers and Labour MPs solicitors. Indeed, notwithstanding the decline in the number and proportion of working-class Labour MPs, a clear indicator of the Conservative–Labour middle-class divide is that Labour MPs are much more likely to have working-class antecedents, often being first-, or at most second-generation middle class in origin. And it is a difference that matters in that where MPs come from in socio-economic terms is likely to contribute significantly to their political views and therefore the choice of party through which they seek to realise their political ambitions.

If MPs are increasingly middle class, they are also largely middle aged. The median age of Conservative MPs in 2001 was 48, Labour MPs 50 and Liberal Democrats 47. Only five MPs were under 30 and only ten over 70. This is hardly surprising: most would-be MPs are expected to have some sort of established career before being elected for a winnable parliamentary constituency and the introduction of a pension scheme for MPs from 1964 means that most now retire at or around normal retiring age.

The Commons is no more representative in respect of ethnic minorities. Only seventeen black or Asian MPs have been elected to Parliament, the first in 1892, but none between 1905 and 1922 or between 1929 and 1987, when there were four, rising to five in 1992 (four Labour and one Conservative). Nonetheless, 2001 saw the largest number ever – twelve, all Labour, although the Conservatives have one Anglo-Indian MP. Even so, this was still substantially below the 5.8 per cent of black and Asian and the 7.2 per cent of other ethnic minorities in the population of Great Britain.[4]

The House of Commons is thus not a representative body in relation to those who elect it, nor, for that matter of those who select candidates or those who vote for particular candidates or parties. Does it matter? That question is better answered in the wider context of both Houses of Parliament, Lords as well as Commons.

The House of Lords

Until 1999 the House of Lords was a virtually unique legislative body in that nearly three-fifths of its members had the right to membership by virtue of their birth – these were the hereditary peers. Most of the remaining members were life peers, plus the 26 senior bishops of the Church of England and small number of Law Lords (also holders of life peerages), whose task it was to fulfil the judicial functions of the House of Lords. It also had a very large membership – 1,290 in November 1999, although the number of regular attenders comprised only about a third. However, in December 1999, following the passing of the House of Lords Act, all but 92 of the hereditary peers lost their right to sit in the Lords, reducing the membership at that point to 670 and resulting in life peers comprising four-fifths of the members. In spite of the removal of most of the hereditary members, the House of Lords remains distinct from most other second chambers in several respects. It is one of only three appointed second chambers in western liberal democracies – the others being the Canadian Senate and the German Bundesrat; all others are either directly elected or indirectly elected by bodies such as state legislatures or local councils.

By removing most of the hereditary peers, the 1999 Act considerably reduced the number of Conservative peers, since many of the hereditaries took the Conservative whip, but more significantly narrowed the gap between Conservative and Labour (see Table 5.7). That gap, however, had already been narrowed by Tony Blair using his prime ministerial powers of patronage to recommend the creation of a large number of additional Labour life peers. In fact, at a rate of more than sixty a year, Blair has been responsible for the creation of more life peers than any other Prime Minister. The second stage of

Table 5.7   *The membership of the House of Lords before and after the House of Lords Act, 1999*

	1999*	2004*
Type of peerage		
Hereditary	58.6	13.5
Life	37.2	78.2
Bishops	2.0	3.8
Law Lords	2.2	4.4
Total	100.0	99.9
Party		
Conservative	39.9	31.4
Labour	16.0	27.1
Lib-Dem	6.0	9.6
Crossbench	29.2	27.1
No affiliation	8.8	4.8†
Total	99.9	100.0

Source: House of Lords, Annual Report and Accounts, 2000–01, and www.parliament.uk.

Notes: * Female peers: 1999 – 7.1%; 2004 – 16.6%; † Includes bishops.

Lords' reform was intended to fulfil Labour's 1997 and 2001 election manifesto pledges to make the upper house more representative and democratic. Later in 2001, the government therefore published a White Paper proposing an elected element of 20 per cent, but this encountered considerable opposition, especially from Labour backbenchers in the Commons. However, in 2003 MPs rejected each of seven options on the composition of the Lords, ranging from a fully elected through various mixes of elected and appointed, to a fully appointed second chamber, although there was a clear majority in favour of an elected element. Conversely, peers voted for a fully appointed House. By this time, it was clear that the Prime Minister preferred a fully appointed body but legislation to achieve this and remove the remaining 92 hereditaries was postponed until after the general election.

The removal of most of the hereditary peers also massively increased the Prime Minister's powers of patronage, since membership now depends almost entirely on the Prime Minister of the day, although most recommendations made by the Leader of the Opposition and the Leader of the Liberal Democrats are usually accepted by the Prime Minister. Of course, the 1958 Life Peerages Act considerably increased prime ministerial patronage, but it also facilitated the appointment of women, more Labour peers and a significant number of distinguished individuals with no party affiliation. However, it was also used by Conservative Prime Ministers to reward supporters and maintain a steady stream of Conservative recruits to the upper house. Royal peerages apart, only three hereditary peerages have been created since 1964, two of which became extinct with the death of the holders, but until 1999 hereditary peerages continued to provide new members for the Lords who owed nothing to prime ministerial patronage. Following a recommendation of the Wakeham Commission on reform of the second chamber an independent Appointments Commission was set up, but its role is limited to vetting party recommendations on narrow propriety grounds and recommending a small number of so-called 'people's peers'; prime ministerial patronage remains intact.

How much the socio-economic composition of a reformed second chamber will differ from the current House remains to be seen, although this it difficult to judge in any case, since recent aggregate data on most aspects of the socio-economic background of peers is not available. Data is available on average age – 68 in 2004 – and the proportion of women members – 16.6 per cent (113) in 2004. Other than that, the most recent data was produced as long ago as 1981. However, a reasonable idea of the educational and occupational composition of the upper house can be gained by looking at life peers in 1981.

Educationally in 1981 life peers, like MPs, constituted a fairly exclusive group, closer to Conservative and Liberal MPs than to Labour – 44.8 per cent had attended public schools, 69.4 per cent were graduates, and 48.8 had been to Oxford or Cambridge. That exclusivity will have been reduced by the increased number of Labour life peers created since 1981, especially since 1997, but hardly to the extent of having transformed educational profile of the House of Lords. The removal of most of the hereditary peers has also had a significant impact, actually increasing the proportion of graduates but substantially reducing the number who had been to public school, especially the Clarendon schools. This has not only made the upper house less socially exclusive but made it a much more meritocratic body, arguably more so than the Commons. This meritocratic picture is reinforced if the occupational experience of life peers in 1981 is examined.

Unfortunately, because the data in Table 5.8 record more than one occupation for individual peers, a direct comparison with MPs is problematic. A further complication is that more than a third had been engaged in political service, mainly as former MPs and ministers. Even more – nearly three-fifths – have been involved in public service and administration, but in many cases it was serving as paid members of public bodies, some full-time, some part-time, and usually for a limited period. In terms of 'normal' occupations, more than a quarter came from a variety of business backgrounds, followed by nearly a fifth from education and a similar proportion from the law, with rather more than one in ten from journalism, writing and publishing, and less than one in ten from manual or non-manual work, although, if full-time trade union officials are added to the latter, the proportion rises to one in seven. The main impact of the removal of most of the hereditary peers has been a substantial reduction in the number of landowners and farmers and those with a military

Table 5.8   *Occupational experience of life peers, 1981*

Occupational experience	%
Public service/administration	58.0
Political service	34.9
Industrialist/service/manufacturing/retail	26.5
Teaching (all levels)	18.8
Legal (judge/barrister/solicitor)	18.3
Civil service (incl. diplomatic)	16.1
Landownership/farming	14.6
Journalism/writing/publishing	10.7
Manual and non-manual workers	8.8
Banking and finance	7.8
Churches	7.6
Military (regular)	6.1
Full-time trade union official	4.9
Arts/entertainment/sport	4.1
Engineering	3.2
Medical	3.4
Accountancy/economist	2.4
Advertising/public relations	1.5
Scientist	1.5

Source: Adapted from unpublished PhD, N. D. J. Baldwin, University of Exeter, 1985.

Note: Total exceeds 100 per cent because a significant number of peers had experience of more than one occupation.

background and to increase those with business, educational, civil service and administrative experience. Not surprisingly, given that many life peers have already had distinguished careers, the proportion previously involved in various forms of public service rose more than any other grouping, quite apart from those who had been MPs. Socio-economically, the House of Lords is not a representative body and this is made all the more so precisely because most peers have extensive careers before becoming members of the upper house, clearly reflected in their average age of 68.

Originally, of course, the House of Lords represented the church and the aristocracy: it had an inclusive membership dependent on social rank; all above a particular rank were included, all below that rank excluded. It represented the interests of the established church, the wealthy and the aristocracy, not all of whom were members. With the decline of landed wealth and of the aristocracy, it became increasingly anachronistic as a representative body, but survived and carved out a significant role for itself. In a sense, it now represents no one – the Anglican Church has its own representative body, the Synod, although Parliament retains some residuary responsibilities for church legislation. In socio-economic terms the House of Lords is less representative than the Commons. The question again arises, does it matter?

Parliament, representation and democracy

Parliament, more particularly the House of Commons, is regarded as the key institution in the UK's system of representative government. Yet MPs are socio-economically representative of neither the electorate nor the general adult population. The House of Lords is even less representative. Since there is little no support for a Parliament consisting of equal chambers, it is reasonable to assume that the Commons will retain its primacy over the Lords and that some issues relating to representation and democracy will continue to be the exclusive preserve of the lower house. In particular, the survival of the government, short of the introduction of a separation of powers, will continue to rest on its ability to retain the confidence of the House of Commons and, with it, continued primacy in financial matters. It may also be assumed that the Lords will continue to defer to the Commons in cases of significant disagreement over legislation, though arguably this could become less certain were the second chamber wholly or substantially elected. Even then, the government could resort to use of the Parliament Acts.

The socio-economic representativeness of Parliament can be viewed in three separate dimensions, each posing a different question. First, would a Parliament in which either or both houses were a microcosm of the adult population more effectively represent the views of that population? Second, would microcosmic chambers be regarded as more legitimate than the existing two houses? Third, would microcosmic chambers be more effective in scrutinising and keeping a check on the government and its policies? None of these questions can be answered definitively, but reasonable parameters to any answer can be set.

To what extent would a microcosmic Parliament better reflect public opinion? The traditional Burkean theory of the MP as a representative rests on the premise that it is perfectly possible for an MP to understand and put forward the views he or she represents; direct experience is not a prerequisite of representation. It is, of course, well known that on various issues – capital punishment, for example – MPs and peers do not reflect majority public opinion. That, however, is the crux of the representative versus the delegate argument. On the other hand, it can be argued that the total absence of particular sections of the population from a representative body is likely to weaken its ability to understand the views of those not directly represented and that more women and more members from ethnic minority groups would make either or both chambers better able to reflect public opinion. However, Parliament is not and cannot be a sort of national 'focus group', able to reflect changes in public opinion from day to day or month to month and, presumably, respond to them. That is a point of view which sits better with arguments for the greater use of initiatives and referendums or the more extensive use of technology to elicit public opinion and, for that matter, 'focus groups', to which Parliament could respond rather than seek to emulate.

To what extent would a microcosmic House of Commons be regarded as more legitimate? This is largely a matter of perception. The legitimacy of the House of Commons rests on a number of factors, such as whether elections are seen as fair and free and on the integrity and behaviour of its members, as well as whether it is seen as genuinely representative body. For example, there was widespread resentment in Scotland in the 1980s and early 1990s that it was being governed by a government the Scottish electorate did not elect. In fact, the last election in which the Conservatives won a relative majority of the votes cast in Scotland (and a majority of the seats) was 1955 and thereafter Conservative strength in Scotland declined to the point that in 1997 the party won no seats at all. Nonetheless, the claim that Conservative governments lacked legitimacy in Scotland was not made between 1959 and 1964 or between 1970 and 1974. Moreover, Labour has won a relative majority of votes and seats in Wales in every election since 1922, but the legitimacy of non-Labour governments was not questioned. What started in Scotland as a political ploy became a widespread perception, and perceptions are crucial in the context of legitimacy. More broadly, if the electoral system is widely perceived as being unfair, then it is likely to undermine the legitimacy of any body elected by it. The same could be said for a House of Commons that is unrepresentative in terms of gender or ethnicity: if sufficient women or particular ethnic groups feel that their views are not adequately represented because they are numerically and proportionately under-represented, then that may lead those individuals or groups to deny it legitimacy. If such feelings were sufficiently widespread, the legitimacy of the Commons would be seriously undermined. Similarly, allegations of 'sleaze' in the 1990s damaged the reputation not only of MPs but also of the House of Commons as an institution.

The question of legitimacy also affects the House of Lords, though less because of its composition and more because of the way its members are chosen. Consequently, a wholly or substantially elected second chamber would probably be seen as having greater legitimacy than the current House and, moreover, see itself as having greater legitimacy, leading it to be more willing to challenge the Commons over legislation. Such legitimacy would probably be enhanced were the Lords elected by PR and MPs continued to be elected by the FPTP. Elected members of the second chamber would also raise the same issues of socio-economic representation that apply to MPs.

Legitimacy is also linked to the public's view of the effectiveness of Parliament and its trust in politicians: the less effective the public perceives Parliament to be and the lower the lower the level of public trust it has in politicians, the lower the likely legitimacy of Parliament. That, however, is a matter that will be discussed in Chapter 10.

And would a microcosmic Parliament be more effective in keeping a check on the government? It is not unreasonable to argue that a more represent-ative Parliament in terms of gender and ethnicity, with a wider range of occupational experience and less exclusive educationally would provide a deeper and broader pool of knowledge and experience with which to carry out the scrutiny function. Debates and committee work could be better-informed, ministers asked more penetrating questions, policies made more effective, government departments and agencies more efficient, better value achieved for tax-payers, but neither a more representative Parliament nor even a microcosmic one would be a guarantee of any of these things.

Ultimately, composition and functions cannot be entirely separated – the one affects the other. Microcosmic representation would guarantee nothing other than statistical representativeness. What Parliament needs is members with the skills and capabilities to fulfil its functions, which involves know-ledge, and organisational ability, both of which can be acquired, but it also requires a desire and willingness to fulfil those functions. There is no simple template against which would-be parliamentarians can be measured; some will be better able to perform one function than another, but the whole must be able to fulfil all Parliament's functions.

The socio-economic composition of Parliament matters: it matters because if affects Parliament's legitimacy; it matters because Parliament, especially the House of Commons, is the pool from which almost all ministers are drawn; it matters because it affects Parliament's ability to carry out its functions. Yet it should not be forgotten that the most important determinant of the behaviour of most MPs and a significant proportion of the members of the House of Lords is not their socio-economic background, but their parties. Socio-economic background plays an important role in determining the personnel of Parliament, but the majority are first and foremost members of parties and the partisan role lies at the heart of the organisation and operation of Parliament.

Notes

1 Pippa Norris and Joni Lovenduski, *Political Recruitment: Gender, Race and Class in the British Parliament*, Cambridge, Cambridge University Press, 1995, p. 122.
2 *Ibid.* pp. 106–22.
3 Michael Rush, *The Selection of Parliamentary Candidates*, London, Nelson, 1969, pp. 99 and 206.
4 Office of National Statistics, 2001.

6

The professionalisation of Parliament[1]

Introduction

The growth of government in the nineteenth and twentieth centuries inevitably increased the demands on Parliament. It sought to respond to these demands in a number of ways – by changes in procedure and operation, by meeting more frequently, and by increasing the resources available to members, both individually and collectively. A major consequence of the first of these changes is that the government's ability to secure the passage of its business increased and the sheer volume of legislation passed grew almost beyond recognition. On the other hand, the time available to the official opposition was formalised and that available to backbenchers substantially reduced and fragmented. This is reflected in an increase in the number of Commons' standing orders on public business from 6 in 1830 to 163 in 2002. Although the number of days the Commons sat during the nineteenth century varied from fewer than 100 to more than 140, in the twentieth century it increased to between 160 and 170. Later, these changes were accompanied by a massive increase in the resources available to Parliament and its members and to what being a Member of Parliament entailed and, to a lesser extent, a member of the House of Lords. Parliament became more and more professionalised, marked by a shift from part-time to full-time MPs and increasingly busy members of the Lords, the payment of MPs, expense allowances for peers, and the provision of a growing range of resources in the form of staff and various allowances, services and facilities in both Houses. However, these changes affected the Commons much more than the Lords and came much earlier in the lower house.

The payment of MPs

Members of Parliament were not paid a salary until 1912. In medieval times constituents sometimes paid their Members and met some of the expenses of sending an MP to Westminster (or wherever Parliament was sitting), but the practice died out by the end of the seventeenth century and thereafter MPs needed personal wealth or a wealthy patron in order to sustain a political career. In the eighteenth century and later, when the Commons met every year, it did so for six or seven months, usually concentrated in the period February to August, and membership could easily be combined with another occupation. This was also facilitated by the parliamentary day, which began in the afternoon, with the principal business being dealt with in the evening, when any important votes also took place. This particularly suited lawyers and those with financial or business interests. On the other hand, until 1918 parliamentary candidates were responsible for meeting the administrative costs in the constituencies they contested and, before the elimination of widespread corruption, following the passing of the Corrupt and Illegal Practices Act in 1883, contesting elections could be a very expensive business. As demands for working-class representation increased, so did demands for the payment of MPs. One of the earliest came from the working-class Chartist Movement in 1838 and proposals for paying MPs were debated five times in the Commons between 1870 and 1895 and formally adopted as party policy by the Liberal Party in 1891, but it was the rise of the Labour Party that gave the demand for payment its final impetus. Early Labour MPs were mostly supported financially by trade unions, but this was successfully challenged in the courts in 1909, leading directly to the introduction of a salary for MPs in 1912.

However, as the notes to Table 6.1 show, pay became entangled with the expenses of fulfilling parliamentary responsibilities, although from 1924 MPs were able to travel free between their constituencies and Westminster. MPs' salaries almost inevitably became a political football – there was never a 'right time' to increase salaries and the decision ultimately lay with MPs themselves. In 1931 the salary was actually reduced by 10 per cent as part a wider reduction in public expenditure during the depression of the 1930s. Extra-parliamentary bodies were twice set up to examine the question of MPs' pay and allowances, the first in 1963–64, the second in 1971. The first reported that many MPs were legitimately claiming expenses against their salaries for tax purposes, thereby significantly reducing their net pay. The second reinforced this finding and recommended that a clear distinction be drawn between the Member's salary and the expenses incurred carrying out parliamentary duties. This recommendation was duly accepted, but the Top Salaries Review Body (TSRB) (now the Senior Salaries Review Body (SSRB)) also made a crucial observation: 'By any reasonable standard ... most Members must be considered as working on a full-time basis, and we consider that the level of remuneration should be assessed accordingly.'[2] Since its first

Table 6.1   *MPs' salaries, 1912–2004 (selected years)*

Year	Salary (£)	Year	Salary (£)
1912	400[a]	1957	1,750[d]
1931	360[b]	1964	3,250[e]
1934	380	1972	4,500
1935	400	1982	14,510
1937	600	1992	30,854
1946	1,000	2002	55,118
1954	1,250[c]	2004	57,485

Source: House of Commons Information Office, *Factsheet M5: Members' Pay, Pensions and Allowances*, 2004.

Notes: [a] From 1912 £100 was exempt from income tax, being regarded as an average allowance for necessary parliamentary expenses. [b] In 1931 the salary was reduced by 10 per cent as an economy measure, half of which was restored in 1934, half in 1935. [c] In 1954 the £100 tax-free allowance was abolished and a sessional allowance averaging £250 was substituted and included in the salary. [d] The sessional allowance was abolished in 1957 and replaced by an additional sum of £750 to cover parliamentary expenses. This was included in the salary. [e] £1,250 of the salary was regarded as an expense allowance.

report, the TSRB/SSRB has reviewed salaries and allowances once during every normal length Parliament, leaving MPs to vote on its recommendations at the beginning of a new Parliament, but between general elections MPs' salaries have been linked to civil service pay and annual increases have therefore been automatic. However, during the 1970s, 1980s and 1990s governments limited or sought to limit increases, not always successfully. In addition, in 1965 (backdated to 1964) a parliamentary pensions scheme for all MPs was introduced.

Apart from ministers, who, of course, receive salaries in that capacity (in addition to their parliamentary salaries), the Speaker and the two Deputy Speakers are paid salaries, as are the Leader of the Opposition, the Opposition Chief whip and one assistant whip, but in 2003 its was agreed that the chairs of select committees should be paid an additional salary of £12,500 a year. This applies to the chairs of all departmental committees and of the Environmental Audit, European Scrutiny, Public Accounts, Public Administration, and Regulatory Reform Committees, and the Commons' chairs of the Joint Committees on Human Rights and Statutory Instruments.

In contrast to MPs, members of the House of Lords (other than a small number of office-holders) are not paid a salary, nor are they regarded as full-time. This also contrasts with the members of second chambers in other comparable countries, such as Australia, Austria, Belgium, Canada, France, Ireland, Italy, Japan, Spain, Switzerland and the United States. In all these countries members of the second chamber receive a full salary and, with the exception of the Irish Senate, are regarded as and expected to be full-time members of the legislature. Members of the German Bundesrat are an exception in that they are not paid as members of the second chamber, but this is because they are 'nominated by and represent the Land governments and, as such, are paid salaries and provided with pensions schemes by those governments'.[3]

The payment of ministers

Ministers, whether MPs or peers (or occasionally neither), are also paid salaries, although before 1831 some ministers received fees and gratuities rather than a salary. Ministers were therefore paid long before MPs qua MPs received any remuneration at all. Since 1971, like those of MPs, the salaries of ministers have been reviewed by the TSRB/SSRB, which also reviews the pay of senior civil servants, judges and senior ranks of the armed services.

Ministers who are MPs continue represent their constituents and between 1946 and 1957 those with a ministerial salary of less than £5,000 received a tax-free allowance of £500 to meet the expenses involved. In 1957 this was increased to £1,250 and extended to all minister-MPs, who also became entitled to other allowances to MPs, such as the secretarial allowance, when they were introduced. In 1970, the TSRB concluded that 'to pay ministers the full parliamentary salary ... without abatement would be over-generous' and recommended two-thirds of the full salary (£3,000), but added that it 'did not mean to imply the same fraction will always be appropriate in the future'.[4] Similarly, in 1983 it noted that ministers and other paid office-holders in the Commons 'remain fully responsible ... for constituency matters throughout their period of office', but that the 'responsibilities of office inevitably limit the individual's ability to undertake the full range of parliamentary activities other than those entailed by the office'.[5] Yet, in 1996 the SSRB asserted, 'a minister retains the full responsibilities of an MP'[6] and recommended that minister-MPs and the Speaker and two Deputy Speakers should receive the *full* parliamentary salary. This, of course, ignores that that fact that they neither are nor can be engaged in the scrutiny role of the Member of Parliament. Nonetheless, the recommendation was accepted, substantially increasing what MPs holding ministerial or other posts were paid without increasing their ministerial or other salaries. Ministers and parliamentary office-holders in the House of Lords receive salaries for the posts they hold, but do not, of course, receive a parliamentary salary, since members of the upper house are unpaid. The salaries of ministers and other paid office-holders is shown in Table 6.2.

The highest paid minister is not, as might be expected, the Prime Minister but the Lord Chancellor. However, this is because he is paid as Head of the Judiciary and Speaker of the House of Lords, as well as a minister, but this will change when the three roles are separated and the office of Lord Chancellor becomes more limited. Otherwise, ministerial salaries are hierarchical, with Cabinet ministers paid the most, Ministers of State the next highest, and so

Table 6.2   *Salaries of ministers and other office-holders, 2004*

Office	Ministerial salary (£)	Parliamentary salary (£)	Total (£)*
Ministers			
Cabinet			
Prime Minister	121,437	57,485	178,922
Lord Chancellor†	207,736	n.a.	207,736
Cabinet minister (Commons)	72,862	57,485	130,347
Cabinet minister (Lords)	98,899	n.a.	98,899
Non-Cabinet			
Minister of State (Commons)	37,796	57,485	95,281
Minister of State (Lords)	77,220	n.a.	77,220
Parl. Under Sec. (Commons)	28,688	57,485	86,173
Parl. Under Sec. (Lords)	67,255	n.a.	67,255
Law Officers			
Attorney General	103,461	Currently in Lords	103,461
Solicitor General	63,486	57,485	120,971
Advocate General for Scotland	63,486	57,485	120,971
Whips			
Govt Chief Whip (Commons)	72,862	57,485	130,347
Govt Chief Whip (Lords)	77,220	n.a.	77,220
Govt Dep. Chief Whip (Commons)	37,796	57,485	95,281
Govt Dep. Chief Whip (Lords)	67,255	n.a.	67,255
Govt Whip/Asst. Whip (Commons)	24,324	57,485	81,809
Govt Whip (Lords)	62,191	n.a.	62,191
Opposition office-holders			
Leader of the Opposition (Commons)	66,792	57,485	124,277
Leader of the Opposition (Lords)	67,255	n.a.	67,255
Opp. Chief Whip (Commons)	37,796	57,485	95,281
Opp. Chief Whip (Lords)	62,191	n.a.	62,191
Deputy Opposition Whip (Commons)	24,324	57,485	81,809
Parliamentary officers			
Speaker	72,862	57,485	130,347
Chair of Ways and Means (Dep. Speaker Commons)	37,796	57,485	95,281
Chair of Committees (Dep. Speaker Lords)	77,220	n.a.	77,220
Dep. Chair of Ways and Means (Commons)	33,218	57,485	90,703
Principal Dep. Chair (Lords)	72,243	n.a.	72,243

Source: House of Commons Information Office, *Factsheet M6: Ministerial Salaries*, 2004.

Notes: * In addition, all ministers (except those with an official residence or any in the Lords receiving a Night Subsistence Allowance) receive a £1,618 London Supplement. † The present Lord Chancellor, Lord Falconer, has elected to receive a Cabinet minister's salary, pending the limitation of the office of Lord Chancellor.

on, down to government whips. The only exceptions are the three Law
Officers, the Attorney General, Solicitor General and the Advocate General for
Scotland.

The full-time Member of Parliament

There have long been parliamentarians whose principal activity was being a
politician, mostly MPs but some members of the Lords too. In many instances,
from time to time they held ministerial office and a few could reasonably
described as full-time, but most were not, even though they were first and
foremost politicians. However, as government activity expanded, the demands
on MPs in particular increased, both within Parliament from their parties and
outside Parliament from their constituents. More and more MPs spent most
of their time on their political and parliamentary work. This was recognised
by the TSRB, following a survey conducted for it in preparation for its first
report in 1971. It found that as many as 70 per cent of MPs had outside
occupations, but this was offset by the fact that most of the time devoted to
such jobs was relatively low and considerably less than the time they spent on
their parliamentary activities. Subsequent TSRB surveys found that the amount
of time devoted to outside occupations had declined yet further.

The figures in Table 6.3 relate only to the parliamentary session and do
not cover recesses, when the Commons is not sitting. The 1982 and 1996
surveys, however, did ask about hours worked during recesses: in 1982 these
amounted to 40 hours for backbenchers and 50 for opposition frontbenchers;
the corresponding figures for 1996 were 50 and 53 hours. Even allowing for
a degree of exaggeration, although it is a remarkably consistent exaggeration,
such hours, whether during the parliamentary session or recesses, constitutes

Table 6.3   *Average hours per week spent by MPs (backbenchers and opposition
frontbenchers) on parliamentary work during the parliamentary session, 1971–96*

Session	No. of hrs.
1971	63
1975	70
1978	66
1982	67
1996	70

Sources: 1971 – TSRB, *Report No. 1*, Cmnd., 4836, December 1971, Appendix A, Table 6;
1975 – TSRB, *Report No. 8*, Cmnd. 6574, July 1976, Appendix A, Table 15; 1978 – TSRB,
Report No. 12, Cmnd. 7598, June 1979, Appendix C, Table 19; 1982 – TSRB, *Report No. 20*,
Cmnd. 8881-II, May 1983, Section I, Table 4; 1996 – SSRB, *Report No. 38*, Cm. 3330-II, July
1996, pp. 30–1.

a full-time commitment by any standard. A more recent survey conducted on behalf of the Hansard Society in 2000 produced an average figure in the range of 61–70 hours per week during the session. It is also the view of most MPs that being a Member of Parliament should be a full-time job, although a significant minority of Conservatives believe that it should be part-time, though they accept that the demands of the job are now such that it amounts to a full-time job.[7]

Parliamentary career patterns

Career patterns in the Commons

The transformation from part-time to full-time MPs is reflected in their career patterns. Parliamentary careers have become longer and less fragmented. In the eighteenth century the average length of service in the Commons was fifteen years, growing longer as the century went on, but not always continuous service. Membership might be interrupted by electoral defeat but was quite commonly interrupted by voluntary retirement, followed by a later period in the House, not least because pursuing a parliamentary career was expensive. In the nineteenth century the average length of service actually fell to ten years, although it rose slowly with the greater political stability after 1868. Election under the age of 30 was by no means unusual before 1832 and continued well beyond then, particularly among the landed gentry and aristocracy and second-generation wealthy manufacturers and businessmen. However, it was also by no means unusual to be first elected at the age of 50 or more – frequently the case with individuals who had had a career in manufacturing, commerce, finance or one of the professions, but were then wealthy enough to embark on a political career. A significant minority of Labour MPs, particularly between 1918 and 1945, were 50 or over when first elected, but this was the result of fewer electoral opportunities earlier in the century, as well as the need to earn a living outside politics. MPs have also increasingly ended their careers in the Commons by voluntary retirement at or around the normal retirement age, especially since the introduction of the parliamentary pension scheme from 1964. Of course, some MPs continue their political careers by becoming members of the House of Lords – in 2002 a quarter of the latter were former MPs, but these are the exception to the general rule. Having a career as a Member of Parliament has to a significant degree become 'normalised', become more like a conventional job or occupation. The job of the MP has become full-time, starting rather later than a normal career – most MPs are first elected between 35 and 45, continuing for nearly twenty years – shorter than the 'normal' career but longer than in the past, and ending with 'normal' retirement at or around 65. All this can be seen in the data shown in Table 6.4.

Table 6.4   *Age at which MPs entered and left the House of Commons and length of service, 1945–97, and 1997–2001*

Age at which first elected

Age	1945–97			1997–2001 (%)
	Cons. (%)	Lab. (%)	Lib/LD (%)	
Under 30	7.5	3.2	7.1	1.0
30–49	80.7	74.1	73.8	80.0
50 or over	11.8	22.7	19.0	19.0

Age on leaving the House of Commons

Age	1945–97			1997–2001 (%)
	Cons. (%)	Lab. (%)	Lib/LD (%)	
Under 30	0.1	0.2	–	–
30–49	20.4	18.4	41.0	11.4
50 or over	79.5	81.3	59.0	88.6

Length of service in the House of Commons

No. of years	1945–97			1997–2001 (%)
	Cons. (%)	Lab. (%)	Lib/LD (%)	
Less than 5	6.6	7.3	10.2	15.9
5–9	19.9	23.9	25.6	8.5
10–14	18.3	16.4	23.1	14.9
15–19	18.8	18.7	12.8	21.3
20–24	15.4	13.6	12.8	14.9
25 or more	21.0	20.0	15.4	24.5

Source: 1945–97 – Rush, *The Role of the Member of Parliament, Since 1868*, Oxford, Oxford University Press, 2001, Tables 5.7 and 5.8.

In the period 1945–97, in by-elections between 1997 and 2001, and at the 2001 general election, very few MPs were first elected under the age of 30. Labour actually had a higher proportion than usual in 1997 – 2.4 per cent, but this was because its landslide victory brought in a number of young candidates who were not expected to win. On the other hand, although more MPs were first elected at the age of 50 and over, most were between 30 and

49. In fact, the mean ages of newly elected Conservative MPs between 1997 and 2001 and in 2001 was 39.6 (median 39), Labour 42.7 (median 42), Liberal Democrats 45.7 (median 47), and those of minor parties 44.5 (median 44). Most would-be MPs have been active in their parties some years before securing selection for a winnable constituency and most have had a non-political occupation to sustain their political activity financially. Conservatives and Liberal Democrats have frequently fought earlier elections unsuccessfully before being elected to Parliament, though this is much less true of Labour MPs. For many Labour and Liberal Democrat MPs, election is preceded by experience as a local councillor: in 2001, for example, this was the case with 64.1 per cent of Labour MPs and 59.6 per cent of Liberal Democrats, but only 34.1 per cent of Conservatives. Generally speaking, however, Conservatives make the transition from political activists to MPs faster than members of other parties and this is reflected in the age at which most Conservatives are first elected.

Historically and not surprisingly, MPs commonly had close connections with the constituencies they represented: in 1868 56.5 per cent had direct connections with their constituencies, substantially more in the case of Conservatives – 66.9 per cent, rather fewer in the case of Liberals – 48.3 per cent. However, local connections tended to decline and by 1979 only a quarter had direct connections, but now it was Labour and Liberal MPs who most commonly had such connections. Indeed, the proportion has tended to rise since 1979 and in 2001 nearly half of all MPs (47.5 per cent) had direct connections – 58.0 per cent Labour, 67.3 per cent Liberal Democrats but only 12.0 per cent of Conservatives. For many Labour and Liberal Democrat MPs this took the form of local government experience. A handful of MPs – thirteen between 1979 and 1999 – had been elected to the European Parliament before election to Westminster and a number had unsuccessfully fought Euro-elections to gain electoral experience, but the European Parliament has not become a significant pathway to Westminster. Nor is it likely that the Scottish Parliament and the National Assembly for Wales will provide many recruits for Westminster. Initially, a number of Scottish and Welsh MPs moved from the latter to Edinburgh or Cardiff – 23 to the former, 10 to the latter, but neither the European Parliament nor the devolved legislatures in Scotland and Wales should be seen in the same light as local government is for would-be MPs – a stepping stone to Westminster. The Scottish Parliament and the National Assembly constitute crucial elements of semi-autonomous political systems and are likely to remain so. So also does the Northern Ireland Assembly, but it presents a different picture of the dual mandate – members of both the Assembly and the Westminster Parliament and, in some cases, a triple mandate – members of the European Parliament too, which serve unionist and nationalist interests in Northern Ireland politics.

Just as most MPs were within a relatively narrow age range when first elected, so there a similar consistency about the age at which they ended their

Table 6.5   *Participation in parliamentary activity, 1871–1995*
(selected sessions)

Session	Frontbenchers	Backbenchers
1871	81.1	25.5
1901	68.8	29.0
1928	68.8	46.7
1947–48	82.0	59.0
1994–95	83.9	89.6

Source: Michael Rush, *The Role of the Member of Parliament Since 1868*, Oxford, Oxford
University Press, 2001, Table 6.4.

careers in the Commons. For some, their careers were brought to a premature
end by electoral defeat or death and a smaller number resign during the course
of a Parliament, but for most it is retirement that ends their career as a
Member of Parliament. Excluding the Westminster MPs who were elected
to the Scottish Parliament (MSPs) or National Assembly for Wales (AMs) in
1999 and subsequently left the Commons, retirement accounts for three-fifths
(62.8 per cent) of those whose Commons careers ended between 1997 and
2001. Length of service followed a similar pattern, with the mean number of
years served, including MSPs and AMs, being 17.8 years, rising to 18.6 years
if the latter are excluded.

In addition to age of entry and exit, and length of service, the extent to
which the role of the MP has been professionalised is reflected in levels of
participation in the House of Commons. The figures shown in Table 6.5 are
based on an analysis of *Hansard* indexes and committee records for the
sessions concerned and represent participation in two out of three activities
in the Commons – debates, asking parliamentary Questions and committee
attendance. Not surprisingly, frontbenchers, that is, ministers and frontbench
spokespersons, had high activity levels in each of the sessions, but backbenchers, whether government or opposition showed lower levels, with figures
comparable to frontbenchers only in the most recent session analysed. This
pattern of activity is analysed in more detail in Table 6.6.

The data in Table 6.6 show extensive activity on the part of ministers,
opposition frontbenchers, government and opposition backbenchers. Ministers and opposition frontbenchers were more or less equally active – their
lower committee activity is explained by that fact neither are members of
investigatory committees. In addition, of course, ministers do not ask parliamentary Questions but answer them. Government and opposition backbenchers also show similar levels of activity, although until relatively recently
opposition backbenchers tended to be more active than government backbenchers – the latter were expected 'to turn up and shut up' and this remains

Table 6.6   *Parliamentary activity by frontbenchers and backbenchers,*
1994–95

Ministers and opposition frontbenchers

Activity	Ministers			Opposition frontbenchers		
	% partic.	Mean no.	% 20+	% partic.	Mean no.	% 20+
Debates	96.5	20.6	39.6	100.0	22.4	46.9
Comms.	68.5	9.9	19.8	75.5	9.0	21.3
PQs	–	–	–	98.9	147.2	85.1
Overall	97.7	–	–	100.0	–	–

Government and opposition backbenchers

Activity	Government backbenchers			Opposition backbenchers		
	% partic.	Mean no.	% 20+	% partic.	Mean no.	% 20+
Debates	97.1	21.0	42.8	99.4	23.4	42.6
Comms.	94.7	25.1	59.2	85.8	20.8	65.3
PQs	96.3	37.0	56.7	97.2	111.2	75.0
Overall	99.6	–	–	100.0	–	–

Source: Michael Rush, *The Role of the Member of Parliament Since 1868*, Oxford, Oxford
University Press, 2001, Tables 6.8–6.10.

true for legislative committees, whereas opposition backbenchers were
expected 'to turn up and speak up'. MPs of parties other than Conservative or
Labour tend to be more active, particularly in debates and asking Questions,
partly reflecting the 'frontbench' activities of most Liberal Democrats and partly
out of a need to work harder to get their message across. A more detailed
analysis of MPs' parliamentary activity would undoubtedly show considerable differences among them, some much more active than others, some more
active in one type of activity than another, some active in ways not included
in the analysis, such as the signing of motions or the introduction of Private
Members' bills. MPs are also constrained by procedure and practice: there are
limits on the number and type of Questions for oral answer, but none on those
seeking a written answer; membership of committees is decided by the parties,
not individual MPs; participation in debates is dependent on 'catching the
Speaker's eye'; and some activities are controlled by a ballot of MPs. Nonetheless, the picture of extensive activity that emerges is clear and, quite apart
from other legitimate activities, such as dealing with the demands of constituents, goes a considerable way to explaining why MPs claim to work the

Table 6.7   *Proportions of MPs and peers serving as ministers, 1900–2001*

	1900	1920	1940	1960	1980	2001
MPs	55.0	71.6	78.4	79.1	180.4	78.6
Peers	45.0	28.4	22.6	20.7	19.6	21.4
Total (n)	60	81	74	82	107	112

Source: 1900–1980 – David Butler and Gareth Butler, *Twentieth Century British Political Facts*, Basingstoke, Macmillan, 8th edn, 2000, p. 1; 2001 – *Dod's Guide to the General Election, June 2001*, pp. 1–15.

hours they do and why most regard the job of being a Member of Parliament as full-time.

Beyond the role of backbencher lies that of frontbencher, especially that of minister, and holding ministerial office is widely seen as pinnacle of a political career (see Table 6.7). For much of the nineteenth century, the number of ministerial posts varied between fifty and sixty, but as government expanded so did the number of posts and since 1964 the number of ministers has exceeded a hundred. The constitutional conventions requiring that ministers are responsible to Parliament has meant in practice that, with a few and usually temporary exceptions, ministers have been drawn from Parliament. However, in 1830 more than half the ministerial posts were held by peers; only gradually did MPs come to fill the overwhelming majority of posts, and since 1945 MPs have held four-fifths of ministerial posts. It is therefore MPs who have benefited most from the expansion of government. In 2001 the government consisted of 112 ministers, of whom nearly four-fifths were MPs. Since the mid-nineteenth century the chances of an MP being appointed a minister or holding a parliamentary office in the Commons have increased considerably: between 1868 and 1900, 14.3 per cent of Conservatives and 14.6 per cent of Liberals became ministers or Speaker or Deputy Speaker; between 1945 and 1997 39.0 per cent of Conservative and 31.3 per cent of Labour MPs secured ministerial or parliamentary office. In the meantime, of course, the opportunities for Liberals had declined sharply.[8] There has also been a marked increase in the number of Parliamentary Private Secretaries (PPSs) – MPs acting as unpaid aides to ministers, widely regarded as the first rung of the ministerial ladder. In 2002 there were 57 PPSs, compared with a mere 9 in 1900.

The chances of ministerial office have increased, but how ambitious are MPs for office? The survey conducted for the Hansard Society Commission on Parliamentary Scrutiny found that nearly half the MPs surveyed thought that serving as a junior minister (48.3 per cent) or a Cabinet minister (49.6 per cent) was 'very important' or 'quite important', but more than a third regarded it as 'not important' or 'not at all important' (35.0 per cent as junior ministers, 37.4 per cent as Cabinet ministers). Not surprisingly, more thought serving in the Cabinet 'very important' (24.5 per cent as a junior minister, 30.9 per cent as a Cabinet minister). Compared with this, rather fewer thought serving as chair of a select committee (seen by some as an alternative career path) 'very' or 'quite important' (36.9 per cent).[9] Of course, regarding serving as a minister as important is not the same as wishing to be a minister: surveys conducted by the Study of Parliament Group throw more light on the ministerial ambitions of MPs, suggesting a significant difference between Conservative and Labour MPs first elected in 1992 and 1997. These found that 64.1 per cent of Conservatives in 1992 and no fewer than 92.9 per cent in 1997 said they hoped to be ministers, compared with 43.1 per cent of Labour MPs in 1992 and 48.1 per cent in 1997. Indeed, in neither case did any newly elected Conservative deny ministerial ambitions, although a number said it was 'too early to say', whereas 18.2 per cent of newly elected Labour MPs in 1992 and 18.5 per cent in 1997 denied that they hoped to achieve ministerial office.[10]

Career patterns in the Lords

Until the passing of the Appellate Jurisdiction Act, 1876, all members of the House of Lords were hereditary peers. The 1876 Act provided for the appointment of two (now twelve) Law Lords to carry out the judicial role of the upper house as the final court of appeal. The Law Lords remain members of the House after retiring as Lords of Appeal, their membership continuing until death, although under government proposals to set up a Supreme Court they will no longer be members of the upper house. They were therefore the first life peers, but it was not until the 1958 Life Peerages Act that others could hold peerages for life. For those who objected to hereditary peerages as a basis for membership of Parliament, especially in the Labour Party, the 1958 Act provided a partial solution by enabling those unwilling to accept a hereditary peerage to become members of the Lords. However, it did not solve the wider problem, nor the particular problem of MPs who were heirs to a peerage, whose membership of the Commons automatically ended when they inherited their titles, since there was no way in which a peerage could be renounced. Their plight was dramatically illustrated by the case of Anthony Wedgwood Benn (now more familiarly known as Tony Benn), MP for Bristol South-East, who became Viscount Stansgate on the death of his father in 1960. Benn was disqualified and his seat declared vacant, but he fought and won the resulting by-election. He was able to do this because the disqualification applies to MPs, not candidates. However, he was again disqualified and his Conservative opponent declared MP for Bristol South-East. This was clearly an unsatisfactory situation and the Conservative government of the day introduced and secured the passage of the Peerages Act, 1963, which not only allowed the heir to a peerage to disclaim it within a year of inheriting it (within a month for sitting MPs) but allowed existing peers to disclaim their peerages. Benn immediately disclaimed his title and was re-elected for his Bristol seat at a further by-election in 1963, brought about by the resignation of the sitting Conservative MP. One of the unintended consequences of the 1963 Act was that it opened the way for the Earl of Home to disclaim his peerage and, as Sir Alec Douglas-Home, succeed Harold Macmillan as Prime Minister in November 1963. The Act had been passed earlier in 1963 before anyone could have known that Macmillan would later resign as Prime Minister for health reasons, but the original draft of the Act had provided for it to come into effect at the date of the next general election, which had to be held no later than October 1964. However, this was changed during its passage through the Lords, so that it came into effect as soon as it received the royal assent – an excellent example of the role of accident in politics.

The Life Peerages Act had a profound effect on the House of Lords. It rejuvenated it, not in terms of age (life peers were and are on average older than hereditary peers) but in terms of activity. The upper house became a much more active body, carving out an increasingly important role for itself as a revising chamber and as a scrutiniser of government policy and administration. Equally importantly, it facilitated a shift in the party balance in the Lords. It was now much easier for the Labour Party to find recruits for the upper house and, from a chamber with an overwhelmingly Conservative majority, the House of Lords became a more evenly balanced body, especially among its regular attenders. The Conservatives remained the largest single party and was still able to use an overwhelming majority on particular occasions by summoning its 'backwoodsmen' – the mostly Conservative irregular attenders – to vote, but they could not be relied upon and used at will. Of course, this did not solve the fundamental and widely held objection that membership of the legislature, carrying with it the right to have a direct say in the passing of laws and in the governing of the country generally, should depend on the accident of birth. However, this objection was largely met by the passing of the House of Lords Act, 1999, which removed all but 92 of the hereditary peers. All these changes, especially the introduction of life peers and the removal of most of the hereditaries, have had an impact on career patterns in the Lords.

The House of Lords offers far more limited career opportunities than the lower house, partly because by convention some ministerial offices must be held by MPs, notably those of Prime Minister and Chancellor of the Exchequer, but also because most heads of government departments are in practice drawn from the Commons, with only the occasional exception. Thus in June 2003, twenty-two ministers were members of the House of Lords, of whom three were members of the Cabinet (the Leader of the House, the Secretary of State for Constitutional Affairs and Lord Chancellor, and the head of one government department – Secretary of State for International Development), and one held the post of Attorney General, the government's senior Law Officer.

Table 6.8   *Attendance in the House of Lords, 1950–2002 (selected sessions)*

Session	Average daily attendance	% of membership (approx.*)
1950	86	10
1959–60	136	15
1971–72	150	14
1980–81	296	25
1992–93	379	32
1997–98	417	35
1998–99	446	35
1999–2000	352†	53
2000–01	340	49
2001–02	370	54

Source: www.parliament.uk/faq/faq2.cfm.2003.

Notes: * They are approximate because they are based on then total membership for the calendar year nearest to the session concerned. † First session after the House of Lords Act, 1999 i.e. following the removal of all but 92 of the hereditary peers and consequent reduction in the size of the House.

The opportunity to achieve Cabinet office as a member of the Lords is therefore limited, but outside the Cabinet the ratio of MPs to peers is marginally better – about one in five, compared with one in seven. Put another way, at any one time about one in seven MPs are ministers, compared with one in thirty peers. However, about a quarter of the members of the Lords are former MPs, half of whom have held Cabinet office, leading some observers to describe the upper house as 'a retirement home for MPs'. Ministers in the Lords (and a small number of office-holders) are, of course, paid, but other members of the upper house are not. Peers will therefore normally have to establish themselves in another career which can continue to sustain them financially or have some other source of income to enable them to pursue a political career in the upper house.

The figures in Table 6.8 provide an indication of the extent to which Members of the Lords are actively involved in its work. They do not distinguish between different types of participation but they show clearly that attendance has increased significantly, especially as the Life Peerages Act began to make an impact, with as few as 10 per cent in 1950 to more than a third in the 1990s. The removal of most of the hereditary peers in 1999 resulted in a fall in attendance, but the number attending was more than half the total membership. The figures also included ministers, opposition frontbenchers and various office-holders, such as Chair of Committees (or Deputy Speaker), who are effectively full-time politicians, but most are backbench peers. Many are retired or semi-retired, enabling them to devote a considerable amount of time to the House. Other backbenchers have sufficient income from various outside occupations (or have private means) and sufficient time available to allow them to be active members. In short, as many as half the membership of the Lords are pursuing political careers (though mostly part-time), whether it is a continuation of an existing political career or embarking on such a career later in life. In this, the House of Lords contrasts with most other second chambers in comparable countries, where the members are usually paid and regarded as full-time politicians.

Resourcing Parliament

Both Houses of Parliament and their members are provided with a range of resources to enable them to fulfil their parliamentary functions, but there is a marked contrast between Lords and Commons. Not only are MPs paid a salary and peers not, but the level of resources for MPs is much greater than that for peers and the same is true of the collective resources provided to each House. That said, extensive resources for MPs are a relatively recent development. Furthermore, although the two Houses co-operate in the provision of some services, such as telephone and postal services, and many aspects of security, most services and facilities are provided and funded separately.

The Palace of Westminster

Parliament has met at Westminster since medieval times, although it also sometimes met elsewhere – Winchester, Lincoln, York and Oxford, for example, and the old Palace of Westminster did not become the regular meeting place until the reign of Henry VIII. The old palace was almost entirely destroyed by fire in 1834, only Westminster Hall and the crypt surviving. The existing Palace of Westminster was built in the middle of the nineteenth century and officially opened in 1852, although the Lords' chamber was first used in 1847 and the Commons' in 1850. The new palace was purpose-built to enable Parliament to fulfil its functions and MPs and peers their roles. Apart from the plenary chambers and a number of committee rooms for the two Houses, the Palace had the atmosphere and most of the accoutrements of a gentlemen's club: it had dining rooms and bars, smoking rooms, a chess room, and two libraries. Living quarters were provided for the Speaker of the Commons and his counterpart in the Lords, the Lord Chancellor, and for the two senior officers of the two Houses, the Clerk of the House of Commons and the Clerk of the Parliaments. In addition, the Prime Minister had an office and the Leader of the Opposition what a nineteenth-century MP described as 'a kind of small den'. However, there were no rooms or 'offices' for individual members of either House; none was thought necessary.

As a royal palace, Westminster long remained under the control of the Crown, represented by the Lord Great Chamberlain, although he delegated responsibility for some matters, notably office and other accommodation, to each of the two Houses. In 1965, however, control of almost all the Palace was transferred to Parliament, but each House has its own arrangements. In the case of the Commons, control is vested in a House of Commons Commission, chaired by the Speaker, and consisting of the Leader of the House and his or her 'shadow' counterpart, and three other MPs. The Commission is responsible for overall policy, with day-to-day running operating through a Board of Management and the heads of the various departments, advised by a number of specialised committees. Control of the Lords rests with the House Committee, chaired by the Lord Chairman of Committees, with day-to-day responsibility in the hands of the Clerk of the Parliaments and other senior officials, operating through a Board of Management.

The House of Commons

As noted earlier, until 1972 no distinction was drawn between the salary paid to MPs and the expenses they incurred in carrying out their parliamentary responsibilities. The only allowance they received covered travel between London and their constituencies, introduced in 1924. Telephone facilities were limited to calls within the London area and postal facilities to communications with ministers, government departments and a number of public bodies. All other costs, such as paying for secretarial help, other telephone and postal costs, and subsistence while in London, had to be met from the Member's salary or private resources. Although from the outset a proportion of the salary was treated as a tax-free allowance for necessary parliamentary expenses, in practice this became increasingly inadequate, resulting in the ludicrous situation in which some MPs with sufficient income from other sources were legitimately claiming sums equal to their parliamentary salaries against tax. However, growing criticism of this state of affairs, both inside and outside Parliament, led in 1969 to the introduction of a secretarial allowance and free telephone and postal services for parliamentary business within the UK and, in 1971, to the setting up of the TSRB (SSRB) to review MPs' pay and allowances. In addition to recommending a clear distinction between pay and expenses, the TSRB recommended a subsistence allowance to cover the cost of living in London during the parliamentary session. A pension scheme had already been introduced with effect from 1964 and this, with other changes, set MPs firmly on the road to professionalisation (see Table 6.9).

Even before the introduction of a secretarial allowance in 1969, only 12 per cent of MPs had no regular secretarial help, but only about a fifth had any full-time staff and two-fifths shared secretarial assistance with one or more other MPs.[11] After the introduction of the allowance the proportion of MPs with no regular secretarial help fell to 6 per cent and the proportion with full-time staff rose to more than a quarter, leaving two-thirds using part-time assistance.[12] By the early 1990s, over 90 per cent of MPs had one or more

Table 6.9   *MPs' allowances, 2004*

Allowance	Intro.	Provision in 2004
Staffing allowance	1969	£66,458–£77,534 (linked to RPI)†
Incidental exp. all.* (IEP)	2001	£19,325
IT equipment		£3,000 (centrally provided)
Telephone and postage	1969	Free on parliamentary business within the UK
Travel	1924	Free to and from constituency and between home and Westminster, plus some provision for family, car mileage and bicycle allowance
Subsistence (additional costs all.)	1972	Allowance when the House is sitting: £1,618 London supplement (inner London MPs) *or* maximum of £20,902
Pension	1965§	Payable at 65 (60 with reduced benefit) according to length of service; minimum of 4 years' service
Resettlement grant	1974	Lump sum equivalent to 50–100% of salary, depending on age and service

Source: House of Commons Information Office, *Factsheet M5: Members' Pay, Pensions and Allowances*, 2004.

Notes: * The IEP is intended to cover other expenses e.g. office rental, staff travel. † Varying according to type of post and whether staff work in London or elsewhere. There is also provision for a contribution equal to 10 per cent of each employee's gross salary to fund pensions. § Backdated to 1964.

full-time staff and the average number of staff per Member in 2003 was 3.5. This figure includes secretarial staff, personal assistants and research assistants.[13] In 1971 less than 10 per cent of MPs had a research assistant, but by the early 1990s three-fifths had. Some staff are located at Westminster, others in the Member's constituency, with Conservatives more likely to have more staff at Westminster and Labour MPs more in their constituencies.

There were, however, other developments in the provision of resources for MPs, particularly in office accommodation for both members and staff and in extending information and research services. In 1950 few backbench MPs had even desk spaces at Westminster and none had offices. By 1960 the number of desk spaces had increased to nearly a hundred and about a dozen single rooms were available for backbenchers. Utilising space in the various nooks and crannies of the Palace and taking over a number of nearby buildings, resulted in seventy single rooms being available in 1971 and a total of nearly two hundred desk spaces altogether, two-thirds of which were outside the Palace itself. By 1982 the comparable figures were two hundred single rooms and over six hundred desk spaces, two-fifths outside the Palace, plus more than 350 desk spaces for Members' staff.[14] However, with yet further offices being provided in buildings near the Palace and the opening of Portcullis House, the long-planned new parliamentary building, in 2000, individual office accommodation was available to all MPs.[15]

In addition to the provision of resources to individual MPs, there has been a considerable expansion in the staff of the House of Commons. Excluding staff in the Refreshment Department, for whom figures were not available in 1972, the Commons' staff increased by 168 per cent between 1972 and 2000[16] and the total in 2002 was 1,163. The total in 2002, including catering staff, was 1,430.[17] Apart from various ancillary staff vital to the operation and administration of the Palace and its environs, these include clerks, who provide crucial procedural information and advice and are a responsible for running of committees, and the staff of the House of Commons Library, who provide MPs with invaluable information on all aspects of government policy and its implementation. The staff of these two departments in particular have risen from 95 and 55 respectively in 1972 to 282 and 209 in 2003.[18] The clerks advise and assist MPs with the tabling of parliamentary Questions, amendments to bills and motions and the library staff deal with reference enquiries from Members and their staff – more than 60,000 a year, longer research enquiries – some 15,000 a year, and briefing papers on almost all government bills and a wide range of policy matters – some 96 in 2001–02. Apart from the services provided to MPs individually, the Commons' staff also play a major role in supporting the work of the House in the Chamber, the additional debates since 1999 known as Westminster Hall sittings, and, of course, the extensive legislative and scrutiny work undertaken by committees.

Apart from the Public Accounts Committee, which is served by the 800-strong National Audit Office, most select committees engaged in the scrutiny of government policy and administration are assisted in their work by part-time specialist advisers, of whom there were 157 in 1999–2000 and 223 in the longer than normal session of 2001–02. They are drawn from universities, 'think-tanks', various research bodies and the like. Some act as general advisers within a committee's remit, but most are engaged for particular enquiries.

All these services are provided on a politically neutral basis and, although they could be said to constitute the Commons 'civil service', the staff are not civil servants but employed by the House of Commons and have their own career structures. Nonetheless, there is also provision for supporting the various opposition parties. This is known as 'Short money', after the Leader of the House, Edward Short, who was responsible for its introduction in 1975. The amount allocated is related to the number of seats and votes won by each party at the previous general election. The bulk of it goes to the Official Opposition: in 2002–03 Short money totalled £5m, of which nearly two-thirds went to the Conservatives and nearly a quarter to the Liberal Democrats. The purpose is threefold – to fund the costs of the Leader of the Opposition's office, to provide research staff and other backing for opposition parties in carrying out their parliamentary responsibilities, and to assist with travel and other related expenses. This is, of course, over and above the payment of salaries to the Leader of the Opposition, the Opposition Chief Whip and one Assistant Whip.

MPs, individually and collectively, and the House of Commons as a whole have undergone a professionalisation process which recognises that being a Member of Parliament is a full-time job and that without adequate resources neither MPs nor the House of Commons as a whole can hope to fulfil their responsibilities. All services and facilities are subject to periodic review and most salaries and allowances are linked to the RPI. Whether they are adequate and whether additional resources are necessary will always be a matter of opinion, but one thing is clear – the professionalisation of the MP and of the House of Commons is an accomplished fact and any proposals for yet more resources should be seen clearly in that context.

The House of Lords

It would be easy to characterise the House of Lords as the amateur part of Parliament, more akin to the House of Commons of the nineteenth and early twentieth centuries, not least because (ministers in the Lords and a few other office-holders apart) members of the upper house are unpaid. This, however, would be misleading since, like the Commons, the Lords has been undergoing a process of professionalisation as a consequence of its increased activity and the role it has carved out for itself since the passing of the 1958 Life Peerages Act. Average daily attendance increased from fewer than a hundred in 1950 to nearly three hundred in 1980–81 and to over four hundred before the removal of most of the hereditary peers in 1999 – equivalent to more than a third of the eligible members. After 1999, average attendance fell back and in 2001–02 was 370, but this was the equivalent of more than half the membership (see Table 6.8). However, even before the 1958 Act, limited expenses allowances were introduced. In 1946 an allowance to cover rail travel between a peer's main place of residence and London was introduced, but was subject to an 'assiduity' rule that claimants must have attended at least a third of the possible sittings (though, after 1947, not applied to peers living in Scotland) and this was not abolished until 1972, it being argued that infrequent attenders could and did make a significant contribution to the work of the House. It was not until 1961 that a car allowance was introduced, but in 1957 an expense allowance to cover other costs – subsistence, secretarial help and the like – had become available, but there was confusion about what it did and did not cover and this was not resolved until 1975. In due course the system was further refined, notably to allow some expenses for non-sitting days to be claimed for attendance at committees. In 2001 peers were allowed to claim free postage on parliamentary business and in 2003 some of the

Table 6.10   *Peers' allowances and services, 2004*

Allowance	Provision
Day subsistence	£64.00 per day.*
Overnight subsistence	£128.00 per day.†
Secretarial assistance	£53.50 per day.§
Travel – home to Westminster	1st class rail fares, air travel or car mileage all
Telephone and postage	Free on parl. business in UK
Visiting EU institutions and national parliaments	Various costs covered

Notes: * Maximum of £10,880 (170 sitting days). † Maximum of £21,760 (170 sitting days). § Maximum of £11,235 (170 sitting days, plus 40 non-sitting days for committees).

expenses arising from visits on parliamentary business to EU institutions and the national parliaments of EU members and candidate countries (see Table 6.10).

Just as office accommodation for MPs has, until recently, been a scarce resource, so it has for peers, but even more so: even in 1988–89 only 150 desk spaces were available, but the situation has improved dramatically since then and in 2003 desk spaces were available to 90 per cent of peers, although these are mostly in shared rooms.[19] In terms of staffing, the Lords also provides a contrast to the Commons: as activity has increased, so have staff numbers, but in 2002 the House of Lords had only 404 staff (382 in 2001), less than a third of the Commons' 1,430. It is, of course, important to remember that, unlike MPs, peers do not have constituents and the constituency role undoubtedly makes considerable demands on the time and resources of MPs. As with the Commons, the most important staff are the clerks and library staff, both fulfilling roles similar to those of their counterparts in the Commons, though on a more limited scale, particularly in the case of the library. In 2002 the latter had a staff of thirty, including two-part-time, compared with more than two hundred in the House of Commons library. Even so, in 2001–02 library staff were able to deal with more than 17,000 enquires from peers, but in other respects cannot match the scale of the services provided for MPs.

Again lagging behind the Commons, funds to support the opposition and, in the case of the Lords, crossbench peers in carrying out their parliamentary responsibilities were not introduced until 1996. Known as 'Cranborne money', after the then Leader of the House of Lords, it is on a smaller scale, amounting in 2002–03 to £621,000 (some 12 per cent of Short money in the Commons), with the greater part, more than three-fifths, going to the Conservatives and nearly a third to the Liberal Democrats (House of Lords 2001–02). Nonetheless, although the resources available to peers and to the upper house

Table 6.11   *Cost of the House of Commons and the House of Lords*

	2001–02 (£)	2002–03 (£)
House of Commons	254m (119m)	275m (134m)
House of lords	56m (10m)	57m (13m)
Total	310m	332m

Source: House of Commons Commission, 2001–02 and House of Lords 2001–02 and House of Lords, *Annual Report and Accounts, 2001–02.*

Notes: The figures in parentheses exclude MPs' salaries and expenses for both MPs and peers.

collectively are much more limited than those available to MPs and to the Commons, they have increased and will continue to do so, especially as the demands on the House of Lords and its members increase.

Financing Parliament

Institutions such as Parliament do not come cheaply and the cost has inevitably risen with the professionalisation of both houses, especially the Commons. In 1973–74 the House of Commons cost £13m, a figure not reached by the House of Lords until 1988–89,[20] but by 2002–03 the cost of the Commons had risen to £275m and that of the Lords to £57m (see Table 6.11). Of course, a significant part of that increase is accounted for by inflation, but the greater part is due to the expansion of the resources allocated to both houses.

As Table 6.11 shows, the House of Commons costs between four and five times as much as the House of Lords, but it is important to note that nearly half the cost of the Commons is taken up by MPs' salaries and expenses, whereas peers' expenses constitute less than a quarter of the Lords' total cost.

Compared with lower chambers in other parliaments, particularly those in comparable European countries, such as France, Germany and Italy, but less so compared with Australia, Canada and, especially, the US Congress, British MPs are about half-way up the international league in terms of salaries, services and facilities, better-off in some respects, worse-off in others.[21] The House of Lords, however, is less well-resourced than a number of second chambers in comparable countries: 'There is no doubt that the resources available to Australian, Canadian, French and American Senators are extensive, especially to the latter in terms of staff.'[22] Of course, Australian and American Senators are elected and have constituents, yet not only has the House of Lords become much busier in recent years, it also meets more often than any other legislative chamber, save the Commons and in 1999–2000 actually met one day more than the Commons. Given that its members are unpaid and are provided with much more limited resources than MPs, it can be argued that the UK gets it second chamber on the cheap. Were the second stage of Lords' reform to result in a fully- or substantially elected upper house, the pressure for full-time, salaried, adequately resourced members would be considerable and resisting that pressure would be unwise, however tempted the Treasury or others might be. But with an appointed second chamber appearing to be the most likely outcome of further changes in the composition of the Lords, it would be easier to leave the upper house resourced much as it is at present. However, like the Commons, the House of Lords has been experiencing professionalisation: some of its members are in practice full-time; the demands on staff are less than in the Commons but growing; the services provided are more limited but expanding. In short, like the Commons, the professionalisation of the Lords is a continuing process. It is, furthermore, a process that is taking place in most modern legislatures, not only at the national level but the sub-national level – witness the salaried, full-time membership and substantial resources of the Scottish Parliament, National Assembly for Wales and the Northern Ireland Assembly.[23] The history of the resourcing of Parliament has been haphazard and piecemeal and it is a history that shows every sign of continuing.

Notes

1 Parts of this chapter were published as Chapter 16, 'Parliament: Pay and Resources', in Nicholas D. J. Baldwin (ed.), *Parliament in the 21st Century*, London, Politico's, 2004.

2 Top Salaries Review Body, *First Report: Ministers of the Crown and Members of Parliament*, Cmnd. 4836, December 1971, para. 25.

3 Michael Rush, 'Socio-Economic Composition and Pay and Resources in Second Chambers', in Nicholas D. J. Baldwin and Donald Shell (eds), *Second Chambers*, London, Frank Cass, 2001, p. 33.

4 Top Salaries Review Body, *First Report*, Cmnd. 4836, December 1971, para. 87.

5 Top Salaries Review Body, *Report No. 20*, Cmd. 8881, May 1983, 24.

6 Senior Salaries Review Body, *Report No. 38*, Cm. 3330-I, July 1996, para. 43.

7 Michael Rush, *The Role of the Member of Parliament Since 1868: From Gentlemen to Players*, Oxford, University of Oxford Press, 2001, p. 119.

8 *Ibid.*, Table 5.10.

9 Hansard Society, *Report of the Hansard Society Commission on Parliamentary Scrutiny: The Challenge for Parliament*, London, Vacher Dod, 2001, Appendix 4, Table 3.11.

10 Rush, *The Role of the Member of Parliament*, p. 135.

11 Anthony Barker and Michael Rush, *The Members of Parliament and His Information*, London, Allen & Unwin, 1970, p. 171.

12 Michael Rush and Malcolm Shaw (eds), *The House of Commons: Service and Facilities*, London, Allen & Unwin, 1974, p. 276.

13 The House of Commons Commission, *Annual Report*, 2003.

14 Michael Rush (ed.), *The House of Commons: Services and Facilities, 1972–1982*, London, PEP, 1983, p. 82.
15 The House of Commons Commission, *Annual Report*, 2002.
16 Rush, *The Role of the Member of Parliament*, p. 129.
17 The House of Commons Commission, *Annual Report*, 2002.
18 Rush, *The Role of the Member of Parliament*, p. 129, and the House of Commons Commission, *Annual Report*, 2003.
19 Donald Shell and David Beamish (eds), *The House of Lords at Work: A Study based on 1988–89 Session*, Oxford, Oxford University Press, 1993, p. 316, and House of Lords, *Annual Report and Accounts, 2001–02*.
20 Rush and Shaw, *The House of Commons*, p. 28 and Shell and Beamish, *The House of Lords*, p. 313.
21 Senior Salaries Review Body, *Report No. 38: Vol. 2 – Surveys and Studies*, Cm. 3330-II, July 1996, Sections 3a and 3b.
22 Rush, 'Socio-Economic Composition and Pay and Resources in Second Chambers', p. 35.
23 Senior Salaries Review Body, *Report No. 42*, Cm. 4188, March 1999, Appendix E.

7

The organisation of business

Parliament and adversary politics

Parliament is dominated by two monolithic political parties, one normally forming the government, the other the official opposition. Much of what Parliament does and how it is organised is predicated on the confrontation between government and opposition. It applies to the control of the parliamentary agenda and the distribution of parliamentary time, to the conduct of proceedings and, indeed, to the physical layout of the chambers of Lords and Commons and to many, though not all committees. This physical domination, however, should not be seen as simple cause and effect, since it preceded the government–opposition dichotomy, even though it now contributes powerfully to it. All this is far more evident in the Commons than the Lords, but it is no less important in explaining and understanding the operation of the upper house. Though the two major parties dominate Parliament and are essentially the engines that drive the legislature, they do so through the roles of government and opposition, which have been institutionalised into what is commonly called adversary politics which can be shown in a number of ways.

Parliamentary time and the initiation of business

The figures in Table 7.1 tend to underplay the extent to which the government dominates the agenda in the House of Commons in that almost all of what the opposition does and much of what backbenchers do are reactions to government policy. Moreover, although backbenchers take the initiative in a quarter of the time available, this time is fragmented between a large number of Members and through the parliamentary year, week and day, whereas government time comes in much larger chunks. Another way of emphasising this is to note that government business takes precedence on every day except

Table 7.1   *Distribution of time and initiative of business on the floor of the*
House of Commons and House of Lords

Initiator	House of Commons (% time) 1999–2000	House of Lords (% time) 2000
Government	61.5	66.2
Opposition	9.5	9.2
Backbenchers	22.7	21.5
Private business	0.6	0.1
Other business	5.7	3.0
Total	100.0	100.0

Source: Commons – House of Commons, *Sessional Digest, 1999–2000*; Lords – adapted from
Wheeler-Booth, in R. Blackburn and A. Kennon, *Griffith and Ryle on Parliament*, London, Sweet
& Maxwell, 2003, p. 684.

Fridays. The setting up of the Westminster Hall sittings has increased the time
allocated to backbenchers by about 25 per cent, but it too is fragmented
between individual backbenchers, broken down into relatively small parcels
on subjects chosen by backbenchers. Indeed, both for Westminster Hall debates
and other backbench business, the competition for time is such that its allocation is decided by ballot.

A similar picture emerges regarding the House of Lords, with somewhat
more time being allocated to government business, particularly government
bills, and a little less to backbenchers. In the Commons, of course, the government can normally use its majority to control the distribution of time, but not
in the Lords, since no party holds a majority. However, the agenda, both in
term of initiative and the distribution of time follows a regular pattern, varying
little from session to session, partly enshrined in the standing orders of each
House and partly stemming from usage, even though in the Lords government business does not have precedence over other business. Within these
parameters the day to day and week to week use of time is negotiated between
the parties through what are euphemistically known as 'the usual channels'.

The physical setting

The physical layout of the House of Commons' Chamber reinforces the
adversarial nature of Parliament (see Figure 7.1): the government and its
supporters sit on one side of the House and the official opposition and its
supporters, together with other opposition parties, on the other, directly confronting each other. This is seen vividly and dramatically at Question Time,
with ministers and 'shadow' ministers facing each other, separated only by
the Clerks' table, and even more so at Prime Minister's Questions every

Figure 7.1 *A simplified plan of the Chamber of the House of Commons*

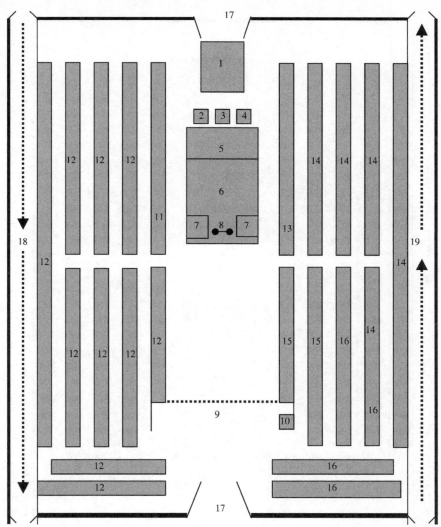

Key: 1 Speaker's Chair.
2 Clerk of the House.
3 Clerk.
4 Clerk.
5 Clerks' Table.
6 Table of the House.
7 Despatch Box.
8 Mace.
9 Bar of House.
10 Serjeant at Arms.
11 Government frontbench.
12 Government backbenches.
13 Opposition frontbench.
14 Opposition backbenches.
15 Liberal Democrats.
16 Other opposition parties.
17 Entrances to the House.
18 Aye lobby.
19 No lobby.

Figure 7.2   *A simplified plan of the Chamber of the House of Lords*

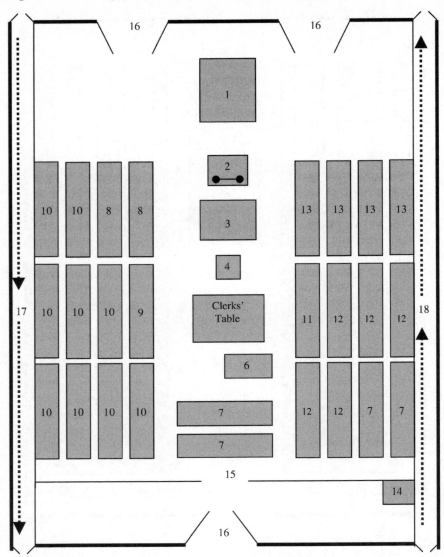

Key:
1 Throne.
2 Woolsack and Mace.
3 Judges' woolsack.
4 Lord Chairman's chair.
5 Clerks' Table.
6 *Hansard* reporters.
7 Crossbenches.
8 Bishops' benches.
9 Government frontbench.
10 Government backbenches.
11 Opposition frontbench.
12 Opposition backbenches.
13 Liberal Democrat benches.
14 Black Rod.
15 Bar of the House.
16 Entrances to the House.
17 Contents lobby.
18 Not contents lobby.

Wednesday. Members on opposing sides vociferously support their leaders and jeer their opponents. The practice of the government supporters sitting to the Speaker's right and its opponents to his or her left can be traced back to at least the mid-eighteenth century, possibly earlier to the late seventeenth century, with the growth of party, and when a change of government occurs the leaders of the two main parties and their supporters exchange sides.[1] However, this owed much to the nature of the former St Stephen's Chapel, meeting place of the Commons from 1547 until its destruction by fire in 1834. St Stephen's was rectangular in shape, with most of the benches set out facing each other and the practice of Privy Councillors, advisers to the monarch, sitting on the frontbenches either side of the Speaker dates back to at least the sixteenth century.[2] There is a further feature that contributes to the adversarial nature of the Commons – both St Stephen's Chapel was and the present Chamber is remarkably small, and the benches can seat little more than half the Members, although additional seating in the side galleries means that there is room for about two-thirds of the 659 MPs. This gives the Chamber an intimate atmosphere, adding to its confrontational nature, especially when it is crowded. Following the two occasions when the Chamber was destroyed – 1834 and 1941, it was decided to retain both the layout and size of the Chamber and, during the debate in 1943 on the rebuilding of the Commons, Winston Churchill remarked: 'We shape our buildings and our buildings shape us.' However, it is a mistake to attribute the adversarial politics which characterises parliamentary government in the UK (and most other parliamentary systems) simply to the physical layout of the Chamber, important as that is; it owes far more to the fierceness of the partisan clash.

The relative significance of the physical layout can be judged by looking at the Chamber of the House of Lords (see Figure 7.2). It is essentially similar the Commons' Chamber, with government facing opposition, but the partisan confrontation in the upper house is much less in evidence and the whole tenor of Lords' proceedings much gentler. This reflects a difference in culture, illustrated by the names of the division lobbies in the two Houses: in the Commons they are the 'Aye Lobby' and the 'No Lobby', in the Lords the 'Contents Lobby' and the 'Not Contents Lobby'. However, physical layout can also indicate the degree of confrontation, as the layout of standing committees, select committees and the Westminster Hall sittings show.

Standing committees (see Figure 7.3), most of which deal with the committee stage of bills, are laid out in exactly the same way as the Chamber itself, with government facing opposition, and are miniatures of the whole House, devices for dealing with half-a-dozen mostly government bills at once, and operate essentially in the same adversary fashion as the Chamber. Select committees (see Figure 7.4), on the other hand, are laid out in a horseshoe fashion and are not confrontational in appearance or, for the most part, operation.

Figure 7.3   *A simplified layout of a standing committee room*

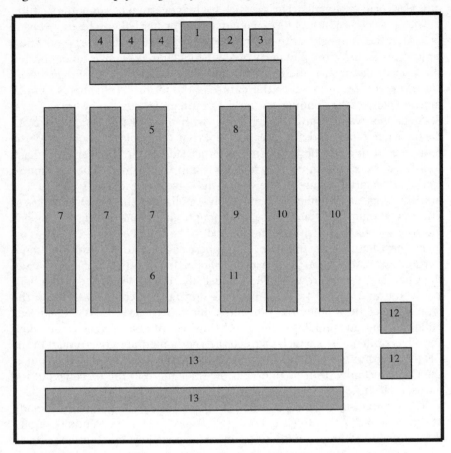

Key: 1 Chair of the committee.   7 Government backbenchers.
       2 Clerk of the committee.   8 Opposition 'Shadow minister'/spokesperson.
       3 *Hansard* reporter.   9 Opposition whip.
       4 Civil servants.   10 Opposition backbenchers.
       5 Ministers.   11 Third party spokespersons.
       6 Government whip.   12 Press seats.
                                        13 Public seats.

The Westminster Hall sittings offer yet another physical variation (see Figure 7.5), with a hemi-circular layout intended to create a less confrontational atmosphere. However, that depends more on the nature of the business they deal with than on simple layout. Because standing committees deal mostly with government bills they tend to replicate the adversary politics more typical of the Chamber, but select committees mostly investigate government policy and administration on a largely non-partisan basis and

Figure 7.4   *A simplified layout of a select committee room*

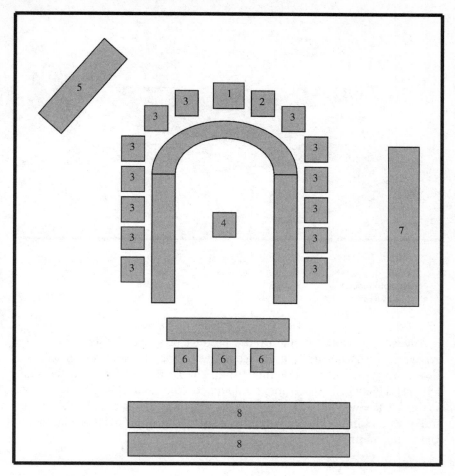

Key: 1 Chair of the committee.   5 Committee advisers and staff.
2 Clerk of the committee.   6 Witnesses.
3 Members of the committee.   7 Press seats.
4 *Hansard* reporter.   8 Public seats.

only occasionally operate in a strongly partisan fashion. Westminster Hall
debates vary in character – MPs may well contribute from a clearly party
viewpoint, but party is often less evident or even unapparent. Furthermore,
the same can be said of debates in the Chamber itself – much depends on
what is being discussed: the fiercely confrontational nature of Prime Minister's Questions lie at one extreme of the partisan continuum and proceedings
like the invariably non-partisan adjournment debates at the end of the day at
the other.

Figure 7.5   *A simplified layout of Westminster Hall sittings*

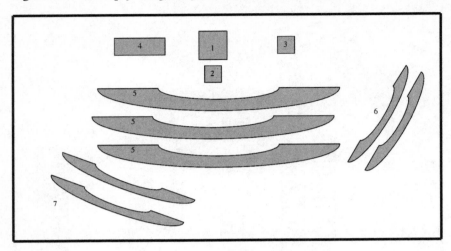

Key: 1 Chair.   5 Members' seats.
        2 Clerk.   6 Press seats.
        3 Hansard reporter.   7 Public seats.
        4 Civil servants.

Adversarial politics is mainly the product of a party system dominated by two large parties and varies according to the business concerned. It is also more typical of the Commons than the Lords, but here too the main conflict is between government and opposition and this manifests itself further in the way in which the parties organise themselves in Parliament and in the setting of the parliamentary agenda through what are known as 'the usual channels'.

Party organisation in Parliament

Each of the parties represented in the two Houses has its own organisational arrangements, but those of the two main parties are the more elaborate. The Conservative Party's principal parliamentary body in the Commons is the 1922 Committee, originally formed in 1923 by Conservative MPs first elected in 1922 who felt a need to meet regularly to discuss party policy, but 'The 1922' quickly became a general backbench body. It meets weekly on Wednesdays during the parliamentary session to discuss forthcoming parliamentary business and to act as a forum for backbench views. It is chaired by a senior backbencher elected annually by its members. When the party is in office the 1922 Committee is confined to backbenchers and ministers attend by invitation, but in opposition it consists of all Conservative MPs except the party

Leader. Until 1965 the Leader of the Conservative Party 'emerged' from discussions among senior members of the party, whether in government or opposition, but following dissatisfaction over the way in which Sir Alec Douglas-Home 'emerged' as Leader in 1963 a system of election by Conservative MPs was introduced. This lasted until 1998, when William Hague, elected Leader after the 1997 election, introduced a system by which a shortlist of two MPs is chosen by Conservative MPs with the final choice decided by a ballot of the full party membership in the country. This procedure was used to elect Iain Duncan Smith, following Hague's resignation after the 2001 election, but when Duncan Smith was forced to stand down as Leader after losing a vote of confidence among Conservative MPs, his successor, Michael Howard, was the sole nominee and therefore declared Leader. Once elected, and when in opposition, the Leader invites leading members of the parliamentary party in both Houses to form a Shadow Cabinet, formally called the Consultative Committee, usually consisting of about twenty members. However, when he became Leader, Howard opted for a smaller Shadow Cabinet of eleven. Additional frontbench spokespersons are also appointed, but the Shadow Cabinet forms the nucleus of any future Conservative government, although the Leader is under no formal obligation to appoint all its members to the Cabinet when forming a government. Backbench Conservatives in the Lords have their own organisation, the Association of Conservative Peers, which operates in a similar fashion to the 1922 Committee and meets weekly.

Labour's party arrangements in the Commons centre on the Parliamentary Labour Party (PLP), consisting of all Labour MPs and meeting every Monday during the session to discuss the following week's business, hear what the party's position will be on various matters, including divisions, and allow an exchange of views between the party leadership and backbenchers. It is chaired by a senior backbencher elected annually by the PLP. When the party is in opposition the PLP also annually elects the eighteen members of the Parliamentary Committee, which, with the Leader, Deputy Leader, Chief Whip in the Commons, Shadow Leader of the House, and Chief Whip in the Lords, forms the Shadow Cabinet, chaired by the Leader. Until 1981 the Leader and Deputy Leader were elected by the PLP, but since then they have been elected at the Party Conference by an electoral college, consisting of one-third Labour MPs and MEPs, one-third individual party members, and one-third affiliated organisations (mainly trade unions). Under Labour Party rules members of the Shadow Cabinet will be appointed to the Cabinet when the party takes office, but there is no mechanism for enforcing this rule and in 1997 Tony Blair offered two members of the Shadow Cabinet ministerial posts outside the Cabinet, one of whom accepted and one declined. When the party is in office, the Parliamentary Committee comprises eighteen members, four ex officio – the Leader, Deputy Leader, Chief Whip in the Commons, and Chair of the PLP, six backbench MPs elected by the PLP, one elected backbencher from the Lords, and four ministers, three from the Commons and one from the

Lords, chosen by the Prime Minister. In opposition the Parliamentary Committee's task is to organise the party's role as the official opposition; in office its task is to liaise between the government and its backbenchers. Labour members of the Lords also meet weekly but are entitled to attend PLP meetings, though few do.

For many years the Conservative and Labour Parties have also operated a range of party committees or subject groups broadly paralleling government departments, but Michael Howard decided to reduce their number to four policy groups, covering home, foreign, economic and environmental affairs respectively. Labour's subject committees meet fortnightly and the Conservative policy groups monthly. The importance of these bodies varies: they can and do sometimes influence party policy, whether in government or opposition, but much depends on the attitude of the party leadership and the backbenchers who run them, but the available evidence suggests that they are more important in the Conservative Party.

The smaller parties in the Commons also meet weekly, with the two nationalist parties, the Scottish National Party and Plaid Cymru, meeting jointly to discuss matters of mutual interest and parliamentary tactics. Because of their small size, they do not operate any subject committees, although the Liberal Democrats have periodic discussion days away from Westminster. All members of the smallest parties act as frontbench spokespersons and the Liberal Democrats have their Shadow Cabinet of about twenty members. In the Lords the Liberal Democrats meet weekly and the crossbench peers also meet to discuss forthcoming business, though not, of course, in order to adopt any particular point of view.

'The whip'

Every week during the parliamentary session each of the parties in both Houses circulates 'the party whip' to all its members. The whip provides details of the next week's business, of meetings of the party's subject committees or policy groups, and of other information the party leadership wishes to convey to its supporters. Most importantly, it contains explicit instructions about which divisions are expected, with their relative importance indicated by being underlined once, twice or three times (as shown in Figure 7.6). A three-line whip means that all the party's MPs (or peers) are expected to support the party, regardless of pre-existing commitments and all but the most serious illness, although in situations when the government has only a small majority (or even lacks a majority) or its majority is threatened by a backbench rebellion, seriously-ill MPs have been brought to the parliamentary precincts to have their votes 'nodded through' by the party whips. The government normally decides whether a particular division should be subject to a three-line whip, but the opposition sometimes forces the government's by deciding to impose a three-line whip on its own supporters. Divisions subject to a

Figure 7.6   *'The whip': three-line, two-line and one-line whips*

Three-line whip
Important divisions will take place and your attendance at (time) for (time) is essential.
▬▬▬▬▬▬▬▬▬▬▬▬▬▬▬▬▬▬▬▬▬▬▬▬▬
Two-line whip
Important divisions will take place and your attendance at (time) for (time) is essential unless you
▬▬▬▬▬▬▬▬▬▬▬▬▬▬▬▬▬▬▬▬▬▬▬▬▬
have received authorised absence from the Deputy/Assistant Chief Whip.
▬▬▬▬▬▬▬▬▬▬▬▬▬▬▬▬▬▬
One-line whip
Your attendance is requested.
▬▬▬▬▬▬▬▬▬

two-line whip are also regarded as important and MPs' attendance as 'essential', but they may miss the division with the permission of the whips. Two-line whips are usually subject to 'pairing', by which the agreed absence of a government MP is cancelled out by the absence of an opposition MP, thus preserving the government's overall majority. However, since winning its huge majority in 1997 and again in 2001, pairing has not operated, but would return in the event of a government with a smaller majority being elected. Indeed, Labour's majority has allowed the party managers to give its MPs 'time off' from parliamentary commitments to concentrate on constituency work, especially during the 1997–2001 Parliament. A one-line whip means a hotly contested division is not expected and MPs may absent themselves at will. In practice, the government whips will ensure that enough government supporters are available to win any such divisions and to avoid the loss of government business through a failure to maintain a quorum in the House. Some divisions are not subject to whipping at all. This is the case with all Private Members' bills, although supporters and opponents of such bills may organise their own, informal whipping and the government seek to defeat a particular bill, again by informal whipping.

Any MP who feels unable to support the party in a division is expected to discuss his or her concerns with the party whips, who will try to persuade them to toe the party line. On matters concerning the MP's constituency the whips may allow an abstention or, rarely, a vote against. Abstentions are not formally recorded, although a Member may ostentatiously abstain by sitting in the Chamber during a division, and abstentions are often handled discreetly. Issues of conscience are sometimes dealt with in a similar fashion. However, clear defiance of the whip may lead to disciplinary action, ranging from a warning about future conduct to withdrawal of the whip, formally excluding the MP from the parliamentary party. Ultimately, the government whips are intent on securing the passage of the government's business and the opposition

Table 7.2   *The party whips, 2004*

Government	No.	Off. opp. (Cons.)	No.	Lib-Dems.	No.
The House of Commons					
Parl. Sec. to the Treasury (Chief Whip)	1	Chief Whip	1	Chief Whip	1
Treasurer of HM H'hold (Dep. Ch. Wh.)	1	Deputy Chief Whip	1	Deputy Chief Whip	1
Comptroller of HM H'hold	1	Assistant Chief Whip	1	Whips	4
Vice-Chamb. of HM H'hold	1	Whips	11		
Lords Comm. of the Treasury	5				
Assist Whips	7				
Total	16		14		6
House of Lords					
Capt. of the Gentlemen at Arms	1	Chief Whip	1	Chief Whip	1
Capt. of the Queen's Bodyguard of the Yeoman of the Guard	1	Deputy Chief Whip	1	Deputy Chief Whip	1
Lords/Baronesses in Waiting	5	Whips	11*	Whips	3
Total	7		14		5

Source: www.parliament.uk.

Note: * Also act as frontbench spokespersons on particular policies.

whips in making life as difficult for the government as possible, but all parties have a strong interest in maintaining party cohesion – splits and divisions in the party ranks are anathema to the party leadership, not least because parties perceived by the electorate as divided tend to lose rather than win elections.

The whips are at the heart of the party organisation in Parliament; they are the warrant officers and NCOs of the system (see Table 7.2). They were, in fact, preceded by 'the whip', the earliest example of which can be found in 1621, when supporters of James I were sent a written appeal underlined six times and in the eighteenth century the patrons of some boroughs issued whips to MPs representing 'their' seats. However, it was also during the seventeenth century that whips as party personnel came into being, first with the government, later with the opposition, but usually only a single person in each case, and pairing has been be traced back to 1730. The Tories had a chief whip in the Commons between 1802 and 1832, and from 1835; the Whigs/Liberals had a chief whip from 1830. After 1832 the number of whips in the Commons increased but the number of government whips did not reach double figures until 1964 and was still only five in the Lords.

The post held by the Government Chief Whip in the Commons is that of Parliamentary Secretary to the Treasury and other senior government whips formally hold posts in the royal household, while middle-ranking whips are Lords Commissioners of the Treasury. In none of these cases do the holders of these posts have any substantive role in the Treasury or the royal household. The Conservative and Labour whips are organised on a regional basis, with a separate whip for all MPs representing constituencies in a particular region. Both parties also have a pairing whip and an accommodation whip. All the other parties have only a single whip, except for the Liberal Democrats, who have a chief whip, deputy chief whip and four other whips.

There are fewer whips in the Lords but, like the Commons, the government whips have grandiose titles – the Captain of the Gentlemen at Arms (the Government Chief Whip), the Captain of the Queen's Bodyguard of the Yeomen of the Guard (the Deputy Chief Whip), and Lords (or Baronesses) in Waiting – seven in all. The official opposition actually has nearly twice as many whips – eleven, but this is because they are also assigned frontbench policy responsibilities. The Liberal Democrats again have fewer than the two main parties – five in all. There is also a Convenor of the Crossbench Peers, a position set up in 1965 to act as a spokesperson for crossbench interests in the House. The Convenor represents the crossbenchers on domestic committees in the Lords and is consulted through the usual channels.

The whips at work

The whole purpose of the party organisations in Parliament is to ensure that the relationship between the party leadership and its supporters in both Houses operates as smoothly and effectively as possible. The party leadership is particularly concerned about maintaining party cohesion and from time to time takes disciplinary action against members who undermine that cohesion, but there is also a two-way process at work. It is a foolish leadership that ignores the views of its supporters and party meetings and subject committees or policy groups are an important part of that two-way process in which the whips play a crucial role. They are the eyes and the ears of the leadership but it is not simply their task to enforce party discipline; they also gauge party opinion to feed back backbench views and concerns to the leadership and alert it to any discontent. It is their job to warn the leadership, when a particular line cannot in their judgement be held and, ultimately, though rarely, to tell party leaders that his or her position is at best under threat, at worst untenable. The Conservative Party has always been more ruthless with its leaders than Labour and it was loss of support in the parliamentary party that ended the leadership careers of Edward Heath in 1975, Margaret Thatcher in 1990 and Iain Duncan Smith in 2003.

Most of the time the party leaderships are able to carry their supporters with them and, although backbench dissent has been more common since the 1960s, cohesion is the norm, a norm owing much to the efforts of the whips. It has already been noted that all the parties have disciplinary powers at their disposal. These include withdrawal of the whip, deselection as a party candidate, and expulsion from the party. However, these are used sparingly and, in some circumstances, are actually counter-productive. In fact, for many years the Conservative Party did not withdraw the whip from any Conservative MPs and, when it was used by John Major against Euro-sceptic rebels in the 1992–97 Parliament, it weakened rather than strengthened his position. On the other hand, Labour used withdrawal of the whip more extensively between 1945 and the early 1960s, but then decided that it was not particularly effective except in particular cases and now rarely uses it. The Labour Party also expelled a number of left-wing MPs in the 1945–50 Parliament but has made little use of the power since. The Conservatives have used deselection against candidates, usually on the extreme right of the party, but not against sitting MPs, whereas Labour has from time to time deselected candidates and MPs. However, MPs are usually under greater threat of deselection from their local parties, should they fall out with them, than from the national leadership. Most disciplinary action is taken by quieter means, since the whips have at their disposal a number of sticks and carrots.

The whips largely control the membership of committees and, although the competition for serving on a standing committee dealing with government legislation can hardly be said to be fierce, that for select committees investigating government policy and administration is. Conversely, resisting nomination for a standing committee or poor attendance is viewed negatively by the whips, especially the government whips, since these committees are crucial to the passage of the government's legislative programme. Membership of parliamentary delegations to bodies like the Inter-Parliamentary Union and the Commonwealth Parliamentary Association are much coveted, meeting as they often do in attractive overseas locations. Denial of pairs, when pairing is operating, is another weapon available to the whips, as is the allocation of office accommodation, hence the appointment of an accommodation whip. Indeed, coming to Westminster with a 'reputation' can affect how the whips treat newly elected MPs, as Ken Livingstone, former Labour MPs for Brent East and now Mayor of London, found after he was first elected in 1987. One newly elected Labour MP in 1992 said that the best advice he received from an experienced Member was, 'Be nice to Ray Powell', then Labour's accommodation whip. Above all, however, the whips, especially the chief whips, have the ear of the party leader and can influence the career prospects of their charges. This is particularly important in the choice of ministers, both when a government is first formed but even more so at times of periodic ministerial reshuffles, which now tend to take place annually. Of course, party 'heavyweights' can make their own way, though even they usually need a helping hand in the early stages of their parliamentary careers. However, with nearly a hundred ministerial posts available to MPs, plus some sixty unpaid Parliamentary Private Secretaries (the first step on the ministerial ladder), the Prime Minister cannot hope to know well all the party's MPs, so that there is plenty of scope for the whips.

The other side of the coin is that ambitious MPs can do much to help themselves by co-operating with the whips, who are only too glad to suggest a Question or motion a keen backbencher might table, possible interventions in debates, a Private Member's bill to sponsor, a possible appearance on radio or television to defend the party's point of view, or simply urge attendance in the Chamber to provide vocal support to the leadership, while volunteers to serve on a standing committee are especially welcome. Some MPs are more susceptible to the blandishments of the whips than others, but all are aware that their political careers lie within the party, not outside it. All parties have their mavericks but most MPs support their parties, especially against their rival parties, and most of the time see the whips as allies not enemies. As such, the whips can assist MPs, particularly government backbenchers, in securing policy concessions, help with constituency issues and other matters that might concern individual MPs. The whips also work hard to persuade MPs of the party's case, to allay the concerns of doubters, avoid public dissent and, above all, ask whether 'this' is the issue on which they should openly defy the party line. A handful of MPs become sufficiently disillusioned to quit party politics altogether, but any MP disillusioned with his or her party but wishing to continue their political career normally has to 'cross the floor' and join another party.

What applies to the Commons, however, is somewhat less applicable to the Lords. Here too the whips work hard to ensure party cohesion, but necessarily rely far more on persuasion than coercion. Fewer carrots are available in the Lords and even fewer sticks, with fewer ministerial and frontbench opportunities, a significant number of peers towards the end of their political careers, no possibility of deselection and withdrawal of the whip or expulsion from the party of little or no use, and crossbenchers entirely beyond the range of the whips. Partisan conflict is low key in the upper house and three-line whips are less common, though more widely used by Labour than the Conservatives, but, like the Commons, those peers who take a party whip more usually vote with their parties than not.

In both Houses the whips also play a more mundane role in monitoring the progress of government business, whether from a government or opposition viewpoint, on a day-to-day, sometimes hour-to-hour, basis co-operating where necessary or appropriate across the party divide through the usual channels.

The whips are crucial to the operation of a Parliament dominated by party, more so in the Commons than the Lords, but also crucial in maintaining and explaining adversary politics.

Setting the parliamentary agenda: 'the usual channels'[3]

'The usual channels' is the term used to describe discussions between party representatives in the House of Commons and House of Lords to determine the agenda of each House. There are, in fact, separate usual channels for Lords and Commons and, where necessary, discussions take place between the relevant personnel of both Houses. They can be traced back to at least the early twentieth century – the term 'usual channels' was first used by Arthur Balfour in 1905, when he was Prime Minister and Leader of the House of Commons, but various examples of informal arrangements between the parties can be found in the nineteenth century. By 1909, the practice of asking the government to announce the following week's business had been established and by 1914 the term 'the usual channels' was in regular use. Gradually they became more elaborate and systematic, particularly in the Commons with the appointment of a private Secretary to the Government Chief Whip, the origins of which date back to 1919, although the position was not fully established until 1931. The holder is not a party appointee but a civil servant who remains in post when there is a change of government. He is the key figure in the usual channels: Richard Crossman, Leader of the House of Commons 1966–68, described the Private Secretary to the Chief Whip as a 'key man because he's the little round ball-bearing which makes the huge joint work that links the Opposition and Government Whips' offices'.[4] However, as Figure 7.7 shows, the Private Secretary is at the centre of a network in which there are other important figures. These are the Leader of the House of Commons,[5] who is the government's business manager and a member of the Cabinet, the Government Chief Whip, also a member of the Cabinet,[6] the 'Shadow' Leader of the House, the Opposition Chief Whip, and the Liberal Democrats' 'Shadow' Leader of the House and their Chief Whip. However, the usual channels operate bilaterally rather than multilaterally, in that they function separately between the government and the official opposition, between the government and the Liberal Democrats and, insofar as they are consulted at all, between the government and each of the other parties. In addition, discussions sometimes take place between the various opposition parties, although again on a bilateral basis. The initiative is firmly in the hands of the government: each week the Private Secretary, the Leader of the House and the Government Chief Whip draw up a draft agenda and timetable for the following two weeks, which is then presented to the Opposition Chief Whip for discussion. The latter, in consultation with the Shadow Leader, may seek a debate on something not on the agenda or a longer debate on something that is on

Figure 7.7 *'The usual channels' in the House of Commons*

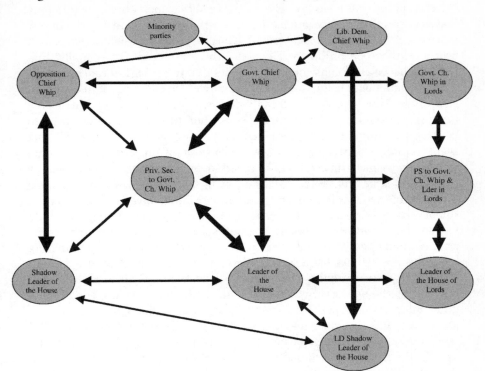

Source: Michael Rush and Clare Ettinghausen, *Opening Up the Usual Channels*, London, Hansard Society, 2002.

the agenda and raises other matters, but the opposition cannot normally force the government's hand. A separate meeting is held between the government and the Liberal Democrats, who may have had a meeting with the official opposition to discuss matters of mutual interest. The order of business is then agreed by the Leader of the House, the Chief Whip and Private Secretary and shown separately to the Shadow Cabinet and Liberal Democrats, before final approval by the Cabinet. A formal business statement is made by the Leader of the House after Question Time each Thursday, setting out the programme for the next week and the Monday following, with information about business for the second week, should the Leader think it appropriate. The official opposition and other parties may seek changes in the programme, and these are possible but not common.

Since the government's main concern is to secure the passage of its bills and other business through the House, the usual channels are also used for day-to-day negotiation between the party whips, but they are used for other purposes too, such as negotiating the membership of committees or filling casual vacancies, to discuss possible changes in procedure or the operation of the Commons, or the election of a new Speaker or appointment of a Deputy Speaker. In all these operations, however, the usual channels are entirely informal: no minutes or formal record of meetings or discussions are kept and, crucially, they depend on trust between those involved. Occasionally, that trust breaks down because one side believes that the other has reneged on an understanding or is being totally unreasonable. This may result in a suspension of the usual channels and the withdrawal of co-operation, but seldom for long, since both government and opposition need the usual channels to operate smoothly and effectively. Indeed, some see the usual channels as a silent conspiracy between government and opposition, not least because sooner or later they expect their roles to be reversed. Furthermore, it is a conspiracy that operates largely to the exclusion of backbenchers, with only limited inclusion of the Liberal Democrats and little or no involvement of the other, smaller, parties. Above all, the usual channels illustrate the importance of party, for ultimately their smooth operation depends on the ability of the government and opposition to deliver on their undertakings, especially in keeping to the agreed timetable. Since they depend on parties, much in turn depends on relative party strengths. The huge majorities won by Labour in 1997 and 2001 or by the Conservatives in 1983 and 1987 place the government in a much more powerful position vis-à-vis the opposition than where the government has a much smaller majority, as did the Conservatives between 1992 and 1997, and even more so where the government actually lacks a majority, as with the Labour governments of March–October 1974 and 1976–79. In the latter circumstances, the official opposition can make life very difficult for the government, but it is often the other, smaller parties who are able to exert influence greater than their numbers merit, since the government may be only too willing to grant concessions in return for support in the division lobbies. Thus, during the 'Lib–Lab Pact' of 1977–78, the Liberals supported the minority Labour government and were able to extract important policy concessions, while the Ulster Unionists were also able to exploit the situation. In such circumstances, the usual channels become even more important.

The House of Lords, as Figure 7.8 shows, has it own usual channels, which, while broadly similar to those in the Commons, operate somewhat differently and under different circumstances. The main difference in personnel is that the Lords' equivalent of the Private Secretary to the Government Chief Whip in the Commons is not a civil servant but one of the Lords' Clerks or officials and serves both the Leader of the House of Lords, a member of the Cabinet, and the Government Chief Whip in the upper house. However, it is principally the circumstances that the make the operation of the usual channels in the Lords different: first, for many years no government has had an overall majority in the Lords among the regular attenders (even though the Conservatives have been the largest single party); second, more than a quarter of the members of the upper house are crossbenchers, with no party affiliation, and there

Figure 7.8   *'The usual channels' in the House of Lords*

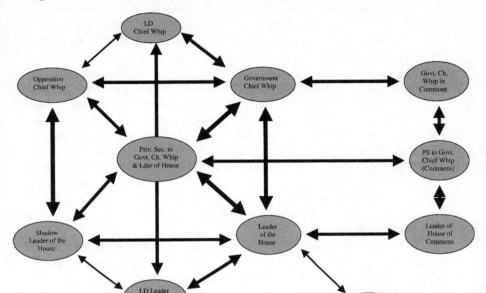

Source: Michael Rush and Clare Ettinghausen, *Opening Up the Usual Channels*, London, Hansard Society, 2002.

are marginally more Liberal Democrats in the Lords than the Commons; third, much of what the House of Lords does is in reaction to what has happened in the Commons, particularly over legislation; and, fourth, government business has no precedence under the standing orders of the Lords. Thus, while the government essentially retains the initiative, it cannot dominate the upper house in the way it does the lower. The usual channels in the Lords are therefore necessarily characterised by more negotiation, more give and take, and the Liberal Democrats have more influence than in the Commons. As for the crossbenchers, they are not normally consulted through the usual channels, since they cannot 'deliver' their members in support of any arrangement agreed through the usual channels, but they play a crucial part in the work of the Lords and provide an element of uncertainty seen in the Commons only when a significant rebellion among government backbenchers is in the offing. As in the Commons, the usual channels operate informally, with no records being kept, and bilaterally but with a greater reliance on ad hoc meetings between ministers and opposition frontbenchers, necessary to facilitate the passage of government legislation. These discussions result in the weekly production of a 'Forthcoming Business' document covering the agenda for the week ahead, a provisional agenda for the week following and sometimes beyond. This document contains estimates of the amount of time to be devoted to particular items and preliminary lists of speakers in debates. Differences between the usual channels in Lord and Commons are evidence of the extent to which the two Houses enjoy a substantial degree of autonomy in their operation.

The existence of the usual channels at Westminster illustrates not only the dominance of party but the institutionalisation of government versus opposition: if the parties are the engines of Parliament, the usual channels are the lubricant which ensure its smooth-running most of the time. But this also depends significantly on the personalities of those who operate the usual channels and, from time to time, they work less well because of personality clashes. However, also underlying the working of the usual channels is the general acceptance that the government is ultimately entitled to secure the passage of its business or, to put it more succinctly, that the government gets its way but the opposition has its say.

Unlike many other legislatures, including the Scottish Parliament and the National Assembly for Wales, which have created formal Business Committees to set their agendas, Westminster has always resisted such formalisation, arguing that it is precisely because they operate in private that the usual channels work effectively and that a more public process would make life intolerable for the party business managers. In practice, formal Business Committees also depend upon private discussion, but differ from the usual channels at Westminster in that the agenda is ultimately subject to approval by the full legislature. Even though the latter may seldom reject or modify the agenda agreed in a Business Committee, the formalisation of the usual channels would reduce the ability of the government and the opposition to control the parliamentary agenda, a prospect neither is likely to relish, particularly the government.

The parliamentary timetable

The parliamentary year

The parliamentary year or session straddles calendar years, running from the autumn of one year to the autumn of the next, most commonly from November to November. This has been the pattern since the 1928–29 session, except in years when a general election takes place. General elections normally result in the truncation of the session in which Parliament is dissolved and the prolongation of the first session of the new Parliament. These shorter and longer sessions have tended to become more pronounced since 1979, with general elections being held in the spring or early summer. The 1996–97 session, for example, was 86 days, the 1997–98 session 241 days, 2000–01 83 days and 2001–02 201 days. Not surprisingly, given the growth in government activity, the number of sitting days has tended to rise, averaging

Table 7.3   *Sitting days per session, 1955–2001*

Parliament	House of Commons (mean no.)	House of Lords (mean no.)	Ratio: Commons to Lords
1955–59	163	106	1.5:1
1959–64	164	120	1.4:1
1964–66	170	123	1.4:1
1966–70	174	128	1.4:1
1970–74	170	130	1.3:1
1974	174	128	1.4:1
1974–79	176	135	1.3:1
1979–83	174	148	1.2:1
1983–87	170	147	1.2:1
1987–92	169	148	1.1:1
1992–97	160	148	1.1:1
1977–2001	161	159	1.01:1

Source: David Butler and Gareth Butler, *Twentieth Century British Political Facts, 1900–2000*
Basingstoke, Macmillan; House of Commons, *Sessional Returns* and House of Lords, *Annual Reports*.

between 130 and 140 days in the nineteenth century, nearly 150 between 1906 and 1945, and more than 160 since 1945, although there have invariably been variations from Parliament to Parliament, usually related to some governments being more active than others. Moreover, in the nineteenth century the session normally began in January or February and ended in July or August, but from the early twentieth century the session has been spread through the year.

The session applies to both Houses of Parliament, but, since they operate autonomously, the number of days each meets per session varies and there are some days when one House is sitting and the other is not. Until recently, the Commons always sat more frequently than the Lords, as Table 7.3 demonstrates.

In the mid-1950s the Commons was meeting one-and-a-half days for every day the Lords met, but this ratio has gradually become more or less equal and in some recent sessions the Lords has actually met more frequently than the Commons: 1998–99: Commons 149 days, Lords 154; 1999–2000: Commons 170 days and Lords 176. Although they have separate agendas, the two Houses necessarily co-ordinate their operation through the usual channels. Indeed, to a significant degree the Lords' agenda is driven by that of the Commons, especially on legislation, waiting for bills to pass through the Commons and for the latter's response to any amendments the upper house may have made, although one in three government bills start in the Lords rather than the Commons. However, the financial supremacy of the Commons means that the Lords spends very little time on financial business and focuses its

Table 7.4 *The 1999–2000 parliamentary session*

House of Commons		Constituency days	House of Lords	
Dates	Sitting days		Dates	Sitting days
17 Nov.–21 Dec.	21	3	17 Nov.–16 Dec.	18
22 Dec.–9 Jan.	Christmas Recess	–	17 Dec.–9 Jan.	Christmas Recess
10 Jan.–22 Feb.	29	3	10 Jan.–20 Apr.	62
23–25 Jan.	Constituency week	–		
28 Feb.–20 Apr.	38	0		
21 Apr.–1 May	Easter Recess	–	21 Apr.–1 May	Easter Recess
2–25 May	18	0	2–25 May	16
29 May–2 June	Whitsun Recess	–	29 May–2 June	Whitsun Recess
5 June–28 July	37	3	5 June–27 July	37
29 July–22 Oct.	Summer Recess	–	28 July–26 Sept.	Summer Recess
23 Oct.–30 Nov.	27	2	27 Sept.–30 Nov.	43
Total	170	12		176

Source: House of Commons, *Sessional Information Digest*, 1999–2000, and Lords' *Hansard*.

legislative attention on other bills, as a result of which it is often able to devote more time to these than the Commons.

There is, in fact, a regular pattern to the parliamentary session (see Table 7.4), rather like the school year, with breaks or recesses at Christmas, Easter and summer and some shorter breaks in between. Until recently, it was the practice to announce the dates of recesses at various stages during the session, sometimes at short notice. However, this became increasingly inconvenient and longer notice began to be given, leading eventually to the full sessional timetable being announced in advance of the session. Then, from the 2002–03 session, the sessional pattern was modified, so that Parliament returned for a short period in September, adjourned for the party conference season and resumed again in October.

The session usually opens in November, with the Speech from the Throne, outlining the government's legislative programme for the year. This is delivered in the Lords' Chamber by the Queen in person, with the Commons present at the bar of the House, having processed from their House. This is followed by debates in both Houses on the government's proposals, but thereafter the pattern in the two Houses diverges somewhat. The Commons has some financial business to deal with, including the Chancellor of the Exchequer's Pre-Budget Report, essentially an assessment of the economic situation and its implications for the presentation of the Budget itself the following spring. In addition, some government bills will be started on their way in the Commons, with others starting in the Lords, but the upper house deals with none of this financial business and is therefore able to spend more time debating

Table 7.5 *The distribution of business in the House of Commons and House of Lords, 1999–2000*

Type of business	House of Commons	House of Lords
Debates	32.2	15.4
Parliamentary Questions	9.7	13.3
Primary legislation	45.4	62.1
Delegated legislation	2.4	2.8
Other	10.2	6.4
Total	99.9	100.0

Source: House of Commons, *Sessional Return for 1999–2000* and House of Lords, *Sessional Statistics, 1999–2000*.

other matters. As the session progresses, particularly after the Christmas Recess, more time is spent in both Houses on government legislation, but the Commons again spends a good deal of time on financial matters, with the Budget in late March. This period also sees the earlier stages of backbench Private Members' bills in the Commons. This pattern is repeated after the Easter Recess, leading to the approval of expenditure and taxation by the Commons in the summer and the completion of the passage of government bills through the lower house, including those passed first by the Lords. Meanwhile, the upper house becomes increasingly busy with government legislation and has less time for debates on other matters. Then, following the Summer Recess, both Houses return to Westminster for a 'tidying up' period before the session comes to an end. This is an especially busy time for the Lords, since it will be dealing with the final stages of government bills, often resulting in bills going back and forth between the two Houses before finally approving them or, occasionally, resulting in a bill not being passed.

The pattern of business that the parliamentary year produces can be seen in Table 7.5, which shows that the Commons spends more time on debates than the Lords, the latter more on primary legislation. The first statistic is somewhat misleading, however, since one form of Questions in the Lords initiates short debates, so that the true figure for Lords' debates is 21.3 per cent. On the other hand, increased government legislation has resulted in the upper house spending more time on primary legislation at the expense of debates, other than in election years, when fewer government bills reach the Lords, but the actual number of debates has grown because they tend to be shorter. Other differences result simply from the amount of time regularly allocated, such as the hour's Question Time in the Commons, compared with half-an-hour in the Lords. Length of sitting can also vary, but overall the number of sitting hours in 1999–2000 was 1,443 in the Commons and 1,325 in the Lords. However, these totals ignore time spent on committee activity, which considerably increases the amount of parliamentary time, especially that devoted in the Commons to legislation and to scrutiny in both Houses. For instance, standing committees dealing with the committee stage of bills in the Commons added a further 729 hours, amounting to more than half the hours spent in the Chamber, and another 353 hours were taken up by Westminster Hall sittings. In addition, Commons' select committees engaged in the scrutiny of policy and administration held 895 meetings in 1999–2000. A significant amount of committee activity also takes place in the Lords, although the House seldom uses committees for the committee stage of bills and the level of select committee activity is less than in the Commons simply because the number of peers regularly attending limits the number of committees the upper house can sustain. Not surprisingly, just as the parliamentary year in the two Houses produces variations, so also do the parliamentary week and day.

The parliamentary week and day

As with the parliamentary year, there is no requirement or need for Lords and Commons to have the same pattern of sittings. Indeed, in the late 1950s and for some time after, the House of Lords concentrated its sittings on Tuesdays, Wednesdays and Thursdays, with occasional Monday and rare Friday sittings. From the later 1980s, however, it began to meet on most Mondays and more frequently on Fridays, depending on the pressure of business. In comparison, the House of Commons has long met on most days of the week, but from 1994 a number of Fridays (traditionally backbench time) became non-sitting days. These are known as 'constituency days' and intended to allow Members to spend time in their constituencies.

Similarly, there have long been variations in sitting hours. From the sixteenth century to the mid-eighteenth century the Commons sat in the mornings, but gradually the practice of starting in the afternoon and adjourning at 10.30 p.m. or later became the norm. This continued to be the basic pattern (the Second World War excepted) until January 2003, other than starting and finishing earlier on Fridays. Experiments with morning sittings took place in 1967, but proved unpopular and were quickly abandoned, only to be used again from 1995 to 1999 with greater success. However, the massive influx of newly elected Labour MPs in 1997 produced growing pressure to change to what were termed 'family-friendly' hours of sitting. Meeting in the afternoon undoubtedly suited the mostly part-time MPs of the nineteenth century and much of the twentieth, particularly those with business interests, legal practices, journalistic careers or other outside jobs. As MPs became increasingly full-time in practice, so the pressure for adopting a 'normal working day' increased. This led, first, to Thursday sittings being changed from 11.30 a.m. to 7.30 p.m., and then, from January 2003, sittings began at 11.30 a.m. on Tuesdays, Wednesdays and Thursdays, finishing at 7.30 p.m. on Tuesday

Table 7.6 *The weekly and daily timetable of the House of Commons*

Time	Monday	Tuesday	Wednesday	Thursday	Friday
9.30 a.m.					Prayers Petitions Private Members' bills or Government Adjournment debate
10.30 a.m.				Prayers Oral Questions	
11.00 a.m.			Prayers Oral Questions Questions to the Prime Minister (12 noon)	Urgent Questions* Ministerial Statements Presentation of bills Main business	Statements Urgent Questions*
11.30 a.m.					Private Members' bills
12.30 p.m.			Urgent Questions* Ministerial Statements Presentation of bills Ten-minute rule bills Main business	Main business (cont.)	Private Members' bills
2.30 p.m.	Prayers Oral Questions	Prayers Oral Questions	Main business (cont.)	Main business (cont.)	Exempted business† Adjournment Debate Adjournment (3.00 p.m.)
3.30 p.m.	Urgent Questions* Ministerial Statements Presentation of bills Main business	Urgent Questions* Ministerial Statements Presentation of bills Ten-minute rule bills Main business		Main business (cont.)	
6.00 p.m.	Main business (cont.)	Main business (cont.)	Main business (cont.)		
6.30 p.m.	Main business (cont.)	Main business (cont.)	Main business (cont.)		
7.00 p.m.	Main business (cont.)	Main business (cont.)	Exempted business† Adjournment debate		
7.30 p.m.	Main business (cont.)	Main business (cont.)	Adjournment	Exempted business† Adjournment debate	
10.00 p.m.	Exempted business† Adjournment debate	Exempted business† Adjournment debate		Adjournment	
10.30 p.m.	Adjournment	Adjournment			

Notes: * Known as Private Notice Questions until January 2003. † Various types of business which may be taken after the normal time of adjournment e.g. various types of delegated legislation. Finance Bills.

Table 7.7   *Westminster Hall sittings*

	Monday	Tuesday	Wednesday	Thursday	Friday
Mornings	No sitting	9.30–11.30	9.30–11.30	No sitting	No sitting
Afternoons	No sitting	2.00–4.30	2.00–4.30	2.30–5.30	No sitting

Source: www.parliament.uk.

and Wednesday and 6.30 p.m. on Thursdays, with Monday and Friday sitting hours remaining the same.

Ironically, no sooner had the new, 'family-friendly' system been introduced than nearly two hundred MPs signed a motion seeking a return to the earlier arrangements, arguing that the change had 'adversely affected' the business of the House and a review was subsequently set in train. In January 2005 this resulted in Tuesday sittings reverting to 2.30–10.30 p.m. and Thursday sittings starting an hour earlier at 10.30 a.m. – to take effect after the general election (see Table 7.6).

The pattern of business on Mondays to Thursdays is essentially the same, whereas Fridays are devoted almost entirely to backbench or Private Members' business, principally Private Members' bills. Of course, within this pattern the actual business varies from day to day. Thus, while Question Time is a daily set piece, except on Fridays, as are the short half-hour adjournment debates, on most days there are no Urgent Questions, bills are not necessarily introduced every day, and whether there is a ministerial statement on some issue varies. More importantly, however, the main business can vary considerably: it may be a major debate on an aspect of government policy, one of the stages of a government bill, a debate on a matter raised by an opposition party, various types of financial business, and so on. In addition, Westminster Hall sittings are held on three days a week – Tuesdays, Wednesdays and Thursdays, as shown in Table 7.7. These are used almost entirely for debates chosen by backbenchers.

Until the changes introduced in 2003, the pattern of sitting hours in the Lords was similar to that of the Commons, starting at 2.30 p.m. and finishing at 10 p.m., except for Fridays (see Table 7.8). This pattern is retained for Mondays, Tuesdays and Wednesdays, but in 2003 the start of the Thursday sitting was brought forward to 11 a.m., followed by break between 1.30 p.m. and 2.30 p.m., with adjournment at 7.30. However, the more important difference between Lords and Commons relates to the pattern of business. In the Lords, Question Time is shorter and limited to five Questions and legislation normally takes precedence on all days except Wednesday, which is generally reserved for debates on other matters. In addition, what are known as unstarred Questions are Questions intended to give rise to a debate, the equivalent to the

Table 7.8 *The weekly and daily timetable of the House of Lords*

Time	Monday	Tuesday	Wednesday	Thursday	Friday
11.00 a.m.					Prayers Introduction of new peers Private Notice Questions Ministerial Statements Private Bills Business Motions Public bills Affirmative Statutory Instruments
1.30 p.m.					Public bills etc. (cont.)
2.30 p.m.	Prayers Starred Questions Introduction of new peers Private Notice Questions Ministerial Statements Private bills Business Motions Public bills Affirmative Statutory Instruments	Prayers Starred Questions Introduction of new peers Private Notice Questions Ministerial Statements Private bills Business Motions Public bills Affirmative Statutory Instruments	Prayers Starred Questions Introduction of new peers Private Notice Questions Ministerial Statements Private bills Business Motions Debates on motions by opposition parties and crossbenchers	Starred Questions Public bills etc. (cont.)	Public bills etc. (cont.)
3.00 p.m.	Public bills etc. (cont.)	Public bills etc. (cont.)	Debates (cont.)	Public bills etc. (cont.)	Public bills etc. (cont.) Adjournment
7.30 p.m.	Public bills etc. (cont.) Unstarred Questions	Public bills etc. (cont.) Unstarred Questions	Debates (cont.) Unstarred Questions	Unstarred Questions Adjournment	
8.30 p.m.	Public bills etc. (cont.) Unstarred Questions	Public bills etc. (cont.) Unstarred Questions	Public bills etc. (cont.) Unstarred Questions		
10.00 p.m.	Adjournment	Adjournment	Adjournment		

Source: www.parliament.uk.

Commons' adjournment debates. These differences in the pattern of business also illustrate the significance of the rules and procedures of the two Houses.

The significance of rules and procedures

Rules and procedures matter. They matter in the same way as constitutions and constitutional arrangements matter because they are a crucial part of the context within which Parliament operates. However, they operate at two levels – in the day-to-day working of Parliament, on the one hand, and as the means by which Parliament seeks to fulfil its functions.

At the first level, the rules and procedures of the two Houses set out the details of various mechanisms, such as Question Time, various types of debate and the legislative process, and the work of committees. Of no less importance are the rules and procedures which set out the rights and responsibilities of the members of both Houses, individually and collectively, including those of the majority and various minority parties and, crucially, of the government and the official opposition. However, because the Lords and Commons operate separately and determine their own rules and procedures, there are some important differences between them. In particular, as the political focal point of Parliament, the Commons has had to adopt its rules and procedures much more than the Lords to the growth of government: in 1810 the House of Commons had a mere seven standing orders; by 1870 it was seventy, by 1897 nearly a hundred, and in 2003 163, plus temporary and sessional orders. Thus, far from being immutable, rules and procedures have been adapted to changing circumstances, with increasing precedence given to government business in the Commons. But the increase in Commons' standing orders also reflects the growing dominance of party, a factor always of greater importance in the Commons than the Lords. Closure, the bringing of a debate to an end by a vote, has been part of the standing orders of the Commons since the 1880s and the timetabling of debates on bills soon became the norm, sometimes imposed, but mostly agreed through the usual channels. However, although the provision for closure can also be found in the House of Lords, it is, in the words of the House's *Companion to the Standing Orders*, 'a most exceptional measure', last used in 1927. Moreover, although the length of debates may be agreed through the usual channels in the Lords, there is in practice no means of enforcing a timetable. Proceedings in the Lords are self-regulating and the Lord Chancellor, in his capacity as Speaker of the House, has no disciplinary powers, unlike the Speaker in the Commons, who regulates debates and enforces the rules of the House. There is in both Houses a constant battle between the government, intent on getting its programme through Parliament, and the opposition parties, intent on making life difficult for the government by exposing that programme and government policies and administration generally to public scrutiny. The cliché that all's fair in love and war is equally applicable to politics, and the ingenuity of parliamentarians knows few if any boundaries. Governments seek to outmanoeuvre oppositions and vice versa and attempts at partisan manipulation of rules and procedures are a feature of the operation of Parliament, more overtly in the Commons, less so in the Lords. It is therefore not surprising that both Houses keep their rules and procedures under constant review through permanent Procedure Committees and ad hoc committees and working groups on particular aspects of their operation. Immediately after the 1997 general election, for example, the Labour government set up a Select Committee on the Modernisation of the House, whose work continued into the 2001 Parliament, while the House of Lords, at the invitation of the then Leader of the House, the late Lord Williams of Mostyn, set up a Working Group on the Working Practices of the House in 2001. Underpinning the operation of Parliament at this level are the party organisations within the two Houses, and the presence of party does much to explain how Parliament works, not least its adversarial nature.

At the second level, rules and procedures contribute crucially to the ability of Parliament to fulfil its functions, particularly the legislative, financial, representative and scrutiny functions to the point that they are the very basis of parliamentary government – the sustaining of a government and the calling of it to account. The balance between the two is a fine one and some observers argue that it has shifted too much in favour of the government, a matter that will be explored in more detail in later chapters.

Notes

1 Edward Porritt, *The Unreformed House of Commons: Parliamentary Representation Before 1832*, Cambridge, Cambridge University Press, 1909, Vol. I, pp. 506–7.
2 *Ibid.*, p. 426.
3 This section is based on Michael Rush and Clare Ettinghausen, *Opening Up the Usual Channels*, London, The Hansard Society, 2002.
4 Richard Crossman, *The Diaries of a Cabinet Minister: Vol. 2 – Lord President and Leader of the House of Commons* (ed. Janet Morgan), London, Hamish Hamilton and Jonathan Cape, 1976, p. 23.
5 Until 1942 the position of Leader of the House of Commons was usually held by the Prime Minister, provided he was a member of the Commons rather than the Lords. In the latter case, a leading member of the government party in the Commons held the post.
6 Between 1974 and 1976 the Government Chief Whip was a member of the Cabinet, but before 1974 and between 1976 and 1997 attended Cabinet meetings, though not a member. This practice goes back to at least 1951.

8

The legislative role

Parliament and legislation

Parliament is often described as a legislature, but it is more accurate to say that it plays a crucial part in the legislative process, since the initiative in most of the legislation that is passed annually comes from the government rather than Parliament, but the government's legislative proposals require parliamentary approval. Of course, in most modern legislatures it is the executive which takes a significant amount of the initiative, but an important distinction can be made between what have been called 'transformative' and 'arena' legislatures[1] or 'active' and 'reactive' legislatures.[2] Transformative or active legislatures are those 'that possess the independent capacity, frequently exercised, to mould and transform proposals from whatever source into laws'; arena or reactive legislatures 'serve as formalised settings for the interplay of significant political forces in the life of a political system'.[3] The prime example cited of a transformative or active legislature is the United States Congress, that of an arena or reactive legislature, the UK Parliament. Between these extremes can be found other examples of less transformative and less reactive legislatures – in the Netherlands, Germany, Italy, and France under the Fourth Republic (1946–58), resulting from factors such as the prevalence of coalition government, or electoral instability. Of course, it can be argued that Parliament does have influence over legislation put forward by the government – some bills may be passed unamended, but others do not and from time to time a government bill is defeated or withdrawn. Essentially, Parliament is an arena legislature in which the two major parties confront each other through the roles of government and opposition; it is also a reactive legislature, spending much of its time responding to government proposals. Furthermore, government business has precedence on most sitting days in the House of Commons, governments normally have majority support in the lower house, and the House of Lords rejects few government bills outright, and most government proposals become law.

Types of legislation

As noted in Chapter 3, Parliament deals with two basic types of legislation – primary, consisting of bills, which if passed become Acts of Parliament, and secondary, consisting of rules and regulations issued under the authority of Acts of Parliament and, since 1973, rules and regulations emanating from the European Union. These two basic types then sub-divide into various sub-types, as shown in Table 8.1. Some measure of the scale of the legislative output of Parliament can be given by noting that in 1999 35 Acts of Parliament, comprising 2,096 pages, and 3,491 statutory instruments (SIs), comprising 10,754 pages, were passed. The number of Acts passed each year varies, as does their length, and the average from 1997 to 2000 was 49 and 2,600 pages and average number of domestic regulations nearly 3,300, comprising nearly 9,000 pages. In addition, Parliament considers about 1,200 EU documents a year, many of which are draft regulations or policy proposals leading to regulations.

Primary legislation is divided into public and private Acts of Parliament. The former consist of acts of general application and the latter of acts of limited geographical or personal application. Although public and private bills go through similar stages in Parliament, private bills are dealt with separately and are subject to different procedures. There are also what are known as hybrid bills, parts of which have general application and other parts affect particular limited or private interests, and the latter are subject to private bill procedure.

Private bills

Private bills are now few in number but in the nineteenth century and earlier far outnumbered public bills. Historically, they were of particular importance during the industrial revolution because parliamentary approval was necessary to authorise the construction of roads, canals and railways and, later, of reservoirs, gas and electricity supplies, there being no general law permitting such developments. The passing of private bills was also necessary for personal matters, such as divorce and naturalisation, and remains necessary to resolve for example, certain legal problems with estates and allowing the marriage of individuals not normally permitted by existing law but for which reasonable case can be brought. However, most private legislation nowadays is passed to allow local authorities to build tramways, light railways, or marinas, but since 1992 most such developments are authorised by ministerial order under the Transport and Water Act and do not require separate bills. The remaining matters still requiring private bills result in half-a-dozen acts a year.

Unlike public bills, which are introduced by the government or a member of either of the two Houses, private bills are initiated by a petition from the organisation, person or persons seeking their passage. The presenters of

Table 8.1 *Types of legislation*

Primary Legislation	Secondary Legislation
Public bills	*Statutory Instruments*
Bills intended to have application to the whole of the UK or specifically to England and Wales, Wales, Scotland or Northern Ireland and to the whole population of those areas	Regulations issued by a minister under powers conferred by an Act of Parliament to implement or modify policy
Government bills	*Orders in Council*
Bills introduced in Parliament by a Minister of the Crown	Orders issued by ministers under the authority of the royal prerogative to e.g. transfer responsibilities from one government department to another or from a UK minister to one of the devolved assemblies
Private bills	
Bills intended to have application to a named geographical area, organisation or person or persons	
Local bills	*Orders under the Transport and Works Act 1992*
Bills intended to have application to a named geographical area or organisation	Orders made by ministers to authorise proposals for limited local developments
Personal bills	*European*
Bills intended to apply to a named person or persons	European documents e.g. draft regulations produced by the Council of Ministers, policy proposals produced by the European Commission
Hybrid bills	
Bills parts of which are intended to have general application and parts local application	

private bills normally employ the services of a parliamentary agent. These are firms, of which there are half a dozen, specialising in the preparation and presentation of such bills. As with public bills, private bills undergo a formal first reading or presentation in Parliament, followed by a second reading, committee stage and report or consideration stage, but unlike public bills, private bills are subject to fees. The work on private bills is divided equally between the two Houses, except that bills of a mainly financial character usually start in the Commons. They are debated at second reading only if opposed and are then referred to an opposed or unopposed bill committee. It is at the committee stage that private bills are treated differently, since the committee operates like a civil court. With unopposed bills, the parliamentary agent presents the case for the bill and in that of opposed bills the case for and against is usually put by lawyers representing those concerned, who may call evidence in support of their case. The members of private bill committees must not have an interest in the bill concerned, nor, if they are MPs, may their constituents, and attendance at committees is obligatory. A bill may be amended at the committee stage and any amendments are reviewed at the consideration stage, followed by a final examination of the bill at third reading, after which it proceeds to the other House. Any amendments made by the latter are then considered by the House in which the bill was first introduced and, if passed, the bill proceeds to royal assent. In 1999–2000 five private bills were passed, although there are always others bills in process, since they can be carried over from one session to the next or Parliament to Parliament.

Public bills

All public bills, whether government or Private Members' bills (PMBs), go through essentially the same process in Parliament, but there are variations in that process, allowing Parliament a degree of flexibility in how it deals with bills (see Table 8.2). However, apart from the fact that most bills can be introduced in either the Commons or the Lords, most of these variations apply to government bills rather than PMBs. The major constitutional exception is that financial bills – basically those proposing taxation or expenditure – must originate in the Commons in recognition of its financial primacy and the Lords give only minimal consideration to such bills. Thus all bills are formally presented at a first reading and not debated, except that one of the procedures for allowing MPs to present a PMB gives the proposer and an opponent ten minutes each to put their case, thereby providing a limited de facto first reading debate, but procedurally the MP is seeking leave to introduce the bill. Not all bills proceed beyond first reading – most that do not are PMBs, but the principles or basic proposals of all that do are debated at second reading. If this hurdle is passed, the bill goes to the committee stage, at which its detailed proposals are discussed. It is at this stage that the bill may be amended or new

Table 8.2 *The legislative process: the stages of a public bill*

House of Commons

Pre-legislative	First reading	Second reading	Committee stage	Report stage	Third reading	Lords' amdts.	Royal assent	Post-legislative
White Paper Consultation Paper ('Green Paper') Draft bill (ref. to deptl. select comm.; ad hoc select comm.; joint comm.)	Formality, except for ten-minute rule bills	Floor of House Second reading comm. Grand comm.	Whole House Standing comm. Special stand. comm. Divided between floor and stand. comm. Select comm. Joint comm.	Floor of House Standing comm. Grand comm.	Floor of House	Floor of House	Formality	Dept. select comm. Ad hoc select comm. Joint comm.

House of Lords

Pre-legislative	First reading	Second reading	Committee stage	Report stage	Third reading	Lords' amdts.	Royal assent	Post-legislative
White Paper Consultation Paper ('Green Paper') Select comm. Joint comm. Draft bill	Formality	Floor of House	Floor of House Grand comm.* Public bill comm. Select comm. Joint comm.	Floor of House	Floor of House	Floor of House	Formality	Select comm. Ad hoc select. comm. Joint comm.

Note: * An 'open' committee in that any peer may attend and participate, but no divisions may take place and only unanimously agreed amendments may be made.

clauses introduced. The bill is then brought back to the House for its report stage, at which further changes are possible, and finally examined as a whole at third reading. Of course, a bill may fail to complete any of these stages, but, again, this is a fate normally reserved for PMBs rather than government bills. Only if a bill completes all its stages in one House does it proceed to the other, where it goes through essentially the same process. Once it has been passed by both Houses, it proceeds to the formality of the royal assent, which has not been refused since 1707 when Queen Anne refused to sign a Militia Bill relating to Scotland, having also refused to sign a bill containing similar provisions passed by the then Scottish Parliament in 1703. Once a bill has received the royal assent, it as an Act of Parliament and either comes into force immediately or at a date laid down in the Act itself, or at a later date specified by a minister issuing a commencement order bringing the whole or parts of the Act into operation, as appropriate.

Government bills

Government bills must be seen in the context of the data in Table 8.3. Put simply, government bills almost always become Acts of Parliament. Given that governments normally have a majority in the House of Commons and the House of Lords does not normally reject government bills, this is hardly surprising. However, the extent of government control over the parliamentary agenda is shown by noting that, in 1977–78, 86.0 per cent of government bills still passed, even though the government lacked a majority. Most government bills are foreshadowed in the annual Queen's Speech in November, but both before and after the speech there is a pre-legislative stage involving

Table 8.3   *The success rate of government bills, 1992–2001*

Session	Success rate
1992–93	100.0
1993–94	100.0
1994–95	94.9*
1995–96	97.7
1996–97	100.0
1997–98	98.1
1998–99	87.1†
1999–2000	97.5
2000–01	60.8§

Source: *House of Commons Sessional Returns.*

Notes: * One bill withdrawn and one hybrid bill carried over (then possible only with hybrid or private bills). † One bill carried over under new procedure. § Short session due to general election.

varying degrees of discussion within the government and with various interests outside government and Parliament, as well as the actual drafting of
legislation.

In practice, government bills originate from a variety of sources, most obviously from the governing party's election manifesto and specific election
pledges. For example, in its 1997 manifesto Labour promised to introduce a
national minimum wage, to remove hereditary peers from the House of Lords,
to incorporate the European Convention on Human Rights into UK law,
and to introduce devolution in Scotland and Wales, resulting in the passing of
bills to fulfil each of these pledges. Bills of this type are to a significant degree
ideologically driven and therefore among the more controversial, at least as
far as the battle between government and opposition is concerned. This is not
to say that other bills cannot be highly controversial, as the efforts of the Blair
government to pass bills limiting the right to be tried by jury have shown.
Similarly, legislation to regulate scientific experiments with human embryos
and human fertilisation treatment has been massively controversial, but not
in a partisan sense. Some bills, notably those approving public expenditure
and implementing the annual Budget, have to be passed every year and normally follow a regular cycle; other matters require periodic legislation, such
as the renewal of the BBC's Charter. The UK's membership of the EU also
generates the need for legislative action, most of it in the form of delegated
legislation directly from Brussels, but some requires primary legislation, such
as bills implementing the Maastricht, Amsterdam and Nice Treaties, or the
introduction of elections to the European Parliament and various policy matters requiring changes in UK law. Most government departments also gener-
ate proposed bills, as civil servants become aware of action needed to improve
policy implementation, administrative structures and, increasingly, accountability through codes of practice, or respond to decisions by the courts, especially in the process of judicial review. Most government departments have a
range of advisory committees consisting mainly of experts in appropriate fields
and these too contribute to the demand for legislation. The government also
has to react to royal commissions, judicial and other inquiries it may have set
up. For example, the Labour government established royal commissions
on the possible reform of the electoral system (the Jenkins Commission) and
on the reform of the House of Lords (the Wakeham Commission), judicial
inquiries following two rail crashes and to investigate the Metropolitan
Police's handling of the murder of the black teenager, Stephen Lawrence, two
inquiries to examine the government's handling of foot-and-mouth outbreak
in 2001, and the Hutton inquiry into the death of the chemical and biological
weapons expert, Dr David Kelly in 2003. Not all such inquiries result in
reports recommending legislation, but they remain an important source of
bills. In addition to ad hoc commissions and inquiries, there are a number
of permanent bodies that keep particular areas of policy and the law under
review, notably the Royal Commission on Environmental Pollution, the Law

Commission, and the Criminal Law Review Committee. The Law Commission, for instance, is a major source of what are called consolidation bills, that is, bills which tidy up the statute book by bringing all existing legislation in a particular field into a new Act, repealing redundant bills or parts of bills.

All these sources of legislation are either part of the governmental machine or closely connected with it, but there are two other important sources outside that machine – pressure or interest groups and the public (or particular sections of it). It is impossible to say how many pressure groups there are, partly because some are short lived and can come and go with bewildering speed but more especially because they are difficult to define. Thus, organisations like the Campaign for Nuclear Disarmament, the Abortion Law Reform Association, the Society for the Protection of Unborn Children, the League Against Cruel Sports, the Countryside Alliance are clearly pressure groups by any definition, but others, such as business groups and trade unions engage in pressure politics but are also involved in other activities that lie outside this sphere. Moreover, there are also many organisations that seldom if ever engage in politics, but which, if they feel that their interests are affected, will make political representations or mount a public campaign. Nonetheless, pressure groups and other organisations regularly demand changes in the law, governments listen and, if convinced, act. For example, following Labour's return to power in 1974, trade unions demanded and secured the repeal of the Conservatives' Industrial Relations Act, though they were less successful after 1997 in persuading the Blair government to repeal other industrial relations legislation passed by the Thatcher and Major governments between 1979 and 1997. Similarly, ASH – Action on Smoking and Health has persuaded successive governments to pass legislation limiting tobacco advertising and the Ramblers' Association persuaded the 1997 Labour government to legislate for greater access to the countryside. On the other hand, both Conservative and Labour governments have been reluctant to legislate on matters like abortion, preferring to leave some issues to be dealt with by Private Members' bills. The same view was taken on the banning of hunting, but in the 2002–03 session a government bill was introduced but failed because of disagreements between Lords and Commons.

Public opinion may also persuade governments to introduce legislation, particularly in areas such as immigration and crime, but also on specific matters, such as dangerous dogs. Indeed, legislation to control dogs provides an example of just how dramatic the impact of public opinion can be. A Dangerous Dogs Bill was passed as a Private Member's bill in 1989, but a series of attacks on adults and children by breeds such as rottweilers and pit bull terriers in 1991 led to demands for stronger controls. The Home Secretary, Kenneth Baker, refused to take any further action but public pressure via the media and Parliament was such that two days later the Prime Minister, John Major, announced that the Dangerous Dogs Act would be amended, as it was by the end of July 1991. Similarly, the tragic murder of sixteen primary school children and one of their teachers in the Scottish town of Dunblane in 1996 led to swift legislative action to ban the private ownership of guns. Although legislation was delayed by a judicial inquiry, the Firearms Act (Amendment) Bill received its first reading on 31 October 1996 and received the royal assent on 27 February 1997. Governments also react to events without waiting for public opinion to express itself fully and clearly, most obviously in response to events like terrorist bombings in Birmingham in 1974 and Omagh in 1998 or the 9/11 attacks in New York and Washington in 2001.

Once the government has decided in principle that it wishes to introduce a bill on a particular matter, the legislative process is set in train. It is likely that there will already have been some discussions within and between relevant government departments and possibly some with some outside interests, but it is at this point that the pre-legislative stage gets fully underway. In some cases the process will move quickly to the introduction of a bill, either because it is urgent or fairly straightforward requiring little or no consultation inside or outside government. In many cases, however, there is a gestation period of varying lengths, sometime involving private consultations with outside interests, sometimes public consultation, sometimes both. Consultation, whether public or private, has become much more common and, relatively speaking, less haphazard. Indeed, when Labour returned to power in 1997, the government set up nearly three hundred 'task forces' and more than two hundred internal reviews, usually with representatives of various non-governmental organisations, as well as civil servants.[4] Most did not result directly in the production of bills, but they played their part in the pre-legislative stage. Previous governments had developed the practice of producing 'Green Papers' or consultative documents, setting out the problem or issue, raising questions and, sometimes, offering solutions. However, these were not part of a regular or systematic consultation process and their use declined in the 1990s. Nevertheless, Green Papers are still used but there is no longer a clear distinction between them and what are called 'consultative documents'. Thus, the Blair government has published Green Papers on planning, identity cards, the education of 14 to 19 year-olds, and pensions but produced many more consultative documents – for example, on the quality and provision of early education and childcare and on health inequalities in 2001, on digital television and on alcohol abuse or harm in 2002, on racial equality, marine conservation, the development or air transport, corporation tax reform, the appointment of judges, and the second stage or Lords' reform in 2003. Overall in 2002, government departments engaged in more than six hundred national consultations.[5]

However, in cases where the government is firmly committed to action and to how it wishes to achieve its objective, 'White Papers' are published, setting out its proposals in more detail – on, for instance, local government (1998 and 2001), policing (2001), NHS reform, immigration, and regional government in 2002, and higher education in 2003. The sequence of White Papers, bills, Acts of Parliament and policy implementation can be seen clearly in the setting up of the Scottish Parliament and the National Assembly for Wales: following election pledge on devolution, the Blair government published White Papers on Scotland and on Wales in July 1997, held referendums seeking approval for the proposals in September and had the necessary legislation on the statute book in 1998, ready for the first elections in May 1999 and the transfer of power from 1 July 1999.

In addition to Green Papers, consultative documents and White Papers, it has become increasingly common for the government to present bills to Parliament in draft form, a practice that began under the 1992–97 Major government but has become more extensive under the Blair government. Draft bills are considered by various committees – one or more of the appropriate departmental select committees, another established select committee, a joint select committee or an ad hoc select committee of either House set up for the purpose, as shown in Table 8.4. This opens up the legislative process, since select committees are able to take oral and written evidence from ministers, civil servants, experts in the field and organisations representing outside interests. Not only does this practice have the potential for improving the quality of legislation but it sometimes results in criticism of the government's proposals, as happened when the draft Communications Bill was referred to a joint committee in 2002 and the committee was especially unhappy about the bill's media ownership provisions.

Each government department will have its legislative priorities, but is constrained by the knowledge that it will only be able to cope with one or two bills, particularly if one is a major piece of legislation. The Prime Minister's views will, of course, carry great weight and ministers compete for his or her support. However, there are always more bills proposed than there is parliamentary time available and each bill must compete with others for time in the government's legislative programme for the session concerned. Ultimately, this is in the hands of the Cabinet's Queen's Speech and Future Legislation Committee, which decides the priority to be given to proposed bills. Not all bills included in the government's legislative programme are mentioned in the Queen's Speech and, of course, other bills are sometimes added during the year. Once a proposed bill has been accepted for inclusion, an outline is sent to the Office of the Parliamentary Counsel, whose lawyers will prepare a draft in accordance with departmental instructions. Unless a bill is presented to Parliament in draft form, Parliament is not directly involved until a bill is presented for its first reading, following which it is printed and the parliamentary process proper begins. The printed bill is accompanied by explanatory notes, outlining its purpose and each of its clauses, together with its financial implications. In addition, since the passing of the Human Rights Act, 1998, each bill must be accompanied by a statement that it conforms with the provisions of the European Convention on Human Rights (or rarely, that it does not and why).

Table 8.4 *Draft bills presented to Parliament, 1997–2002*

Session	Bill	Examined by
1997–98	Pensions Sharing in Divorce Bill	Social Security Committee
1998–99	Local Government and Marketing Bill	Joint select committee
	Liability Partnerships Bill	Trade and Industry Committee
	Electronic Communications Bill	Trade and Industry Committee
	Financial Services Regulation Bill	Treasury Committee
	Railways Bill	Environment, Transport and Regional Affairs Committee
	Local Government (Organisation and Standards) Bill	Joint select committee
	Financial Services and Marketing Bill	Joint select committee
	Food Standards Bill	Ad hoc select committee
1999–2000	Insolvency Bill	Trade and Industry Committee
	Government Resources and Accounting Bill	Public Accounts Committee
	Freedom of Information Bill	Public Administration Comm. and House of Lords Delegated Powers and Regulatory Reform Committee
2000–01	Water Bill	Environment, Transport and Regional Affairs Committee
	Export Control and Non-Proliferation Bill	Defence, Foreign Affairs, International Development, and Trade and Industry Committees
2001–02	Communications Bill	Joint select committee
	Local Government Bill	Transport, Local Government and Regions Committee

Source: House of Commons, *Sessional Information Digests*.

Bills, other than financial bills, may be introduced in either House, although major government bills usually go first to the Commons, especially if they are likely to be strongly opposed by the opposition parties. The advantage of starting some bills in the Lords is twofold: first, it gets some bills on their way early in the session and reduces the legislative burden on the upper house later in the session, as the queue of Commons' bills builds up; and, second, it often saves time for the Commons, as the Lords will have done most of the donkey-work on such bills. There is, however, a potentially important disadvantage – bills introduced first in the House of Lords are not subject to the Parliament Acts, 1911 and 1949, so that the Commons cannot override the Lords' veto should serious conflict arise over such bills. This happened in the 1999–2000 session with the Criminal Justice (Mode of Trial) Bill, which sought to limit the right to trial by jury. Although the bill passed its second reading in the Lords, it was withdrawn by the government at the beginning of the committee stage, when what is known as a 'wrecking amendment' was passed. The government then reintroduced the same bill in the Commons, as the Criminal Justice (Mode of Trial) (No. 2) Bill, but this time it was rejected on second reading by the Lords and again withdrawn to allow further discussions on the proposals to take place. Eventually, yet another attempt was made in the 2003–04 session and became law, but only after further clashes between the two Houses. This, however is the exception to the rule and all governments start off a significant number of bills in the House of Lords, although Conservative rather than Labour governments are more willing to do so, since Labour is more likely to propose legislation that will attract serious opposition in the upper house. Thus, in the 1992–97 Parliament 39.4 per cent of government bills started in the upper house, compared with 30.7 per cent in the 1997–2001 Parliament.

The first substantive stage of any bill is its second reading. In most cases, as the data relating to the 1999–2000 session in Table 8.5 shows, this is taken on the floor of the House, exclusively so in the House of Lords. Two other alternatives are available in the Commons – a second reading committee or one of the grand committees. Second reading committees are intended to save the full House time and are normally used for a small number of non-controversial bills, such as the Royal Parks (Trading) Bill and the Trustee Bill in 1999–2000. For some years five or six bills were referred to second reading committees, but, apart from four bills in 1994–95, they have been much less used since the early 1990s. In one case in 1994–95, an apparently non-controversial bill, the Family Homes and Domestic Violence Bill, was dealt with by a second reading committee, but subsequently withdrawn when it encountered strong opposition from backbenchers who had not been members of the committee. The second reading of bills exclusively concerned with Scotland (of which there have been few since the Scottish Parliament was established in 1999), Wales or Northern Ireland can be taken in the Scottish, Welsh or Northern Ireland Grand Committees, but these committees mostly

Table 8.5 *Government bills, 1999–2000*

House	Second reading		Committee stage		Report stage		Third reading		Commons/Lords amdts.	Bill withdrawn	Royal assent
Commons	Floor of House	38	Whole House	8	Sep. rep. stage	2	Sep. 3rd rd.	2	20	1*	39
	2nd rd. com.	1	Stand. comm.	29	Rep and 3rd rd.	36	Rep and 3rd rd.	36			
	Both	1	Split	2	No rep. stage	1	No 3rd rd.	1			
Total		40		39		39		39		1	39
Lords	Floor of House	41	Whole House	29	Sep. rep. stage	33	Sep. 3rd rd.	33	16	2†	39
			Grand comm.	8	Rep and 3rd rd.	4	Rep and 3rd rd.	4			
			Both	2	No rep. stage	1	No 3rd rd.	1			
Total		41		39		38		38		2	39

Notes: * Criminal Justice (Mode of Trial) Bill (No. 2) – passed all its Commons' stages, but withdrawn after second reading in the Lords. † Criminal Justice (Mode of Trial) Bill – introduced in House of Lords, but withdrawn during committee stage and Criminal Justice (Mode of Trial Bill) (No. 2) – withdrawn after second reading in the Lords.

deal with other business and the occasional statutory instrument and are seldom used for bills. Any bill given a second reading in either a second reading committee or a grand committee receives a second reading in the whole House without debate, unless the committee recommends against second reading. Second reading debates are wide-ranging, covering any aspect of the bill but not allowing any amendments, which are a matter for the committee and later stages. Major bills are usually debated as the main business on one parliamentary day (i.e. six hours) or, occasionally, two days (twelve hours), less important bills for a shorter period, before being sent for their committee stage. It is rare for a government bill to be rejected at second reading, the last occasion in the Commons being the Shops Bill in 1986, proposing that shops be allowed to open on Sundays.[6]

The purpose of the committee stage is to examine bills in detail and, if appropriate, pass amendments to existing clauses or introduce new ones. Although each clause and schedule must be approved, only new clauses and those for which amendments have been tabled are actually debated, so that any number of clauses may be approved without debate. It is therefore misleading to describe the committee stage as a line-by-line examination of the bill. Moreover, in the Commons bills are subject to strict timetables, either agreed through the usual channels or imposed by the use of a guillotine motion normally enforced by the government's majority. There is also an important procedural difference between committee stage debates and all other debates in that only in a committee stage debate may an MP or peer speak more than once, other than to raise a point of order or in other limited circumstances. This is to facilitate detailed consideration of a bill. The committee stage in either House may be taken by the full House – a proceeding known as committee of the whole House – or in a committee (a standing committee in the Commons, a public bill committee or the Grand Committee in the Lords). In the Lords most bills are taken in a committee of the whole, but the reverse is the case in the Commons, as the data in Table 8.5 shows. Using a committee to take the committee stage is simply a means of enabling the House concerned to deal with more than one bill at a time or to allow other business to be taken in the floor of the House, but the pressure on the Lords to make more use of committees has been much less than on the Commons. However, the Lords began to make more use of public bill committees, but they proved unpopular with peers because they limited participation to the members of the committee, so the device of the Grand Committee was introduced in 1994. Any peer may attend and participate but no divisions may take place and only unanimously agreed amendments may be made, so that the practice is confined to non-controversial bills, as agreed through the usual channels. In the 1997–2001 Parliament, twenty-two, mostly government bills, were dealt with by the Grand Committee procedure, including eight government bills in 1999–2000. Occasionally in the Lords, a bill is referred to a select committee to hear expert evidence before being committed to a committee of the whole

House, but in most cases these are Private Members' bills rather than government bills. Joint committees may be similarly used, but the only existing example is the Tax Law Rewrite Committee, which takes the committee stage of tax simplification bills.

The decision in the Commons as to whether a bill is taken on the floor of the House or in a committee depends on the bill concerned. Major constitutional bills, such as Representations of the People Bills, those on devolution, and the Human Rights Bill, or those in which a large number of MPs are interested will normally be taken in a committee of the whole House. So also will non-controversial bills that require little parliamentary time, since referring them to a committee will take longer, and bills, controversial or not, of a particularly urgent nature are similarly taken on the floor. It also depends on political circumstances in that, although a government with a majority is entitled to a majority on any committee, a small government majority may make control of the committee more difficult and therefore easier to take the bill on the floor of the House. Some evidence of this can be found in that the 1992–97 Conservative government, which began with a majority of twenty-one, only to find it gradually reduced by by-election losses, referred 46.9 per cent of its bills to standing committees, whereas between 1997 and 2001, with its massive majority, the Labour government referred 62.9 per cent of its bills. There are usually seven or eight standing committees, each comprising between sixteen and fifty members (in practice mostly between twenty and thirty), in proportion to party representation in the House. As noted in Chapter 7, standing committees are essentially miniatures of the House both in procedure and appearance, reproducing the adversarial confrontation of the Chamber. The term 'standing' is a misnomer, for, although they were standing or permanent committees when first used in the late nineteenth century, in practice a new committee is appointed for each bill referred. Standing Committee A, B and so on therefore have a shifting membership, partly reflecting expertise and interest in the bill concerned and partly members appointed by the whips to make up the necessary numbers. Procedurally, the members are appointed by a Committee of Selection, but the committee basically accepts the nominations put forward by the whips. Unlike other committees, ministers and opposition frontbenchers are members, leading for the respective sides, and party whips also serve on standing committees, as do the overwhelming majority of backbenchers. The standing committees make a major contribution to the legislative work of the Commons, meeting for about half the total time spent in the Chamber. They have no powers to take oral or written evidence, but since 1980 there has been a provision for special standing committees, which do have such powers. However, after an initial flurry between 1980 and 1984, they have been little used – twice in 1992–97 and only once in 1997–2001, although the Adoption and Children Bill was referred to a special standing committee in 2001–02. The reason is not so much the time taken – a maximum of only three additional sittings are allowed – as the potential for opening or re-opening matters the government regards as having settled at the pre-legislative stage through consultation. The committee stage may also be taken by a select committee, as happened with the Armed Forces Bill and the Adoption and Children Bill in 2000–01, the latter being reintroduced in the first session of the 2001 Parliament. However, where the committee stage of a bill is taken by a select or joint committee, the bill is then referred to a committee of the whole House before proceeding to its final stages. Finally, bills may be divided between a standing committee and the floor – the normal practice for Finance Bills but also used, for instance, for the Political Parties, Elections and Referendums Bill in 1999–2000.

Once a bill has completed its committee stage, it proceeds to the report stage and third reading. Both are taken on the floor of the House. The purpose of the report stage is to accept the bills as amended in committee, not to go over ground covered in the committee stage (although the government may take the opportunity to reverse changes made in committee) but new amendments and clauses can be proposed. In many cases this is to fulfil undertakings made by ministers in committee: the government may specifically promise to bring forward an amendment or new clause, or it will have undertaken to consult outside interests, or merely to look again at a provision in the bill. Such undertakings may also be given with the intention of proposing changes after the bill has been sent to the other House; this is particularly the case with bills passed first by the Commons.

The purpose of the third reading is to take a final look at the bill, but, whereas in the Commons the third reading normally follows immediately upon report to the point that they are taken together, as Table 8.5 shows, and amendments are rare. In the Lords these two stages are usually separate and amendments on third reading are the norm. A further important difference at both report and third reading in the Commons is that amendments are selected by the chair, with some being rejected and others grouped together for discussion. This is done in a politically neutral fashion, governed to a considerable extent by detailed procedural rules. In the Lords, however, there is no selection and all amendments can be debated, although, as in most of its proceedings, the upper house operates a self-denying ordinance that militates against filibustering. Therefore, should a majority in the Lords strongly oppose a bill, it will not be talked out but be amended against the government's wishes, particularly at the committee and report stages.

Having completed all its stages in one House, a bill is then passed to the other and goes through a similar process. About 50 per cent of government bills first introduced in the Commons are amended in the Lords and about 40 per cent of those first introduced in the Lords are amended in the Commons. These changes may be accepted or rejected by the other House or some compromise agreed, in which case the bill will proceed to the formality of the royal assent, but in the event of an impasse the bill cannot proceed further, unless the Parliament Acts are invoked. In practice, as Table 8.3 clearly shows, few government bills fail to complete their passage through Parliament and, until 1991 the 1911 Parliament Act had been used on only three occasions – twice in 1914 and then to pass the 1949 Parliament Act. Of course, conflict between the two Houses has always been far more likely when the Labour Party is in office, but the operation of the Salisbury Convention from 1945, by which the Lords did not oppose the second reading of bills fulfilling manifesto commitments, nor usually prevent the ultimate passing of a bill by using wrecking amendments, undoubtedly helped. Moreover, although the Lords reserve the right to amend manifesto bills and to oppose bills not fore-shadowed in the manifesto, when conflict over Lords' amendments persist the upper house usually gives way. Nonetheless, in 1968–69 and twice during the 1974–79 Parliament the House of Lords effectively killed two bills by refusing to back down. Even then, the latter two bills were passed after amend-ments were agreed and the bills reintroduced the following session. In 1990, however, the Lords rejected the Conservative government's War Crimes Bill and in 1991, for the first time since 1949, a bill was passed using the Parlia-ment Acts. And then, in 1999 the Parliament Acts were used to pass the European Parliament Elections Bill and again in 2000 to pass the Sexual Offences (Amendment) Bill. This renewed willingness to use the Parliament Acts and the removal of most of the hereditary peers in 1999, has increased the likelihood of conflict between the Lords and Commons. Greater use of the Parliament Acts may encourage the Lords to refuse to pass government bills it strongly opposes and the removal of most of the hereditaries appears to have given the upper house a greater sense of legitimacy.

That said, compromises between Commons and Lords – in effect between the government and the upper house – are also brought about by pressures of legislative time, especially towards the end of a parliamentary session, since a bill must normally pass all its stages in both Houses within a single parlia-mentary session, otherwise it dies. In such circumstances, the government may reluctantly accept Lords' amendments or agree a compromise solution. This pressure towards the end of the session has been partly relieved by the introduction of the carry-over of bills from one session to the next. This was introduced initially in 1998 and first used on the Financial Services and Mar-kets Bill, which had partially completed its passage through the Commons in 1998–99 and was reintroduced in 1999–2000, eventually receiving the royal assent. The principle of carry-over was incorporated in Commons' standing orders in October 2002 for an experimental period, but can only be used if the House passes a specific resolution for the bill concerned and only for one additional session. This provision, however, applies only to bills in the Com-mons, not the Lords, and the carry-over of bills in the Lords can be used only on bills that have been subject to pre-legislative scrutiny in the upper house – another example of the significance of the procedural autonomy of the two Houses. In practice, the carry-over of bills has not yet had a major impact on the handling of legislation – only two bills were carried over from 2002–03 to

Table 8.6   *Number of amendments* to government bills, 1968–69 and 1970–71*

Amdt moved by	Amdts moved	Amdts passed	% passed
House of Commons			
Government	2,649	2,648	99.9
Govt backbenchers	253	30	11.9
Opposition	1,930	97	5.0
Total	4,832	2,775	57.4
House of Lords			
Government	1,042	1,040	99.8
Govt backbenchers	57	11	19.3
Opposition/crossbenchers	900	132	14.7
Total	1,999	1,183	59.2

Source: J. A. Griffith, *Parliamentary Scrutiny of Government Bills*, Allen & Unwin, London, 1974, Appendices 1–3.

Note: * Including new clauses.

2003–04 and the earlier return of the Commons in September is likely to ease but not remove the end of session log-jam.

What effect does all this legislative activity in Parliament have on government bills? Because most, sometimes all, government bills are passed does not mean that they are unamended. Some, of course, are not, but most are, some extensively. However, to answer this question more precisely is more difficult: Parliament, especially the Commons, now publishes far more information about its working than it has since the late nineteenth and early twentieth centuries, but not so much on the crucial legislative stages of committee and report in both Houses and the third reading in the Lords. The most detailed study available covering one or more sessions was published in 1974 and covered three sessions in the Commons and two in the Lords. Table 8.6 shows amendments made to government bills in 1968–69 and 1970–71.

The data shows clearly that large numbers of amendments were made or new clauses inserted in the two sessions, but it also shows that the overwhelming majority were government amendments, to the point that virtually all government amendments are approved. Furthermore, more detailed analysis showed that most were drafting amendments rather than changes of substance. Of course, changes in wording are not necessarily trivial, usually having the intention of clarifying the consequent law, an important factor in the implementation of policy. On the other hand, some changes of substance are made, most of which result from representations made by outside interests or from points raised during the passage of bills through

Table 8.7   *Number of amendments* to the Broadcasting Bill, 1990*

Amdt moved by	Amdts moved	Amdts passed	% passed
House of Commons			
Government	567	561	98.8
Govt backbenchers	174	5	2.9
Opposition	674	20	3.0
Total	1,415	586	41.4
House of Lords			
Government	771	761	99.7
Govt backbenchers	139	5	3.6
Opposition/crossbenchers	674	20	2.6
Total	1,250	586	62.0

Source: The Hansard Society, *Making the Law: The Report of the Hansard Society Commission on the Legislative Process*, Hansard Society, London, 1992, Appendix 5.

Note: * Including new clauses.

Parliament. More recent data simply reiterates the picture that emerges from the 1974 study, as the figures for changes to the 1990 Broadcasting Bill show (see Table 8.7).

That a similar situation prevails can be illustrated by pointing out that the Criminal Justice and Public Order Bill in 1994 attracted nearly 800 amendments, with 96.7 per cent of government amendments being passed but only 18.8 per cent of amendments moved by others[7] and by noting that government bills continue to substantially amended in the House of Lords (see Table 8.8).

Yet further evidence that government bills are changed as they go through Parliament is the extent to which they grow longer: in 1996–97 the length of government bills increased by 9.5 per cent and in 1999–2000 by 30.4 per cent, and the 1998 Finance Bill tripled in length.[8] It is therefore an assumption that the dealing with government bills in Parliament is little more than a rubber-stamping process. Only rarely does a government fail to secure the passage of a bill because it cannot carry its backbench supporters with it. In 1968–69 the then Labour government managed the unusual feat of losing two bills – one on Lords' reform and the other on the reform of industrial relations – and in 1986 Conservative backbenchers defeated their government's attempt to change the law on Sunday trading, but these are exceptions to the general rule. Changes to government bills as they go through Parliament are the norm and governments listen to criticism from inside and outside Parliament and are open to persuasion. Consequently, governments will often accept detailed changes that do not affect the main policy thrust of the bill.

Table 8.8   *Amendments* to government bills made in the House of Lords, 1999–2000*

Bills passed by the Commons			Bills introduced in the Lords		
Amdts tabled	Amdts passed	% passed	Amdts tabled	Amdts passed	% passed
8,715	3,794	43.5	2,267	942	41.6

Source: House of Lords, *Sessional Statistics, 1999–2000.*

Note: * Including new clauses.

Table 8.9   *The formal timetabling of bills, 1945–2001*

Period	No. of bills	Guillotine motions	Programme motions	Total timetabling motions
1945–74	28	33	–	33
1974–97	73	103	–	103
1997–2001	63	41	55	96

Source: House of Commons Library, *Factsheet Series P No. 10: Guillotine and Timetabling Motions,* 2001 and House of Commons, *Sessional Information Digests.*

That said, the extent to which bills are changed is also a sign of that many bills are not sufficiently well-prepared when presented for their first reading.

The willingness to listen and the under-preparation of bills is part of the explanation for the amending of government bills, but another important reason is time. The government's legislative programme is always crowded and all bills are timetabled, formally or informally. Moreover, timetabling has increased since 1945, as Table 8.9 shows. As the volume of government legislation has expanded, so the pressure on parliamentary time has increased, but in most Parliaments since 1945 the actual number of bills subject to guillotine motions was small, not reaching double figures until the 1974–79 Parliament, when the Labour government was in a minority for most of the time and found it necessary to use the guillotine. However, the more frequent use of the guillotine continued in succeeding Parliaments, especially that of 1987–92. Much depends generally on the extent to which the opposition chooses to oppose particular government bills, but two other factors also contributed to this trend. The first was the guillotining of the second reading of some bills and, the second, the growing activism of the upper house, resulting in the guillotining of Lords' amendments.

Bills not formally timetabled are mostly timetabled by agreement through the usual channels, but there has been growing support for the regular timetabling of all or most government bills[9] and, the Modernisation Committee, set up after the 1997 general election, proposed the formal programming of bills. This was through programme motions agreed by government and opposition. In 1997–98 more bills were subject to agreed programme motions than to guillotine motions, but the process began to break down in the following session, with more bills guillotined than programmed, and from 1999–2000 most programme motions were imposed by the government, since the opposition concluded that they were too helpful to the government. From the government's point of view, programme motions are more flexible than guillotine motions because they are more easily modified as the bill proceeds. However, although timetabling may help the government get bills through the Commons, it does not necessarily result in effective scrutiny of government legislation. John Griffith's analysis of the 1967–68 and 1968–69 sessions showed that half the bills considered took up between 8 and 9 per cent of the time, whereas 28 per cent of the bills took between 75 and 81 per cent. There is no reason to believe that the picture has changed significantly since then. In practice, this means that with many bills some parts are not discussed at all and others are inadequately discussed during their passage through the Commons, leaving a good deal of work to be done on them as they go through the Lords. The adage that 'the opposition gets its say, but the government gets its way' has much truth in it, although the opposition would likely argue that the guillotine and programme motions significantly reduce its say.

In fact, the problem goes deeper. It is not just governments trying to cram as much legislation as they can into the parliamentary year, but also of the whole legislative process being rushed. Consultation is more widespread and systematic but often inadequate or with important gaps; this in turn means that bills are often inadequately drafted, quite apart from the time pressure on the parliamentary draftsmen; not enough bills are presented to Parliament in draft form, often because to do so prolongs the legislative process; arrangements for the implementation of policy contained in bills often amount to little more than assigning political and administrative responsibility to government departments and agencies; and the implications of a particular policy or set of proposals, especially for other policy areas, are not always fully addressed. Through its various non-legislative scrutiny mechanisms, Parliament can check policy implementation, whether an Act of Parliament has achieved its objectives and is working well, but there is no systematic post-legislative process and it may not be until those affected, directly or indirectly, by a particular policy make their feelings known that the government becomes aware of any problems. Governments wish to make their mark, to implement changes and pursue policies they believe to be right, but time becomes of the essence: the former Labour Prime Minister, Harold Wilson, once remarked that 'a week in politics is a long time'; as the next general election looms, four or five years seem even shorter.

There is, however, another perspective, an important one. Whatever its imperfections, the legislative process in Parliament exposes government bills to public scrutiny by forcing the government to explain and defend the policies it seeks to implement through that process. Government bills normally pass but not without explanation, even though the quality of that explanation could be improved by more effective scrutiny.

Private Members' bills

Nearly three times as many public bills are introduced by backbenchers than by the government, but whereas the government expects to see all its bills become acts, only 15 per cent of Private Members' bills (PMBs) became law in 1992–97 and only 5.7 per cent in 1997–2001. Moreover, government bills are introduced with the clear intention of changing the law; PMBs may be introduced for a variety of reasons. Some, of course, are introduced in the hope that the law will be changed by the end of the session, but others are used as part of a long-term campaign for a change in the law, or to secure publicity on a particular issue or cause, or to make a partisan or ideological point. For example, following the drowning of several young people from his constituency in a canoeing tragedy, David Jamieson, MP for Plymouth (Devonport), introduced a bill to regulate activity centres, which failed through lack of time, but in 1995 he successfully piloted the Activity Centres (Young Persons' Safety) Bill through Parliament, after coming second in the Members' ballot for PMBs. A longer-running campaign was that of Lord Lester and other peers in seeking the incorporation of the European Convention on Human Rights into UK law by introducing a series of Human Rights Bills before it became government policy, following Labour's election victory in 1997 and the enactment of the Human Rights Act, 1998. MPs regularly, and peers less often, also table bills clearly reflecting their partisan or personal ideological views – bills to secure the UK's withdrawal from the EU or to secure referendums on this or other controversial issues are common and, Tony Benn, former Labour MP, regularly tabled bills to bring about major constitutional changes he favoured. In short, PMBs can simply be a means by which MPs express their views, in the same way as they do by tabling motions; they can also be used by MPs to secure publicity and claim to be taking action over some issue, even though the chances of action taking place are minimal. Peers, however, make less use of PMBs, using them either in an effort to change the law as quickly as possible or as part of a longer-term campaign.

The tactical considerations of securing the passage of government bills and PMBs are also different. Once in the government's legislative programme, government bills are normally assured of majority support and enough parliamentary time to secure their passage, but PMBs must win majority support and compete for very limited parliamentary time – a mere thirteen Fridays

Table 8.10   *Types of Private Members' Bills*

Type	Procedure
Ballot bills	Ballot, open to all backbench MPs, held at the beginning of each parliamentary session. Twenty names drawn, with the order determining priority for second reading, but not for later stages
Ten-minute rule bills	Opportunity for MPs to introduce a bill after parliamentary Questions and ministerial statements on Tuesdays and Wednesdays. The proposer is given ten minutes to state the case for the bill and one MP (if any) is given ten minutes to state the case against. The House then votes on it without further debate and, if passed, it joins the queue of existing Private Members' bills
Presentation bills	Any backbench MP may present a bill without a debate or a vote on any sitting day. It is then printed and joins the queue of existing Private Members' bills
Bills from the House of Lords	Any peer may introduce a Private Members' bill and time is normally found for its consideration. If it passes all its stage in the Lords, it proceeds to the Commons, where it joins the queue of existing Private Members' bills

per session. Little is left to chance with government bills, but chance plays a massive role in the fate of PMBs.

In the House of Commons, PMBs may be introduced by any Member, but by convention ministers, whips and opposition frontbenchers do not normally do so. The same applies to the House of Lords, but whereas a peer simply tables a bill and time will be found for its consideration, MPs may use one of three methods (Table 8.10) – by winning a place in the annual ballot to introduce a bill, by what is known as 'the ten-minute rule', or by simply tabling or presenting a bill – and these have a considerable affect on a bill's chances of success. This is because, in effect, bills form a queue, with balloted bills initially taking precedence, followed by ten-minute rule and presentation bills in that order. Some bills will be rejected at second reading, others will fail to complete it and go to the end of the queue, allowing lower-ranked ballot bills, ten-minute rule and presentation bills to move up the queue. Tactics are of great importance, both in deciding when to move the particular stage of a bill and in securing support and minimising opposition. One of the problems faced by the sponsors and supporters of a bill is that their opponents may prolong proceedings on another bill ahead of it in the queue and, to secure a vote on his or her bill, the sponsoring Member must find a way of ensuring that at least a hundred MPs are available to vote. PMBs are not formally subject to party whipping, so that sponsors must do their own whipping.

Table 8.11   *The success rate of Private Members' bills, 1992–2001*

Session	Ballot	Presentation	10-minute	Lords	Total
1992–93	30.0	4.8	2.7	55.6	7.8
1993–94	40.0	5.4	0.0	60.0	13.8
1994–95	45.0	3.1	5.8	44.4	15.0
1995–96	60.0	5.9	2.3	33.3	19.1
1996–97	70.0	0.0	3.8	100.0	28.9
1992–97	*49.0*	*3.5*	*2.9*	*56.8*	*15.2*
1997–98	25.0	7.4	1.1	16.7	6.8
1998–99	35.0	0.0	0.0	25.0	7.7
1999–2000	25.0	0.0	0.0	85.7	5.8
2000–01	0.0	0.0	0.0	0.0	0.0
1997–2001	*21.3*	*2.4*	*0.4*	*36.0*	*5.7*

Source: House of Commons, *Factsheet L2: Private Members' Bills Procedure.*

What is absolutely crucial, however, is the attitude of the government. If the government is opposed to a bill, it will almost certainly fail: formal whipping may not take place but informal whipping can and ministers will normally make it clear whether or not they favour a bill. In some instances, the government may take stronger action against a bill, encouraging its backbenchers to speak and vote against it. In 1994, the then Minister of State for Social Security, Sir Nicholas Scott, was forced to admit that his department had provided government backbenchers with amendments to the Civil Rights (Disabled Persons) Bill, leading it to run out of time, and was forced to apologise to the House of Commons. It is also the case that bills strongly opposed by other backbenchers will often fail, not necessarily because a majority votes against them but because time constraints and procedural obstacles make it easy to prevent a bill making progress.

PMBs introduced and passing all their stages in the Lords before coming to the Commons are the most likely to succeed, as the figures in Table 8.11 show, but these need to be seen in the context of the few bills that come to the Commons by this route and the far smaller number of PMBs introduced in the Lords – a mere 44 compared with 540 in the Commons in the 1992–97 Parliament and 32 compared with 393 in the 1997–2001 Parliament. These aside, ballot bills offer the greatest chance of success. Ballot bills therefore receive a good deal of attention from various organisations and individuals wishing to see changes in the law and, as soon as the results of the annual ballot are announced, the MPs with the first ten or so slots will be inundated with offers of possible bills to promote. A major source, in fact, is government departments, almost all of whom have bills that did not secure a place in the government's legislative programme, usually of a non-controversial nature, and the department concerned will provide drafting assistance and advice. These include bills drafted by the Law Commission or the Criminal Law Review Body, proposing limited but sometimes important changes in the law. Then there are pressure groups, often with bills already drafted and willing to provide advice and other support as the bill goes through Parliament. MPs who were not successful in the ballot are another possible source. Much also depends on the personal interests of individual MPs: most backbenchers put their names into the ballot each session and some have a proposal firmly in mind, others not, but the latter will often choose bills that reflect their particular concerns or interests, whether it is a departmental bill, a pressure group one, or taking up a current issue. Many MPs relish the opportunity to get a bill onto the statute book and some will choose one that is likely to pass, rather than one strongly opposed.

Ultimately, the three key factors are time, tactics and the attitude of the government. Most PMBs fail simply through lack of parliamentary time, not because they lack merit or support; tactics are crucial, especially if the bill is at all controversial; but it is the government's attitude that matters most. From the mid-1950s through to the late 1970s and in a limited number of cases, governments were willing to provide government time for particular bills, either because they favoured the bill concerned or felt that MPs should be given the opportunity to decide whether to change the law on a particular issue. This was the case with nine bills between 1956 and 1976. A number concerned social or moral issues in which governments preferred to avoid direct involvement, such as obscene publications, the abolition of the death penalty, homosexuality, abortion and divorce, all which were addressed by PMBs passed during this period. They were also issues on which MPs did not divide on party lines. However, governments became increasingly reluctant to provide time and, since 1988, they have seldom done so, although in the final shortened sessions of the 1987–92 and 1992–97 Parliaments the Conservatives did provide time for MPs to decide the fate of PMBs that had completed most of their stages. The Labour government elected in 1997 made it clear that it was not prepared to provide government time for PMBs, although the occasional exception has occurred – for example, for the Census (Amendment) Bill (1999–2000), while the Tobacco Advertisement and Promotion Bill was adopted as a government bill in 2002. The long struggle to secure the passage of a bill to ban fox and stag hunting provides a different example. In its 1997 election manifesto Labour promised to ensure that MPs would have the opportunity to vote on the issue, as indeed they did, but the first attempt to pass a hunting bill failed, like many other bills, through lack of time. A subsequent bill failed to pass the Lords and Labour repeated its pledge to allow MPs to vote on the issue, eventually introducing a government bill incorporating options to ban hunting, on the one hand, or to regulate it, on the other. MPs voted for a ban, peers for regulation, and the ban became law using the Parliament Acts. This tactic of taking up issues formerly left to PMBs by incorporating choices in a government bill has also been used for Sunday trading law and lowering the age of consent in homosexual relationships.

What can be said more broadly is that PMBs provide a means of directly changing the law, and therefore policy, on matters for which the government has not found parliamentary time, so that changes take place earlier than would otherwise be the case, and to deal with issues that governments are reluctant to address (see Table 8.12). But they can also be used to get issues on to the policy agenda or move them up that agenda, either as part of a longer-term campaign or drawing attention to an issue of more immediate public concern. Governments may be forced to act, sometimes sooner, sometimes later, or at least say why the law should not be changed. Between 1945 and 1948, Attlee's Labour government took over most Private Members' time, including that normally available for PMBs, for government business saying that its programme of economic and social reform required it. Whether this action was justified is a matter of opinion, but there are reasonable grounds for arguing that PMBs make a positive contribution to Parliament's legislative function. Cynics might well say that this is because many of the PMBs that pass are really government bills, but that supports the argument more than it undermines it.

Secondary legislation

Secondary or delegated legislation has become an increasingly important part of the legislative output of government: from less than a thousand in 1900, the annual number of statutory instruments (the main form of domestic secondary legislation) normally exceeds three thousand. There is, in addition, a constant and growing flow of legislation from the EU, which national parliaments are expected to scrutinise, though not directly to approve. Parliament has therefore developed mechanisms to deal with both.

Domestic delegated legislation

Although the long-term trend is upward, the figures in Table 8.13 show that the number of statutory instruments (SIs) remained steady during the period 1995–2002. However, this ignores the impact of devolution: from July 1999 the Scottish Parliament and the National Assembly for Wales became responsible for dealing with delegated legislation within the areas of their legislative competence,[10] but this has had little effect on the number of SIs issued by the UK government. The higher figure for 2001 reflects the 597 SIs the government issued to deal with the outbreak of foot-and-mouth that year. The actual volume of domestic delegated legislation exceeds that of primary legislation by a factor of more than three – some 10,000 pages a year, compared to 3,000. Like Acts of Parliament, SIs divide into those that have general and those that have local application but, unlike Acts, with about half the SIs falling into each category.

Table 8.12 *Examples of successful Private Members' bills*

Act	Purpose
Matrimonial Causes Act, 1937	Extend the ground for divorce
Obscene Publications Act, 1959*	Relax censorship laws
Murder (Abolition of Death Penalty) Act, 1965*	Suspended the death penalty for murder. Later made permanent
Sexual Offences (Amdt) Act, 1967*	Legalised homosexual acts between consenting adults
Abortion Act, 1967*	Legalised abortion
Unsolicited Goods and Services (Amdt) Act, 1975	Regulated the sending of unsolicited goods and services to private individuals
Sexual Offences (Amdt) Act, 1976*	Provided for anonymity in rape cases
Housing (Homeless Persons) Act, 1977	Placed a requirement on local authorities to house homeless persons
British Nationality (Falkland Islands) Act, 1983	Conferred British nationality on Falkland Islanders, following the Argentine invasion of 1982
Video Recordings Act, 1984	Regulated the sale of 'video nasties'
Access to Personal Files Act, 1986	Providing individuals with right of access to their records on e.g. health, education, housing, employment, social services and welfare held by various organisations
Scotch Whisky Act, 1988	Defining and regulating the production and sale of Scotch whisky
Marriage (Registration of Buildings) Act, 1990	Allowing various buildings in addition to churches, other religious buildings and register offices to be licensed for marriage ceremonies
Chiropractors Act, 1994	Regulating the practice of chiropracty
Theft (Amdt) Act, 1997	Correcting an anomaly in the law, following a ruling by the Law Lords
Pesticides Act, 1998	Extending the powers of local authorities to regulate and control the use of pesticides
Protection of Children Act, 1999	Compilation and maintenance of a list of persons unsuitable to work with children

Note: *Given government time.

Table 8.13   *Number of statutory instruments, 1995–2002*

Year	Number
1995	3,345
1996	3,291
1997	3,114
1998	3,323
1999	3,343
2000	3,202
2001	3,806
2002	2,959

Source: www.hmso.gov.uk/si-statistics.htm.

Table 8.14   *Examples of statutory instruments*

SI (no.)	Type
	General instruments
2713	The Access to the Countryside (Exclusions and Restrictions) (England) Regulations 2003
2743	The Offshore Installations (Safety Zones) (No. 3) Order 2003
2747	The Individual Savings Account (Amendment) Regulations 2003
2762	The Motor Vehicle Tyres (Safety) (Amendment) (No. 2) Regulations 2003
2775	The Judicial Pensions and Retirement Act 1993 (Qualifying Judicial Offices) (Amendment) Order 2003
2779	The Child Support (Miscellaneous Amendments) (No. 2) Regulations 2003
	Local instruments
2711	The Road Traffic (Permitted Parking Area and Special Parking Area) Metropolitan Borough of Wirral) Order 2003
2724	The Lancaster Port Commission Harbour Revision (Constitution) Order 2003
2769	The City of Birmingham (Electoral Changes) Order 2003

Source: www.parliament.uk.

The examples shown in Table 8.14 give some idea of the enormous range of matters covered by delegated legislation. About four-fifths of the local instruments are orders dealing with roads and road traffic, bridges, and rights of way, but general instruments range more widely. In 2002, for instance, 310 related to the NHS, 151 to education, 88 to social security, 59 to road traffic, and 48 to taxation. In fact, delegated legislation impinges on people's lives far more than primary legislation, since it is concerned with the implementation of policy, whether it relates to NHS services, education, social services, pensions, welfare and other benefits, transport, planning and the environment, and so on. Nonetheless, it can also include politically controversial issues, such as 'bovine spongiform encephalopathy (BSE), the sale of food with genetically-modified ingredients, the outlawing of the use of imperial measurements in shops, the powers of the Home Secretary to detain dangerous paedophiles in custody, drink-driving laws, the Child Support Agency, highly-contested road schemes, drought orders and cold weather payments to old age pensioners'.[11] Less often, it can be used to effect a major shift in government policy, as happened when the then Ministry of Education issued Circular 10/65 requiring local education; authorities to draw up plans for comprehensive secondary education; and in areas like entitlement to benefits, taxation and immigration rules, more limited but nevertheless important shifts in policy can occur. Parliament, however, is not required to deal with local instruments, so that what follows relates to the parliamentary scrutiny of general instruments.

Except for SIs on financial matters, which like their equivalent in primary legislation, are dealt with by the Commons, both Houses scrutinise delegated legislation. This scrutiny takes the two forms – technical and substantive. The technical is concerned with whether each SI meets a number of legal and other criteria and is carried out by the Joint Committee on Statutory Instruments (JCSI), the Commons' half of which deals with financial SIs. The committee has fourteen members, drawn equally from the two Houses and by convention is chaired by an opposition MP. It has legal advice available through the Speaker's Counsel and the Counsel of the Lord Chairman of Committees and may require government departments to submit explanatory memoranda or to send witnesses in response to concerns expressed by the committee on any instrument. The grounds on which the committee may draw the attention of Parliament to a particular instrument are shown in Box 8.1.

The JCSI expresses concern about a fairly small proportion of SIs, mostly on the grounds of defective drafting, with others requiring further explanation or where the authority to issue an instrument is in doubt. A much smaller proportion are mentioned because of delay (see Table 8.15).

Box 8.1   The technical scrutiny of statutory instruments (SIs)

Grounds for drawing special attention to statutory instrument

1 Imposes a financial charge.
2 Excluded from challenge in the courts.
3 Retrospective effect.
4 Unjustifiable delay in publication or laying before Parliament.
5 Ultra vires.
6 Requires elucidation.
7 Defective drafting.

Table 8.15   *Reasons for drawing attention to SIs, 1992–2000*

Reason	1992–97	1997–2000
Defective drafting	52.2	64.8
Elucidation required	22.2	10.8
Vires in doubt	16.3	12.5
Delay	1.2	4.5
Other	8.1	7.3
Total reported	16.6	8.0

Source: Robert Blackburn and Andrew Kennon, *Griffith and Ryle on Parliament: Functions, Practice and Procedures*, London: Sweet & Maxwell, 2nd edn, 2003, pp. 335–6.

Page argues that the technical scrutiny of SIs is not a problem, other than making the important observation that the JCSI is overworked, but goes further by suggesting that the committee has an impact that goes beyond those SIs that are reported: 'The likely reaction of the JCSI is in the minds of those that draft any SI, since what they draft will be eventually referred to it.'[12]

Those SIs which require parliamentary approval are subject to one of two procedures, affirmative or negative procedure (see Box 8.2). Under affirmative procedure an instrument will not take effect unless approved by both Houses of Parliament, unless it concerns finance, in which case it must be approved by the Commons alone. This is subject to a time limit of 28 or 40 days, depending on what is laid down in the enabling or parent act. Negative procedure means that an instrument will come into effect on a specified date unless either House refuses to approve it. Only about one SI in eight is subject to affirmative procedure, usually those dealing with important matters, such as levels of social security benefits, tax changes between Budgets, local government finance, and issues likely to arouse some controversy. In the Commons, affirmative instruments are automatically considered by a standing committee on delegated legislation, unless the minister concerned proposes that they be debated on the floor of the House. Those referred to a standing committee, which, like those on the committee stage of bills, are set up anew for each referral – between ten and twelve are appointed each year, are debated for a maximum for $1\frac{1}{2}$ hours. However, a committee may not amend an instrument, merely reporting to the House that it has considered it. There then follows a $1\frac{1}{2}$-hour debate in the House, but again the instrument may not be amended, only accepted or rejected. In practice, rejection is rare. Negative procedure in the Commons is similar, except that an SI is referred to a standing committee or debated in the House only if an MP tables a motion, known as a 'prayer', against it. In practice, the proportion of negative instruments prayed against is small, averaging less than 10 per cent in the 1997–2001

Box 8.2   Parliamentary approval of SIs

Affirmative procedure

The SI must be approved by both Houses (except for those on financial matters, which need only Commons' approval) within 28 or 40 days, according to the enabling act, to come into effect.

Negative procedure

The SI will come into effect on a specific date unless either House (except for those on financial matters, which need only Commons' approval) passes a motion calling for its annulment (usually within 40 days).

Scrutiny process

House of Commons
The SI is automatically referred to a Standing Committee on Delegated Legislation unless the minister concerned tables a motion for it to be debated in the House.

Scrutiny process

House of Commons
The SI may be referred to a Standing Committee on Delegated Legislation or, if the minister concerned tables a motion, debated in the House.

House of Lords
May be debated on the floor of the House.

House of Lords
May be debated on the floor of the House.

Table 8.16   *Consideration of statutory instruments by the House of Commons, 1999–2000*

Action	Affirmative instruments	Negative instruments
SIs laid	180	1,241
Considered by House	17	4
Considered by stand. com.	157	16

Source: Robert Blackburn and Andrew Kennon, *Griffith and Ryle on Parliament: Functions, Practice and Procedures,* London: Sweet & Maxwell, 2nd edn, 2003, 348–9.

Parliament, and is declining for reasons that are unclear.[13] Moreover, it is important to note that, while the government normally accedes to 'prayers' from the opposition frontbench, those tabled by backbenchers often go unanswered. Even here, the government is reluctant to allow time on the floor of the House, so that most 'prayers' are dealt with in standing committees. The operation of both procedures is shown in Table 8.16.

In the House of Lords all proceedings on SIs take place on the floor of the House, but as with the Commons few are actually debated and only rarely is an SI rejected. However, in 2000 the Lords rejected two orders regarding elections to the Greater London Assembly, 'flushed with the new legitimacy which was said by ministers to have followed' the removal of most of the hereditary peers by the House of Lords Act 1999.[14] It should also be noted that the government cannot use the Parliament Acts to override the rejection of an instrument by the upper house, a situation the Blair government has said it will alter.

As with primary legislation, much delegated legislation is in practice subject to consultation with those likely to be affected by it. Page found that 85 per cent of more than 300 outside organisations he surveyed said that they were consulted about SIs – most of the time' (54 per cent) or 'some of the time (31 per cent), only 9 per cent saying 'rarely' and 3 per cent 'never'. In addition, more than two-thirds said that government departments either 'listen and usually make changes' (5 per cent) or 'listen and sometimes make changes' (66 per cent), although a quarter (26 per cent) replied that departments 'listen and rarely make changes', leaving 3 per cent saying that departments 'don't listen to us'.[15] In some cases the enabling legislation requires consultation to take place, but the principal incentive for the government to consult outside interests is that their support makes it easier to implement regulations. It is also important to note that this process works largely because it takes place behind the scenes in what Page describes as the mundane world of 'everyday politics' or 'low politics', rather than in the much more confrontational and public world of 'high politics'. The extent and nature of the consultation – usually before the presentation of SIs to Parliament – goes some way to meeting the principal criticism of the parliamentary scrutiny of delegated legislation, that Parliament is put in a take-it-or-leave-it situation, since it has no power to amend SIs. The Commons' Procedure Committee has on a number of occasions recommended improvements in the scrutiny of delegated legislation, including the laying of some instruments for affirmative approval in draft, a period of 60 rather than 40 days for those subject to negative procedure, and the on the length of debates on referred SIs. The Hansard Society Commission on the Legislative Process had earlier made similar recommendations, but also recommended that Parliament should be able to amend SIs.[16] In 2002 a Group on the Working Practices of the House of Lords recommended that there should be a Lords' committee empowered to examine the merits of SIs and this was set up in December 2003.

Other steps were taken in this direction in 1994, with the passing of the Deregulation and Contracting Out Act (now superseded by the Regulatory Reform Act 2001). The object of the Act was to reduce the burden of rules and regulations on businesses and the professions. Since this involved using secondary legislation to amend primary legislation, a special procedure had to be established. This led to the setting up of the Deregulation and Regulatory

Reform (now Regulatory Reform) Committee in the Commons and extending the remit of the Delegated Powers and Regulatory Reform Committee (established in 1992) in the Lords. Unlike the other committees dealing with SIs, these two committees examine the purpose of deregulation orders before they are presented in draft form, at which point the committees re-examine the proposals. Furthermore, the period for consultation on such orders is 60 rather than the maximum of 40 days for other SIs. Although the government can normally secure the passage of such orders, especially in the Commons, the wider consideration and longer period for consultation is an improvement on scrutiny arrangements for most delegated legislation. Not surprisingly, the number of deregulation orders was greatest in the years immediately following the passing of the 1994 Act, culminating in 43 proposals and 35 draft orders in 1997–98, but the Regulatory Reform Act in 2001 extended the application of deregulation orders, so that they are likely to continue to be an important part of secondary legislation. Both committees pay particular attention to what are called 'Henry VIII clauses' (so-called because Henry frequently used decrees not requiring parliamentary approval), which allow ministers to use SIs to amend primary legislation. The Lords' committee takes a particular interest in these. Finally, the passing of the Human Rights Act 1998 has led to a similar procedure being used to amend Acts of Parliament to make them compatible with the European Convention of Human Rights. This work is carried out by the Joint Committee on Human Rights, set up in 2001.

European Union legislation

The UK's accession to the European Economic Community, now the European Union (EU), in 1973 meant that legislative proposals put forward by the European Commission in Brussels also needed to be considered by Parliament. In 1974, a Select Committee on European Secondary Legislation (now the European Scrutiny Committee) was set up by the Commons and a Select Committee on the European Communities (now the Select Committee on the European Union) by the Lords. In due course, the range of matters subject to scrutiny broadened, covering not just specific legislative proposals but also other documents prepared by the Commission for consideration of other EU institutions, hence the use of the term 'EU documents'. However, the two committees operate differently, as Table 8.17 shows. The European Scrutiny Committee operates in a similar way to the Statutory Instruments Committee, sifting through documents, referring some to one of three European Standing Committees for further consideration. In 1999–2000 the committee considered 1,205 documents, of which 39.1 per cent were considered in detail as raising matters of legal or political importance. The Lords' European Union Committee operates through six specialised subject sub-committees, drawing on the considerable expertise available in the upper house. These sub-committees examine the policy substance of documents, often taking oral and written

Table 8.17   *The parliamentary scrutiny of European Union documents*

House of Commons	House of Lords
1 Minister lays the document before Parliament	1 Minister lays the document before Parliament
2 The European Scrutiny Committee decides whether it is legally and/or politically significant and whether it should be debated in a European Standing Committee or (rarely) on the floor of the House	2 The Select Committee on the European Union, operating through specialised sub-committees, examines it, taking oral and written evidence from ministers, civil servants, various experts pressure groups and others and reports to the House
3 The minister answers questions and the document is debated in the standing committee	3 The majority of reports are debated in the House, with an oral response from the government
4 A motion to take note of the document is moved on the floor of the House without debate, but with the possibility of a vote and amendment	4 The government makes a written response to most reports

evidence, and issuing reports that are highly regarded at Westminster, in Whitehall and beyond. In 1999–2000, the committee published eighteen reports, but it has become more active since, publishing no fewer than fifty reports in 2002–03, mostly on substantive policy matters. Moreover, it does not confine itself to narrow policy matters but regularly considers the EU Budget and major policy questions, such as relations between the EU and the United States and the proposals for a European Constitution.

However, although both Houses have reasonably effective machinery for examining policy emerging from the EU, only on matters requiring primary legislation, such as the implementation of treaties like Maastricht, Amsterdam or Nice can Parliament reject or amend proposals. Decisions on matters dealt with by the Commons' and Lords' committees are almost all made by the EU Council of Ministers and do not require specific parliamentary approval. Of course, the original European Communities Act 1972 survived bitter opposition in the Commons, as did the legislation implementing Maastricht, but these are exceptions to the rule that Parliament's control over EU matters is severely limited.

The legislative role: an overview

Both Houses of Parliament devote a considerable amount of time and effort to the scrutiny of legislation, both primary and secondary – nearly half the time in the Commons, more than three-fifths in the Lords. Elaborate machinery for this purpose has been developed and refined over many years. Two factors, however, have a crucial impact on the legislative process in Parliament – time and executive dominance. There is always more legislation on the stocks than Parliament has time to consider. This is particularly the case for Private Members' bills, but it is also true of government legislation. Each year ministers compete for the time available in the Commons, over whose agenda and timetable the government has much greater control than it does of the Lords, although in practice the upper house finds time for government bills. Some bills that do not get into the government's legislative programme become PMBs, but only 10 per cent of backbench bills become law anyway. Significant sections of bills may not actually be discussed in the Commons because of the use of programme motions or timetables, although the more limited procedural constraints in the Lords usually allows greater freedom of discussion. However, although the government may be constrained by time, the fact that it normally has majority support in the Commons and the general primacy of the Commons over the Lords places the government in a powerful position. In short, on legislation the government usually gets its way, although how much it gets its way on the detail of bills varies in practice. Even here, the government can often legitimately claim that it has been listening to concerns expressed inside and outside Parliament and is simply responding accordingly. On delegated legislation government control is even greater: Parliament is faced with a take-it-or-leave it situation and seldom goes as far as rejecting secondary legislation. Parliament's role in dealing with EU legislation is not one of acceptance or rejection but only of comment, although such comment is not without its influence when UK ministers participate in the Council of Ministers and EU summits.

There is no doubt that the scrutiny of legislation could be improved procedurally by a variety of means, but elaborate means already exist and ultimately the effectiveness of such scrutiny is in the hands of the members of the two Houses. They have the means, but do they have the will?

Notes

1 See Nelson W. Polsby, 'Legislatures', in F. I. Greenstein and N. W. Polsby (eds), *Handbook of Political Science*, Reading, Mass., Addison-Wesley, 1975, Vol. V, pp. 277–96. Also published in Philip Norton (ed.), *Legislatures*, Oxford, Oxford University Press, 1990, pp. 129–48.

2 See 'Classifying Legislatures', in Michael Mezey, *Comparative Legislatures*, Durham, N.C., Duke University Press, 1979, pp. 21–44. Also published in Philip Norton (ed.), *Legislatures*, Oxford, Oxford University Press, 1990, pp. 149–76.

3 Polsby, 'Legislatures', p. 277.

4 See Tony Barker with Iain Byrne and Anjuli Veall, *Ruling by Task Force: The Politico's Guide to Labour' New Elite*, London, Politico's, 2000.

5 Cabinet Office website, 2003.
6 See Francis Bown, 'The Defeat of the Shops Bill, 1986' in Michael Rush (ed.), *Parliament and Pressure Politics*, Oxford, Clarendon, 1990, pp. 213–33.
7 Paul Silk and Rhodri Walters, *How Parliament Works*, London, Longman, 4th edn, 1998, p. 127.
8 Robert Blackburn and Andrew Kennon, *Griffith and Ryle on Parliament: Functions, Practice and Procedures*, London, Sweet & Maxwell, 2nd edn, 2003, pp. 335–6.
9 See The Hansard Society, *Making the Law: The Report of the Hansard Society Commission on the Legislative Process*, London, 1993, Chapter 7.
10 The average number of SIs per year approved by the Scottish Parliament between 2000 and 2002 was 508 and by the National Assembly for Wales 296.
11 Edward C. Page, *Governing by Numbers: Delegated Legislation and Everyday Policy-Making*, Oxford, Hart Publishing, 2001, p. 3.
12 *Ibid.*, p. 161.
13 Blackburn and Kennon, *Griffith and Ryle on Parliament*.
14 Michael Wheeler-Booth, 'The House of Lords', in Blackburn and Kennon, *Griffith and Ryle*, p. 731.
15 Page, *Governing by Numbers*, pp. 142–3.
16 Hansard Society, *Making the law*, pp. 149–50.

9

The scrutiny role

Parliament and policy

The principle of the government collectively and ministers individually being responsible to the legislature is one of the defining characteristics of parliamentary government. The scrutiny of legislation was dealt with in Chapter 8; this chapter is concerned with the scrutiny of government policy and its implementation. The legislative process in Parliament is, of course, an integral part of the policy process, but it is a particular part, subject to specific and clearly defined procedures and therefore merits separate treatment. Legislation, however, is not an end in itself; it is a means to an end – setting the parameters of a particular policy or modifying an existing one. Whether a particular piece of legislation is likely to achieve its policy objective is a legitimate part of the scrutiny role, but scrutiny goes much further than that. Nor it is it limited to a post-legislative role, important as that may be; it is concerned with the effectiveness of policy, with the challenging of policy and, indeed, with the absence of policy. In any case, neither a newly elected government nor Parliament at the beginning of each session starts with a blank policy sheet. Newly elected governments inherit policies, some of which they may wish, indeed are pledged, to change, but much of what they inherit continues more or less unchanged. Some of the primary legislation passed each parliamentary session is routinely necessary, notably that authorising taxation and expenditure, some introduces new policies, some modifies existing policies, but it constitutes only a fraction of the whole range of policy and Parliament also seeks to scrutinise this, as well as the legislation it is asked to approve. Similarly, much secondary legislation relates to the implementation of existing policy, as well as that emanating from newly passed primary legislation. Parliament has therefore developed a variety of mechanisms in seeking to fulfil its scrutiny role – debates, committees, questions to ministers, and the tabling of motions.

There is, however, one area of scrutiny that straddles the legislative and non-legislative aspects of scrutiny – financial scrutiny. Parliament, more particularly the House of Commons, is required to give annual approval to the government's proposals for taxation and expenditure and these ultimately take the form of bills, but other aspects of financial scrutiny lie outside the legislative process and the two are better looked at holistically rather than separately.

Financial scrutiny

Parliament's financial role can be traced back to medieval times, occasioned by the monarch seeking approval for the raising of new or additional taxes. However, the financial role also extended to the approval of expenditure or supply. Although many early Parliaments were not summoned specifically to approve the raising of taxes or the granting of supply but to seek advice about other matters and to hear pleas for the redress of various grievances, the idea that the raising of taxes in particular required parliamentary consent gave Parliament a powerful weapon in any attempt to control or influence the monarch, even more so when it was linked to the principle of the redress of grievances before the granting of supply. This was explicitly claimed by the House of Commons in 1348, by which time the Commons had also claimed primacy over the Lords in financial matters. It did this on the grounds that it represented those who would pay the taxes, which the House of Lords did not. In 1671 and 1678 the Commons passed resolutions asserting its financial primacy, in particular stating that the House of Lords should not amend proposals for taxation or supply. The upper house did not challenge the Commons' financial primacy until 1860, when it rejected a bill abolishing paper duties, which had a significant impact on the price of newspapers and other print media. The then Chancellor of the Exchequer, Gladstone, promptly made the proposal part of his Budget and the Lords stepped back from such a challenge to the Commons. However, periodic clashes occurred during the nineteenth century, but not over finance until the Lords rejected the Liberal government's Budget in 1909. This culminated in the formal curbing of the Lords' financial powers: financial legislation has to be passed within a month of being introduced in the upper house, otherwise it will proceed to the royal assent without the latter's approval. The House of Lords does not therefore seek to amend financial legislation but does debate it and, in 2001, set up an Economic Affairs Committee, which reports each year on the annual Finance Bill arising out of the Budget, as well as on other aspects of economic policy. In addition, the House of Lords also debates the annual Defence Estimates (or expenditure proposals).

To deal with financial business the Commons developed various procedures and practices, especially as a result of the conflict with the first two

Stuart kings, James I (1603–25) and Charles I (1625–49), both of whom levied taxes without parliamentary consent. In 1641, as part of a series of actions to curb Charles' power, the Commons set up specific means of exercising its financial role. These took the form of two committees of the whole House, the Committee of Supply to deal with proposed expenditure and the Committee of Ways and Means to deal with proposed taxation. Committees of the whole House are not chaired by the Speaker but by another member of the House and operate under less restrictive rules of procedure, especially that of speaking more than once on the same motion, thus providing greater freedom of debate. The Chancellor of the Exchequer presented the annual Budget, containing the government's taxation proposals, to the Committee of Ways and Means and all estimates – the government's annual expenditure proposals – were subject to approval in the Committee of Supply. During most of the nineteenth century the Commons spent a considerable amount of time discussing the estimates, but by the end of the century the number of Supply Days had been limited. More importantly, the time spent on the estimates was increasingly devoted to topics chosen by the official opposition and, in effect, Supply Days became Opposition Days only loosely connected to the discussion of public expenditure. In 1966 and 1967 respectively, the Committee of Supply and the Committee of Ways and Means were abolished and in 1982 Supply Days were renamed Opposition Days, recognising the reality that they had long ceased to be meaningfully related to the scrutiny of expenditure. Three Estimates Days, spread through the session were introduced, but in spite of their name they are used to discuss reports of select committees. Nonetheless, there remains a procedural framework for financial scrutiny, as shown in Tables 9.1 and 9.2. To understand this framework two important factors need to be taken into account. First, the financial year starts and finishes in April and therefore coincides with neither the calendar year nor the parliamentary year. Second, only ministers of the crown are permitted to table motions proposing increases in expenditure or taxation; backbenchers may only propose decreases.

The scrutiny of expenditure

The government's expenditure proposals are prepared by the Treasury in consultation with government departments. However, in this context it is crucial to be aware that the Treasury is not first among equals but the key government department in deciding both the overall level of public expenditure and how much each department will be allowed to spend. Before 1998, the Treasury conducted an annual public expenditure survey in deciding how much each department would be allocated for the following financial year. In 1998, the Labour government replaced this with three-year departmental Spending Reviews leading to Public Service Agreements (PSAs), which set out each department's objectives, specific targets and expenditure over

Table 9.1 *The parliamentary financial cycle: expenditure*

1 Pre-Budget Report	Purpose	Form			
Presented by the Chancellor of the Exchequer in November	Assesses the state of the economy, outlines the aims of the Budget and presents public expenditure proposals	Annual White Paper on Public Expenditure			

2 The Estimates	Purpose	Introduced	Authorised	Legislation
Winter Supplementary	To cover additional expend. in current financial year	November/ December	Not later than 6 February	Consolidated Fund No. 1 Bill
Votes on Account	To cover expend. after end of financial year but before Main Estimates approved	November	Not later than 6 February	Consolidated Fund No. 1 Bill
Excess Votes	Additional expend. not anticipated in previous year's estimates	February	Not later than 18 March	Consolidated Fund No. 2 Bill
Spring Supplementary	Additional expend. required for the current financial year	February/March	Not later than 18 March	Consolidated Fund No. 2 Bill
Defence Votes A	Expend. for the armed forces' personnel for the next financial year	February	Not later than 18 March	Appropriations Bill (Consolidated Fund No. 3 Bill)
Main Estimates	Expend. for the next financial year	March/April	Not later than 5 August	Appropriations Bill (Consolidated Fund No. 3 Bill)
Summer Supplementary	Additional expenditure for the next financial year	April/May	Not later than 5 August	Appropriations Bill (Consolidated Fund No. 3 Bill)

a three-year cycle. Although covering three years, the Spending Reviews are conducted biennially to allow an overlap of one year to review the progress of PSAs. Other adjustments may be made, such as allocating more money to fund particular policies or new initiatives, or responding to changing circumstances. Nonetheless, the government's proposals for public expenditure must be approved each year by Parliament and the Chancellor of the Exchequer outlines the proposals soon after the opening of the new parliamentary session in November in the Pre-Budget Report. At the same time, the government publishes its annual White Paper on Public Expenditure. The detailed proposals are presented to Parliament in the form of supply estimates for each department, broken down into separate 'votes' to cover various aspects of expenditure (see Table 9.1). However, the position is complicated by the fact that, although the Treasury maintains contingency funds for emergencies such as natural disasters or the unanticipated use of the armed forces, departments may need additional expenditure. For the current financial year this is provided for by winter and spring supplementary estimates and, for the next financial year, by summer supplementary estimates. Other funds may also be needed to cover expenditure not anticipated in the previous year's estimates and these are authorised in the form of 'excess votes' and, finally, to cover the time between the end of the financial year in April and the approval of the main estimates by early August, votes on account are authorised.

Apart from scrutiny on the floor of the House, expenditure is also subject to scrutiny by committees. In 1912, a Select Committee on Estimates was established to examine the estimates in detail, largely in recognition of the fact that this had long ceased to be the case through Supply Days. However, the Estimates Committee could only examine a small proportion of the estimates and had no staff other than a clerk to assist it. In practice, the committee used the estimates to examine the policies they funded and did so reasonably effectively through a series of sub-committees focusing on particular policy areas. In 1970, the Estimates Committee was replaced by a Select Committee on Expenditure, also operating through specialised sub-committees, but it too focused largely on policy rather than the expenditure involved and the logic of this was recognised in 1979 when the specialised departmental committees were set up, with a remit to scrutinise all policy and administration, including expenditure. But, because they control their own agendas, the departmental committees have tended to pay only limited attention to the expenditure proposals of their respective departments. This may be in the process of changing for three reasons. First, since 1991 all government departments have been required to submit annual reports to Parliament containing more easily understood details of departmental plans, targets and expenditure than can easily be deduced from the estimates. Second, resulting from a process started in 1993, since 2002 all government departments (and other public bodies) have been required to adopt Resource Accounting and Budgeting, which covers not only cash received and spent within a particular year but the full range of resources and assets available to the department, which can be used to scrutinise departmental plans and judge their performance. The financial aspects of departmental reports are based on Resource Accounting and Budgeting and from 2002 departments were required to publish two reports, one in the spring covering the next financial year and one in the autumn covering the previous financial year. Third, following proposals from the Modernisation Committee, the Commons passed a resolution in 2002 setting out the core tasks of the departmental committees (see Box 9.2), one of which is 'to examine and report on the main estimates, annual expenditure plans and annual resource accounts' of departments.

That said, scrutiny of expenditure proposals remains a problem. On the one hand, expenditure proposals lie at the heart of every government's programme and, while governments may be willing to make changes at the margins, they rarely, if ever, give way on major aspects of expenditure; on the other, MPs are more interested in policy than expenditure, mostly seeing the latter as a vehicle for policy, not an end in itself. In the nineteenth century, the House of Commons had the means to carry out detailed scrutiny of the government's expenditure proposals in that it could, and to a degree did, examine the estimates in detail, but by the end of the century such scrutiny had virtually been abandoned. Thus the tools for the effective scrutiny of expenditure existed but increasingly the will to use them effectively did not. How effective passing responsibility to the departmental committees will be remains to be seen, but it too depends of the willingness of MPs – in this case the members of each committee – to undertake the task and to take it seriously. The most likely outcome is that it will vary from committee to committee and therefore from department to department.

Thus far attention has been focused on government expenditure *proposals*, but the auditing of expenditure is subject to a different set of arrangements, notably through the Public Accounts Committee (PAC), set up in 1861 by Gladstone when Chancellor of the Exchequer. The PAC's task is to examine the accounts presented to Parliament by government departments and various other public bodies, on the one hand, to check that the funds allocated have been used for the purpose agreed by Parliament and, on the other, that value for money has been obtained. The second of its tasks means that the committee is more than a narrow accounting body and allows it to investigate how effective the policy sustained by the expenditure has been. This latter part of the PAC's remit is an important contribution to the wider scrutiny function and will be discussed later in the chapter.

The PAC is assisted by the National Audit Office (NAO), formerly the Exchequer and Audit Office, headed by the Comptroller and Auditor-General (C&AG), supported by a staff of some eight hundred. The C&AG is not a civil servant but an officer of the House of Commons and is responsible to the Public Accounts Commission, consisting of the Chair of the PAC (who also chairs the Commission) and seven other MPs, none of whom are ministers.

The PAC has sixteen members and the chair is always a member of the official opposition, usually someone who has held office as a Treasury minister. The NAO examines the accounts of all government departments, and more than a hundred executive agencies responsible for delivering services on behalf of departments. In addition, it examines the accounts of the majority of non-departmental public bodies (NDPBs), of which in 2000 there were more than a thousand. These include bodies like environmental agencies, the Health and Safety Executive, the Arts Council, Higher Education Councils, which have executive powers, and a wide range of advisory bodies. The C&AG presents reports to the PAC on a wide range of matters, mostly focused on particular policies but sometimes more broadly over the operation of a government department or other body. These form the basis for PAC inquiries, resulting in between forty and fifty committee reports a year. In 2002–03, for example, there were 48 reports dealing with policies in fourteen different departments, seven executive agencies, and four NDPBs. In most cases, this involved reports on several different policy matters in particular departments: Health – six, Defence – five, Environment and Rural Affairs, Work and Pensions, and the Treasury four each, and the Home Office three. PAC reports are taken very seriously by the Treasury and by the departments and other bodies concerned, not least because of their value-for-money focus. Crucially, rather than challenging government expenditure proposals, the PAC operates from an ex post facto position of strength, examining not whether policy will work but whether it has worked. This makes the PAC one of, if not the, most effective of parliamentary committees.

The scrutiny of taxation

It is a similar story with the parliamentary scrutiny of taxation in that the government will not normally give way on the main thrust of its taxation proposals any more than it will on expenditure. However, with the details of taxation and other matters in the Budget there is always room for manoeuvre and the Chancellor will listen to representations from inside and outside Parliament, especially on the implementation of proposals, and concessions are invariably made.

As with expenditure proposals, the Budget starts its way through Parliament in November in the form of the Pre-Budget Report (see Table 9.2). However, between then and the actual presentation of the Budget in late March, nothing further happens within Parliament, but outside Parliament it is a period of intense activity both by the Chancellor and various pressure groups seeking to influence its contents. It is important to appreciate that economic policy generally and the Budget in particular are very much the responsibility of the Chancellor of the Exchequer. However much influence the Cabinet may have – something that varies from government to government – it only rarely has a major influence on economic policy. Crises involving serious cuts in

Table 9.2   *The parliamentary financial cycle: taxation*

Period	Details	Location	Legislation
November	Pre-Budget Report by Chancellor of the Exchequer	Chamber of House of Commons	
Late March	Chancellor presents the Budget and publishes the Financial Statement and Budget Report ('The Red Book')	Chamber of House of Commons	Resolutions (under Provisional Collection of Taxes Act 1968) giving immediate approval to tax changes
Post-Budget Day	4-day debate on the Budget	Chamber of House of Commons	
April	Finance Bill to implement the Budget introduced	Chamber of House of Commons – 1-day debate on second reading	Finance Bill
April–July	Remaining stages of the Finance Bill in Commons	Committee stage split between floor of House and standing comm. Report stage – 2 days Third reading – 1 day or second day of report stage	Finance Bill
July	Finance Bill in Lords	A sub-committee of the Economic Affairs Committee considers the Bill and issues a report which informs a one-day debate in the Chamber on all stages. Under Parliament Act 1911 may not amend it	Finance Bill

public spending have sometimes been influenced by the Cabinet, but that is the exception to the rule, and expenditure is largely a matter between the Chancellor and individual departmental ministers. Even more so with the Budget, which is very firmly in the hands of the Chancellor, usually in consultation with the Prime Minister, much depending on who holds each post. Thus, even Tony Blair, widely seen as a powerful Prime Minister, is faced with a very powerful Chancellor in Gordon Brown, as the main driving force in economic policy.

As soon as the Chancellor has presented the Budget, a detailed Financial Statement and Budget Report, known as the Red Book from the colour of its cover, is published, and the House of Commons passes a series of resolutions implementing any proposals requiring immediate action, such as changes to fuel tax or the duty on alcohol or cigarettes. This is done under the Provisional Collection of Taxes Act 1968. There then follows a four-day debate in the Chamber, focusing on the Chancellor's proposals as a prelude to the introduction of the Finance Bill to implement the Budget. The bill follows the same legislative procedure as other public bills, except that, whereas the committee stage of most bills is taken either on the floor of the House or in a standing committee, the committee stage of the Finance Bill is always divided between the floor and a standing committee. A small number of important and more controversial clauses – seven in 1999–2000, chosen mainly by the opposition, are taken on the floor and the rest – 150 in 1999–2000 – in a standing committee. Once the bill has completed all its stages in the Commons, it is debated in the Lords but cannot be amended and passes all its stages in single day. Since 2001, however, the Finance Bill has been examined by a subcommittee of the Economic Affairs Committee and its report is used to inform the debate in the Lords.

The Budget debates, especially in the Commons, inevitably produce broader scrutiny of the government's economic policy, as well as discussing the Chancellor's detailed proposals, but once attention turns to the Finance Bill the focus is largely on the details of the Budget. However, the Chancellor's Pre-Budget Report in November and his Budget Statement in March are also reported on by the Commons' Treasury Committee. In the latter case, it publishes its report in time for the debates on the Finance Bill. In addition, it is open to other select committees to conduct inquiries into those parts of the Budget affecting matters within their remit, but they usually prefer to focus on policy matters, taking up budgetary issues incidentally rather than specifically or regularly.

Any secondary legislation involving financial matters is, as noted in Chapter 8, referred to the Commons' Select Committee on Statutory Instruments and in 2001 a Joint Committee on Tax Law Rewrite to which bills revising taxation legislation are referred was set up.

Financial scrutiny: an overview

Overall, Parliament deals fairly effectively with taxation and, although parliamentary approval is seldom in doubt because governments normally have an overall majority in the Commons, the government is usually persuaded to make changes in detail. Of course, if the government lacks a majority, it may be forced to make important concessions: this happened in 1977, when two Labour backbenchers supported by the Conservative opposition, secured an amendment to the Finance Bill providing for the automatic indexation of personal tax allowances with the rate of inflation. Even with a government majority, such changes can take place because it is easy for MPs to focus on particular aspects of taxation and because governments are prepared to listen and, not infrequently, respond. This contrasts with the inability of the Commons to influence government expenditure proposals. On the other hand, the ex post facto examination of expenditure by the PAC is highly effective, checking propriety and value for money. This exposes government expenditure to genuine scrutiny, even though it is after the money has been spent. Ultimately, the effectiveness of financial scrutiny depends on the willingness of MPs to engage in what is often tedious and largely unrewarding work and on the willingness of government to listen. That dichotomy, however, lies at the heart of effective parliamentary scrutiny generally, not just financial scrutiny in particular.

Non-legislative scrutiny

Parliament has available to it a number of mechanisms for the scrutiny of non-legislative matters. Furthermore, unlike the minimal role it plays in financial scrutiny, the House of Lords makes major contribution to non-legislative scrutiny. Essentially, these mechanisms fall into four categories: parliamentary Questions, debates, motions, and investigatory committees. However, as Table 9.3 shows, in each category there are different types and there are also differences between the two Houses.

Parliamentary Questions

With the possible exception of the State Opening of Parliament once a year, Question Time is almost certainly the aspect of Parliament with which most people are familiar. Prime Ministers' Questions (PMQs) is broadcast on television each week and is frequently shown on news and current affairs programmes. However, in terms of the sheer number of Questions MPs ask ministers – nearly 5,000 in 1999–2000, Questions to the Prime Minister constitute only about 15 per cent, but because far more Questions are asked than the Prime Minister can possibly answer they amount to little more than 1 per cent of the Questions *answered*. In addition, PMQs usually shows the Commons at its most adversarial, particularly with the confrontation between the Prime Minister and the Leader of the Opposition. Question Times involving other ministers are, of course, often adversarial but usually less gladiatorial than PMQs. More importantly, the overwhelming majority of Questions in

Table 9.3   *Non-legislative scrutiny mechanisms*

House of Commons	House of Lords
Parliamentary Questions	
Oral answer	Starred (oral answer)
Written answer	Written answer
Urgent	Private Notice Questions
Westminster Hall	Unstarred (debates)
Debates	
Government initiated	Government initiated
Opposition initiated	Opposition initiated
Backbench initiated	Backbench initiated
Motions	
Early Day Motions (EDMs)	
Investigatory committees	
Departmental	Permanent
Other permanent	Ad hoc
Ad hoc	Joint
Joint	

both Commons and Lords are those for written answer and there are important differences between the two Houses.

In practice, there are four types of parliamentary Questions (see Table 9.4). First, Questions for oral answer (known as starred Questions in the Lords), not all of which in the Commons receive an oral answer because of insufficient time at Question Time. Any unanswered Questions receive a written answer, unless, in the Commons, the MP concerned chooses to defer or withdraw the Question. There are, however, limits on the number of Questions each MP may ask and on the period of notice. Members are limited to eight Questions over ten sitting days, with not more than two for any one day, and Questions must normally be tabled not more than a fortnight and up to three sitting days before the Question Time concerned (account is taken of recesses and adjournments). The three-day limit was introduced in January 2003 (it was previously ten days) to facilitate more topical Questions. However, because there are always more Questions tabled than can be answered in the hour-long Question Time, Questions are drawn at random electronically, a process known as 'the shuffle'.

In the Commons, Question Time is the first substantive business every day except Friday, when only Urgent Questions (discussed below) are taken, and normally last just under an hour. Before 1997 the Prime Minister answered

Table 9.4   *Number of parliamentary Questions answered in the House of Commons and House of Lords, 1999–2000*

House of Commons	No.	%	House of Lords	No.	%
Oral replies*	5,343	(2,095)12.9	Starred (oral)	630	12.0
Urgent Questions (PNQs)	9	0.02	Private Notice Questions	9†	0.2
Written replies	36,067	87.1	Written replies	4,511	86.1
			Unstarred (debates)	87	1.7
Total	41,419		Total	5,237	

Source: House of Commons Library, *Sessional Information Digest, 1999–2000* and House of Lords, *Sessional Statistics, 1999–2000*.

Notes: * Including supplementary Questions; figure in brackets excluding supplementary Questions. † This was an unusually high figure; the normal number of PNQs is between one and three.

Questions twice a week, on Tuesdays and Wednesdays, but Tony Blair changed this to a half-hour session on Wednesdays when he became Prime Minister. Apart from the Prime Minister, Question Time operates on the basis of a departmental rota, so that the ministers concerned appear once every four weeks, with larger departments allotted more time than smaller. In 1999–2000, for instance, apart from the Prime Minister, most oral Questions were answered by the Foreign and Commonwealth Office, followed by Environment, Transport and the Regions, Health, Social Security, and the Ministry of Defence. Almost all PMQs ask the Prime Minister to list his or her official engagements for the day concerned or sometimes invite the Prime Minister to visit the Member's constituency, whereas most Questions to other ministers must be substantive and relate to the minister's departmental responsibilities. When the minister has answered, the Member asking the original Question is allowed a supplementary Question and, at the discretion of the Speaker, other Members may also ask supplementaries, but the Speaker will not allow a debate to develop, although what amounts to a mini-debate sometimes does. Generally speaking, oral Questions are used by the opposition, particularly frontbench spokespersons, to attack government policy and by government backbenchers to defend it, particularly by the use of supplementary Questions. Indeed, with PMQs it is only when the first supplementary is asked that the Prime Minister knows for certain what Question is being asked, although all Prime Ministers come to Question Time well-briefed by their staff on a range of possible topics. Of course, although government backbenchers usually support the government, sometimes by asking 'patsy', not to say sycophantic Questions (sometimes at the instigation of the whips), some can and do ask searching and critical Questions of their government. Nonetheless, Question Time in the Commons, and PMQs in particular, is usually Parliament at its most partisan.

Question Time in the House of Lords is very different, largely lacking the adversarial atmosphere of the Commons, shorter and strictly limited on the number of Questions asked. Questions for oral answer in the Lords are known as starred Questions (indicated by an asterisk on the Order Paper). As in the Commons Question Time takes place every day except Fridays, but in the Lords it is limited to thirty minutes on Mondays and Thursdays, when a maximum of four Questions may be asked, and forty minutes on Tuesdays and Wednesdays, when the maximum is five. No departmental rota operates and there is a provision for topical Question tabled earlier in the week on Tuesdays, Wednesdays and Thursdays. As in the Commons, however, more members of the House wish to ask Questions than there is time available and peers may not table more than one starred Question per day and no more than two topical Questions per session. Unlike the Commons, however, where Questions for oral answer are often used for party point-scoring, starred Questions are used to secure information and, as a former Clerk of the Parliaments has observed, Question Time in the Lords is 'less stage-managed ... [and] ... less party political'.[1] Supplementary Questions are allowed and Questions and answers on the matter concerned may last as long as ten minutes and, as Wheeler-Booth notes, 'many are asked by experts in their own specialities, where they wish to prod the government into action, with support from experts in all parts of the House. If a minister has a weak case, the seven or eight minutes allowed for each Question will show it.'[2]

There is also provision in both Houses for asking urgent Questions, known as Urgent Questions in the Commons (Private Notice Questions (PNQs) until June 2003) and still called PNQs in the Lords. These are for Questions on matters that have arisen since the previous sitting and for which no opportunity is likely to be available very soon. In the Commons the Speaker decides whether to allow an Urgent Question; in the Lords the Leader of the House, who is, of course, a minister, decides, subject to the agreement of the House, which usually accepts his or her decision. Understandably, the number of such Questions is small, especially in the Lords (the figure in Table 9.7 for 1999–2000 is unusually high), although it varies more from session to session in the Commons. In addition, UQs are quite often used in the Commons by opposition frontbenchers and, traditionally, the Leader of the House always responds to a UQ from his or her opposition 'shadow' in announcing the future business of the Commons on Thursdays.

Far more Questions are tabled for a written answer – 87.1 per cent of all Questions answered in the Commons and 86.1 per cent in the Lords in 1999–2000. Considerably more than half the Questions tabled for oral answer in the Commons are not answered at Question Time and mostly receive a written response: in 1999–2000, 5,747 Questions were tabled for oral answer and 2,095 (36.4 per cent) received such answers, the rest constituting about 10 per cent of the Questions receiving written answers. All Questions receiving a written answer, regardless of whether they were originally tabled for such an answer, are printed in *Hansard* and therefore available to MPs, peers and public alike. Most Questions for written answer are asked to extract factual information from the government. In some cases it is information the government would prefer not to reveal, but in most it is information not readily available.

The government refuses to reply to about 1 per cent of the Questions asked, most obviously on security grounds, commercial sensitivity or other reasons of confidentiality, but also sometimes because of the cost involved. In 2002, it was estimated that the cost of answering a Question for oral answer was £299 and for a written answer £135, with an advisory maximum cost limit of £600 for written answers but none for oral answers.[3] While parliamentary Questions generally have been a growth area of parliamentary activity, most of the growth until the second half of the twentieth century was in Questions for oral answer; 1966–67 was the last session in which more Questions for oral than written answer were tabled. Although it has been possible to table Questions for written answer since 1902, they were not widely used until after the Second World War; by 1976–77 they exceeded 25,000, 31,000 in 1984–85 and 41,000 in 1989–90, averaging 38,000 in normal length sessions since. Although there is no limit on the number of Questions for written answer an MP may table, the Member may request a reply on a particular or 'named day', in which case there is a limit of five such Questions tabled at a minimum of three days' notice. 'Named day' Questions are used by MPs to secure information in time for a debate or to meet a local newspaper, radio or television deadline. Almost all MPs who are not ministers use Questions for written answer, some prolifically, and there is no doubt that they are an important means of scrutiny, placing in the public domain an enormous quantity of information about government policy and administration, including much statistical data.

Table 9.5 shows the use made by MPs of parliamentary Questions, but in analysing the data on oral Questions account needs to be taken of the Speaker's obligation to secure a balance between the parties in parliamentary

Table 9.5   *The use of parliamentary Questions by MPs, 2001–02 (%)*

Party	Oral PQs	Suppl. PQs	PMQs	Written PQs
Cons.*	30.9	44.1	43.9	43.4
Lab.†	55.4	39.0	38.1	33.3
Lib-Dem†	10.0	11.3	13.6	18.8
Other	3.7	5.6	4.4	4.5
Total	100.0	99.9	100.0	100.0

Source: House of Common Library, *Research Paper 03/02*.

Notes: * Frontbenchers and backbenchers. † Backbenchers only.

proceedings. Thus, although Labour MPs tabled 55.4 per cent of the Questions tabled for oral answer in 2001–02, reflecting Labour's massive majority, Conservatives were allowed more supplementaries, especially in proportion to their numbers in the House. The same applied to the Liberal Democrats and minority party MPs. However, in the use of Questions for written answer, unaffected by the Speaker's obligations, Conservative MPs were even more active, asking 10 per cent more than Labour backbenchers. If Questions per MP are examined, then Conservatives asked twice and Liberal Democrats three times as many Questions for written answer as Labour backbenchers. This in part reflects the practice of opposition party frontbenchers using such Questions to secure information they need for their frontbench responsibilities, but it is also the result of the widespread use of written Questions by opposition MPs as a means of scrutiny. Some backbenchers, including government backbenchers, use both oral and written Questions to probe extensively into particular issues, sometimes to the extent of conducting a campaign, as the Labour backbencher, Tam Dalyell, did in the 1980s over the sinking of the Argentinian cruiser *The General Belgrano* during the Falklands War.

The use of Questions for written answer in the House of Lords follows a similar procedural pattern but, as Table 9.4 shows, at a much lower level of activity: the ratio of Questions receiving written answers in the Commons compared with the Lords is 8:1. Nonetheless, their use by peers has increased markedly from fewer than a hundred before 1970 to well over four thousand in recent sessions. Like MPs, peers find Questions for written answer a valuable means of extracting information not otherwise available.

The House of Lords also has another type of Question, known as unstarred Questions, which lead to short debates. However, these will be dealt with in the following section on debates.

Debates

Both Houses spend most of their time debating various matters, but the greater part of this debating time is spent on legislation, especially government legislation. Non-legislative time accounts for about 35 per cent of the time on the floor of the House in the Commons and 28 per cent in the Lords. In addition, since 1999 the Commons has held sittings in the former Grand Committee Room off Westminster Hall, known as Westminster Hall debates, which add about a further 25 per cent to the time available to backbenchers. Although there are various types of debates, it makes more sense to discuss them on the basis of on whose initiative they take place – that of the government, the opposition parties, or backbenchers. Again, there are significant differences between Commons and Lords in both types of debates and who has the initiative.

As Table 9.6 shows, the government has the initiative in more than half the time allocated to non-legislative debates in the Commons, with the

Table 9.6   *The initiative in non-legislative debates*

House of Commons	1999–2000*	House of Lords	1989–90
Government	52.9	Government	25.5
Opposition parties	25.4	Parties	33.2
Backbenchers	21.6	Backbenchers	41.3
Total	99.9	Total	100.0

Sources: House of Commons, *Sessional Digest, 1999–2000* and D. Shell, *The House of Lords,*
Table 7.1 (more up to date figures are not readily available, but the distribution remains
essentially similar in the Lords).

Note: * Excluding Westminster Hall debates.

opposition parties a quarter and backbenchers a fifth. In contrast, backbenchers in the Lords have two-fifths of the time, the parties (including government
backbenchers) a third, leaving the government with a quarter. This reflects
three factors. First, the government has much greater control over the Commons' agenda. Government business, whether legislative or non-legislative,
takes precedence on all days in the Commons except Fridays and, although
time is allocated to the opposition parties, its use is subject to negotiation with
the government through the usual channels. Similarly, time on the floor of
the House is also allocated to backbenchers, but it is fragmented and comes
mostly at the end of the parliamentary day. In contrast, the Lords' agenda is
much more the result of negotiation through the usual channels, especially
on non-legislative matters. Second, politically the government needs to have
various matters debated by the Commons. Quite apart from introducing primary and secondary legislation to implement its policies, the government is
expected to give the Commons, as the elected representatives of the people,
the opportunity to consider policy proposals and their subsequent operation, as
well as to debate matters of concern. In some cases, politically it will need the
approval of the Commons; in others, the opportunity to debate the matters
concerned is sufficient. The House of Lords also welcomes the opportunity
to debate government policy but, as the constitutionally and politically lesser
of the two Houses, its imprimatur is much less important to the government
on non-legislative matters. Third, the less adversarial atmosphere of the Lords,
differences in party representation and the presence of a significant block of
crossbenchers facilitates a more flexible allocation of non-legislative time.

   Government initiatives in both Houses take the form of government
motions, on which a vote may or may not be take place, or ministerial statements, which give rise to a short debate but are not followed by a vote. In fact,
the parliamentary year starts with major debates in Commons and Lords on the
government's proposals for the forthcoming session presented in the Queen's
Speech. In both Houses the debate is held over five days. In the Commons the

first day is a general debate, followed by topics agreed through the usual channels on the second and third, and amendments tabled by the opposition parties on the fourth and fifth. In the Lords the time is divided between debates on foreign affairs and defence, home affairs, health and social policy, and environmental, agricultural and economic policy. Debates arising out of government motions in the two Houses range widely in subject-matter, some occurring each session, notably various aspects of foreign affairs and defence, others varying from session to session according to current issues. In the Commons most such debates do not end with a vote or division and, in that sense do not usually directly decide anything. In 1999–2000 the government tabled 25 substantive motions, but only five related directly to government policy – on fisheries, two Defence White Papers, the EU's Common Agricultural Policy, and the Coal Operating Aid Scheme. Others were tabled on public expenditure and reports of the PAC, but most concerned non-policy matters, such as procedural changes, the internal organisation of the House, the MPs' pension scheme, and tributes to Betty Boothroyd on her retirement as Speaker and Queen Elizabeth the Queen Mother on her hundredth birthday. The procedural motion, in fact, brought about important changes, such as the programming of bills and placing Westminster Hall sittings on a permanent footing. Other important policy matters, including White Papers on rural and urban policy, issues scheduled for discussion at EU Council meetings, the work of the intelligence and security services, various defence and foreign affairs issues, and further reform of the House of Lords, were all discussed on formal adjournment motions. Even where votes take place, the government rarely if ever loses and the main purpose is to provide MPs, including opposition frontbenchers, with the opportunity to discuss government proposals, ongoing policy or issues of current concern. From time to time, however, crucial votes do take place, such as those on the use of military force in Iraq in 1991 and 2003.

Government-initiated debates in the Lords are usually on a 'take-note' motion and therefore do not end with a division, although a substantive resolution can be tabled to enable a vote to take place. As in the Commons, such debates vary according to government business and the issues of the day, but the absence of a government majority in the Lords means that discussions via the usual channels assume a much greater significance in deciding what is and what is not debated. Essentially, debates on government motions in the Lords take place on matters that the government feels should be debated and the House wishes to debate.

The government has a variety of ways of announcing policy initiatives and keeping Parliament informed about its policies. These include White Papers setting out government proposals on a particular issue and various forms of consultation documents, although the distinction between the two is sometimes blurred. Such documents are sometimes accompanied by a ministerial statement in Parliament, but ministerial statements are used to make policy announcements without the full panoply of a White Paper to report on the outcome of international discussions or meetings, to bring Parliament up to date on some policy matter, in response to sudden events at home or abroad or to a continuing crisis situation. For example, the Chancellor's Pre-Budget Report is one such statement and the Prime Minister regularly reports to the Commons following meetings of the EU Council of Ministers (as do other ministers in particular policy areas). Similarly, a natural disaster, such as widespread flooding in some part of the UK or a major earthquake abroad invariably result in statements, and continuing crises, such as that over BSE ('mad cow disease') in 1995–96 or the outbreak of foot-and-mouth disease in 2001, produce a series of statements.

Statements are normally made in the Commons by the minister concerned and most, though not all, are repeated in the House of Lords. Which statements will also be made in the Lords is decided through the usual channels, with the attitude of the opposition usually being the crucial factor. Thus, in 1999–2000 288 statements were made in the Commons and 243 in the Lords. Statements are normally followed by questions and comments from the floor of the House, to which the minister responds – in effect a limited form of debate. In the Commons most statements and the ensuing debate take up less than an hour, but rather more than a quarter last longer. In the Lords proceedings on statements are limited to a maximum of 40 minutes, divided equally between frontbenchers and backbenchers. Overall, ministerial statements take up about 5 per cent of the time in the Commons and 4 per cent in the Lords.[4]

Ministerial statements are an important and flexible way of bringing various matters into the public domain and giving Parliament, especially the Commons, an opportunity to subject the matter concerned to a degree of scrutiny. In particular, they enable the government to respond quickly to events and allow Parliament to be involved at an earlier stage than is often the case with many other scrutiny devices. It was also the practice until 2003 for ministers to publish statements in response to what are known as 'inspired' Questions for written answer, in effect a Question planted by the government whips. However, these written statements are now published on the Order Papers of the two Houses, which has the advantage of drawing them more directly to the attention of MPs and peers.

As noted earlier in this chapter, the former Supply Days eventually became days when the official opposition chose the subject for debate, although a procedural link with the estimates was retained, and in 1982 were renamed Opposition Days. There are now twenty of these, of which seventeen are available to the official opposition and three to the Liberal Democrats, although up to one of these days may be used by one of the smaller parties. Opposition Days are in practice spread through the session and are mostly used for half rather than full-day debates. As with government-initiated debates, the topics vary considerably but are much more likely to be driven by current policy concerns and, of course, be on matters that the opposition parties believe the government to be vulnerable to criticism, as shown in Box 9.1. There are,

Box 9.1   Opposition Day debates, 1999–2000

Official opposition	*Liberal Democrats*	*Ulster Unionist Party*
Full-day debates	*Half-day debates*	*Half-day debates*

Official opposition	*Liberal Democrats*	*Ulster Unionist Party*
Full-day debates		
1 Investment in the London Underground.	1 Meeting the needs of pensioners.	1 The Patten Report on policing in Northern Ireland.
2 The National Health Service.	2 Protecting Post Office services.	
3 The relationship between Parliament and the executive.	3 Tax cuts and public services.	
	4 Equal opportunities in Britain.	
Half-day debates	5 Britain's strategic interests.	
1 Health care.	6 Pensions and pensioners.	
2 Running costs and accountability of central govt.	8 Privatisation.	
3 Asylum and immigration.		
4 Development policy.		
5 Education.		
6 The Millennium Dome.		
7 The NHS.		
8 Small businesses.		
9 Mozambique.		
10 The future of the Rover company.		
11 The future of sub-post offices.		
13 Asylum seekers.		
14 UK manufacturing and enterprise.		
15 The future of the teaching profession.		
16 Govt policies on tackling crime.		
17 Transport taxation, spending and investment.		
18 Pensions.		
19 GM crops.		
20 Football hooliganism.		
21 Planning, house-building; the development of greenfield sites and the decline of cities.		
22 The govt's early release of prisoners.		
23 Committee on Standards in Public Life: recommendations on ministers and special advisers.		
24 Fuel protests.		
25 The supply and recruitment of teachers.		
26 The London Underground – Public Private Partnership.		
27 The Millennium Dome.		

however, other occasions when the opposition parties can take the initiative and seek a debate. Indeed, the selection of government-initiated debates is partly driven by opposition representations made through the usual channels, but if the official opposition tables a motion of censure the government is obliged to provide debating time. If a censure motion is carried, the government must, by convention, either resign forthwith or call an election. The last time this occurred was in 1979, when the Labour government was defeated by 311 votes to 310, leading directly to the general election of 1979. However, censure motions are not very common – three in the 1974–79 Parliament, including the one that was carried, two in 1979–83, one 1983–87, two in 1987–92 and none since 1991, although the government may table a motion of confidence, as John Major's Conservative government did in 1993 after it was defeated on the Social Policy Protocol of the Maastricht Treaty, or make it known that divisions on particular items of business will be treated as matters of confidence, as Major did over the European Communities (Finance) Bill in 1994. Except when the government is vulnerable, as the 1974–79 Labour government was (especially during the period of minority government between 1976 and 1979), governments normally defeat censure motions or win confidence votes. Censure motions are also possible in the Lords but rare – the last, which was defeated, was in 1983 – and largely pointless, since passing such a motion would have no direct effect, given the primacy of the Commons.

There are no Opposition Days in the Lords but time is allocated through the usual channels to each of the parties to decide topics for debate. In 1999–2000 this was eighteen days – four to Labour, eight to the Conservatives, three to the Liberal Democrats, and three to the crossbenchers. Topics are chosen by party meetings, not the party leadership, in the House and through the weekly meeting of crossbenchers. Debates vary in length from one to five hours but are mostly two-and-a-half hours, usually on what is called a 'motion for papers'. This formally requests the government to lay papers on the subject concerned before the House, giving the mover of the motion the right to reply at the end of the debate, at which point the motion is withdrawn and no vote takes place. As in the Commons, topics vary considerably but are often linked to current issues.

Backbenchers have a variety of opportunities to initiate debates as individuals, but practice in the two Houses differs. Before 1999, thirteen Fridays a session were allocated for motions tabled by backbenchers, but these have been transferred to the Westminster Hall sittings, so that the only time now available on the floor of the House for debates initiated by backbenchers are the daily adjournment debates. These take place at the end of each day's sitting immediately following the main business and last half an hour. This is exclusively backbench time and Members are chosen by ballot to table motions. Adjournment debates are commonly used to raise constituency issues and there is always a minister from the relevant department present to reply. The equivalent in the House of Lords are unstarred Questions, which are taken either for an hour between 7.30 and 8.30 p.m. ('the dinner break') or for one-and-a-half hours after the main business. Unstarred Questions are not subject to a balloting procedure but are dealt with on a first-come, first-served basis, subject to agreement between the member concerned and the Government Chief Whip on a suitable day, since the government needs notice in order to respond. Unstarred Questions give rise to short debates involving the original questioner and other peers who wish to participate, followed by a reply from the minister. In 1999–2000, 87 unstarred Questions were tabled. Backbench peers also have the opportunity to initiate debates via a ballot and such debates have precedence over other business on one Wednesday a month from the beginning of the session to the Whitsun recess, after which the upper house becomes increasingly busy with government legislation. The House of Lords also provides time for the debating reports of its European Union and Science and Technology Committees.

There are yet further debating opportunities for backbench MPs, first through the Scottish, Welsh and Northern Ireland Grand Committees, all of which hold debates on matters continuing to be the responsibility of Parliament, following the setting up of the devolved bodies in these parts of the UK. In the 1999–2000 the Scottish Grand Committee held eight debates and debated four ministerial statements, the Welsh Grand Committee held six debates and debated four statements, and the Northern Ireland Grand Committee three debates. In 1999, however, a major development for backbench initiatives took place with the introduction of the Westminster Hall sittings, which expanded backbench time by about 25 per cent and take place in the Grand Committee Room off Westminster Hall.

Although the government uses a limited amount of Westminster Hall time for debates and ministerial statements, it is essentially backbench time, as is the time devoted to select committee reports (see Table 9.7). Most of the sittings are adjournment debates, sixty or ninety minutes in length, on subjects chosen by a ballot of backbenchers. As with Questions for oral answer,

Table 9.7   *Westminster Hall debates, 1999–2000*

Type of business	Time (hrs : mins)	%
Government	45 : 28	12.9
Balloted	249 : 20	70.7
Debates on sel. comm.reps.	53 : 44	15.2
Points of order	0 : 02	<0.1
Government responses	4 : 06	1.2
Total	352 : 40	100.0

Source: House of Commons Library, *Sessional Information Digest, 1999–2000.*

departments operate a rota and, like regular adjournment debates, Westminster Hall debates are attended by ministers who respond to the debate. In 2002 a further type of Westminster Hall debate was introduced – cross-cutting Questions involving ministers from a range of departments covered by the topic for debate. This was a response to concerns expressed by a number of select committees and by the government itself over what has been termed 'joined-up government' – policies in which several departments are involved. Although they were set up partly to compensate for debates on motions formerly debated on Fridays not devoted to Private Members' bills and also four Consolidated Fund Bill debates (also in practice backbench time), Westminster Hall sittings have extended the time available for debates initiated by backbenchers. In addition, as noted in Chapter 7, the hemi-spherical layout used for the sittings is intended to build on and further encourage the less partisan nature that characterises many backbench-initiated debates.

The House of Commons, but not the Lords, provides one further opportunity for debates intended to scrutinise government policy – emergency debates. Any Member may seek a debate 'on a specific and important matter that should have urgent consideration' (Standing Order 24). Applications may be made on any day except Fridays. The Speaker must be convinced that the proposed subject is of national importance and that an opportunity to debate it in the reasonably near future is unlikely, but successive Speakers have been reluctant to grant emergency debates and this is reflected in the sharp decline in the number of applications. In the 1974–79 Parliament applications for emergency debates each sessions averaged 48, rising in the next two Parliaments to 62 (1979–83) and 70 (1983–87, but falling to 37 in 1987–92, to seven in 1992–97 and three in 1997–2001. If successful, however, a debate normally takes place at the start of main business the next day (or on the following Monday, if granted on a Thursday), although on extremely urgent matters the debate starts at 7 p.m. the same day. Any debate normally concludes with a vote. A recent emergency debate was in 2002 over the deployment of British troops in Afghanistan and was the first since 1993, both having been granted to opposition frontbenchers. Even when more applications were made, few were granted – 3/66 in 1978–79, 3/84 in 1983–84, for example, only four since 1987 and no backbencher has successfully applied for an emergency debate since 1987. Emergency applications, however, do offer MPs an opportunity to draw attention to an issue and this largely accounts for the large number of applications in the 1970s and 1980s, but the Member has only three minutes in which to state a case and the failure to secure debates appears to have depressed the number of applications. Occasionally, the government agrees to a debate on an urgent matter which might otherwise form the basis for an emergency application, as it did in 1986 when a debate on the US bombing of Libya was held. The government may also recall Parliament to debate an emergency situation when its feels MPs and peers should be given the chance to express their views. This happened, for instance, in 1982 over the Argentinian invasion of the Falklands, in 1990 over Iraq's invasion of Kuwait, in 2001 following the 9/11 terrorist attacks in the United States, and in 2002 over possible military action against Iraq. Parliament is sometimes recalled for other purposes, as it was in 2002 to pay tributes to Queen Elizabeth the Queen Mother, following her death.

In general, non-legislative debates do not formally decide anything; in many cases no vote takes place and, where it does, the government, certainly in the Commons, does not expect to lose the vote, any more than the opposition expects to win. Furthermore, different debates have different purposes: the rare emergency debates and most recalls of Parliament are to deal with urgent matters; most debates on government motions are to allow Parliament to discuss government proposals on policy; Opposition Days subject the government to scrutiny on matters chosen by the opposition parties; adjournment debates are mostly about backbench constituency concerns; Westminster Hall sittings are mainly for backbench scrutiny initiatives. The two Houses also differ: debates are mostly more partisan in the Commons, less partisan in the Lords, but even here it depends on the type and subject of debate, especially in the Commons; there is no provision for emergency debates in the Lords, nor a direct equivalent of unstarred Questions in the Commons. Ultimately, debates are about subjecting the government to public scrutiny, bringing matters into the public domain, and providing MPs and peers with opportunities to give voice to public opinion and the absence or curtailment of debate reduces Parliament's ability to fulfil one of its major functions.

Early day motions

Early day motions (EDMs) are a device available to MPs, but not to peers, to express their views on any matter they wish. As such, they receive a good deal of media attention, usually prefaced by 'A hundred MPs have signed motion ...'. In spite of their name, EDMs are rarely debated and, most of the few that are, are in fact 'prayers' for the annulment of SIs. The rest are mainly backbench expressions of opinion, although EDMs can be and are used for essentially non-political purposes, such as congratulating an individual or a team or group of people on a sporting performance or other achievement, or congratulating all those concerned on the fiftieth anniversary of the BBC Radio serial, *The Archers*, to the point that the term 'parliamentary graffiti' has been applied to some EDMs. However, most have a political purpose: some are all-party motions on matters such as pensions, child abuse, environmental issues, abortion, or human rights; some relate specifically to constituency matters; some are attempts by government backbenchers to persuade the government to change policy or by opposition backbenchers to pressure their leaders; government backbenchers use them to attack opposition party policies and opposition backbenchers to attack government policies. Moreover, the rules on the subject-matter of EDMs give MPs greater freedom than for example, is the case with tabling Questions, which must be directed at a particular minister and be on a subject for which he or she has ministerial responsibility (although parliamentary ingenuity often finds a way round such restrictions). Apart from judicial matters which are sub-judice, EDMs may criticise individuals, address matters which are not specifically the responsibility of national government, or demand that bodies like local authorities should take action, and so on.

The fact that EDMs are rarely debated is not the point: they are a simple, speedy and effective way of expressing backbench opinion, particularly to the government of the day. There is no limit on the number of EDMs that a Member may table, nor to the number of signatories, with the possibility of additional signatories as long as the motion remains on the Order Paper, which it will until the end of the session. Thus EDMs have been used by Labour backbenchers since 1997 to express concern about welfare benefits, misgivings over military action in Afghanistan and Iraq, and university tuition fees. All-party views on reform of the House of Lords have also been expressed effectively via EDMs. They are not, of course, limited to non-legislative scrutiny and EDMs on tuition fees played their part in securing concessions on the implementation of the policy. Although they expect to be consulted about political EDMs before they are tabled, there is little the whips can do to prevent a Member from doing so, nor to prevent other Members from signing them. It is not therefore surprising to find that EDMs have become an increasingly popular means of expressing backbench opinion: before 1951–52, there were fewer than a hundred, varying in succeeding sessions but averaging more than a thousand per session in the 1983–87 Parliament, rising to more than 1,500 in 1992–97, but falling to a sessional average of 1,156 in 1997–2001.

Investigatory committees

Parliament has long used committees to investigate government policy and administration and their use for this purpose was widespread during the nineteenth century. In the Commons the oldest permanent investigatory committee is the Public Accounts Committee, but most other committees were set up for specific inquiries and were disbanded once these had been completed. In 1871, for instance, eighteen investigatory committees were set up and held 237 meetings. In comparison, although a similar number of legislative committees were used (17), these resulted in only 73 meetings. However, as the government's control over the Commons increased, more use was made of legislative and less of investigatory committees. Thus, in 1947–48 there were 21 legislative committees (mostly standing committees taking the committee stage of bills), holding 140 meetings, compared with only 2 investigatory committees, holding 38 meetings, but in the 1950s there were growing demands for extending parliamentary scrutiny through investigatory committees (see

Table 9.8   *The growth of investigatory committees in the House of Commons*
(selected sessions)

Session	No. of committees	No. of meetings	No. of inquiries
1956–57	3	120	11
1968–69	9	371	27
1977–78	11*	456	51
1985–86	16	555	148
1999–2000	19	895	274

Source: Select Committee Returns for each session.

Note: * In 1977–78 there were six investigatory committees, but the Select Committee
on Expenditure operated through six sub-committees, one general and five specialised.
For comparative purposes it has been treated as six committees, giving a total of 11.

Table 9.8). Governments strongly resisted these demands but did tentatively
concede a Select Committee on Nationalised Industries in the 1950s.

The late 1960s and the 1970s saw increasing experimentation in the
use of investigatory committees. The Nationalised Industries Committee continued to operate but committees scrutinising education, science and technology, agriculture, race relations, overseas aid, and Scottish affairs were set
up in the 1960s. In addition, a committee was established to monitor the work
of the Parliamentary Commissioner for Administration (now the Parliamentary
Ombudsman), whose post was created in 1967 to investigate complaints from
the public against government departments. Then, in 1970, the Estimates
Committee was replaced by a Select Committee on Expenditure, operating
through specialised sub-committees on a wide range of government responsibilities. The Agriculture Committee had been disbanded in 1969 after it had
trodden on the Labour government's toes over the UK's application to join
the European Common Market, but agriculture became the responsibility
of one of the Expenditure Committee's sub-committees, as did education, so
that, apart from Scottish Affairs (abolished in 1972), the other committees
survived until 1979. The Expenditure Committee was ostensibly a financial
committee but, like the Estimates Committee, it used expenditure as a vehicle
for scrutinising policy. As such, and along with the other committees, it
considerably extended the scrutiny of policy and administration, although
its impact on public expenditure was negligible. However, demands for a
comprehensive committee system covering the whole range of government
responsibilities continued and, in 1978, the Procedure Committee produced
a major report recommending the creation of departmental committees.
Its recommendations were implemented in 1979 by the newly elected Conservative government and the present system dates from then. However, as
new departments are created, others abolished or merged, the number and

responsibilities of the departmental committees change: in 1979 there were fourteen, in 2003 eighteen. For example, since 1997 responsibility for transport has shifted several times, the work of the former Scottish and Welsh Offices has been much reduced, the Ministry of Agriculture, Fisheries and Food has been replaced by the Department of the Environment, Food and Rural Affairs and the Lord Chancellor's Department by the Department of Constitutional Affairs. In 1997 the cross-departmental Environmental Audit Committee was set up and the work of the departmental committees is further supplemented by the PAC and the Public Administration Committee, which has replaced the Select Committee on the Parliamentary Commissioner for Administration, and, following the Human Rights Act 1998, a joint committee on Human Rights has been established (see Table 9.9).

The House of Lords also operates a number of investigatory committees, but is not able to sustain as many committees as the Commons because most of its members are part-time rather than full-time (see Table 9.10). It has therefore created a small number of sessional, essentially permanent, committees – on the Constitution, Economic Affairs, the European Union, and Science and Technology, but supplements these by appointing ad hoc committees to conduct particular inquiries, of which there was one in 2003, on Religious Affairs. Other, recent ad hoc committees have included Central–Local Government Relations (1994–96), the Public Service (1996–97), the Monetary Policy of the Bank of England (1999–2001) and Stem Cell Research (2001–02). Proposals by members of the House for new ad hoc committees are considered each year by the House of Lords' Liaison Committee, which consists of the chairs of all select committees.

The membership of investigatory committees is decided through the usual channels in both Houses, with the views of the party whips playing a crucial role. In the Commons most committees have eleven members but some have more, to accommodate a wide range of responsibilities – Environment, Food and Rural Affairs, for instance; others to accommodate a wider range of parties – Constitutional Affairs, and Northern Ireland, and Environmental Audit, for example. Neither ministers nor opposition frontbenchers are members of investigatory committees, except in the cases of Environmental Audit and the PAC, whose membership includes the Minister for the Environment and the Financial Secretary to the Treasury, but neither attends, so that in practice each committee has fifteen members. There is more variation in membership in the Lords, partly due to the practice of using co-opted members, especially by the European Union Committee, and partly because the less partisan operation of the upper house allows greater flexibility. Membership is allocated in proportion to party representation in each House, including crossbenchers in the Lords. Eleven-member committees in the Commons therefore comprise seven Labour, three Conservative and one Liberal Democrat MPs, but the absence of a single-party majority in the Lords usually leaves Conservative and Labour with equal numbers – three to five, the Liberal Democrats with

Table 9.9 *Investigatory committees in the House of Commons, 2003*

Committee	Remit	Members	Chair	Sub-comms.
Departmental				
1 Constitutional Affairs	Dept. of Constl. Affairs	12	LD	No
2 Culture, Media and Sport	Dept. of Culture, Media and Sport	11	Lab.	No
3 Defence	Ministry of Defence	11	Lab.	No
4 Education and Skills	Dept. for Education and Skills	11	Lab.	No
5 Environment, Food and Rural Affairs	Dept. for Environment, Food and Rural Affairs	17	Cons.	2 (ad hoc)
6 Foreign Affairs	Foreign and Commonwealth Office	11	Lab.	No
7 Health	Department of Health	11	Lab.	No
8 Home Affairs	Home Office	11	Lab.	No
9 International Development	Dept. for International Development	11	Cons.	No
10 Northern Ireland	Northern Ireland Office	13	Cons.	No
11 Office of the Deputy Prime Minister	Housing, planning, local govt and regions	11	Lab.	1 (Urban Affairs)
12 Science and Technology	Office of Science and Technology and research councils	11	Lab.	No
13 Scottish Affairs	Scotland Office	11	Lab.	No
14 Trade and Industry	Dept. of Trade and Industry	11	Lab.	No
15 Transport	Dept. for Transport	11	Lab.	No
16 Treasury	Treasury, Inland Revenue and Customs and Excise	11	Lab.	1 (ad hoc)
17 Welsh Affairs	Wales Office	11	Lab.	No
18 Work and Pensions	Dept. for Work and Pensions	11	LD	No
Others				
1 Environmental Audit	All depts. and agencies	16†	Cons.	No
2 Public Accounts	All depts. and agencies	15†	Cons.	No
3 Public Administration	Ombudsmen, civil service	11	Lab.	No
Joint				
Human Rights	Human rights in the UK* and remedial orders under the Human Rights Act, 1998	12–6 MPs and 6 peers	Lab.	No

Source: www.parliament.uk.

Notes: * Excluding individual cases. † Including Minister for the Environment as a member of the Environmental Audit Committee and the Financial Secretary to the Treasury as a member of the PAC, neither of who attends in practice.

Table 9.10   *Investigatory committees in the House of Lords, 2003*

Committee	Remit	Members	Chair
Sessional (permanent)			
1 Constitution	Examine constitutional bills and keep operation of constitution under review	12	Cons.
2 Economic Affairs	Economic policy	13	Lab.
(a) Sub-Committee on the Finance Bill	Examine and report on annual Finance Bill	8 + 3 co-opted	Lab.
3 European Union 7 sub-committees:	EU documents and other matters relating to the EU	18	Crossbench
(a) Economic and Financial Affairs and International Trade		3 + 4 co-opted	Lab.
(b) Internal Market			
(c) Foreign Affairs, Defence and Development Policy		3 + 7 co-opted	Lab.
(d) Agriculture and Environment		3 + 7 co-opted	Cons.
(e) Law and Institutions		3 + 7 co-opted	Crossbench
(f) Home Affairs		2 + 7 co-opted	LD
(g) Social and Consumer Affairs		1 + 8 co-opted	Crossbench
4 Science and Technology	Science and technology policy	15	Crossbench
Ad hoc			
Religious Offences	The law on religious offences	12	Crossbench
Joint			
Human Rights	Human rights in the UK* and remedial orders under the Human Rights Act, 1998	12–6 MPs and 6 peers	Lab.

Source: www.parliament.uk.

Note: * Excluding individual cases.

two or three, and crossbenchers with two to four, depending on the size of the committee. Membership also reflects interest and expertise, with the latter particularly evident in the Lords. Committee chairs are similarly allocated via the usual channels. In the Commons this again reflects party representation, with the government deciding which its party will chair. In 2003 Labour chaired fourteen of the twenty-one investigatory committees in the Commons, including the Treasury Committee which is normally chaired by a government backbencher, the Conservatives five and the Liberal Democrats two. The choice of committee chairs is usually made by the Chief Whip of the party concerned, but from time to time one of the Commons' committees rejects the nominee and makes it own choice. As with membership, there is more flexibility in the Lords, with party being a major factor but expertise and experience playing an important part too, reflected in the fact that crossbenchers chaired three committees and two European Union sub-committees in 2003.

All investigatory committees are select committees and therefore have the power to take oral and written evidence, to appoint specialist advisers to assist them in their work, and, if they think necessary, to hold hearings anywhere in the UK and travel abroad on fact-finding trips, and a number make use of sub-committees. As noted in Chapter 7, Commons' select committees do not adopt the adversarial procedure of standing committees but meet and operate in a much less partisan atmosphere, while the Lords generally is less partisan than the Commons. Select committees also differ from standing committees in being empowered to take oral and written evidence, although special standing committees may do so but are seldom used, and to employ specialist advisers. It is, however, the ability to take evidence in particular that enables the investigatory committees in both Houses to engage in meaningful parliamentary scrutiny, but whom they may question and what they may see is subject to important limits. Although the attendance of witnesses or the production of papers from those outside Parliament and government can, if necessary, be enforced by either House, such witnesses seldom refuse and many welcome the opportunity to give oral and written evidence. Indeed, some written evidence is unsolicited in that when a committee announces an inquiry it issues a general invitation to submit evidence, as well as approaching particular individuals or organisations from whom it especially wishes to receive evidence. The occasional refusal to give evidence is usually resolved by an order to attend. In 1978, for instance, Sir Charles Villiers, Chair of the British Steel Corporation, refused to give evidence to the Nationalised Industries Committee on the grounds of commercial sensitivity, but subsequently appeared before the committee in a private session. Similarly, Arthur Scargill, then President of the National Union of Miners, refused to appear before the Energy Committee because he thought it would serve no useful purpose, but subsequently did when summoned to attend. In practice, pressure groups in particular are often keen to have the chance to present their views.

The taking of evidence from ministers, civil servants, and ministers' special advisers is a different matter, however, sometimes arousing controversy. Committees cannot require ministers, civil servants or special advisers to give evidence and can only request them to do so. Ministers normally give evidence when requested, but difficulties can arise over the formal responsibilities of particular ministers. For example, in 1976 the government became involved with a rescue package for the motor manufacturer, Chrysler UK, formal responsibility for which lay with the Secretary of State for Industry, but another Cabinet minister, Harold Lever, Chancellor of the Duchy of Lancaster, had been closely involved with the policy, even though he had no formal responsibility for it. The Prime Minister, Harold Wilson, therefore refused to allow Lever to appear before the relevant sub-committee of the Expenditure Committee. More recently, in 2001–02 the government refused to allow a Treasury minister to give evidence to the then Transport, Local Government and the Regions Committee on the Public–Private Partnership funding of the London Underground, resulting in the committee saying that the Secretary of State for Transport 'has been little more than a messenger'. Ultimately, it is for the Prime Minister to say whether a particular minister should appear before a committee. Similarly, it is ministers who decide which civil servants should give evidence and civil servants are provided with detailed guidance, known as the Osmotherly Rules, on giving evidence and may advise a committee that particular questions (such as what advice they have given to ministers) should be addressed to the minister rather than civil servants. When, in 1986, for instance, the Defence Committee wished to take evidence from named civil servants on the Westland affair, over which two Cabinet ministers resigned, the Cabinet Secretary gave evidence instead. Nor may committees have direct access to Cabinet papers or departmental files – written evidence from the Cabinet Office and departments normally takes the form of memoranda.

Ministers' special advisers have presented a particular problem for committees, especially as the number of special advisers has increased considerably. In 1974 there were 28 special advisers to ministers and 38 before Labour came to power in 1997. However, since then the number has more than doubled: in 2001 there were 81 special advisers, 28 of whom were in the Prime Minister's Office or the Cabinet Office. In many cases these advisers play only a limited role in the policy-making process and committees are unlikely to seek evidence from them. However, in a number of cases they play a crucial and major part, such as Jonathan Powell, the Prime Minister's Chief of Staff, and Alastair Campbell, the former Director of Communications, Andrew Adonis, Head of the No. 10 Policy Unit, or Ed Miliband, special adviser to the Chancellor of the Exchequer, from whom evidence was likely to be of considerable interest and value in committee inquiries. However, apart from the occasional exception, the Prime Minister has refused to allow special advisers to give evidence on the grounds that, as with civil servants, policy discussions

Table 9.11   *The number and type of witnesses appearing before investigatory committees, 1999–2000*

Type of witness	No.	%
Cabinet ministers	63	2.2
Other ministers	109	3.9
Civil servants/public bodies	991	35.4
MPs, peers, etc.*	24	0.9
From outside Parliament	1,609	57.5
Total	2,796	99.9

Source: House of Commons, *Sessional Return, 1999–2000*.

Note: * Including members of the Scottish and Welsh Executives and of the National Assembly for Wales.

within the government and any advice given is confidential. Thus, attempts by the Public Administration Committee to secure the appearance of several special advisers have been unsuccessful, as were the efforts by the Transport, Local Government and the Regions Committees to secure evidence from Lord Birt, the Prime Minister's adviser on transport policy.

It may seem surprising that nearly three-fifths of the witnesses appearing before investigatory committees in 1999–2000 were from outside Parliament, such as academics and other experts, and representatives of pressure groups, and that only 6.1 per cent were ministers, given that the committees are scrutinising government policy (see Table 9.11). But much of that scrutiny is focused on how policies are working or whether proposed policies will work, so that the second largest grouping, 35.4 per cent, comprises civil servants, representatives of public bodies such as executive agencies, health trusts and various commissions. Moreover, the global figures in Table 9.11 mask considerable variations between committees, relating partly to their remits and partly to what they are investigating in a particular session, so that there can be variations between sessions as well as committees. Some committees are more likely to take much of their evidence from witnesses outside Parliament – Culture, Media and Sport, the former Environment, Transport, Local Government and the Regions, Public Administration, the former Social Security, and Trade and Industry, for example; others from civil servants and other officials – Defence and Public Accounts, for instance; with, in 1999–2000, ministers appearing most often before Agriculture, Environmental Audit, International Development, Scottish Affairs and Treasury. In addition, considerable amounts of written evidence are received – 6,067 memoranda in 1998–99.[5] Similarly, the number of reports published by each committee varies, from the twenty produced by Defence and fourteen by Trade and Industry in 1999–2000 to the four by Health, Home Affairs, and Public Administration, three by Welsh

Affairs, and one by Scottish Affairs, although the last two had had their remits lessened by devolution. However, some of these reports were extensive, accompanied by one, sometimes two, volumes of evidence, others were the result of short, sharp inquiries into topical matters. This is, of course, apart from the much larger number of reports published by the PAC, assisted by the NAO – 47 in 1999–2000.

To assist them in their work each committee has one or more clerks responsible for its operation and administration and committees are also permitted to employ specialist advisers, either generally or for specific inquiries. In 1999–2000, for instance, the investigatory select committees employed 96 clerks and ancillary staff and 157 special advisers. The last figure does not, of course, include, the staff of the NAO who work for the PAC, but it was agreed in 2002 that the NAO would assist other committees, particularly in inquiries related to expenditure. Also in 2002, a full-time Scrutiny Unit with, some dozen staff and headed by a senior clerk, was set up to assist with consideration of the estimates and with pre-legislative scrutiny.

Although the party whips play an important part in deciding the membership of select committees and who is appointed chair, once established the committees are largely autonomous. In particular, they decide the topics for inquiries, although these are inevitably driven to some extent by political events. Thus issues such as the Millennium Dome, the supply of arms to the government of Sierra Leone in 1998, the government's handling of the outbreak of foot-and-mouth disease in 2001, or various aspects of the war against Iraq in 2003 and 2004 are bound to be investigated, but much also depends on the committee chair and the interests of the members, especially where the a committee's remit covers diverse policy areas. Committees sometimes conduct inquiries into matters for which the government has no responsibility, as the Culture, Media and Sport Committee has done when inquiring into the future of professional rugby and the future of ITV's *News at Ten*. Other committees, like the Public Administration Committee inquiry into the reform of the House of Lords, have arguably stretched their terms of reference. In fact, one of the criticisms made of select committees is that they are not sufficiently systematic in scrutinising government policy and administration within their remit and, in 2002, following recommendations by the Modernisation Committee, the House of Commons passed a resolution setting out the 'core tasks' of the departmental select committees (see Box 9.2).

Although most of the departmental committees carry out most of these tasks, it remains to be seen whether their work has become more systematic and comprehensive in practice. What can certainly be said is that investigatory committee activity and thus detailed scrutiny of government policy and administration continues to grow, as the figures in Table 9.12 show.

How effective are investigatory committees? A frequent criticism is that their impact is limited because their reports are seldom debated and, when they are, almost all those taking part are members of the committee concerned.

Box 9.2   The core tasks of departmental Select Committees

Task

1   To consider major policy initiatives.
2   To consider the government's response to major emerging issues.
3   To propose changes where evidence persuades the committee that present policy requires amendment.
4   To conduct pre-legislative scrutiny of draft bills.
5   To examine and report on the main Estimates, annual expenditure plans and annual resource accounts.
6   To monitor performance against targets in the Public Service Agreements.
7   To take evidence from each minister at least annually.
8   To take evidence from independent regulators and inspectorates.
9   To consider the reports of Executive Agencies.
10 To consider, and if appropriate report on, major appointments by a Secretary of State or other senior ministers.
11 To examine treaties within their subject areas.

Source: Modernisation Committee, *First Report*, HC 224-I, paras 31–5, and resolution of the House of Commons, 14 May 2002 (HC Deb., 385, 14 May 2002, c.715).

Table 9.12   *Number of meetings held and reports published by departmental committees, 1979–2000*

Parliament	Meetings*	Reports†
1979–83	2,140	193
1983–87	1,789	218
1987–92	1,968	323
1992–97	2,748	366
1997–2001	2,759	472

Source: Select Committee Returns.

Notes: * Including sub-committees. † Excluding special reports (mostly government responses to substantive reports).

Certainly, it was the case until recently that the opportunities to debate select committee reports were severely restricted, mainly to the three Estimates Days per year, allowing the debating of about six reports. However, the use of some morning sittings between 1995 and 1999 and, more importantly, some West-minster Hall sittings, has extended the number of opportunities considerably, allowing approximately thirty reports to be debated each session, although debates till tend to be limited to the committee members. This sort of criticism implies that it is only committee reports that are debated which have an impact, but ignores that fact that, by convention, the government normally replies reports within two months, recommendation by recommendation. Not all recommendations are accepted, but that too implies that committees are right and governments are wrong, whereas the reality is more complex. In terms of the sheer amount of information made available about government policy and administration, particularly in the form of oral and written evidence, there can be no doubt that they are effective. Much of the information brought into the public domain by committee activity is not available elsewhere and often would not be available were it not for the work of the committees. Assessing the impact on government policy on their reports is much more difficult. The Commons' Liaison Committee has suggested that their inquiries contribute to policy formation and assessment in four important ways: first, influence on longer-term policy and development in departments; second, in throwing light on topical issues arising out of particular events; third, in contributing to debates on particular issues, including those which cut across departmental responsibilities; and in conducting policy post mortems.[6] However, most committee reports make recommendations and whether these are accepted or not provides some measure of the impact of the committee. Research on the recommendations made by the former Education, Science and Arts Committee and the Social Services Committee in the 1979–83 Parliament found that 26.5 per cent and 35.1 per cent respectively were accepted, 27.1 per cent and 19.7 per cent rejected, with the remainder being kept under review.[7] These excluded recommendations not directly the responsibility of the government but which, in many cases, were passed to those concerned. There are also particular examples, such as the Home Affairs Committee on the abolition of the 'sus' law, the PAC on delays in issuing passports, several other committees on the operation of the Child Support Agency, the Treasury Committee on the way that government expenditure plans are presented to Parliament, and various committees on government procurement policy. One the other hand, governments have also rejected major recommendations – over the privatisation of naval dockyards, the UK's withdrawal from UNESCO, and criticism of arms sales to the government of Sierra Leone. Nonetheless, reports critical of government policy and administration, whether accepted or not, contribute importantly to the scrutiny process. Examples of such reports can be found in Table 9.13.

It is important to place the work of investigatory committees in a broader context. First, they are part of the wider policy networks that develop around issues and various policy areas. Second, in addition to providing a greater volume and range of information, the committees subject ministers and civil servants to greater scrutiny than in the past. Third, their longer-term impact is likely to be significant, especially as committees review earlier recommendations and return to particular issues. Fourth, more MPs than ever before

Table 9.13   *Examples of select committee reports critical of government policy and administration, 1999–2002*

Subject matter	Committee	Session
Private Finance Initiatives (PFIs) and Private Partnerships (PPPs)		
The new Dartford Tunnel PFI	Public Accounts Committee	1999–2000
National Air Traffic System PPP	Environment, Transport and the Regions Committee	2001–02
The Royal Armouries Museum at Leeds PFI	Public Accounts Committee	2001–02
The refurbishment of the Treasury Building PFI	Public Accounts Committee	2001–02
The London Underground PPP	Environment, Transport and the Regions Committee	
Arms to Sierra Leone	Foreign Affairs Committee	1998–99
	Foreign Affairs Committee	2001–02
The Ilisu Dam project in Turkey	Trade and Industry Committee	1999–2000
	International Development Committee	1999–2000
	Trade and Industry Committee	2000–01
	International Development Committee	2000–01
State Earnings-Related Pension Scheme (SERPS)	Public Accounts Committee	1999–2000
	Public Administration Committee	2000–01
	Public Accounts Committee	2000–01
Delays in the renewal of passports in 1999	Public Accounts Committee	1999–2000
The Millennium Dome Project	Culture, Media and Sport Committee	1999–2000
	Public Accounts Committee	2001–02
The Wembley Stadium Project	Culture, Media and Sport Committee	1999–2000
	Culture, Media and Sport Committee	2001–02
The collection of excise duty	Treasury Committee	2000–01
The Criminal Records Bureau	Home Affairs Committee	2000–01
Equitable Life and the life assurance industry	Treasury Committee	2000–01
The National Probation Service	Public Accounts Committee	2001–02
The future of Gibraltar	Foreign Affairs Committee	2001–02
The Channel Tunnel Rail Link	Public Accounts Committee	2001–02
The disposal of refrigerators	Environment, Food and Rural Affairs Committee	2001–02
The self-assessment tax scheme	Treasury Committee	2001–02

Table 9.14 *How effective is Parliament in scrutinising government activity in the following areas?*

Area	Very effective/quite effective	Not effective/not all effective	+/−
Government expenditure	31.6	32.2	−0.6
Other public services	25.4	36.4	−11.0
Departmental policy-making	26.4	38.5	−12.1
Central govt and the Cabinet Office	14.4	50.0	−35.6
Executive agencies	8.1	65.9	−57.8
Cross-cutting issues	4.0	67.2	−63.2
Utility regulators	6.4	75.6	−69.2
The EU Council of Ministers	4.1	82.8	−78.7
Quangos	1.7	83.9	−82.2
Overall	27.3	31.8	−11.0

Source: Hansard Society Commission on Parliamentary Scrutiny, 2001, Appendix 4, Table 2.5.

are involved in the work of investigatory committees, enlarging the pool of specialised knowledge available for scrutiny, knowledge that can be and is used beyond the confines of committee work into other areas of parliamentary scrutiny.

Non-legislative scrutiny: an overview

In a survey conducted on behalf of the Hansard Society Commission on Parliamentary Scrutiny, MPs were asked how effective they thought Parliament was in scrutinising various areas of government activity. The results are shown in Table 9.14.

The responses in Table 9.14 make depressing reading as a judgement on effective parliamentary scrutiny, but they need to be interpreted in the light of three factors. The first is the same MPs' judgement about the effectiveness of various scrutiny mechanisms (see Table 9.15).

These responses show a much more positive view of the effectiveness of various mechanisms in scrutinising government policy and administration, especially select committees and Questions for written answer, Urgent Questions and ministerial statements. Not surprisingly, PMQs rate very poorly. The second factor is that, following the massive 40 per cent turnover in membership in 1997, most MPs, especially backbenchers, have only a limited experience of the Commons: following the 2001 general election, half the Members had been elected since 1992, including 55.8 per cent of Labour MPs, 35.5 per cent of Conservatives and 76.9 per cent of Liberal Democrats.

Table 9.15 *How effective are the following mechanisms in securing information and explanations from government?*

Area	Very effective/quite effective	Not effective/not at all effective	+/−
Select committee hearings	86.2	3.4	+82.8
Written PQs	51.7	15.9	35.8
PNQs (Urgent Questions)	44.0	18.3	+25.7
Ministerial statements	46.0	20.4	+25.6
Departmental Question Time	25.6	40.3	−14.7
Opposition Days	23.4	48.0	−24.6
PMQs	8.0	73.1	−65.1

Source: Hansard Society Commission on Parliamentary Scrutiny, 2001, Appendix 4, Table 2.4.

This means that they lack a longer-term perspective, not least how much more extensive parliamentary scrutiny is now compared with the situation before 1979, let alone earlier. On the other hand, who better than MPs to judge how effectively they scrutinise government policy and administration? Yet, in a sense they are probably too close to the action, conscious more of the limitations of scrutiny than of its effectiveness. This is, in turn, related to the third factor: it is doubtful whether the responses in Table 9.14 take much account of scrutiny by the House of Lords. Quite apart from partisan views about the upper house as it is at present constituted, MPs are much more likely to focus on the actions of the Lords in dealing with government legislation than with non-legislative scrutiny. It is also a moot point as to how well informed MPs, including not a few ministers, are about what the House of Lords does.

The scrutiny role: horses for courses?

A different way of looking at non-legislative scrutiny is to shift the focus from effectiveness to purpose when looking at the various mechanisms available. Just as the various mechanisms for legislative scrutiny are intended to subject primary and secondary legislation to particular forms of scrutiny, some on principle, some on detail, some on legal propriety, so also do the various non-legislative scrutiny mechanisms. This is no better illustrated than by looking at parliamentary Questions, which come in a variety of forms within and between the two Houses of Parliament. Prime Ministers' Questions are often cited as Question Time at its worst, the Commons at its most adversarial and characterised by 'yah-boo' politics, as the Prime Minister and the Leader of the Opposition confront each other and their supporters bay at each other. Yet they serve the purpose, as indeed Question Time sometimes does on other occasions, of highlighting the partisan and ideological confrontation in general and in Parliament in particular. Some debates perform a similar function. Politics is in part about that confrontation, but only part, and other types of Question perform different functions. Those for written answer are used mainly to extract information; Urgent Questions or PNQs are a way of getting information and comment on a matter of immediate concern. Questions in the Lords are different again: Questions for written answer serve the same information-extracting purpose, but starred Questions – those for oral answer – are less partisan and more measured than is often the case in the Commons; and unstarred Questions are vehicles for initiating limited debates.

This same thread runs through other scrutiny mechanisms: the elaborate procedures developed to deal with financial business should not be lumped together as a whole but considered in their various parts. The Chancellor's Pre-Budget Report in the autumn of each year provides a valuable assessment of the state of the economy, but subsequent examination of public expenditure is woefully inadequate, yet the post-expenditure work of the PAC is highly praised. The Budget debate also provides not only a further opportunity to assess the economic situation but subjects the government's handling of the economy and the policies that flow from it to extensive scrutiny. Of course, parts of it and the later scrutiny of the Finance Bill are highly partisan, but other parts are not, especially those that focus on detailed proposals.

Other debates similarly vary in purpose: some of those initiated by the government and most of those by the opposition parties are strongly partisan, but at the same time focusing attention on issues that should be openly debated; backbench-initiated debates can also be partisan, but most are not, raising issues important to constituents, probing the working of government policy in detail. Debates in the Lords provide yet a further dimension, drawing on the wide range of expertise available in the upper house, sometimes duplicating topics covered in the Commons but often not, or approaching similar topics from different perspectives. Ministerial statements in both Houses offer further debating opportunities, though on a more limited basis.

Backbench opinion in the Commons is widely expressed through EDMs and, notwithstanding their use as parliamentary graffiti, enable the government to gauge parliamentary opinion on government policy and the political agenda generally, especially among its own supporters but also where opinion crosses the party boundaries. EDMs also enable MPs to give voice to public concerns more quickly than most other parliamentary procedures allow.

Investigatory committees, however, are widely regarded as the most effective form of scrutiny, with their ability to probe policy and administration in depth through the questioning of ministers, civil servants and other public officials and to open up parliamentary scrutiny to those outside Parliament, whether experts or those affected by government policy. The least partisan of the mechanisms available, they offer a more sober and considered form of scrutiny and their expansion in use and, more particularly, range, has added greatly to their value. They are less partisan because the government can afford to allow them to be: with the important exception of draft bills, no government business is dealt with procedurally by investigatory committees that leads governments to assert greater party control over them. Even draft bills do not present a problem: they can easily be 'retrieved', committee recommendations on them can be rejected; and the fate of bills does not depend on select committee proceedings.

Ultimately, it is a matter of 'horses for courses': oral Questions and some debates place ministers on the ideological spot, Questions for written answer and other debates extract information, motions express backbench opinion, investigatory committees probe in depth. How effective they are as means of scrutiny is a matter of judgement and, no doubt, ways of improving them or additional mechanisms could be suggested. In the end, their effectiveness depends on the willingness of MPs and peers to use them and to use them effectively; and that means securing a balance between the partisan and scrutiny roles.

Notes

1 Michael Wheeler-Booth, 'The House of Lords', in Robert Blackburn and Andrew Kennon, *Griffith and Ryle on Parliament: Functions, Practice and Procedures*, London, Sweet & Maxwell, 2nd edn, 2003, p. 685.
2 *Ibid.*, p. 685.
3 House of Commons, *Factsheet P1: Parliamentary Questions*.
4 Blackburn and Kennon, *Griffith and Ryle*, pp. 471–5 and 690–2.
5 *Ibid.*, p. 599.
6 See Liaison Committee, *First Report: Shifting the Balance – Select Committees and the Executive*, HC 300, 1999–2000 and *First Report: Shifting the Balance – Unfinished Business*, HC 321, 2000–02.
7 Michael Rush, 'The Education, Science and Arts Committee' and 'The Social Services Committee' in Gavin Drewry (ed.), *The New Select Committees: A Study of the 1979 Reforms*, Oxford, Clarendon, 2nd edn, 1989, Tables 5.3 and 13.2.

10

Parliament and the people

Introduction

The Parliament Act 1911 stipulates that the maximum life of a Parliament is five years, unless both Houses approve an extension beyond that period, as happened in the First and Second World Wars. However, because the UK does not have fixed-term elections, the Prime Minister may decide on an earlier dissolution of Parliament, usually when he or she thinks it most likely the governing party will win. As noted earlier, governments are rarely forced into elections and there are occasions when, faced with adverse opinion polls, the Prime Minister allows a Parliament to run its full course, as John Major did with the 1987–92 and 1992–97 Parliaments. However, general elections usually take place about every four years. In his book, *The Social Contract*, Rousseau asserts: 'The people of England regards itself as free; but it is grossly mistaken; it is free only during the elections of Members of Parliament.'[1] Rousseau's concern was that periodic elections were not a sufficient condition for democracy; there had to be a means of giving continuous expression to popular consent. In short, in what ways could popular consent be elicited *between* elections?

The equally short answer is, by a number of means, though they could hardly be said to amount to continuous popular consent. A number of these means were mentioned in Chapter 4 – referendums, initiatives, recalls, opinion polls, e-democracy, pressure politics, and legislative representation. Referendums are used only rarely in the UK. The initiative has had limited use locally and the recall is not used at all. These will be discussed further in the final chapter. This chapter is concerned with legislative representation, particularly the MP's constituency role, and with pressure politics and Parliament, although it will briefly examine what people think of Parliament as an institution. Before doing so, however, the existence of other elections, often held between general elections needs to be discussed. Each general election normally produces a full complement of MPs for the House of Commons; very occasionally, for instance, a candidate dies during the actual election campaign and a further election in that constituency becomes necessary. However, between general elections casual vacancies occur, most commonly nowadays because of the death of a Member, but also through resignation or being appointed to a post incompatible with continued membership of the Commons and, very occasionally, through the disqualification of a Member. Such vacancies are filled through a by-election in the constituency concerned: between 1945 and 1997 the average number of by-elections per year was 8.3, but by-elections have become less frequent, as electors in the constituencies concerned often took the opportunity to express their dissatisfaction with the government. Consequently, the number of 'unnecessary' vacancies created by appointing MPs to various positions incompatible with continued membership has declined sharply: between 1945 and 1970 the average number of by-elections per year was 11.2, but from 1970 to 1997 it was only 5.7. By-elections, however, are an unsatisfactory means of expressing public opinion, since they are limited to the constituency concerned, although the message they send can be remarkably powerful. In March 1962, for instance, the Conservatives lost the very safe seat of Orpington in Kent to the Liberals in a by-election and in July the Prime Minister, Harold Macmillan, sacked a third of his Cabinet and made 24 changes altogether in his government. Orpington was not the direct cause but it was a major factor. The 1974–79 Labour government found its majority whittled away through by-elections and the Conservatives failed to win a single by-election throughout the 1992–97 Parliament, in both cases contributing to the delaying of the following general election. But by-elections are too few and too haphazard a means of gauging public opinion between general elections.

Other elections, however, can provide a more reliable indicator, even though that is not their purpose. Local elections have long been seen as widespread tests of opinion, with opposition parties often gaining support at the expense of the governing party. Similarly, the same could be said of elections to the European Parliament, though not necessarily of elections to the Scottish Parliament and the National Assembly for Wales, vis-à-vis the UK government. Even so, while all these elections provide a better test of opinion than by-elections because of their wider geographical spread, they suffer from the same disadvantages as by-elections. Local, European and devolved elections are intended to elect representatives to particular bodies and use of them as 'protest' votes is not in the interests of effective local, European or devolved politics. As expressions of opinion, however, they are blunt instruments, difficult to be certain whether they reflect general dissatisfaction or concern about specific policies. In the latter case, there are far better ways of influencing policy.

The constituency role

Apart from university seats (first established in 1603 and abolished from 1950), MPs have always represented territorial constituencies. It is therefore hardly surprising that their constituents should expect Members of Parliament to respond to their concerns and one of the earliest means of expressing such concerns was by petition. Petitions, however, preceded Parliament and were originally addressed to the monarch, who dealt with them in a variety of ways, later referring some to Parliament, particularly the Commons. Most early petitions sought redress for individual grievances, including groups of individuals from a particular city, town or locality. These were the origin of private bills. In due course, wider petitions began to develop, sometimes arising from individual petitioners becoming aware that they had common grievances and then combining their efforts to increase the pressure for redress, but eventually leading to common petitions with more widespread support. It was in common petitions that public bills had their origin, though, of course, not all petitions required legislation. The number of petitions presented to Parliament has varied historically, but rose dramatically in the nineteenth century: in 1785 there were 298 but by 1833 the number had risen to 10,394 and was causing problems with the organisation of business in the Commons, as debating petitions had precedence over other business and were used by MPs to debate matters of their choice rather than the government's. This problem was solved in 1842 by referring all petitions to a select committee, although the number of petitions continued to rise, reaching well over 30,000 by the end of the century and used increasingly to express views on political issues. Thereafter, they declined sharply to the point that in 1939–40 there was only one. However, a revival occurred in the 1980s and early 1990s, culminating in 2,651 in 1992–93, followed by a further decline to about a hundred a year. Petitions can only be presented via a Member, who is not obliged to do so, but usually will when requested. Two-thirds of petitions are formally presented on the floor of the House, but no debate is allowed; the remaining third are informally presented via a petition 'bag' behind the Speaker's Chair. Petitions are then passed to the government department concerned and about two-thirds receive a response in the form of a departmental 'observation'. The modern importance of petitions is as a means of drawing attention to an individual grievance, usually from a constituent, or publicising a more widespread grievance or matter of concern over government policy, often though not necessarily exclusively from constituents. In practice, there are more important and effective ways of dealing with constituency concerns, whether arising from individual grievances or matters affecting constituents more generally.[2]

There is, in fact, ample historical evidence that MPs have expected and have responded to the pleas and demands of constituents. The constituency role is not therefore a modern phenomenon; what is modern is its scope and universality. In medieval times and after, some MPs were faced with and paid far more attention to demands from their constituents than others, depending on both constituents and their interests, on the one hand, and the inclinations of individual MPs, on the other. As the pace of economic and social change quickened, especially under the impact of the agricultural and industrial revolutions, so constituency demands increased and the constituency role expanded. Edmund Burke, as noted in Chapter 3, famously declared that he was not the 'Member for Bristol' but a 'Member of Parliament' and in 1778 supported an Irish Trade Bill which a number of his constituents opposed. However, Burke felt obliged to explain to his constituents why he favoured the bill.[3] More positive evidence can be found of MPs acting on behalf of their constituents before 1832 in the case of Liverpool, where Sir Thomas Johnson (MP for Liverpool 1701–23) Bamber Gascoyne (1780–96) and his brother, Isaac Gascoyne (1796–1831) defended the city's trading interests in the Commons, both in debate and by promoting bills.

Similar activities can be found for MPs representing other cities and parts of the country, leading Lord North, when Prime Minister, to comment: 'The representatives of the trading towns and manufacturing counties are fully apprised of the sentiments and wishes of their constituents.'[4] MPs were also channels for patronage – jobs, sinecures, pensions and honours in the gift of the government, although an important part of this patronage largely disappeared following civil service reforms begun in 1854 and the introduction of open competition in 1870. However, some MPs, both before and after 1832 had little or no contact with their constituents. Porritt, drawing a contrast between the county Member, who 'was usually answerable to the public opinion of his county' and those representing constituencies with major commercial interests, such as London, Bristol and Liverpool, on the one hand, and those elected for smaller boroughs, on the other: 'Many of these boroughs were never visited by their Members from the election of a Parliament to its conclusion. In some it was not even necessary that a candidate should attend the election; while in others ... it was stipulated by patrons that Members should not go near their constituencies.'[5] This continued to varying degrees after 1832, declining only with the gradual elimination of nomination boroughs, further extensions of the franchise and growing government intervention, which stimulated demands on MPs from constituents. Under the impact of social and economic change constituents increasingly raised individual complaints or problems with MPs, as well as the more traditional matters relating to the collective interests of the constituency. The former included 'dismissals from posts in the public service, the provision of pensions to particular individuals, taxation disputes, various cases involving members of the army and navy, and, frequently, criminal cases'.[6] Collective interests concerned 'trade, industry, commerce, agriculture, and employment ... [but with] ... the development of the postal, telegraph, and telephone services, these too figured prominently in the constituency matters raised by Members'.[7] Yet more government intervention served merely to increase the scope and extent of the constituency role, particularly with individual constituents' problems. For example the introduction of the old age pension in 1909 and sickness and unemployment benefit in 1911 had a clear impact: 'the 1909 *Hansard* index contains 157 named pensions cases, that of 1910 251, falling to 53 in 1913. The national insurance benefits produced similar listings and the number of cases increased yet further during and after the First World War'.[8] Nonetheless, even in the inter-war period some MPs continued to resist constituents' demands or at least be reluctant constituency MPs and it was not until after the Second World War, with the massive expansion of the welfare state and enormous growth of the public sector, that the constituency role came to be fully recognised by the overwhelming majority of MPs, developing into what became known as 'the welfare officer role'. Even as later as 1967, a survey of MPs found 11.9 per cent of the opinion thought that 'the "welfare officer role" has been taken too far'.[9]

Various ways of tracing the growth of the constituency role have been used, but none is entirely satisfactory, since no broad overall measure exists. Anecdotal material, drawing on memoirs, biographies, autobiographies and various historical studies of Parliament, provides a useful source but not a systematic measure. A somewhat more systematic measure over time is the number of letters received by MPs, particularly from constituents, and the number of letters between Members and ministers. Even here, estimates, different methods of counting, not always distinguishing between parties, and not drawing a distinction between letters from constituents and non-constituents blur the picture. In his comprehensive study, *Parliament*, Sir Ivor Jennings cites select committee evidence in 1920 of MPs replying to at least 50 letters a week from constituents and in 1945 receiving an average of 80 a week from all sources.[10] In 1967, Barker and Rush found that 61.5 per cent of MPs received between 25 and 74 letters a week from constituents, a further 25 per cent 75 or more, and only 13.5 per cent fewer than 25. This was a marked contrast with the letters received from non-constituents: 50 per cent received fewer than 25 per week and only 15.2 per cent between 25 and 74, although 34.8 per cent said it varied. In general, Labour MPs received more letters from constituents and non-constituents, though not overwhelmingly so.[11] A survey conducted by the Letter Writing Bureau in 1986 found that nearly half the Members (47 per cent) received between 120 and 210 letters a week and more than a quarter (28 per cent) between 216 and 300, with three-quarters (73 per cent) saying that more than half came from constituents.[12] By 2000, when the Hansard Society survey was conducted, four-fifths of Members were receiving more than a hundred letters, half (49.3 per cent) more than two hundred, and nearly a fifth (18.4 per cent) more than three hundred.[13] These latest figures do not include e-mails or responding via MPs' websites and it is worth noting that in 2003 four-fifths of MPs had publicly accessible e-mail addresses and three-fifths had websites (see Table 10.1). Most

Table 10.1   *MPs with e-mail addresses and websites accessible to the public,*
2003

Party	E-mail	Website
Cons.	72.8	55.4
Lab.	85.3	64.8
LD	90.7	89.3
SNP	100.0	60.0
PC	75.0	50.0
Other	60.0	30.0
Total	81.9	63.3

Source: www.parliament.uk.

MPs receive less than a hundred e-mails a week from constituents, but this is likely to be an increasingly common way of contacting MPs.[14]

In addition to contacting their MPs by letter, e-mail or through a website, constituents may also telephone Members or their staff at Westminster or in the constituency, where most MPs have offices or contact numbers. They may then be asked to put details of their problem or complaint in writing or offered a meeting with the Member at a constituency 'surgery'. The holding of regular sessions or 'surgeries' at which constituents can discuss their problems is a long-standing practice, going back to at least the inter-war period, and itself preceded by MPs meeting particular constituents by arrangement. How widespread the practice was before the Second World War is difficult to say but, writing in 1939, Jennings suggests: 'Even before 1924 [when free rail travel to and from the constituency was introduced] many MPs were compelled to visit their constituencies nearly every week.'[15] However, it is doubtful whether 'many' meant 'most' and it was almost certainly more common among Labour and Liberal than Conservative MPs. After 1945 surgeries became increasingly common: in 1963 Robert Dowse found that 84.1 per cent of MPs, including ministers, held surgeries[16] and by 1967 90.7 per cent of MPs, excluding ministers, did so: 'Surgeries were slightly more common among Labour MPs, but more Conservatives saw constituents by appointment and less than 2 per cent of all MPs did not hold surgeries.'[17] The availability of surgeries is usually advertised in the local press and places such as public libraries, civic centres or local authority offices, as well as on Members' websites. In general, direct contact with constituents has been enhanced by the introduction after 1997 of 'constituency Fridays', when the House is not sitting.

The extent to which the constituency role has grown can also be shown by the amount of time MPs devote to it (Table 10.2). Although the overall time on parliamentary business during the session increased only marginally between 1982 and 1996, there was a marked shift in the proportion spent on

Table 10.2 *Time spent by backbenchers on constituency and non-constituency work, 1982 and 1996 (hours per week (%))*

1982 and 1996

	1982	1996	1982	1996
	In session	In session	In recesses	In recesses
Constit. work	13 (19.4)	27 (38.6)	23 (57.5)	31 (62.0)
Non-constit. work	54 (80.6)	43 (61.4)	17 (42.5)	19 (38.0)
Total	67 (100.0)	70 (100.0)	40 (100.0)	50 (100.0)

Source: 1982 and 1996: TSRB, *Report No. 20*, Cmnd. 8881-II, May 1983, Section I, Table 4 & SSRB, *Report No. 38*, Cm. 3330-II, July 1996, 30–1.

2000

	Range (hrs per week (%))
Constit. work	28–46 (63.6–62.2)
Non-constit. work	16–28 (36.4–37.8)
Total	44–74

Source: 2000: adapted from *Report of the Hansard Society Commission on Parliamentary Scrutiny*, Survey of MPs, Tables 3.7 and 3.10.

constituency work from one to two-fifths; and, while the *proportion* of time spent on constituency work during recesses remained around three-fifths, the average number of hours increased from 23 to 31. Moreover, by 2000 constituency work took up more time than non-constituency work overall, a mark of the emphasis that MPs now place on the constituency role, as well as its growth.

All these measures of the growth in the constituency role are reflected in an analysis of *Hansard* indexes in selected sessions between 1871 and 1995. Bearing in mind that raising a constituency issue through parliamentary Questions, in debate or sometimes by tabling a Private Members' bill are one of several alternatives open to MPs and not the most common means used, since they exclude private and informal approaches to ministers and departments and the use of Early Day Motions, the figures in Table 10.3 almost certainly represent minimum levels of constituency activity by MPs. Furthermore, although there are differences between parties, especially in the earlier sessions covered, the modern extent of the constituency role is clear – in effect, all MPs are involved.

In dealing with problems raised by individual constituents MPs have four basic choices, depending partly on the nature of the problem and partly on

Table 10.3   *Proportion of backbench MPs raising constituency issues in Parliament, 1871–1995*

Party	1871	1887	1901	1913	1928	1946–47	1961–62	1976–77	1994–95
Cons.	9.6	31.8	34.8	47.5	45.6	84.5	75.4	89.3	85.7
Lib/LD	11.7	43.5	55.2	44.5	55.8	65.0	85.7	100.0	100.0
Lab.	–	–	100.0	60.0	76.2	75.2	88.9	84.4	86.9
All	11.2	45.2	50.1	49.8	54.5	78.2	81.2	87.3	86.6

Source: *Hansard* indexes for each year.

the judgement of the Member. Of course, an initial judgement by the Member may result in the matter being taken no further, perhaps because it is clear that no redress is available, perhaps because it does not fall within the scope of public policy, perhaps because the Member totally lacks sympathy with the complaint, but in all cases a reply would normally be sent. However, this and most other aspects of the constituency role are dealt with in a non-partisan fashion, so that the constituent's political views are not normally a factor as far as the Member is concerned. Similarly, in dealing with individual griev-ances in particular, government MPs do not receive preference over opposi-tion MPs. The four options for dealing with a constituent's case are contacting the minister or government department concerned, contacting a local coun-cillor or local official (or other appropriate persons or bodies), referring the case to the Parliamentary Ombudsman, and raising the matter in Parliament. These are neither sequential nor mutually exclusive options, and the nature of the case and the Member's experience of similar cases will quickly deter-mine which option or options are followed.

If the matter is one of national government responsibility, the most com-monly used option is through a minister or government department. Letters from MPs receive priority in government departments and therefore offer a reasonably quick response. Thus, it is hardly surprising that the number of letters from MPs to ministers has increased considerably: it was estimated that in 1908 the number of letters dealt with by ministers, mostly from MPs, was 'a few thousand', by 1947–48 over a 100,000, and by 1990 250,000.[18] No doubt the level of correspondence has continued to grow, further enhanced by e-mail. Informal contacts with departments by telephone or, in the case of ministers, in the division lobbies, dining rooms and cafeterias and other parts of the Palace of Westminster also take place. Dealing directly with govern-ment departments and securing a letter responding to the problem from a minister is popular with Members because a copy of the letter can be passed to the constituent and MPs are aware that, even in cases in which no redress is offered, a ministerial letter often helps to mollify the constituent's feelings.

Writing to one's MP is a well-known means of seeking help, but people are not always aware of what is a matter for national government as distinct from some other person or body in authority. In any case, even knowing who is responsible for what is no bar to seeking the MP's help, although this has been complicated by the devolution of a wide range of policy and administrative responsibilities to devolved institutions in Scotland, Wales and Northern Ireland. In these cases, Westminster MPs pass on cases or advise constituents to contact their representative in the devolved legislature. This does not, of course, apply to MPs representing English constituencies and MPs have long taken up cases such as housing and education with local authorities, usually involving local councillors and officials. Furthermore, in many welfare cases the MP initially contacts local officials of bodies like the Benefits Agency before, if necessary, taking up the matter nationally.

Yet another alternative is to refer a complaint to the Parliamentary Ombudsman, who has powers to investigate government departments and agencies in cases of alleged maladministration. The office of Parliamentary Commissioner for Administration (or Parliamentary Ombudsman) was established in 1967 and was the first step in setting up an extensive ombudsman system covering most public services, whether provided by government departments or other bodies, including all the privatised industries. However, the Parliamentary Ombudsman differs from other ombudsmen in that complaints must be made through a Member of Parliament, although the Ombudsman will pass on complaints received directly to the constituent's MP, but it is up to the MP to decide whether to ask the Ombudsman to conduct an investigation. All other ombudsmen, including those established by the devolved institutions, may receive complaints directly. The channelling of complaints through MPs was adopted because of fears that the Ombudsman would be overwhelmed with cases and because MPs feared a dilution of their constituency role. In the event, the Ombudsman was not overwhelmed and it is doubtful whether the constituency role would have been adversely affected; on the contrary, the Parliamentary Ombudsman (and the ombudsman system generally) has considerably enhanced the ability of MPs to help their constituents.

The Ombudsman is restricted to complaints of alleged maladministration and cannot investigate complaints about government policy or those for which a remedy is available via a statutory tribunal, such as those on employment or taxation, or through the normal courts, or with the decisions of tribunals or courts, personnel matters, or those involving commercial contracts. Nonetheless, maladministration covers a significant range of matters: in general, it means 'poor advice or the wrong application of the rules', such as 'avoidable delay, faulty procedures or failing to follow the correct procedures', failure to inform the complainant about any rights of appeal, misleading or inadequate advice, 'refusing to answer reasonable questions, discourtesy and failure to apologise properly for errors, mistakes in handling ... claims [and] not offering an adequate remedy where one is due'.[19] Successive Parliamentary Ombudsmen have extended their jurisdiction by creating and following precedents and the Ombudsman's jurisdiction has also been formally extended in various ways since 1967. In 2001–02 the Parliamentary Ombudsman received 2,139 complaints, dealt with 2,582 (including cases carried forward from the previous year), of which just over half (1,358) were rejected and 195 were subject to a full investigation. However, it is important to place these figures in their proper context: all complaints are subject to prime facie investigation, but a significant number are rejected as beyond the Ombudsman's jurisdiction; many other complaints are settled through the good offices of the Ombudsman before reaching the full investigation stage; and of those fully investigated in 2001–02 more than four-fifths were found to be justified – 22 per cent partly justified, 63 per cent fully justified.

Finally, there are various opportunities for Members to raise constituents' grievances in the House – through parliamentary Questions, in debates (especially adjournment and Westminster Hall debates), or by tabling an EDM, which will not normally be debated but will be published and draw attention to the matter. In general, however, Members prefer to deal with constituency cases more privately, through contacting ministers, government departments or other bodies, or, where appropriate, referring a case to the Parliamentary Ombudsman. Using a more public means is sometimes a sign that other options have failed, although MPs may also enlist the help of the media and some cases receive media attention before the MP becomes involved. Dealing with individual constituency grievances takes up most of the time MPs devote to the constituency role – between three-fifths and two-thirds, and more than two-fifths of their time overall, according to the figures in the Hansard Society survey in 2000.[20] As far as the subject-matter of individual constituency cases is concerned, the same survey suggests that dealing with local council and welfare matters are the most common, followed by Child Support Agency and immigration cases. Some issues are perennial, others come and go. Thus the 1986 survey by the Letter Writing Bureau found housing (basically a local authority issue), health and welfare benefits topped the list, but immigration was cited by only 10 per cent.[21]

The constituency role, however, is also concerned with what may be termed collective issues, matters of interest or concern to some or many of a Member's constituents. As with individual problems, some collective issues are perennial, others come and go. For example, persuading the government to approve the building of a local by-pass, seeking to prevent the closure of a local factory, or securing funds for building a new hospital or school are battles which, once won or lost, are either an end to the matter or pushed back down the political agenda. But long-term issues such as economic or environmental interests are always there and MPs are expected to respond to local opinion and to take the initiative in defending and advancing constituency interests. The UK's membership of the EU has increased the importance of such interests, especially with the availability of funds from Brussels. Similarly, the growing dispersal of civil servants and government agencies around the country has opened up yet another dimension. The economic and social make-up of a constituency largely determines the nature of collective constituency demands on the MP. The manufacturing, commercial, agricultural and other interests jostle for attention, often seeking opportunities and changes in policy with wider implications for the constituency, particularly relating to its transport and communication infrastructure, housing stock, leisure amenities and so on, quite apart from demands in these areas in their own right. This is not a new phenomenon, as the history of Parliament's involvement in the agricultural and industrial revolutions demonstrates, but its scope and scale is, and looking after the collective interests of the constituency is as much part of the constituency role as dealing with individual grievances. Like the latter, the collective constituency role is conducted on a largely non-partisan basis. Of course, which party a Member represents will probably result in a greater or lesser sympathy for or identification with particular constituency interests, but not normally to the extent of refusing to help. In addition, collective constituency interests are more likely to be directly affected by government policy and this sometimes gives government backbenchers an advantage, but it can also be a disadvantage if the government is reluctant to make concessions. The party whips generally take a sympathetic view of the Member whose constituency interests conflict with party policy, sometimes quietly allowing an abstention in a division or even voting against the party line. In addition, it is not unusual for MPs from constituencies with common interests within a particular city or part of the country or more generally to co-operate, sometimes across party lines.

Philip Norton has provided a valuable overview of the individual and collective aspects of the constituency role (see Table 10.4) – the 'powerful friend' and the 'promoter of constituency interests', but points to other dimensions of the constituency role – the 'safety valve', the 'information provider', the 'advocate', the 'local dignitary', and the 'local benefactor'. There is little doubt that contacts with constituents provide MPs with valuable feedback on government policy and administration, particularly 'where the shoe pinches' but also on wider issues of public concern. All MPs receive letters from constituents and non-constituents on policy matters, some more than others, especially where they are identified with a particular cause or point of view. In addition, pressure groups frequently urge their members to contact their MPs by various means – letters, e-mails, attending a constituency surgery, lobbying them at Westminster. Such activity often enables MPs to gauge local and sometimes national opinion. Conversely, MPs are in a position to inform and advise constituents about government or party policy, creating a two-way channel of communication. Many MPs write columns for their local newspapers and frequently take part in local and regional radio or television broadcasts. Some issues are also of special concern to a Member's constituents, sometimes because of the socio-economic make-up of the constituency, more commonly because particular events, such as tragic accidents or legal cases such as child abuse or gun crimes. Historically, MPs were also seen as local benefactors, not

Table 10.4   *The constituency role of the Member of Parliament*

Role	Function
Powerful friend	The MP seeks to redress an individual constituent's grievance by contacting a minister, government department or agency, local authority or other body, utilising direct contacts, parliamentary procedures, or the Parliamentary Ombudsman. *Active.*
Promoter of constituency interests	The MP seeks to promote, advance or defend local economic, cultural, environmental and other interests. *Active.*
Safety valve	Constituents are able to express their views on public policy to the MP. Enables the MP to gauge local and possibly national public opinion. *Largely passive.*
Information provider	Constituents able to seek information and advice from the MP about government or party policy *Semi-active.*
Advocate	The MP identifies with a particular cause centred in or with support in the constituency. Includes local constituency party activity. *Passive/active.*
Local dignitary	The MP attends official and other functions in the constituency ex officio. *Largely passive.*
Benefactor	The MP provides personal help, possibly financial, to an individual constituent or group of constituents (e.g. donations to local organisations). Historically important as a dispenser of and channel for patronage. *Active.*

Source: Adapted from Philip Norton, 'The Growth of the Constituency Role of the MP', in
F. F. Ridley and Michael Rush (eds), *British Government and Politics Since 1945: Changes in
Perspective*, Oxford University Press, 1995, pp. 208–10. Also published in *Parliamentary Affairs*,
47, 1994.

least because many were wealthy and able to help individual constituents
financially or engage in local philanthropy in various ways by funding municipal projects such as local libraries, educational institutions or almshouses,
as well as being dispensers of local and national patronage. The main vestige
of this remains subscriptions to local organisations, although helping secure
funds from various sources – the Millennium Commission, national bodies
like the Arts Council, or European funds have become increasingly important.
Finally, the MP continues to fulfil a role as a local dignitary, attending official
and other functions in the constituency. Furthermore, not only is more time
spent on some aspects of the constituency role than others but some may be
described as active, such as dealing with individual constituents' problems,
and others as passive, such as attending local functions.

Evidence of all these activities is found in the Hansard Society survey, but it also shows that it is with dealing constituents' individual problems that account for the bulk of the time MPs spend fulfilling the constituency role. More significantly, however, the Hansard and the earlier TSRB/SSRB surveys (see Table 10.2) show that the constituency role generally has taken more and more of MPs' time to the point that the Hansard survey found that constituency work occupied as much as three-fifths of the hours MPs work. The earlier surveys of 1982 and 1996 already showed the balance moving in this direction, particularly during recesses, and for some observers is a cause for concern. If the balance between the scrutiny and constituency roles in particular shifts markedly towards one at the expense of the other, particularly towards the constituency role, then the effectiveness with which the scrutiny role is performed may be seriously affected.

Parliament and pressure politics

The context

'There is no such thing as society. There are individual men and women and there are families', Margaret Thatcher once famously said. She might have added that there are also many and often conflicting interests. One of the commonest ways of advancing and defending interests is through pressure groups, which, like parties, are agencies of political mobilisation in that they enable people to combine their efforts and resources in attempting to influence public policy. However, while parties advance and defend a broad range of interests, pressure groups are normally focused on a much narrower range. That said, while some pressure groups clearly represent a single interest, whether it is a particular group of people or a particular cause, others are more difficult to identify. Similarly, political parties are usually easily identified but the boundary between parties and pressures is in practice blurred. Although British politics is dominated by two major parties, plus a significant third party, excluding independent candidates with no party label, the official election return for the 2001 general election lists no fewer than 42 parties. However, at least a dozen were pressure groups masquerading as parties in that they were simply putting up candidates to publicise their cause, such as the Pro-Life Alliance (with 37 candidates) and the Legalise Cannabis Alliance (with 13 candidates). On the other hand, the United Kingdom Independence Party (UKIP) could be said to straddle the boundary. It was formed as the Anti-Federalist League in 1991 to campaign against the UK's membership of the EU, ran 428 candidates in 2001 and won 1.5 per cent of the vote[22] and in that respect was very like the Referendum Party, also opposed to the EU, which had 547 candidates in 1997 and won 2.6 per cent of the vote. Yet, in the elections to the European Parliament in 2004 UKIP secured the election of 12 MEPs and won 16.1 per cent of the vote in Great Britain, pushing the

Liberal Democrats into fourth place on share of the vote. Nonetheless, at least 21 of the 'parties' contesting the 2001 election were parties in the sense that, realistically or otherwise, they were nominating a number of candidates in the hope of securing their election to Parliament and, moreover, had manifestos covering all or most of the principal policy areas. However, only five – the Conservatives, Labour, the Liberal Democrats, the Greens, and the Socialist Labour Party put up more than a hundred candidates for the 659 seats, although the Scottish National Party and Scottish Socialists put up candidates in all the Scottish constituencies, as did Plaid Cymru in all Welsh constituencies, and the Ulster Unionists, Sinn Fein and the Social and Democratic Labour Party fought all Northern Ireland seats.

Lobbying or pressure politics is as old as politics itself, but increasing governmental intervention led to the formation of pressure groups as a means of making lobbying more effective. Trading, commercial, financial and, in due course, manufacturing interests actively lobbied ministers and MPs from the early eighteenth century, but some of earliest pressure groups were those pressing for political and parliamentary reform – the Society for Supporting the Bill of Rights (1769), the Society for Promoting Constitutional Information (1780), and the Friends of the People (1792), plus others in different parts of the country, such as London, Manchester and Sheffield. Another early and ultimately successful pressure group was the Committee for Effecting the Abolition of the Slave Trade, founded in 1787 and achieving its objective in 1807. In addition, various scientific, religious, charitable and philanthropic organisations were set from the late sixteenth onwards – the Royal Society (of London for Improving Natural Knowledge) (1662), the Society for Promoting Christian Knowledge (1699), the Royal Society of Arts (the Encouragement of the Arts, Manufacturers and Commerce) (1754), the Sunday School Society (1785), various missionary societies, the National Society for Promoting Education (1809), the Royal National Lifeboat Institution (1824), the Royal Society for the Prevention of Cruelty to Animals (RSPCA) (1824), and the British and Foreign Temperance Society (1831). The partial repeal of anti-trade union legislation in 1824 opened the way to the formation of trade unions, particularly among skilled workers – the Steam Engine Makers, the National Union of Cotton Spinners, the Society of Carpenters and Joiners, and the Potters' Union, for example, and the setting up of the Trades Union Congress (TUC) in 1868. Employers also organised themselves – the Association of the British Chambers of Commerce (1865), the Railway Companies Association (1867), the National Federation of Associated Employers of Labour (1873), and the British Iron Trade Association (1875), for instance. In 1898, an Employers' Parliamentary Council was set up to 'take action with respect to any bills ... affecting the interests of trade, of free contract and of labour'[23] and 1916 saw the formation of the Federation of British Industry and the National Union of Manufacturers, which merged to form the Confederation of British Industry in 1965. In agriculture, the Central and

Associated Chamber of Agriculture was formed in 1866, the National Agricultural Union in 1982 and the National Farmers' Union (NFU) in 1908. Not surprisingly, the First World War produced a number of ex-servicemen's organisations – the National Federation of Discharged and Demobilised Sailors and Soldiers (1917), the National Union of Ex-Servicemen (1920) and the British Legion (1921).

Three of the most well-known nineteenth-century groups are the Catholic Association, the Anti-Corn Law League and the Chartists, the first two conspicuously successful, the third a failure in its immediate impact. The Catholic Association was formed by Daniel O'Connell, an Irish lawyer, and his supporters to remove the legal barriers against Roman Catholics holding various public offices, including that of Member of Parliament. The Association successfully ran Catholic candidates in a series of by-elections and this, together with the fear of widespread disaffection, led to Catholic Emancipation in 1829, with O'Connell being the first Catholic MP since Catholics were excluded from the Commons in the seventeenth century. The Anti-Corn Law League was founded in 1839 by Richard Cobden and John Bright, both Lancashire cotton manufacturers, to campaign for the repeal of the 1815 Corn Laws, which kept the price of bread artificially high and therefore affected manufacturing costs. Through huge public meetings, pamphleteering and annual bills in Parliament, but ultimately assisted by the failure of the Irish potato crop in 1845 and famine in Ireland, it persuaded the Prime Minister, Sir Robert Peel, to repeal the Corn Laws in 1846, splitting his Conservative Party in the process. The Chartists grew out of the London Workingmen's Association, founded in 1837, and drew up a People's Charter demanding universal manhood suffrage, equal electoral districts, voting by secret ballot, the abolition of the property qualification for MPs, the payment of MPs, and annually elected Parliaments. It too used public meetings and demonstrations, but in particular it sought to persuade Parliament to accede to its demands by presenting huge petitions – in 1839 with more than a million signatures, in 1842 with three million, and in 1848 claiming six million but found to be two million, with many patently false signatures, including those of the Queen, the Prince Consort and the Duke of Wellington. Chartism, it was said was laughed out of existence, although the government took it seriously enough to post troops on the bridges across the Thames to prevent demonstrators from marching on Parliament. Nonetheless, only one of its demands – annually elected Parliaments – had not been realised by 1918. Groups such as these disappear when they have achieved or clearly failed to achieve their objectives, but others survive, such as Anti-Slavery International (founded in 1823 as the British and Foreign Anti-Slavery Society), the RSPCA, the Electoral Reform Society (formed as the Proportional Representation Society in 1884), the NFU, and the Royal British Legion. And, as government intervention increased yet further, more and more pressure groups were set up, especially during the second half of the twentieth century.

Table 10.5   *The growth of pressure groups*

Period formed	%
Pre-1900	8.7
1900–39	13.7
1940–59	10.3
1960–79	27.7
1980–2000	39.5
Total	99.9
	(1,019)

Source: *PMS Guide to Interest Groups*, 2000.

Although the *PMS Guide to Interest Groups* lists only a minority of groups, it covers a wide range and can be regarded as representative. The figures in Table 10.5 clearly show that two-thirds of the groups listed were formed in 1960 or later. Including two-fifths since 1980. Of course, they exclude groups that came and went before 2000, especially the growing number of so-called NIMBY ('not in my back yard') groups set up usually to oppose a development in a particular locality. This expansion is part of a greater awareness and willingness to engage in various forms of political activity, a matter that will be further addressed in the final section of this chapter.

Accompanying the growth of pressure groups has been a growth in the number of political consultants – firms offering clients information and advice on how to advance and defend their interests – in short, how to engage in pressure politics. Research by the Study of Parliament Group in 1986 identified 28 political consultants; the *PMS Guide* lists 58 'public affairs consultants'. Some political consultancy firms operate solely in that field but a number are part of larger firms offering a wide range of public relations and similar services. In addition, some of the larger law firms in London offer political consultancy services and they, and a number of political consultants, also operate in Brussels, dealing with EU matters. Although political consultants are sometimes referred to as 'political lobbyists', few actually lobby on behalf of their clients, but advise them how best to lobby on their own behalf, including, where appropriate, Parliament and parliamentarians.

Assessing the number of pressure groups is much more difficult, partly because they can appear and disappear with bewildering rapidity, having succeeded or failed in their self-appointed task, but not least because a significant proportion reject the description 'pressure group'. Organisations like Compassion in World Farming, the Campaign for Nuclear Disarmament, the Abortion Law Reform Association, the Society for the Protection of Unborn Children, the Howard League for Penal Reform, or the Pensioners' Rights Campaign are clearly pressure groups, but others, such as trade unions, the

Royal National Institute for the Blind, the Automobile Association, the Royal British Legion, or the Cystic Fibrosis Society do not regard themselves first and foremost as pressure groups, even though from time to time they all engage in pressure politics. Beyond these are many organisations seldom involved in trying to influence the government, but will do so if an existing or proposed policy affects their interests. It might be more appropriate to describe such organisations as potential or latent pressure groups and some idea of the number of bodies involved can be gauged by noting that the 2002 edition of the *Directory of British Associations* has nearly 7,000 entries. Most of the time these organisations are simply going about their non-political business, but at any one time a number will be seeking to influence public policy. This means that the government (and others in authority at various levels in the political system) are constantly faced with efforts to persuade it to introduce new policies or abandon or modify existing ones. In short, the government is subject to a great deal of what is commonly called lobbying but better termed pressure politics.

Pressuring Parliament

Logic would suggest that the most important people to lobby are those who make the decision, whether they are ministers, civil servants, local council-lors and officials, or others in authority. In practice, the world of pressure politics is more complex. Access to the decision-makers is greater for some than others; the decision-makers are not always easy to identify and much depends on the perceptions of those doing the lobbying; but there are also alternative routes available – it may be possible to influence the decision-makers by other means, including through Parliament.

With the important but limited exception of Private Members' bills (PMBs) and the occasional free vote, Parliament decides little but formally approves much. However, it can be a very effective channel of influence. On the one hand, this involves seeking to influence specific decisions by Parliament, most obviously legislation, and, on the other, using Parliament as part of the wider policy network in the area concerned. In the first case, groups may seek the rejection or amendment of a bill as it goes through Parliament or the rejection or reconsideration of a statutory instrument. With PMBs, a group may actu-ally sponsor a bill by persuading an MP or peer to introduce a bill, in some cases offering assistance in drafting and advising on amendments during its passage. Of course, other groups may oppose a PMB, as has happened with bills on abortion and the banning of hunting. As part of a policy network, groups may seek to influence the development or direction of policy by giving evidence to select committee inquiries, by working through party committees and all-party groups, by requesting sympathetic MPs or peers to ask parlia-mentary Questions, table motions, participate in debates, or generally provide them with information relevant to the group's interests.

Table 10.6   *Pressure group contacts with Parliament*

Type of contact	%	N
Regular of frequent contact with MPs	74.7	189
Presented written evidence to a select committee	65.6	166
Regular or frequent contact with peers	58.7	148
Presented oral evidence to a select committee	49.0	124
Contacts with all-party groups	47.6	120
Contacts with party subject groups or committees	40.9	103

Source: Michael Rush (ed.), *Parliament and Pressure Politics*, Oxford, Clarendon, 1990,
Table 1.4. The total number of pressure groups responding was 253, representing a response
rate of 73.1 per cent of the sample.

The most systematic research on the use pressure groups make of Parliament was carried out between 1986 and 1989, but it provides a comprehensive picture of Parliament and pressure politics and there is no reason to believe that this picture is significantly different, with the important exception of the relationship between MPs and professional lobbyists or political consultants. Central to the research was a survey of more than 250 pressure groups and the basic picture is shown in Table 10.6.

Table 10.6 shows that pressure groups pay a good deal of attention to Parliament. Moreover, although more attention was paid to MPs and the House of Commons than to peers and the House of Lords, extensive use was made of the latter. Thus, 83.1 per cent of groups had asked an MP to put down a Question, compared with 48.6 per cent making the same request to a peer; 51.3 per cent had asked an MP to table a motion, compared with 33.3 per cent a peer; 37.0 per cent had sponsored a PMB introduced in the Commons, compared with 14.7 per cent in the Lords; and 49.7 per cent had asked an MP to arrange a meeting on their behalf with a minister, compared with 23.2 per cent asking a peer. That said, of those who had used both Houses, about a quarter found the Commons more useful and a quarter the Lords, but nearly half found them equally useful. It was also clear that groups found Parliament a useful means of influencing policy, as the data in Table 10.7 shows.

Of course, as already noted, Parliament decides little and all this activity could be the result of a serious misconception by pressure groups of where the power lies, who makes the decisions that matter to them. However, this does not appear to be the case: when asked who they thought had most influence over public policy, groups showed a firm grasp of the political reality. Only 7.6 per cent placed Parliament first (as indeed it might be for some groups whose interests are most likely to be affected by PMBs rather than government legislation), but 31.6 per cent said ministers and 28.5 per cent civil servants or government departments.[24] For most groups Parliament is a means

Table 10.7   *The value of contacts with Parliament*

Type of contact	% finding 'very useful' or 'useful'
Contact with MPs	92.5
Influencing bills	55.5
Dealing with SIs	45.1
Party committees	73.8
All-party groups	68.9
The House of Lords	81.8
Select committees	85.5*

Source: Michael Rush (ed.), *Parliament and Pressure Politics*, Oxford, Clarendon, Appendix: Survey Results, pp. 280–96.

Note: * 'Significant impact' or 'Some impact'.

to influence the decision-makers and, used skilfully, can be highly effective. It is important to remember that, although some groups are totally opposed to a particular policy and may have little chance of persuading the government to abandon it (short of a change of government in some cases), many groups are more concerned about the detailed provisions of a policy and here governments are far more open to persuasion. Governments want their policies to work and getting the detail right invariably helps, not least in winning the support of those most affected by the policy. It is worth noting that no government has been willing to implement the defence policy advocated by CND: the Labour Party has twice adopted a policy of unilateral nuclear disarmament, only to subsequently abandon it in office or as office loomed. Furthermore, pressure politics also needs to be seen in the long as well as the short term: the suffragists and the more militant suffragettes had a long struggle before seeing votes for women become a reality; the Abortion Law Reform Association was formed in 1936 but the Abortion Act was not passed until 1967; and the League Against Cruel Sports, formed in 1924, did not secure a ban on hunting until 2005.

MPs, peers and pressure politics

One of the obvious ways for pressure groups to keep in touch with political developments, to secure political advice and to influence policy is to acquire the services of an MP or peer, particularly the former. It has long been the case that MPs are required to declare any pecuniary interest when participating in a debate in the Chamber or a standing committee or in questioning a witness before a select committee, and this was formalised by a resolution of the House in 1974. However, this did not prevent MPs from offering advice to those outside the House, including pressure groups and other outside interests, even to be paid for doing so. This is because any pecuniary interest has to be direct and specific and does not, for example, apply to changes in income tax or expenditure on education of health, which in principle apply to everyone. Similarly, members of the House of Lords are expected to declare any personal interest in a subject under debate. Moreover, any MP or peer accepting a bribe or any other inducement to act or vote in Parliament in a particular way would be in contempt of Parliament, as would anyone making such an offer or attempting to intimidate a member of either House. Again, this does not prevent organisations outside Parliament from paying an MP or peer for political advice to represent their interests in Parliament, provided such interests are declared when appropriate. However, in the early 1990s increasing concern was expressed about the relationship between MPs and outside interests, especially with professional lobbyists, leading to the setting up in 1995 of the Committee for Standards in Public Life (originally known as the Nolan Committee, after its chair), whose recommendations led to important changes in that relationship.

Of course, the organisation outside Parliament with the longest-standing representation in Parliament is the established church, the Church of England, whose two archbishops and 24 senior bishops are ex officio members of the House of Lords. In the nineteenth and early twentieth centuries the bishops played an active role in the political work of the Lords, but this declined during the inter-war period and did not revive again until the upper house became increasingly active following the 1958 Life Peerages Act. Understandably, the bishops are most likely to be involved in social, moral or religious matters, such as the law on abortion, homosexuality or divorce, or issues like Sunday trading, religious broadcasting, and religion in schools, but they also were and remain active on aspects of health, education and social welfare. However, while in one sense they are seen as speaking for the church, they act mainly as individuals, although on some issues a number may co-operate and co-ordinate their activities in the House. Other Christian denominations and other religions, such as Judaism, Islam, Hinduism are also represented in the Lords and, like the Anglican bishops, these peers may be seen as speaking for them, but they too act as individuals even though they may co-operate with other peers. They are, of course, appointed as individuals not as representatives of their faiths, although their religion is likely to have been a factor.

Another major set of interests represented in Parliament are trade unions. For much of its history, the Labour Party has provided a parliamentary route for the influence of trade unions. Indeed, the unions played a crucial part in the founding of the Labour Representation Committee, set up in 1900 to secure working-class representation in Parliament. Almost all Labour MPs are members of trade unions, but one of the ways the unions helped Labour in its early days, and for long after, was by sponsoring Labour candidates, which involved paying all or some of their election expenses and, especially before MPs were paid, financially supporting those elected. In fact, union sponsorship

Table 10.8   *Sponsored Labour MPs (selected years)*

Year	Trade unions	Co-operative party	Total
1945	30.5	5.8	36.4
1959	36.0	6.2	42.2
1966	36.4	5.0	41.4
1979	49.1	6.3	55.4
1992	52.8	5.2	58.0

Source: Butler and Butler, *Twentieth Century British Political Facts*, London, Macmillan, 2000, p. 162.

of candidates preceded the founding of the Labour Party and the first two sponsored MPs, Thomas Burt and Alexander Macdonald, were elected as 'Lib–Labs' and supported by their mining unions. In 1918, well over four-fifths (86.0 per cent) of Labour MPs were union-sponsored. Thereafter, the proportion declined as the Labour recruited more MPs from the middle classes and in 1922 it fell to three-fifths (60.6 per cent).

Because many unions sponsored candidates in seats normally held by Labour, the proportion tended to rise when the party did less well at the polls and fall when it was more successful, as the figures for 1945 and 1959 in Table 10.8 show. However, this was subsequently offset by another factor, a significant change in the type of MP sponsored by the unions. Until well after the Second World War almost all union-sponsored MPs were sponsored by industrial trade unions and had occupational backgrounds directly related to their unions, and so were miners, engineers, railwaymen, textile workers, steel workers, and so on. Increasingly, however, more white collar unions began to sponsor MPs and, more importantly, large general unions, like the Transport and General Workers Union and the General and Municipal Workers began to sponsor MPs whose occupational links with their unions were tenuous but who were well educated and often extremely able individuals, among them no fewer than ten members of Tony Blair's first Cabinet in 1997, including the Prime Minister himself. In addition, the Co-operative Party, founded in 1917 as the political wing of the Co-operative Movement, also sponsored Labour MPs and candidates, rather than operating as a separate party, but on a much smaller scale. In 1992 fourteen Labour candidates were elected as Labour and Co-operative MPs. In 1995, however, in the aftermath of the first Nolan Committee report, the Labour Party abandoned the system of sponsored MPs and replaced it with 'constituency plan agreements'. These involved individual unions giving financial support to selected Constituency Labour Parties, mainly in marginal seats, to boost Labour's chances in the 1997 election. Almost a hundred such agreements were made. The formal abandonment of sponsored MPs coincided with and was part of a loosening of the ties between the trade unions and the Labour Party initiated by Tony Blair after he became party leader in 1994. The party became much less dependent on the unions financially and union influence on party policy has declined markedly since the heady days of the 'social contract' between the TUC and the Labour government of 1974–79. Nonetheless, the relationship remains significant: almost all Labour MPs are members of trade unions, though much stronger ties exist with some MPs than others, and policies such as the adoption of the minimum wage and extension of employee rights owe a good deal to union influence. However, that influence was exercised much more through informal links between union and party leaders and through the party conference than via union-sponsored MPs, whose numbers were greater than their influence, even though they could be relied upon to put forward their unions' viewpoints in Parliament. For most of the Labour Party's history their importance stemmed from the solid, loyal backbench support that most gave to the party leadership.

Some other organisations have also sponsored MPs, notably the National Farmers' Union (NFU) between 1922 and 1935 and the National Union of Teachers (NUT) between 1895 and 1974. Neither the NFU nor the NUT were formally allied or affiliated to any party and sought to maintain a balance in their representation. The numbers were always small – never more than four in the case of the NFU and six with the NUT. In practice, all NFU-sponsored MPs were Conservatives, but the NUT almost always had a mixture, though usually with more Labour than Conservative MPs. These Members, unlike union-sponsored and Co-operative Party MPs, were more like the parliamentary advisers, paid or unpaid, used by an increasing number of outside bodies until the first Nolan Report. In fact, after it ceased to sponsor MPs in 1974, the NUT continued to pay two or three as parliamentary advisers. Data before 1975, when the first Register of Members' Interests was published, is not systematically available, but the growth in the number of MPs acting as parliamentary consultants or advisers can be clearly seen from an analysis of the registers after 1975 (see Table 10.9).

Table 10.9   *Backbench MPs acting as parliamentary consultants or advisers, 1975–2004*

Type or organisation	1975	1985	1995	2004
Business	9.0	12.8	17.9	7.6
Pressure groups	5.7	13.4	19.0	2.8
Political consultants	1.1	1.4	4.6	–
Total	15.8	27.6	41.5	10.4
	(86)	(157)	(234)	(59)

Source: House of Commons, *Registers of Members' Interests 1975, 1985, 1995 and 2004.*

Not surprisingly, business interests more commonly employed Conservative MPs as parliamentary consultants or advisers, by ratios of 5:1 in 1975 and 13:1 in 1995, but in 2004 the ratio was less than 2:1, reflecting the closer relations the Labour Party has developed with business under Tony Blair's leadership and, no doubt, a desire to secure the government's ear after 1997. The expansion of paid parliamentary consultants affected both major parties, but the number of Conservative consultants tripled from a much higher base between 1975 and 1995, whereas Labour consultants only doubled in number, and those employed by professional lobbyists were almost exclusively Conservative.

Pressure group activity in Parliament was increasing well before 1975 and in the late 1960s concern was expressed that some MPs were exploiting their parliamentary position for financial gain in return for 'favours' to pressure groups and foreign governments. This resulted in the setting up of a Select Committee on Members' Interests, whose report recommended a tightening up of the procedures regarding the declaration of interests, but did not recommend a register of interests. However, in 1972 allegations that John Poulson had bribed MPs, civil servants, local politicians and other officials to further his architectural practice surfaced. Three MPs, including the then Home Secretary, Reginald Maudling, had received payments from Poulson but denied any wrong-doing. Maudling resigned as Home Secretary to avoid any conflict of interest with the subsequent police investigation and, following Poulson's conviction in 1974, a select committee concluded that Maudling's conduct and that of two other MPs fell short of expected standards, leading to the resignation of one of the MPs. This affair played a major part in persuading the Commons to set up a register of Members' Interests in 1975, but, far from curbing MPs' relationships with pressure groups, the register served to bring them more clearly into the public domain and it was not until further serious allegations erupted in the 1990s that further significant action was taken. These allegations mostly involved Conservative MPs and culminated in two admitting that they had accepted 'cash for Questions' and allegations that two others had accepted bribes. This was the period in which the term 'sleaze' became common currency and to deal with the situation the Conservative government appointed the Committee on Standards in Public Life, chaired by Lord Nolan, one of the Law Lords, in 1994. It reported in 1995 and found no evidence of widespread abuse of their position by MPs, but recommended a Code of Conduct for MPs, the appointment of a Parliamentary Commissioner for Standards to investigate allegations against MPs, and the registration of the details of paid consultancies. The House of Commons accepted the first two recommendations, but went further with the third by banning 'paid advocacy', that is the initiating of various parliamentary proceedings in return for payment. Of particular concern to Nolan and to many Members was the employment of MPs by political consultancy firms who, by definition, had multiple clients rather than representing particular interests. The requirement to register consultancy agreements, the banning of paid advocacy, and the adverse publicity accusations sleaze had attracted led to a sharp fall in the number of MPs paid to act as parliamentary consultants or advisers and to the elimination of arrangements with professional lobbyists.

Even though outside organisations make considerable use of peers in seeking advice and help, only a handful of peers are employed as parliamentary consultants or advisers. The House of Lords was not directly affected by the events leading to the establishment of a register of interests in the Commons, nor tainted by the sleaze that affected the lower house before 1995, but in the aftermath of Nolan a Register of Peers' Interests was set up in 1996. Two categories covered by the register were made mandatory – paid consultancies and financial interests involving lobbying; the declaration of other interests was voluntary. In the first Register, published in February 1996, 22 peers declared paid consultancies, and 5 financial interests involving lobbying, with a further 311 peers voluntarily declaring other interests. The figures did not vary significantly until after the removal of most of the hereditary peers in 1999, although the number of voluntary declarations had reached 464 by 1999. The first post-1999 Register recorded 13 and 10 peers respectively in the 2 mandatory categories, and 382 in the voluntary ones. In 2001, however, the Register was made entirely compulsory and a code of conduct was introduced, bringing the Lords into line with the Commons, although in some respects the Lords' Register is more extensive, including, for example, the financial interests of peers' spouses, relatives and friends. The 2003 Register recorded 12 peers as paid consultants and 8 as lobbyists.

Although as many as two-fifths of backbench MPs were paid consultants or advisers immediately before Nolan, rising from more than a quarter ten years before, the figure is now only one in ten and the number of peers similarly involved has always been small. Nonetheless, MPs who act as paid parliamentary consultants or advisers have always been a minority, although they were a significant minority by 1995, and MPs and peers generally remain important channels of information and influence for pressure groups, mostly because they sympathise with the interests of those who contact them rather than because they are paid to do so.

Parliament and the people

In 1991 a poll found that 59 per cent of people thought Parliament worked 'very well' or 'fairly well'; in 1995 the proportion was 47 per cent, but crucially only 5 per cent in 1991 and 4 per cent in 1995 though it worked 'very well' and the proportion thinking it worked 'very badly' had risen from 4 per cent to 11 per cent.[25] It is hardly surprising, therefore, that the same series of polls between 1977 and 2000 found widespread agreement that Parliament does not have 'sufficient control of the executive' (see Table 10.10).

Table 10.10 *Agreement with the statement that 'Parliament does not have sufficient control over the executive' (selected years)*

	1977	1991	1995	2000
Strongly agree	12	10	13	21
Inclined to agree	31	40	39	32
Neither agree or disagree	25	19	21	20
Inclined to disagree	–	20	15	8
Strongly disagree	12	3	3	4
Don't know	20	9	9	15

Source: Dunleavy *et al.*, *Voices of the People*, London, Politico's, 2001, p. 76.

Table 10.11 *How much power do people want between elections and how much power do you think they have? (2000)*

Opinion	Should	Do
A great deal	25	4
A fair amount	45	15
A little	17	44
None at all	8	32
Don't know	5	5

Source: Dunleavy *et al.*, *Voices of the People*, p. 55.

This concern about the effectiveness of Parliament is matched by similar concerns about the amount of power people should have and actually do have between general elections (see Table 10.11). The relationship between Parliament and the people is ultimately crucial. The sleaze associated mainly with the Conservatives before 1997 focused mainly on MPs, but it had largely been superseded by unease about the actions of the government. The 2000 *Voices of the People* poll found a majority of respondents expressing concern about ministers 'appointing friends to important public posts' (50 per cent), the use of 'spin doctors to manipulate the media' (57 per cent), the appointment of 'large party donors to government committees and task forces' (52 per cent), the 'granting of peerages and honours to people making large financial donations to political parties' (52 per cent), 'ministers favouring major private interests before the interests of ordinary people' (52 per cent), and 'ministers not being truthful' (66 per cent).[26]

The same poll also found that 49 per cent 'strongly agreed' and 32 per cent 'tended to agree' 'that if governments don't listen, peaceful protest, blockades and demonstrations are a legitimate way of expressing people's concerns'.[27]

There is no doubt that members of the public have become more active in pressure politics and that they have also become more willing to engage in various forms of direct action, some legal, some illegal. These included the violent confrontations between striking miners and the police in 1984–85, the poll tax riots in London in 1990, the destruction of genetically modified crops on several occasions, and the petrol blockades by road hauliers and farmers and violent street demonstrations in London against capitalism in 2000, as well as peaceful demonstrations by students and others protesting against tuition fees and pro-hunting marches by the Countryside Alliance. Demonstrations and marches, including those involving violence, should not automatically be seen as antithetical to parliamentary government, unless they are seeking to overthrow the political system or effect a change in government or of a particular policy by force alone. The 2000 poll found minorities of 45 per cent for the petrol blockades, 28 per cent for the destruction of GM crops and 27 per cent for the pro-hunting demonstrations as 'definitely justified', but only 18 per cent for the anti-capitalist demonstrations. However unacceptable or unpalatable they may be to many, such protests remain expressions of public opinion, often shared by many more than those prepared to engage in direct action. Parliamentary government may be government through Parliament, but not to the extent that governments can ignore public opinion all or most of the time with impunity. Elections allow people to have their say about who governs, but there need to be mechanisms allowing people to have their say, and feel that they are not ignored, between elections. Parliament is part of that process, but it is a process that could be improved. It is a process dependent, on the one hand, on the relationship between Parliament and the government and, on the other, on reforming parliamentary government, and it is with these topics that the final two chapters in this book are concerned.

Notes

1 Jean-Jacques Rousseau, *The Social Contract*, London, J. M. Dent, 1913 (trans. with an introduction by G. D. H. Cole), p. 78 (originally published 1762).
2 See House of Commons Information Office, *Factsheet P7: Public Petitions*, 2003.
3 See *Parliamentary History*, London, T.C. Hansard, 1814, XIX, cc. 1100–24.
4 Cited in Edward Porritt, *The Unreformed House of Commons: Parliamentary Representation Before 1832*, Cambridge, Cambridge University Press, 1909, Vol. I, p. 278.
5 *Ibid.*, p. 251.
6 Michael Rush, *The Role of the Member of Parliament Since 1868: From Gentlemen to Players*, Oxford, Oxford University Press, 2001, p. 207.
7 *Ibid.*, p. 208.
8 *Ibid.*, p. 209.
9 Anthony Barker and Michael Rush, *The Member of Parliament and His Information*, London, Allen & Unwin, 1970, p. 416.

10 Sir Ivor Jennings, *Parliament*, Cambridge, Cambridge University Press, 2nd edn 1957, p. 27.
11 Barker and Rush, *The Member of Parliament*, pp. 404 and 412.
12 Cited in Robert Blackburn and Andrew Kennon, *Griffith and Ryle on Parliament: Functions, Practice and Procedures*, London, Sweet & Maxwell, 2003, p. 106.
13 The Hansard Society, *Report of the Hansard Society Commission on Parliamentary Scrutiny: The Challenge for Parliament – Making Government Accountable*, London, Vacher Dod, 2001, p. 147.
14 See Nigel Jackson, 'Vote Winner or a Nuisance: E-mail and British MPs' Relationship with the Constituents', unpublished conference paper, n.d., p. 9.
15 Jennings, *Parliament*, p. 27.
16 Robert E. Dowse, 'The MP and His Surgery', *Political Studies*, 11, 1963, p. 334.
17 Barker and Rush, *The Member of Parliament*, 413.
18 Rush, *The Role of the Member of Parliament*, p. 207.
19 www.ombudsman.org.uk.
20 Hansard Society, *Report*, Appendix 4, Table 3.7.
21 Cited in Blackburn and Kennon, *Griffith and Ryle*, p. 106.
22 House of Commons Library Research Paper 01/54, p. 11.
23 Graham Wootton, *Pressure Groups in Britain 1720–1970*, London, Allen Lane, 1975, pp. 196–7.
24 Michael Rush (ed.), *Parliament and Pressure Politics*, Oxford, Clarendon, 1990, Table 11.4.
25 Patrick Dunleavy, Helen Margetts, Trevor Smith and Stuart Weir, *Voices of the People: Popular Attitudes Towards Democratic Renewal in Britain*, London, Politico's, 2001, p. 76.
26 *Ibid.*, 88–90.
27 *Ibid.*, 142.

11

Parliament and the government

Parliament and the government: the setting

The effectiveness of parliamentary scrutiny, whether legislative or non-legislative, depends ultimately on the relationship between Parliament and the government, especially that between the House of Commons and the government. That relationship depends, on the one hand, on the constitutional responsibility of the government to Parliament and, on the other, on the government's ability to control Parliament, again in practice the House of Commons. To complicate matters further, both factors depend upon sets of circumstances that are by no mean immutable.

Constitutional responsibility is based not on law but convention and is not protected by being entrenched in a written constitution that has precedence over all other laws. Of course, constitutions are open to interpretation, not least by the courts who usually act as the final arbiter, as the Supreme Court does in the United States and the US Constitution has gone through periods of differing interpretations, sometimes to the point of reversing earlier rulings. However, although the role of the courts as arbiter of the British Constitution has been enhanced by a growth in judicial activism and by the passing of the Human Rights Act in 1998, the UK has no equivalent to the US Supreme Court or similar courts in other countries with written constitutions. The politicians are the principal interpreters of the constitution and this becomes crucial in those practices dependent entirely or substantially on constitutional conventions, which, as already noted in Chapter 1, are not enforceable by law. Constitutional lawyers, academics and others may express their view on the constitutional propriety of the actions or proposed actions of the politicians, but it is the latter who decide how, when and in what way to fulfil their constitutional responsibility to Parliament. The electorate may subsequently pronounce its verdict, but unless and until it does the politicians, especially those holding ministerial office, are normally the final arbiters of constitutional propriety. Much therefore depends on their honesty and integrity, as well as on their interpretation of constitutional conventions. Moreover, the latter may change and develop, as the doctrine of ministerial responsibility undoubtedly has.

The ability of the politicians to interpret the constitution is, in turn, greatly affected by the nature of the party system and the extent of party cohesion. Were the UK to have a multi-party system that usually resulted in no single party securing a majority in the House of Commons, so that coalition (or sometimes minority) government were the norm, the existing conventions might operate differently in certain respects and new ones might develop. For example, one of the partners in a coalition might use its position to force the resignation of a minister or a change of Prime Minister, or bring the government down completely, possibilities much less likely under a single-party majority system. Or, were one major party to be more or less permanently in government and the other more or less permanently in opposition, the attitudes towards the roles of government and opposition might change and co-operation between them might no longer be the norm. Change the party system and the way the constitution operates may change. The party system is characterised by high levels of party cohesion in both Houses of Parliament, although more so in the Commons than the Lords. Governments can normally rely on majority support in the Commons, where it is crucial not just for survival but for the passage of its programme. A total or substantial collapse in party cohesion is unlikely, but there has been a marked lessening since the 1960s, so that while it remains the case that the government controls Parliament, especially the Commons, rather than Parliament controlling the government, that control is less certain than it was. Rebellions have become more frequent in the Commons and no government can rely unreservedly on the Lords, even though the upper house gives more trouble to Labour than Conservative governments.

Interpreting ministerial responsibility and assessing the extent and importance of party coherence are crucial to any understanding of the relationship between government and Parliament and, ultimately, to any consideration of whether and how Parliament should be reformed.

Ministerial responsibility in theory and practice

No one disputes that ministers are constitutionally responsible to Parliament, but what does it mean? And does practice accord with theory? In the history of Parliament, ministerial responsibility is a comparatively new development: ministers were originally responsible to the king, not Parliament, and it was only gradually that Parliament sought to exercise control over ministers. Acting against ministers was a means of exercising some control over policy and the most extreme device developed was impeachment, by which a minister (or other persons in authority) could be tried by the House of Lords on an indictment or impeachment brought by the House of Commons. It was not frequently used, however, and from time to time went into abeyance, notably under the Tudor monarchs, only to be revived by Parliament under the Stuarts, particularly against the ministers of Charles I in the prelude to the Civil War. Between 1621, when its use was revived under James I, and the Revolution of 1688, impeachment was used some forty times but then began to decline and was last used in 1806. It was an unwieldy weapon – the impeachment of Warren Hastings, first Governor-General of India, in 1788 resulted in a seven-year trial – but, just as it was falling into disrepute in Britain, it was incorporated in the US Constitution, where it survives as a weapon of last resort by Congress against the President, Vice-President or members of the Cabinet. Much more flexible and effective was the development of the principle that, in order to remain in office the government needed to retain the confidence of Parliament, in practice majority support in the House of Commons. This became the norm during the eighteenth century and the doctrine of ministerial responsibility became increasingly refined during the nineteenth century, to the point that governments not only depended for their survival on Parliament but were accountable to it for their policies and conduct of affairs. This is clearly reflected in the Ministerial Code issued to all ministers on taking office.

The Ministerial Code sets out in detail how ministers should carry out their responsibilities (see Box 11.1). It originated under Attlee in 1945 but has become much more elaborate. The code applies to all ministers, although some parts apply particularly to Cabinet ministers. In addition to a section on the work of the Cabinet and Cabinet committees, there are sections on ministers' responsibilities to Parliament, their departments, their relationship with civil servants, constituency and party interests, ministerial visits, the presentation of policy, and ministers' private interests.[1] However, unlike the Code of Conduct for MPs, alleged breaches of which may be investigated by the Parliamentary Commissioner for Standards and by the Commons' Standards and Privileges Committee, the Prime Minister is the judge and jury on alleged breaches of the Ministerial Code. Ministerial responsibility is therefore a matter of judgement for ministers and, ultimately and where appropriate, the Prime Minister.

What then happens in practice? To what extent do ministers fulfil their responsibilities to Parliament? To answer these questions it is necessary to define ministerial responsibility generally and in its two specific forms, individual and collective ministerial responsibility. In general, ministers must explain and defend their policies and conduct of affairs to Parliament and the government must retain the confidence of a majority in the House of Commons. However, the former obligation focuses largely on the individual responsibility of ministers for their departments and the latter obligation is the ultimate form of collective responsibility.

Box 11.1   Ministers and Parliament

Extract from the Ministerial Code

Ministers of the Crown are expected to behave according to the highest standards of constitutional and personal conduct in the performance of their duties. In particular, they must observe the following principles of ministerial conduct:

i   Ministers must uphold the principles of collective responsibility.
ii Ministers have a duty to Parliament to account, and be held to account, for the policies, decisions and actions of their Departments and Next Steps Agencies.
iii It is of paramount importance that ministers give accurate and truthful information to Parliament, correcting any inadvertent error at the earliest opportunity. Ministers who knowingly mislead Parliament will be expected to offer their resignation to the Prime Minister.
iv Ministers should be as open as possible with Parliament and the public, refusing to provide information only when disclosure would not be in the public interest, which should be decided in accordance with the relevant statute and the government's Code of Practice and Access to Government Information.
v   Similarly, ministers should require civil servants who give evidence before parliamentary committees on their behalf and under their direction be as helpful as possible in providing accurate, truthful and full information in accordance with the duties and responsibilities of civil servants as set out in the Civil Service Code.

Source: Cabinet Office, *The Ministerial Code*, 1997.

Individual ministerial responsibility

Individual ministerial responsibility means that ministers are answerable to Parliament in that they may be called upon to explain any aspect of departmental policy or operation, including executive agencies within the department's remit, and for any other policies or matters the Prime Minister has assigned to the minister concerned (see Box 11.2). However, it also means that ministers may be held responsible, in the sense of being blamed, for any errors in policy or its implementation that may occur, including the actions of civil servants, except where a civil servant disobeys or defies instructions or acts reprehensibly in circumstances of which the minister could not have been aware. With this exception, a civil servant's actions are constitutionally the minister's actions. Ministers are therefore answerable for their departments.

Box 11.2   Defining ministerial responsibility

Ministerial responsibility

General definition

Ministers are constitutionally responsible to Parliament i.e. they must explain and defend their policies and conduct of affairs to Parliament and, ultimately, in remaining in office the government is dependent upon retaining the confidence of a majority in the House of Commons.

Individual ministerial responsibility

Ministers are expected to explain and defend the exercise of their powers and the carrying out of their duties to Parliament, including the actions of civil servants, and any minister who has lost the confidence of the House of Commons can, by vote of censure or informal pressure, be compelled to resign.

Collective ministerial responsibility

All ministers, from the Prime Minister to junior whips, are answerable to Parliament for the government's conduct of affairs. The government is expected to present a united front and any public disagreement with government policy or criticism of the government entitles the Prime Minister to demand the minister's silence or resignation.

In practice, ministerial culpability is usually confined to matters in which the minister was directly and personally involved, either by being strongly identified with a particular policy or by having personally made a decision or approved a recommendation. Some observers, both academics and within Parliament, have sought to draw a distinction in principle between 'account-ability', that is, accounting to Parliament for departmental policy and opera-tion, and 'responsibility', that is, being personally involved in decisions or with particular policies. However, while some cases fall clearly into one cat-egory or the other, the line between them is ultimately blurred and has been further blurred by the creation of the executive agencies. These were set up under the 'Next Steps' Programme, a reference to the 'next steps', to be taken in civil service reform, starting in 1988 and basically completed ten years later. Their purpose was to separate policy advice and development from the delivery of services. Those working in the agencies remain civil servants, but work under a chief executive responsible to the appropriate minister. This has created a situation in which ministers can claim that they are not directly

Table 11.1   *Ministerial resignations on the grounds of individual ministerial responsibility, 1945–2004*

Governing party	No.	No. per year
Conservative	8	0.232
Labour	4	0.169
Overall	12	0.206

responsible for operational matters dealt with by the executive agencies. This was a situation that existed with the former nationalised industries – gas, electricity, the railways and coal mines, for example – ministers were responsible for policy, the boards of the nationalised industries for operational matters. The blurring occurs when operational matters spill over into public concern and ministers find themselves faced with demands for action.

Most of the time individual ministerial responsibility operates routinely and reasonably effectively in that ministers answer parliamentary Questions, participate in legislative and non-legislative debates, appear before select committees (or delegate civil servants to do so on their behalf), and respond to committee reports. Difficulties arise when matters go beyond the routine, especially when the ultimate sanction of ministerial resignation is demanded. A major problem here is that demands for the resignation of a minister because of an alleged error, policy failure, or departmental incompetence are a frequent and regular part of the partisan clash between government and opposition. In practice, such demands are frequent; actual resignations are infrequent, as Table 11.1 shows.

Between 1945 and 2004 there were more than seventy ministerial resignations, but only twelve could be attributed to individual responsibility – 8 Conservative ministers over 34.5 years and four Labour over 23.6 years, producing similarly low ratios of 0.232 and 0.169 per year. Some of the other resignations resulted from personal behaviour rather than policy matters, such as the resignation of Hugh Dalton as Chancellor of the Exchequer in 1947 after he had revealed Budget information to a journalist; or John Profumo, Minister for War, in 1963 for lying to the House of Commons; or Peter Mandelson, Secretary of State for Trade for Trade and Industry, and Geoffrey Robinson, Paymaster General, in 1998 over private financial arrangements; or Peter Mandelson again in 2001, when Secretary of State for Northern Ireland, over allegations that he had used his ministerial position to assist a wealthy Indian businessman secure a British passport. A subsequent inquiry found that Mandelson had not acted improperly but he was not restored to government office. Various sexual scandals have also resulted in ministerial resignations, including a number of Conservatives in the 1990s and Ron Davies, Secretary of State for Wales, following his 'moment of madness' on

Clapham Common. Most, however, concern resignations under the doctrine of collective ministerial responsibility, but these will be dealt with later in the chapter.

The classic post-1945 resignation on the grounds of individual ministerial responsibility was that of Lord Carrington as Foreign Secretary and two other Foreign Office ministers in 1982 over the Argentinian invasion of the Falkland Islands. In his resignation letter, Lord Carrington said:

> The Argentinian invasion of the Falkland Islands has led to strong criticism in Parliament and in the press of the government's policy. In my view, much of that criticism is unfounded. But I have been responsible for the conduct of that policy and I think it right that I should resign. (Letter to the Prime Minister 1982)[2]

Another frequently cited though disputed example is what became known as the Crichel Down Affair, which led to the resignation of the Minister of Agriculture, Sir Thomas Dugdale, in 1954. Crichel Down was a piece of land in Dorset compulsorily acquired in 1937 for defence purposes. Responsibility for the land subsequently passed from the Air Ministry to the Ministry of Agriculture, which, no longer having any use for it, disposed of it without giving the original owner the opportunity to bid for it. For many years, Crichel Down was cited the classic example of a minister taking responsibility for the actions of his civil servants, but it later transpired that Sir Thomas Dugdale had known and approved of the policy. Other examples are the resignation in 1986 of Leon Brittan, then Secretary of State for Trade, over the actions of his civil servants in the Westland Affair – whether to purchase British or America helicopters for defence purposes – and of Edwina Currie, Parliamentary Under-Secretary for Health, in 1988, following her statement that 'most the egg production of this country ... is now infected with salmonella'. Yet more recent cases are those in 2002 of Estelle Morris, as Secretary of State for Education and Skills, over the failure to meet government education targets, of Stephen Byers, as Transport, Local Government and the Regions Secretary, over the 'resignation' of Martin Sixsmith, his department's Director of Communications, and, in 2004, of Beverley Hughes, Minister of State in the Home Office, over the operation of immigration policy. These recent cases, as do a number of others, illustrate the problems surrounding resignations on the grounds of individual responsibility. Estelle Morris's resignation was accompanied by a letter of resignation and television interview clearly suggesting that she was unhappy in her post and had doubts about her capacity as a Cabinet minister, but she had earlier stated in the House of Commons that, if the targets were not met, she would resign. Thus there may be doubts about exactly why a minister has resigned. Stephen Byers illustrates a different facet: Martin Sixsmith's 'resignation' was announced by Byers before it had been agreed and without Sixsmith's knowledge, but the waters were further muddied because Byers had already been tainted by the action of his political adviser, Jo Moore, who had circulated an e-mail as news of the 9/11 attacks in New York and Washington emerged that it would be 'a very good day to get out anything we want to bury'. The pressure on Byers to resign became intense and he eventually did so. Beverley Hughes' resignation came in the midst of growing public concern about and the government's handling of immigration. Hughes denied that she knew that the advice of British consular officials in Bulgaria and Rumania was being ignored and that officials in the Immigration and Nationality Directorate were accepting applications from these countries with minimal checks in order to 'massage' the figures before EU enlargement took place in May 2004, when citizens of the ten new member states would be eligible to move to the UK. She blamed her civil servants and resisted calls for her resignation, strongly supported by the Home Secretary and the Prime Minister. However, she subsequently admitted she had 'unwittingly misled' MPs and resigned. These cases illustrate that resignations on the grounds of individual responsibility are highly political and, whatever may be the facts of the matter, are not simply a matter of enforcing constitutional propriety. Were the latter the case, many more resignations might be expected.

The cases cited in Table 11.2 are not meant to be a categorical list of instances when ministers should have resigned, but when resignations might have occurred. Its purpose is to explore the circumstances in which resignations appear possible but do not take place. Certainly, in a number of cases there was widespread speculation about one or more ministerial resignations. Analytically, five types of explanation for the absence of a resignation can be suggested, but in some instances there is a degree of overlap.

First, resignation may not be appropriate in that it would be unduly harsh relative to the error, especially where the minister was unaware of the matter. In such cases, corrective action normally ensues – the policy is adjusted or steps are taken to prevent a recurrence. Examples include the Buckingham Palace intruder in 1983, although the Home Secretary, William Whitelaw, did offer his resignation; the collapse of Barlow Clowes in 1989, where the fault stemmed from errors made by officials in the Department of Trade and Industry, although the government subsequently agreed to pay compensation to investors following an investigation by the Parliamentary Ombudsman; and passport delays in 1999, in which the Passport Agency failed to carry out an agreed expansion of staff.

Second, the problem of time lag, that is the lapse of time between events taking place (or a failure to act) and the matter coming to light, such that a different minister or even a different party is in office. The minister in office takes responsibility in the sense of taking any necessary steps to deal with the matter but would hardly be expected to take direct blame and resign. Such cases are quite common, partly because the average time spent by a minister in a particular post is about two years and partly because it may be some

Table 11.2 *Individual ministerial responsibility: the absence of resignations*

Date	Case
1947	The fuel crisis (Emmanuel Shinwell)
1949	The groundnuts scheme (John Strachey)
1959	Kenya: Mau Mau – Hola Camp (Alan Lennox-Boyd)
1960	The Blue Streak missile (several)
1964	The Bloodhound missile (several)
Late 1960s and early 1970s	The Crown Agents (several)
1965–70	Evasion of sanctions against Rhodesia (several)
1971	Vehicle & General Insurance (several)
1974	Collapse of the Court Line (Tony Benn)
1982	Invasion of the Falkland Islands (John Nott)
1982	Buckingham Palace intruder (William Whitelaw)
1983	Escape of IRA prisoners from the Maze Prison (James Prior)
1987–90	House of Fraser takeover bid: delay in publishing inspectors' report (several)
1988	Barlow Clowes investment company: failure of regulatory function by Dept. of Trade and Industry and loss of money by investors (Lord Young)
1989	Government sale of Rover car company – undervaluing of assets (Lord Young)
1991	Escape of IRA prisoners from Brixton Prison (Kenneth Baker)
1992	Britain's withdrawal from the European Exchange Rate Mechanism (ERM) (Norman Lamont)
1995	Parkhurst Prison escapes and the dismissal of the Chief Executive of the Prisons Agency (Michael Howard)
1996	Arms to Iraq 1988–90 – the Scott Report, 1996 (Alan Clark, Sir Nicholas Lyell and William Waldegrave)
1986–2000	SERPS: failure of civil servants to inform prospective pensioners of 50% reduction in entitlement (several)
1986–2000	BSE – the Phillips Report, 2000 (several)
1997–2001	The Millennium Dome (Chris Smith, Peter Mandelson, Lord Falconer)
1998	Arms to Sierra Leone (Robin Cook, Tony Lloyd)
1999	Serious delays in issuing passports by Passport Agency (Jack Straw)
2001	Outbreak of foot-and-mouth (Nick Brown)
2003–04	Handling of Dr David Kelly, government weapons adviser, by Ministry of Defence (Geoff Hoon)

years before it is apparent that something has gone seriously wrong. Cases involving a different minister of the same party include the Blue Streak missile cancellation; excess profits by Ferranti on the Bloodhound missile; the long-running dispute over the takeover of the House of Fraser Store Group involving speculation about a ministerial cover-up occasioned by a long delay in the publication of the report on the matter; the undervaluing of assets in the sale of Rover Car Company; and allegations about the mishandling of the building and financing of the Millennium Dome after 1997. Those involving a change of government include the financial mismanagement of overseas aid contracts by the Crown Agents, the collapse of V & G Insurance, the failure to inform beneficiaries of changes to the State Earnings-Related Pension Scheme (SERPS), and the mishandling of BSE, which began in 1986 and culminated with the publication of the Phillips Report in 2000.

Third, other forms of 'punishment' and ways of dealing with the matter are available – a rebuke or warning by the Prime Minister to the minister concerned about future conduct, moving the minister in a subsequent government reshuffle (or dropping the minister altogether) or 'honourable retirement' (sometimes with peerage), all avoiding any overt and embarrassing link between 'offence' and 'punishment'. Again, this is a common way of dealing with criticism of particular ministers. For example, the ministers at the centre of the fuel crisis in 1947 and the failure of the groundnut scheme in Tanganyika in 1949 were both moved to other posts in subsequent reshuffles. A more recent example is that of Nick Brown, Minister of Agriculture during the foot-and-mouth outbreak in 2001, who was demoted to Minister of State in the Department of Work and Pensions in the reshuffle following the 2001 general election, although he still attended Cabinet meetings. He was subsequently dropped altogether in a later reshuffle. Cases of 'honourable retirement' are more difficult to pin down, but that of Alan Lennox-Boyd, Colonial Secretary in 1959 at the time of the deaths of Mau Mau detainees in Hola Camp in Kenya, could be cited as an example. Another possible case is that of Paul Channon, dropped in a reshuffle in 1989 after being criticised over the handling by the Department of Transport in the aftermath of the Lockerbie disaster involving PanAm Flight 103, the fire in King's Cross underground station, and the Clapham rail crash – all within a short time of one another in the late 1980s. However, most ministers leaving office do so because the Prime Minister wishes to bring new blood into the government or simply because they wish to retire, with a few regarded by the Prime Minister as not successful, though not culpable of errors that might lead to resignation.

Fourth, it has become increasingly common to claim a distinction between policy and administration as a defence, arguing that errors by civil servants or other officials are to blame and that the minister should not be required to resign. In 1983, for instance, 38 Republican prisoners escaped from Maze Prison in Belfast, but the Northern Ireland Secretary, James Prior, and the

Parliamentary Under-Secretary, Nicholas Scott, remained in office, saying that the fault lay with members of the Northern Ireland Prison Service. Similarly, in 1991, when two IRA prisoners escaped from Brixton Prison, the Home Secretary, Kenneth Baker, blamed Home Office officials and refused to resign. Again, in 1998, officials in the Foreign Office were blamed for failing to keep ministers informed about developments in Sierra Leone involving the supply of arms to its government in contravention of a UN resolution, although one of the ministers involved, Tony Lloyd, Minister of State at the Foreign Office was subsequently dropped in a reshuffle. The creation of the executive agencies has ostensibly sharpened the distinction between policy and administration, enabling ministers to claim that any failure lies with the chief executive of the agency, a defence successfully used in 1995 by Michael Howard, when Home Secretary, over escapes from Parkhurst Prison, leading him to dismiss the chief executive of the Prisons Agency, but less successfully by Beverley Hughes in blaming the Immigration and Nationality Directorate in 2004.

Finally, collective responsibility acts as a counter to individual responsibility, in that an attack on a minister is seen as an attack on the government as a whole and political solidarity protects the minister, preventing an immediate resignation, sometimes allowing the minister to escape altogether, sometimes postponing 'punishment' until a later date. This is the commonest response of all, often used in combination with one of the other ways of dealing with alleged policy or other failures: the government closes ranks around the minister concerned, hoping to avoid an embarrassing resignation. One of the clearest examples of this was the continuation in office of Norman Lamont as Chancellor of the Exchequer, following the UK's withdrawal from the European Exchange Rate Mechanism (ERM) in 1992, whose position the Prime Minister, John Major, defended by saying that membership of the ERM was government policy and a matter of collective responsibility. However, individual ministerial responsibility at its most cynical can be seen in the resignation of another Chancellor of the Exchequer, James Callaghan, in 1967, after the decision to devalue the pound – a policy Callaghan and the Prime Minister, Harold Wilson, had resisted since coming to office in 1964 – and Callaghan immediately becoming Home Secretary.

Resignations on the grounds of individual ministerial responsibility, or their absence, are invariably matters of high politics. All the cases listed in Table 11.2 (and no doubt others could have been included) illustrate this to varying degrees. Ultimately, resignations depend on three key factors – the minister, the Prime Minister and the government party. If the minister is determined to resign, if the Prime Minister feels that resignation is best in the circumstances, and if the party, especially the parliamentary party, feels that the minister should go, the minister will go. In all probability, if both the Prime Minister and the party favour resignation, the minister will go, but the reality is that ministers are more likely to resist calls for resignation, Prime Ministers make every effort to avoid embarrassing resignations, and parties prefer stout defence to morale-sapping resignations. Much, of course, depends on the circumstances, as an examination of five cases will show.

Sanctions against Rhodesia, 1965–70

In 1965, the white minority government of Rhodesia, led by Ian Smith, declared its independence from Britain, leading to the imposition by the UK and other countries of economic and other sanctions. However, many of these sanctions were evaded, including the oil sanctions. This was known to the British government, which took only limited steps to prevent their evasion, but the sanctions policy was strongly identified with the Prime Minister, Harold Wilson, and it would have been seriously embarrassing had the government admitted that it was engaged in 'covert ... acquiescence'.[3]

The Court Line case, 1974[4]

A rather different case occurred in 1974, when Court Line, a shipbuilding company but also owners of a major holiday firm, sought government financial assistance. This was forthcoming in the form of a proposal to nationalise the shipbuilding operation, but the Secretary of State for Industry, Tony Benn, also sought to assure holidaymakers affected by Court Line's financial problems. The government's acquisition of the firm, Benn stated in the Commons, 'should stabilise the situation ... including the holidays booked for this summer' that the holidaymakers 'should have some reasonable security, and that the government were anxious to help them'. In the event, Court Line collapsed and a large number of holidaymakers lost their holidays and their money. It was suggested that Benn had misled them, a suggestion denied both by Benn and the Prime Minister, Harold Wilson. A report by the Parliamentary Ombudsman was critical of the handling of the matter, but rejected by the government, which survived a division on party lines in the Commons. As it happens, the holidaymakers were compensated by legislation fortuitously going through Parliament at the time.

The invasion of the Falklands, 1982

As noted earlier, Lord Carrington, the Foreign Secretary, Humphrey Atkins, the Lord Privy Seal and spokesman for the Foreign Office in the Commons and also a member of the Cabinet, and Richard Luce, Minister of State in the Foreign Office with responsibility for Latin America, all resigned. However, John Nott, the Secretary of State for Defence, who was responsible for the naval cuts that led the Argentine government to believe that Britain would not seek to recover the Falkland Islands by force, offered his resignation but was persuaded by the Prime Minister, Margaret Thatcher, to remain in office. There is no doubt that the three Foreign Office ministers were determined to resign, in spite of efforts by the Prime Minister to dissuade them, but there was strong feeling in favour of resignations among Conservative backbenchers. Nott was later knighted and retired from politics at the 1983 general election.

Arms to Iraq, 1988–90

Another case that attracted much attention in the 1990s involved allegations about the supply of arms to Iraq during the 1980–88 Iran–Iraq War. During the trial in 1992 of the executives of Matrix-Churchill, an engineering firm accused of breaking an arms embargo against Iraq, the evidence of a former Conservative minister revealed that they had acted with government knowledge and approval, and the trial collapsed. A judicial inquiry by Lord Justice Scott was set up and his report in 1996 concluded that three ministers had given 'inaccurate and misleading' answers to parliamentary Questions in the Commons. One of the ministers concerned was no longer in Parliament, but two others, Sir Nicholas Lyell and William Waldegrave, were and still held ministerial office. However, backed by the Prime Minister, John Major, and most Conservative backbenchers, they strongly resisted calls for their resignation, although the government survived a censure motion in the Commons by a single vote with, unusually in such divisions, three government backbenchers voting against the government.

Dr David Kelly and the Iraq dossier, 2003–04

More recently, the case of Dr David Kelly attracted massive publicity. Dr Kelly was a civil servant and government weapons adviser, whose off-the-record interview with a BBC journalist led to serious doubts about the accuracy of a government dossier published to support its case for military action against Iraq. Dr Kelly subsequently committed suicide, leading to accusations that he had not been adequately supported by his superiors in the Ministry of Defence, for whom he worked. The government appointed Lord Hutton, a Law Lord, to conduct an inquiry in to 'the circumstances surrounding Dr Kelly's death'. His report was mildly critical of the Ministry of Defence, but did not support the accusations. Nonetheless, because Lord Hutton conducted his hearings in public, providing extensive insights into the operation of the Blair government, as well as the handling of Dr Kelly, there was widespread media speculation that the Secretary of State for Defence, Geoff Hoon, would be forced to resign. Given Lord Hutton's conclusions, it is hardly surprising that he did not, although he subsequently conceded that Dr Kelly's case could have been better handled.

Resignations on the grounds of individual ministerial responsibility are thus few and far between and, although a swift resignation may lance the boil, partisan considerations invariably come to the fore, with the opposition parties hoping that if they pursue the matter vigorously they will win a ministerial scalp and the government equally vigorously defending the minister, if necessary throwing the cloak of collective responsibility over his or her shoulders. In some cases, the resort to judicial or other inquiries, often justified and sensible, allows the question of possible resignation to be postponed and ultimately avoided. Yet, it should be remembered that individual ministerial responsibility is the basis of parliamentary scrutiny, the basis of parliamentary Questions, debates and select committee inquiries, without which parliamentary scrutiny would not be possible. Demands for resignations, however legitimate they may be in particular cases, and the partisan battle they provoke obscure this and the fact that for much of the time individual ministerial responsibility works in that ministers answer parliamentary Questions, defend their policies and actions in debates, and submit themselves and their policies to select committee inquires as part of normal parliamentary business, all of which applies as much to the House of Lords as it does to the Commons. Whether there should be more frequent ministerial resignations or whether ministers should have resigned in particular cases is a matter of opinion, but it should not be allowed to hide the fact that individual ministerial responsibility lies at the heart of parliamentary government.

Collective ministerial responsibility

Now, is it to lower the price of corn or isn't it? It is not much matter which we say, but mind, we must all say *the same*.[5]

This is what Lord Melbourne, when Prime Minister, was alleged to have said with his back to the door at the end of a Cabinet meeting, and it epitomises collective ministerial responsibility. Once something has become government policy, it binds all ministers. The government as a whole is answerable to Parliament. It is expected to present a united front and the Prime Minister is entitled to dismiss any minister who publicly disagrees with or criticises government policy. Indeed, collective responsibility extends to Parliamentary Private Secretaries (PPSs), even though they are unpaid and are not technically members of the government. In practice, the dismissal of a minister for failing to observe collective responsibility is rare – only two cases have occurred since 1945. The first was that of Eric Heffer, Minister of State in the Department of Industry, warned by the Prime Minister in 1974 when he criticised the sale of frigates to the Pinochet regime in Chile, and dismissed in 1975 after speaking in the House of Commons against the UK's continued membership of the EEC. The second case was the dismissal in 1981 of Keith Speed, Parliamentary Under-Secretary for the Navy, for publicly condemning proposals for naval cuts. More common is the dismissal of PPSs, of whom 22 were dismissed between 1945 and 2004. Collective responsibility has also come to be operated by the official opposition, resulting in 17 dismissals between 1968 and 2001. For both government and opposition the logic of collective responsibility is

Table 11.3   *The suspension of collective responsibility*

Date	Issue
1912	Franchise Bill introduced by the government to which amendments extending the vote to women were tabled. The Cabinet decided that members of the government should be free to speak and vote as they wished on the amendments, but the Speaker ruled these out order
1932	To allow one National Labour and three Liberal members of the National government to speak and vote against legislation introducing trade tariffs. Became redundant when free traders refused to accept the Ottawa Agreement on protection in 1932
1975	To allow members of the Labour government to campaign against continued membership of the EEC in the 1975 referendum, but not to speak or vote against it in Parliament
1978	To allow members of the Labour government to speak against and abstain in votes on legislation introducing direct elections to the European Parliament

compelling – parties perceived by the electorate as seriously divided do not win elections and so political solidarity tends to be the order of the day.

Occasionally, party divisions are such that the government suspends collective responsibility on a particular issue, but such occasions are rare, as Table 11.3 shows, but they have served as a way of defusing disagreements within the government and preventing a more serious split developing. However, this is not an option chosen by Tony Blair, following his decision in 2004 to hold a referendum on the draft EU Constitution. He announced that, unlike the referendum in 1975 on continued EEC membership, ministers would not be allowed to campaign for a 'No' vote. Governments (and opposition parties) also sometimes allow a free vote on an issue, as the Conservative government did over various options for Sunday trading in 1994, having lost the second reading of the Shops Bill on a three-line whip in 1986, and the Labour government did over its anti-hunting bill in 2003.

Political solidarity may be the norm, but this does not prevent resignations under the doctrine of collective ministerial responsibility. Two features are striking about the data in Table 11.4: first, there are considerably more resignations on the grounds of collective than individual responsibility – a ratio of 3.4:1; and, second, that they are more common under Labour than Conservative governments – about one a year for the former but only one every two years for the latter. Essentially, such resignations are the result of policy disagreements: a minister who does not like or feels unable to support a particular policy, or sometimes the general thrust of government policy decides to resign. Of course, Prime Ministers and parties are no more enamoured with resignations over policy disagreements than over policy failures, but the latter

Table 11.4   *Resignations on the grounds of collective ministerial responsibility,*
1945–2004

Governing party	No.	No. per year
Conservative	15	0.435
Labour	26	1.102
Overall	41	0.706

are potentially more embarrassing, whereas the former are part and parcel of
intra-party politics. The Prime Minister will invariably try to persuade the
minister to stay, but if he or she insists the government will seek to play down
its significance. The classic dismissal of such resignations is that of Harold
Macmillan, when his Chancellor of the Exchequer and two other Treasury
ministers resigned in 1957, describing their departure as 'a little local difficulty'.
Between 1997 and 2003 seven ministers have resigned over government
policy, one over single parent policy, one increasingly unhappy with the 'Blair
project', one over the rejection of his social welfare proposals, and four over the
Iraq war, including two Cabinet ministers, Robin Cook, the Foreign Secretary,
and Clare Short, the International Development Secretary. However, Tony
Blair managed to persuade Clare Short not to resign initially, urging her to
stay and assist with the post-war rebuilding of Iraq, but she became increasingly unhappy in the aftermath of the war and resigned. Such resignations
are accepted as inevitable from time to time, although they may indicate a
government in difficulty or a party seriously divided. Ministers who resign on
such grounds are only too well aware that it may signal the end of their
ministerial career, but some subsequently achieve further office, as did two of
the three Treasury ministers who resigned in 1958 and Michael Heseltine in
1990, after having resigned in 1986. The greater incidence of such resignations among Labour than Conservative ministers almost certainly reflects the
more ideological nature of the Labour Party, in spite of the growth of neo-
liberalism and Euroscepticism in the Conservative Party. Indeed, it disagreements over Europe that accounted for three of the seven resignations of
Conservative ministers between 1979 and 1997, whereas Labour resignations
are more common among ministers to the left of the party's ideological centre.

   The ultimate enforcement of collective responsibility is granting or denying
the government support in the House of Commons, but governments have
rarely lost votes of confidence – the last was in 1979, preceded by 1924 and
1895. That, however, is hardly the point, as the next section of this chapter
argues. Voting against the government is the norm for opposition parties but
not for government supporters and those who fail to support 'their' government
in the division lobbies are calling it to account, as well as expressing their
dissatisfaction. And dissent by government backbenchers has become much
more common since the 1960s.

Backbench dissent

Backbench behaviour in the House of Commons in the nineteenth century was marked by growing party cohesion, in spite of a decline in the middle of the century during the period of party realignment, so that by the end of the century it was close to 100 per cent. For the first sixty years of the twentieth century this remained largely the norm, so that in 1965 an eminent academic observer of British politics, Samuel Beer, suggested that party cohesion 'was so close to 100 per cent that there is no longer any point in measuring it'.[6] Yet, already there were signs of change: the 1959–64 Parliament witnessed 120 rebellions by government backbenchers, ten times the rate in the previous two Parliaments. In the next normal length Parliament, 1966–70, the number was 109, rising to more than 300 in 1974–79, when the Labour government had either a small majority or no majority at all. In the succeeding Parliaments there were fewer rebellions, but there continued to be many more than between 1945 and 1959 (see Table 11.5).

Of course, the number of actual defeats suffered by governments was much smaller (see Table 11.6), depending largely on the size of the government's normal majority, so that the largest numbers occurred in the 1974 and 1974–79 Parliaments, when the Labour government was particularly vulnerable. More particularly, the eleven defeats between 1945 and 1970 all occurred in two short Parliaments with small government majorities, 1950–51 and 1964–66, and none was the result of deliberate attempts by government backbenchers to defeat the government, but were the result of 'poor organisation

Table 11.5   *Number of rebellions by government MPs, 1945–2001*

Parliament*	No. of rebellions	Governing party
1945–50	79	Labour
1951–55	11	Conservative
1955–59	12	Conservative
1959–64	120	Conservative
1966–70	109	Labour
1970–74	204	Conservative
1974–79	309	Labour
1979–83	159	Conservative
1983–87	203	Conservative
1987–92	198	Conservative
1992–97	174	Conservative
1997–2001	96	Labour

Source: P. Cowley and Mark Stuart, '"In Place of Strife": the PLP in Government, 1997–2001', *Political Studies*, 51, 2003, p. 3.

Note: * Excluding the short Parliaments of 1950–51, 1964–66 and March–October 1974.

Table 11.6   *Number of government defeats in the House of Commons,*
1945–2001

Period/parliament	No.
1945–70	11
1970–74	6
Mar.–Oct. 1974	17
1974–79	42
1979–83	1
1983–87	2
1987–92	1
1992–97	4
1997–2001	0

Source: David Butler and Gareth Butler, *Twentieth Century British Political Facts, 1900–2000,*
Basingstoke Macmillan, 8th edn, 2000, p. 201.

by the whips or deliberate opposition ploys' to catch the government out in
the division lobbies,[7] whereas later defeats resulted from deliberate government backbench rebellions. Not surprisingly, the Labour government elected
in 1997 with a massive 179-seat majority suffered no defeats in the 1997–
2001 Parliament, though it has been defeated once in the 2001 Parliament,
when the government sought to exclude two senior Labour backbenchers
from continuing as chairs of departmental select committees, and came within
five votes of defeat in 2003 over proposals to increase university tuition fees.
Indeed, during the first two sessions of the 2001 Parliament, one or more
government backbenchers rebelled in 18.8 per cent of divisions, more than in
any other Parliament since 1945.[8]

What explains this growth in dissent? A variety of explanations have been
put forward – poor party leadership, changes in the types of individuals elected
to the Commons, and the realisation that, contrary to the conventional
wisdom, governments do not normally fall if defeated in the House of Commons. Poor leadership probably explains some rebellions, especially where
there is evidence that the leadership has not listened sufficiently to backbench
disquiet, since the government often seeks to 'buy off' as many rebels as it
can. On changes in types of MPs, although no clear evidence has been found
to suggest that MPs drawn from particular socio-economic backgrounds are
more likely to defy the whips, it is possible to detect a significant change in
attitude. In the 1950s and earlier, both major parties had solid blocs of loyal
MPs on whom the whips could rely. For the Conservatives it was the 'knights
of the shire', MPs from mostly safe, rural constituencies, with limited political
ambitions; for Labour it was the trade union sponsored MPs, again mostly
sitting for safe seats and also with limited ambitions. If either group showed
signs of serious discontent, the whips quickly informed the government and

steps would normally be taken to respond to their concerns: rebellions were unnecessary and largely unthinkable. Both groups were gradually replaced by MPs on both sides of the House who were not content with a largely passive role and were more politically ambitious. Crucially, it has become increasingly apparent that government defeats rarely brought about a dissolution of Parliament or the resignation of the government and, on those occasions when governments made a particular vote a matter of confidence, they normally survived. In addition, potential rebels among government backbenchers found that they could extract policy concessions from the government, especially on legislation, and governments became adept at containing rebellions by making concessions. In short, there has always been a certain amount of give and take between the government and its backbenchers, but dissent and threatened dissent have increased the amount of give and take, and dissent has become more common and more overt. At the beginning of the twentieth century party cohesion was the norm; at the beginning of the twenty-first century it remains the norm, but significantly tempered by backbench dissent.

Parliament and the government: an overview

Parliament does not control the government; the government largely controls Parliament. This is much more the case with the House of Commons than the House of Lords, but the work of the upper chamber is driven principally by the government's agenda. However, put too baldly, this suggests that Parliament is largely ineffective, but the reality is more complicated. That governments with large majorities more easily get their way than those with small majorities is obvious enough, but much depends on the policies the government seeks to pursue. It must be able to carry all or most of its backbenchers with it and, when that is in doubt, it becomes vulnerable to backbench pressure. Crick's definition of parliamentary control describes not the reality but an ideal. Yet, it is not totally divorced from reality – Parliament does influence, it does advise, it does criticise, it does scrutinise, and it does publicise. The question is not whether it does these things but whether and, if so, how it should do them more often and more effectively.

Notes

1 See Amy Baker, *Prime Ministers and the Rule Book*, London, Politico's, 2000.

2 Letter to the Prime Minister, 1982, cited in Robert Blackburn and Andrew Kennon, *Griffith and Ryle on Parliament: Functions, Practice and Procedures*, London, Sweet & Maxwell, 2003, pp. 50–1.

3 Geoffrey Marshall, 'Individual Responsibility: Some Post-War Examples', in Geoffrey Marshall (ed.), *Ministerial Responsibility*, Oxford, Oxford University Press, 1989, p. 129.

4 Roy Gregory, 'Court Line, Mr Benn and the Ombudsman', *Parliamentary Affairs*, 30, 1977, pp. 269–92.
5 Cited in Walter Bagehot, *The English Constitution*, London, C. A. Watts, 1964, p. 68 (original italics) (originally published between 1865 and 1867).
6 Samuel H. Beer, *Modern British Politics: A Study of Parties and Pressure Groups*, London, Faber, 1965, p. 350.
7 Philip Norton, *Dissension in the House of Commons 1945–74*, 7 London, Macmillan, p. xviii.
8 Philip Cowley and Mark Stuart, 'More Bleak House than Great Expectations', *Parliamentary Affairs*, 57, 2003, p. 211.

12

Reforming Parliament

Reform and the political system

Reforming Parliament needs to be seen in the wider context of the political system, partly because parliamentary reform is not just a matter of making procedural and other internal changes in Parliament and partly because more fundamental changes can be made to the system of parliamentary government, but also because change needs to be considered in terms of political reality. Moreover, although not all political change would necessarily affect Parliament, changes in Parliament might well affect the political system.

The Labour Party came to power in 1997 with a massive programme of political reform. It was not, however, a new programme but one which had been developed during its long years in opposition. Indeed, some proposals predated Labour's defeat in 1979, notably devolution to Scotland and Wales, which it had legislated for but which was not implemented. Others had moved on and off and up and down Labour's agenda over the years, such as reform of the House of Lords, state aid to political parties, local government reform and, in the far distant past, electoral reform. The range and varied nature of this programme can be seen in Table 12.1. None of these changes was exclusive to Labour, but few if any were likely to be implemented unless taken up by one of the two major political parties. In a sense they constituted a reform package, but they were not really presented as a set of interlocking constitutional proposals and, more importantly, neither their implications nor exactly what was proposed had been fully considered. The most advanced plans were for devolution to Scotland and Wales, partly because of the abortive attempt at devolution in 1978–79, but even here much of the running was made by the Scottish Constitutional Convention, a forum which included but was neither driven by nor dominated by the Labour Party but involved a wide range of interests in Scotland in favour of devolution. On Lords' reform, Labour knew it wanted to get rid of the hereditary peers as a first step and

Table 12.1   *The Labour Party's manifesto commitments on constitutional reform, 1979–2001*

Subject matter	1979	1983	1987	1992	1997	2001	Action
Devolution: Scotland	X	X	X	X	X		Done
Devolution: Wales				X	X		Done
Lords' reform	X	X*		X	X	X	Continuing
Commons' reform	X	X		X	X	X	Continuing
Local government reform	X	X	X	X	X	X	Continuing
Freedom of information	X	X	X	X	X		Implementing
State aid to parties	X	X	X	X			Considering
Regional government in England			X	X	X	X	Promised
London government			X	X	X		Done
Bill of Rights				X	X		Implementing
Fixed term Parliaments				X			Dropped
Regulating party finance				X	X		Done
Electoral reform				X	X	X	Reviewed and shelved

Source: Labour Party Manifestos, 1979–2001.

Note: *Abolition rather than reform.

make the upper house 'more democratic and representative',[1] but had no detailed plans for the second stage of reform. On London, the picture was clearer: an elected 'strategic authority' and a separately elected mayor were proposed.[2] The commitments incorporating the European Convention on Human Rights (ECHR) into UK law and the introduction of a Freedom of Information Act were clear in principle, but the practical details would be worked out in office. A commission on electoral reform would be set up and there was a firm commitment to hold a referendum on the electoral system. Furthermore, these proposals would have to compete with the rest of Labour's commitments, while some of the constitutional proposals had a higher priority than others, notably devolution. Nonetheless, action was taken on most, much of it in the 1997–2001 Parliament; some commitments have been fulfilled, others are continuing, but electoral reform is the most significant casualty.

A number of those implemented have implications for parliamentary reform. Devolution, for example, has ostensibly reduced Parliament's burden, but has left unresolved the 'West Lothian question' – the continued ability of MPs representing constituencies in Scotland (and to a lesser extent in Wales) to vote on matters affecting England, a situation which is not likely to be resolved were regional government fully introduced in England. The Human Rights Act has meant that Parliament had to devise machinery to ensure that legislation complies with the ECHR. The Freedom of Information Act, not fully operational until 2005, will probably enhance Parliament's ability to extract information from the government. Changes in local government, the restoration of elected government to London, the regulation of political parties (especially their finances), have implications for the liberal democratic system of which Parliament is part. Changes in Parliament itself, both Lords and Commons, have been considerable, though not everyone sees them as 'reforms'. In particular, some are seen not as strengthening but weakening Parliament – the retention of prime ministerial patronage over membership of the House of Lords and the introduction of the more extensive programming of legislation, for example. Parliamentary reform in particular, however, needs to be considered in terms of what has been done and what could be done.

Parliamentary reform in context

Parliamentary reform is hardly a new phenomenon: the very fact that the Representation of the People Acts extending the right to vote in 1832, 1867 and 1884 are commonly referred to as the Reform Acts, that of 1832 as the Great Reform Act, makes the point. However, the other principal focus of reform in the nineteenth century was the strengthening of the executive vis-à-vis the legislature. In the middle of the century, a number of commentators argued that the problem with Parliament was that the government did not have enough control over it, not that it had too much: 'The great and increasing defect in all parliamentary government ... is the weakness of the executive.'[3] Fears were expressed that 'a fluctuating majority in the Commons' would mean that decisions 'will necessarily be ruled by popular passion and feeling, instead of by reason and prudence'.[4] And Gladstone, following his first term as Prime Minister in 1874, worried about Parliament becoming overburdened and the need 'to expedite public business'.[5] Party came to the rescue; party cohesion reasserted itself and increased in scale until it was nearly 100 per cent. By the time 'Mr Balfour's parliamentary railway timetable' was adopted in 1902, the essential characteristics of the modern House of Commons had been set and, with the curbing of the powers of the House of Lords in 1911, the topping out ceremony for the modern parliamentary edifice could take place. While not complete, governmental control of Parliament was the norm. Most other changes until the middle of the twentieth century served to strengthen rather than weaken governmental control. Party cohesion grew even stronger; procedural changes favoured the government rather than MPs and peers; the resources available to the latter remained poor; and pleas for change fell on deaf ears. To be sure, there was much discussion of reform in the late 1920s and early 1930s, the UK was on the verge of adopting the alternative vote when Parliament was dissolved in 1931, and the House of Lords began to carve out a role for itself following the 1958 Life Peerages Act, but there was no 'shifting of the balance'.

Then, slowly at first but gathering pace and attracting more support, the cries for parliamentary reform grew louder, inspiring and inspired by Bernard Crick's *The Reform of Parliament*, and tentatively responded to by Harold Wilson's 1964–70 Labour government. Gradually, important changes took place, especially in the areas of pay and resources for MPs and in the attitudes and behaviour of Members themselves, the one influencing the other. Procedural changes also took place in the Commons, but were of limited importance and paled beside the most important change of all – the creation of a comprehensive system of investigatory committees, centred around the departmental committees. Meanwhile, despite an abortive attempt at Lords' reform in 1968, the upper house quietly increased its activity, especially through the use of committees, and peers became better resourced. The practice of presenting draft bills developed on a modest scale in the early 1990s, better explanatory material on legislation was made available and the presentation of financial information improved. The flow of information from government departments increased and improved and information on government policy and administration from the investigatory committees in both Houses added enormously to the amount of data placed in the public domain.

It would be churlish to suggest that what followed Labour's election in 1997 was simply more of the same, but the post-1997 changes built on those that had gone before, as well as introducing new ones. The cynical view of parliamentary reform is that governments (and oppositions, for they have a vested interest in government) only allow two types of changes – those that will enhance their ability to get their business through Parliament and those that will not make life difficult for the government. The reality is more complex. A number of the post-1997 changes have undoubtedly enhanced the government's ability to get its business – the programming of bills; changes in the working hours of the Commons are of considerable help to ministers; deferred divisions (by which routine votes are postponed to a paper ballot on Wednesdays) are a great help to the government whips, who do not have to ensure the availability of enough government backbenchers 'to keep a House' as much as before; reducing Prime Minister's Questions (PMQs) to a single session, even though the amount of time is unchanged, puts the Prime Minister in the parliamentary 'hotseat' once a week rather than twice and allows him more time away from Parliament; and the removal of hereditary peers without introducing an elected element has enabled the government to adjust the party balance in the Lords but avoiding creating a second chamber that might challenge the Commons. Changes to working hours, popular with many MPs, costs the government nothing; increasing the opportunities for backbench participation through the Westminster Hall debates do not affect the government's ability to get its business; setting out the parliamentary week and year makes sense for MPs and peers, but again not at great cost to the government, which can always change things at the margins if necessary; setting out the core tasks of the departmental committees will depend on how seriously the committees take them; and the Prime Minister agreeing to be questioned twice a year by the Commons' Liaison Committee can hardly be said to be onerous or especially threatening. None without truth, but none entirely true. The timetabling of legislation is basically necessary and sensible; the trick is to ensure that within that timetabling adequate scrutiny takes place. Deferring divisions matters less than ensuring that 'normal' votes take place on issues that matter to MPs. PMQs once a week is less important than ensuring that the Prime Minister can be questioned by MPs (and why not peers?), which the Liaison Committee sessions enhance. The new working hours remain under review and are unpopular with a significant minority of MPs, including some who originally supported them, and any changes may not benefit the government, especially if linked to modification of the parliamentary week and year. Westminster Hall debates may not affect the government's control of business, but they have considerably extended non-legislative scrutiny. Select committees operate with a considerable degree of autonomy and, as various departmental committees have shown since 1979, some are much more active than others, and some make much more of a nuisance of themselves than others – why else would successive governments seek to remove particular committee chairpersons and retain control over appointments to chairs? And neither the removal of hereditary peers from the House of Lords nor the retention of prime ministerial patronage has made the upper house less of a thorn in the government's side.

There have also been other developments to Parliament's benefit: Questions for oral answer in the Commons have been made more topical; the running sore caused by the misconduct of a small number of MPs has been largely healed by the introduction of a Code of Conduct and the office of the Parliamentary Commissioner for Standards (the Lords following suit with their own Code); the Commons' Order Paper or printed agenda has been simplified and is consequently more informative and easier to understand; more draft bills have been introduced and fuller and better explanatory notes provided; and the two votes on the government's policy on Iraq set a crucial precedent on Parliament's role in committing the country to war, much more so than those on the Falklands in 1982 and the first Gulf War in 1990, both of which were made in response to acts of war.

Reforming Parliament: 1997 and beyond

There is no shortage of proposals for parliamentary reform, some limited and specific, others extensive and fundamental, some procedural, others requiring changes in attitudes and behaviour. More broadly, they fall into internal and external reforms, those involving changes in how Parliament operates and those involving changes in the political system that would have an impact on Parliament and parliamentary government in the UK (see Tables 12.2 and 12.3).

Internal reform

Table 12.2   *Reforming Parliament: internal reform – a checklist*

Area	Affecting	Objective
Personnel	House of Commons and House of Lords	To make Parliament, especially the House of Commons, more representative, to enable MPs and peers to fulfil their roles more effectively, and improve the scrutiny function
Pay and resources	House of Commons and House of Lords	To provide MPs and peers and both Houses collectively with adequate resources to perform their functions
Organising Parliament	House of Commons and House of Lords	To organise the parliamentary day, week and year and to give MPs and peers and both Houses collectively greater control over their agendas in ways that will improve the scrutiny function
Legislative scrutiny	House of Commons and House of Lords	To improve further the scrutiny of primary and secondary legislation
Financial scrutiny	Mainly the House of Commons, but to a lesser extent the House of Lords	To develop more effective financial scrutiny, especially over expenditure
Non-legislative scrutiny	House of Commons and House of Lords	To improve the scrutiny of government policy and administration through improving existing mechanisms and developing new ones
Reform of the House of Lords	House of Lords and House of Commons	To improve the effectiveness of the second chamber and enhance the role of Parliament generally

Personnel

Ultimately, Parliament depends on its members, whether elected or appointed. It depends on their quality in the sense of their ability to fulfil their parliamentary roles and its depends on their attitudes towards those roles. Today's MPs and peers are better-educated than their predecessors and drawn from a wider spectrum of experience, although the decline in working-class representation is marked, women remain significantly outnumbered by men in both Houses, and ethnic minorities are under-represented and concentrated almost exclusively in one party. There is, however, no evidence that microcosmic representation in either or both Houses would necessarily make for a more effective Parliament, but a more socio-economically representative Parliament would allow more voices to be heard and would be more likely to be seen as legitimate. Two-party domination has declined, but more in electoral inputs than outcomes, and the composition of Parliament, especially the House of Commons, remains very much in the hands of the parties. Changing the electoral system to some form of proportional representation (PR) would almost certainly have an impact on the Commons, not just in party but in socio-economic terms too, since multi-member constituencies (either generally or in part) would allow parties to be more flexible in their choice of candidates. In the end, however, parties have to find ways of recruiting a wider range of candidates and persuading local parties to select them, unless they are prepared to be much more dirigiste, which is hardly likely to encourage local party activists. Labour has gone some way down this road with its all-women shortlists, now made legal, and practices such as the 'twinning' of constituencies, gender-balanced and in some cases ethnic-balanced shortlists could also help, but engineering other aspects of the socio-economic spectrum is more difficult.

Nonetheless, no matter how socio-economically representative either or both Houses are, it is ultimately attitudes that count, attitudes towards the three major roles of MPs – the partisan, scrutiny and constituency roles. The constituency role is accepted and valued by the overwhelming majority of MPs. Moreover, it is one of the strengths of parliamentary government in the UK, helping constituents and defending constituency interests, on the one hand, keeping MPs in touch with those they represent, on the other. No doubt some are better constituency MPs than others, but it is a role all are expected to fulfil, whereas the partisan and scrutiny roles depend far more on MPs' attitudes. And the scrutiny role in particular depends not only on the attitudes of MPs but on their abilities. Who MPs are, matters. This is no less true of peers, for whom the scrutiny role is equally crucial. Were all or a proportion of members of the upper house elected, the role of the parties in selecting candidates would become even more important. On the other hand, if nomination remains based on patronage, the party leaders, especially of the Conservative and Labour Parties, will need to exercise their responsibilities to the benefit of Parliament as well as their parties. In both Houses, but particularly the Commons, the balance between the partisan and scrutiny roles is the key factor in attitudes. The scrutiny role, however, is both a matter of attitude and ability.

The number of members each House should have has also become a focus of discussion in recent years – the Commons, partly because of devolution, partly in its own right, and the Lords because any reform must take the matter into account. The establishment of the Scottish Parliament and the National Assembly for Wales involved the transfer of responsibilities from London to Edinburgh and Cardiff, though more extensively for the former than the latter. This opened up the possibility of reducing the number of MPs at Westminster, especially with the transfer of considerable primary legislative powers and financial responsibility to the Scottish Parliament, and proposals for a reduction in the number of MPs representing constituencies in Scotland were built into the Scotland Act 1998. Consequently, the number of Scottish seats will in due course be reduced from 72 to 59, but there is no plan to reduce the number of Welsh seats, since primary legislative powers and most financial responsibility remains at Westminster. However, there have also been suggestions that the number of UK MPs should be reduced generally.[6] In most cases, the reduction envisaged is by about a third to between four and five hundred, although there have been suggestions of halving the membership. The intention in the latter case was to encourage MPs to see themselves as a national forum and as legislative scrutineers and pay less attention to the growing constituency role. Some of the more recent supporters of a reduction also favour lessening the burden of the latter, particularly in dealing with individual constituents. However, the constituency role has grown enormously and significantly reducing it, even if MPs wished, would be no easy task. Nonetheless, bearing in mind that members of the devolved legislatures now shoulder part of that burden, the use of new technology and additional purpose-related staff would not make a reduction in the number of MPs impractical. However, a part of the argument advanced in favour of a reduction is based on the false belief that the British electorate is over-represented compared with those of other comparable countries, such as other members of the EU, Westminster-type systems in Australia, Canada and New Zealand, and very different systems, like the United States. The US Congress, it is pointed out, consists of 435 members of the House of Representatives and a hundred Senators, representing some 260m Americans (comparisons of electorates are difficult since criteria differ between countries), that the French National Assembly, the Australian Senate and House of Representatives, the Canadian House of Commons, and the New Zealand House of Representatives are all smaller than the UK House of Commons, some considerably so, while the German Bundestag, though larger, represents significantly more people. In a number of cases this entirely ignores the fact that a number of these countries are federal systems or have regional elected bodies, dividing responsibility between two levels of government and considerably enhancing the actual level of representation. In fact, only the Japanese are under-represented, compared with Britain, even taking into account the devolved legislatures in the UK.

Levels of representation are partly a matter of opinion – often crudely expressed as, 'there are too many politicians' – and partly a pragmatic matter. The constituency role aside, the question is whether the House of Commons would be more or less effective with fewer MPs. An important measure of this is the number of committees the Commons seeks to operate. It is quite clear from the experience of small legislatures in a number of federal states and from the experience of the 129-member Scottish Parliament and 60-member National Assembly for Wales, that the smaller the body the fewer committees it can sustain. The Commons has substantially increased its committee activity, with the growth of standing committees dealing with the committee stage of legislation, other committees to deal with secondary legislation (including that from Brussels), and, from the 1960s, the use of considerably more investigatory committees, and, most recently, more use of joint committees. These committees have, in turn, become busier. In addition, the creation of the Westminster Hall sittings as a further forum has added to the demands on Members. On a more limited scale, the House of Lords also uses more committees and, with the use of the Grand Committee for the committee stage of bills, has similarly increased demands on peers. Indeed, concern has been expressed about whether the upper house can reasonably sustain more than its present complement of committees. Of course, if a reformed second chamber were to consist entirely or substantially of full-time members, more committees could be sustained, but it also emphasises the importance of considering the size of legislative membership against the roles and tasks that membership is expected to fulfil. Another measure of parliamentary activity is the number of sitting days and here it should be noted that both Lords and Commons also meet more frequently than any other legislative chamber and shows no sign of declining.

Reducing the number of members in Commons or Lords is often linked to a reduction in the number of ministers, which has increased from sixty in 1900 to well over a hundred today. With considerably fewer peers holding ministerial office, this has meant that, in 1900, 1 in 20 MPs were ministers, compared with 1 in 7 now. Furthermore, add Parliamentary Private Secretaries (PPSs) and the ratios are 1 in 16 and 1 in 5. Of course, if these ratios are expressed in relation to MPs of the governing party, they are even more striking – 1 in 10 in 1900 and 1 in 3 now. Moreover, in 1900 and since 1997 the governing parties had massive majorities; if they had had majorities of 1, the ratios would be 1 in 8 and 1 in 2.

As noted in Chapter 11, not only are ministers bound by collective responsibility, so also are PPSs, and together they constitute what is known as 'the payroll vote', even though PPSs are unpaid. Since 1950 the number of ministers, including peers, has increased by two-fifths, but the number of PPSs has increased by more than 100 per cent. The increase in ministers is partly explained by the continuing expansion of governmental activity, reflected particularly at the minister of state level, and it is here that much of the increase in PPSs has occurred. Devolution to Scotland and Wales has only had a limited impact on the number of ministers, with the two posts of Secretary of State being held jointly with other Cabinet posts, and a reduction in the number of non-Cabinet ministers to a single parliamentary secretary in each case. The UK has one of the largest governments in the world and, although it beyond the scope of this book, it is pertinent to ask whether so many ministers are needed. Even more pertinently, it can be asked why so many PPSs are needed. They provide communication channels between ministers and Parliament, especially government backbenchers, and their expansion in numbers stems from the use made of ministers outside the Cabinet by dividing departmental responsibilities among the ministerial 'team' – three departments in 2003 actually had 'team PPSs', as well as those attached to individual ministers. It might be better, however, if most ministers, particularly those outside the Cabinet, dispensed with PPSs and themselves liaised with backbenchers, especially on the government side. Reducing the number of ministers and

PPSs would reduce the amount of prime ministerial patronage, and from a parliamentary point of view that would be no bad thing. In any case, the question should not be divorced from any consideration of reducing the number of MPs or members of the second chamber, both of which should be decided in the context of the roles and workloads of the two Houses.

Pay and resources

Reducing the number of MPs has also been linked to the question of pay and resources: cut the number of MPs, so the argument runs, and improve the pay and resources of the rest. It was, however, an argument mainly when pay and resources were less adequate and now carries less weight than it did. The regular reviews of by the SSRB and the linkage to civil service rates between reviews has taken most of the political sting out of the issue of MPs' pay and allowances, although governments are periodically embarrassed when they seek to curb public sector pay and the media has the occasional field day with allowances and pensions; rightly so, since they should not go unquestioned, even though the media sometimes displays remarkable ignorance of the facts. MPs can hardly be said to be badly paid, as they once undoubtedly were, and the resources available to them have changed beyond all recognition compared with the 1960s and earlier. It is therefore largely a matter of adjusting existing provisions, rather than making major changes and it is the resourcing of Parliament as a whole, especially in areas such as committee work, that is likely to require more attention in the future.

Peers in the current House of Lords (office-holders apart) and members of any future second chamber, present a different case. Peers receive allowances but are not paid and the Royal Commission on the House of Lords did not envisage full-time, paid members of a reformed second chamber, but that 'payment should be made for the time members ... devote to their parliamentary duties' and that 'financial support ... should be related to attendance in Parliament', although it did recommend salaries for the chairs of 'significant committees'.[7] Such arrangements would be similar to those made for members of local authorities. That members of the second chamber should be adequately resourced should not be in question, but were they not to be regarded as full-time and paid a commensurate salary, then they would be exceptions to the general rule compared with members of second chambers in other, comparable countries. It is a bullet that, sooner or later, will have to be bitten.

Organising Parliament

Changes to the parliamentary year and week have been broadly welcomed, but further consideration should be given to particular aspects. There may be a case for having shorter and more frequent recesses and spreading sitting days more evenly through the year, but there is a much stronger case to having a committee day each week or committee weeks when the two Houses are not sitting. One of the drawbacks of the 'family friendly' hours is the conflicting pressure of committee meetings and plenary meetings. At present, too much activity is squeezed into too little space and this problem will grow as committee activity continues to increase. In addition, undue emphasis has been placed on 'family friendly' hours, in that most MPs' constituencies are too far away for the change in hours to have much impact on their families, unless the family has moved to or near London. The argument for mainly day-time hours should rest on normalising the job of being an MP and sitting hours that contribute to parliamentary effectiveness by avoiding excessively long or late sittings should be the criterion. Westminster could and should look at the practice and experience of the Scottish Parliament, which does not allow concurrent plenary and committee meetings and sets aside separate times and days for each.

Both Houses now have control over their own affairs as far as finance and provision of services and facilities to their members are concerned. These changes began in the 1960s and the most recent have involved the introduction of modern management techniques in the operation of Parliament. The two Houses remain largely autonomous, while co-operating over some services and facilities and, of course, over the handling of parliamentary business, but it is crucial that each House should retain procedural autonomy and continue to adapt their modes of operation to enhance their parliamentary functions, particularly in calling the government to account. There is, however, one area over which they have less control – their agendas. This is especially true of the Commons, where the agenda is driven largely by the government, though less true of the Lords. Both the Scottish Parliament and the National Assembly for Wales have Business Committees, as do many other legislatures. Having a Business Committee in each House at Westminster would amount to a partial formalisation of the usual channels, but would not preclude a continuation of informal contacts through the usual channels. Indeed, it is doubtful whether an effective Business Committee could operate without co-operation through the usual channels, which could hardly be banned. However, if this route is followed, it needs to give both Houses greater control over their agendas and not merely formalise the existing arrangements. From Parliament's point of view, it might therefore do better to consider the German model, in which the government is not directly represented on the Business Committee (though it has a minister in attendance); representation is based on party strengths and rights of initiative are built in for other parties as well as for the governing party. The system reduces executive control of the agenda and encourages compromise, but does not prevent the government from getting its business. Incidentally, the Bundestag's Business Committee or Parliamentary Council is also responsible for nominating chairs of committees and for various services and facilities, including office accommodation for members. Neither the government nor the opposition (as the putative government) is likely to favour such an arrangement at Westminster, but adopting the Scottish and Welsh arrangements would be a step in that direction.

Legislative scrutiny

There have been some useful improvements in the means available for the
scrutiny of legislation, especially primary legislation. More extensive consultation on proposed legislation takes place and more and better information is
provided when bills are published. More bills are published in draft and referred to an appropriate departmental committee (sometimes more than one),
a joint committee, or a committee set up for the purpose, all of which can take
oral and written evidence. Draft bills have the considerable advantage of
being less set in stone and allow interested parties, whether pressure groups,
other organisations or experts from outside Parliament, to have their say. Little
use has been made of special standing committees, combining the evidence-
taking powers of select committees and the normal standing committee
procedure. Nor are many bills referred to second reading committees. Greater
use could be made of all these practices, but the key lies in flexibility. For
example, publishing all bills in draft should not become the norm, but should
be reserved for complex and for controversial bills. Alternatively, the Scottish
Parliament's practice of sending all bills to a committee before first reading
could be adopted, but this could overburden the departmental committees, as
could referring the committee stage of most bills to them. The departmental
committees might be better used for the committee stage of particular bills –
where there is much outside interest or concern about the detail, for instance.
Again, flexibility should be the determining factor. Similarly, post-legislative
scrutiny could be made more effective, but it needs to be systematic in the
sense that, at an appropriate interval after it came into effect, consideration
should be given to whether a particular Act of Parliament needs such scrutiny
and flexible in that it might normally be done by the appropriate departmental
committee, but some Acts could be referred to a joint committee or a specially
convened committee, particularly on cross-cutting. This could be preceded by
a sifting process carried out by an expanded Scrutiny Unit.

Secondary legislation presents a less satisfactory picture. The technical
scrutiny of statutory instruments is not a problem, but Parliament's inability
seriously to question the substance of delegated legislation and, in particular,
to amend it should be changed. This would make life more difficult for the
government, but it is not Parliament's role to make life easier for the executive. In practice, most statutory instruments would not be challenged and few
would be amended, but that does not mean that the government should not
be rendered more accountable on the detailed implementation of its policies.

Improvements have been made in the handling of secondary legislation
from the EU and, between them, the two Houses scrutinise such legislation
at least as effectively as any other national Parliament in the Union. That,
however, should not preclude further improvements, particularly in examining the substance of proposals considered by the Council of Ministers.
Co-operation between Lords and Commons over the EU could be extended to
the European Parliament, possibly by involving some MEPs in the committee

work on European legislation. Parliament's role in considering policies emanating from Brussels could become more important with the enlargement of the EU, with the consequent reduction of the UK's representation on the European Commission, and by the adoption of the EU Constitution extending the scope of the Union's activity.

Financial scrutiny

Parliament has long struggled to find effective means of controlling proposed public expenditure, largely to no avail. MPs' interests lie less with expenditure and more with the policies it underpins. The inclusion of the examination of the estimates among the core tasks of departmental committees will improve matters only if the committees take the task seriously. One change that might go some way to achieving this would be to empower committees to re-commend the rejection of a particular estimate and also to recommend the reallocation of expenditure within the overall set of estimates being considered. In either case, the government would be required to find time to debate and vote on the recommendations. Governments would hate the idea, but why should the House of Commons? Proposed expenditure might also be more effectively examined in the light of reports on past expenditure in the same area produced by the National Audit Office and the Public Accounts Com-mittee, especially in respect of value for money. Parliament does much better in examining how the money has been spent and this needs feeding back into the policy process to judge whether policies are working effectively.

Scrutiny of taxation is also reasonably effective, particularly on the detailed impact of proposals. The work of the Treasury Committee on the Chancellor's Budget has deepened scrutiny and the tentative steps taken by the House of Lords to scrutinise economic policy without challenging the financial primacy of the Commons should be welcomed. A useful development might be co-operation between the two Houses, enabling the Commons to draw directly on the expertise available in the Lords.

Non-legislative scrutiny

The development of the departmental committees was undoubtedly the most important parliamentary reform of the twentieth century, even though it has not fulfilled the hopes of some of its more extravagant supporters. Through them the government is now more comprehensively called to account than ever before. The debating of reports is probably less important than that they are published and that the government expects, and is expected, to respond. Here the committees could be more systematic by following up what has happened to their recommendations made in earlier reports. It is sometimes suggested that they should have more powers, but any such proposal should be clearly within the context that committees make recommendations, not decisions. Any suggestion of a shift towards the latter is proposing a move away from parliamentary government: it is the government that is responsible for policy and its implementation and giving committees what would amount to an executive role would blur the relationship between government and Parliament. However, an area in which committee powers should be strengthened is in the calling of evidence, particularly oral evidence. Most of the evidence from outside the executive is presented willingly, but it is the government who decides which ministers and which civil servants should appear before committees. It should be for the committees to decide from whom they wish to take evidence, whether oral or written. It has become a particular problem with the growth in the number of special advisers, some of whom play a key role in policy-making and the creation of executive opinion. Such a power would not prevent the government seeking to persuade the committee that a different minister, civil servant or special adviser would be more appropriate, but the decision should ultimately be the committee's.

The resources available to committees have also expanded considerably and, while it is too early to judge how much the setting up of the Scrutiny Unit has helped, the greater use of committees for legislative as well as non-legislative scrutiny and the assignment of core tasks for the departmental committees is likely to increase the need for yet more back-up. In terms of procedural and administrative resources, that should not be a problem – expansion of existing resources should continue, but the area of expert or specialist advice is more difficult. Clearly, engaging the services of advisers for particular investigations, whether legislative or non-legislative, is a sensible practice but the question of whether some or most committees need long-term, full-time specialist advice is a more complex issue and needs careful consideration. In the end, what should be avoided are committees run by specialist advisers rather than their members.

The Blair government has made much of the problem of achieving 'joined-up government' and this is something that parliamentary committees need to take into account. In particular, this can be and to some extent is addressed by joint investigations by two or more departmental committees, but there is also scope for more use of joint committees, again drawing on the expertise found in the Lords, ad hoc committees to deal with particular issues, and consideration should also be given to more permanent committees on the lines of the Environmental Audit and Public Administration Committees.

Although investigatory committees offer the most effective systematic and in-depth non-legislative scrutiny, other mechanisms should not be forgotten, partly because they offer different types of scrutiny and partly because of the opportunities they provide for individual Members. The Westminster Hall sittings have considerably extended backbench opportunities and the introduction of cross-cutting Questions sessions could become a significant contribution to the scrutiny of joined-up government. Making Question Time more topical is also to be welcomed and, no doubt, other procedural changes could strengthen the scrutiny role. The Commons would do well to look at some of the procedures used by the Lords and a watching brief on procedure and practice in Scottish Parliament and National Assembly for Wales, and, for that matter, legislatures in other countries should be part of Westminster's continuing review of its own operation.

Reforming the second chamber

Having completed stage one of Lords' reform, the Blair government has found itself bogged down in stage two. It was not happy with the main thrust of the Wakeham Commission's recommendations for a partly elected, partly appointed second chamber. Meanwhile, Commons and Lords have managed to create an impasse, the former rejecting all the proposals put to it for a reformed membership ranging from all-appointed to all-elected but clearly in favour of an elected element, and the latter voting in favour of an all-appointed House. Further significant changes in composition seem unlikely, at least until a further general election has taken place, but if and when changes do take place they need to be related to what the House of Lords currently does and a future second chamber needs to do. This is more likely to be achieved by appointment than election and a substantial elected element would probably make the second chamber a more partisan body. This should not preclude the introduction of some elected members, but the proportional balance between them and appointed members is likely to be a crucial factor. As it stands, the House of Lords complements rather than rivals the House of Commons and its future composition should preserve and enhance that relationship, building on the upper house's strengths.

External reform

Table 12.3   *Reforming Parliament: external reform – a checklist*

Area	Affecting	Objectives
A written constitution	Parliament as a whole	To clarify the role and functions of Parliament, in particular its relations with the government
A separation of powers	Parliament as a whole	To divide power constitutionally between the three branches of government – the legislature, the executive and the judiciary
Devolution and federalism	Parliament as a whole	To divide power between different levels of government
Electoral reform	House of Commons and possibly the House of Lords	To ensure that parliamentary representation more accurately reflects public opinion as expressed in elections
Referendums	Parliament as a whole	To enable some issues to be decided by the electorate, usually between elections
Fixed-term Parliaments	Parliament as a whole	To remove the partisan element in determining the date of a general election

A written constitution

Many of the UK's constitutional arrangements are written down in the form of Acts of Parliament and other constitutional documents, but none has a higher status than other laws, and changing constitutional arrangements is not subject to a special procedure, as is the norm with written or codified constitutions. The UK is not unique in this regard but is unusual, and there have been calls from various quarters for the UK to adopt a written constitution. One advocate is Charter 88, a constitutional pressure group drawing support widely across the across the political spectrum, though more from the left of centre. Over time, more and more of the UK's constitutional arrangements have been written down, but this is mainly because more of those arrangements have become the subject of statute law. In principle, it would not be difficult to codify the system of parliamentary government operating in the UK, including those constitutional conventions regarded as crucial to its operation. This is precisely what happened with Canada's constitutional arrangements in the Victoria Charter of 1971, in an attempt at constitutional reform. In the event, the Charter remained a paper constitution, but it showed that codification of existing arrangements could be done. A working example can be found in the German Constitution, drawn up in 1949, and setting down detailed rules to establish and operate a parliamentary system that has served Germany well. Many written constitutions are the products of 'revolutions' or some other political crisis, but they do not have to be. What are the implications of a written constitution?

Written constitutions are normally characterised by three crucial features – a higher status for constitutional law, an amending process requiring a higher level of consent than for other laws, and a judicial body capable of interpreting the constitution and ruling on constitution disputes. The second and third features are products of the first. It must be possible to adapt the constitution to changing circumstances, not simply at the will of those holding power at a particular time, but with support for any change drawn more widely. The obvious way to seek and achieve such support is by requiring a higher threshold of approval than that required for other laws. This can be done in a variety of ways. For example, specifying minimum support in the legislature – say two-thirds or by a national referendum, again with a minimum threshold of support and, possibly, a minimum level of turnout. Indeed, it is possible to combine minimum support in the legislature before a proposal is put to a referendum. It is not difficult to devise mechanisms, although the higher the threshold required the more difficult it will be to amend the constitution and building in too great a minority veto is likely to be counter-productive.

More controversial is the interpretation of the constitution. In some cases this is the task of a supreme court, which also acts as the highest court on other matters, but a special constitutional court could be established. It would need to have in theory and practice clear judicial independence and establish itself as a trusted interpreter and defender of the constitution. This in turn means that appointments to such a body, both in personnel and process, are crucial and any taint of bias, especially partisan bias, would seriously undermine its viability. In short, it must be trustworthy and trusted.

An obvious difficulty with a written constitution is that change, including social change, may become so difficult that it produces constitutional, even political stagnation, especially if veto groups in the form of particular sections of the population develop. There must be sufficient adaptability in the constitutional arrangements to accommodate social and political change.

The likelihood of the UK adopting a written constitution in the foreseeable future is not great, but this does not mean it should not be considered, not least because membership of the EU and the incorporation of the ECHR into UK law have introduced features similar to those found in written constitutions – the supremacy of EU law over UK law and the necessity for UK law to conform to the ECHR.

A separation of powers

Drawing up a written constitution opens up the possibility of making more substantial, even fundamental, changes. The Founding Fathers of the United States, for example, adopted a separation of powers to prevent the concentration of power in the hands of a single individual or institution and there are those who have advocated a separation of powers for the UK. This would, of course, mean the abandonment of parliamentary government for a presidential-congressional system. Whether that would be an improvement lies beyond the scope of this book, but it is an assumption that it would simply mean the wholesale importation of the American political system or that a UK system based on the separation of powers would operate in essentially the same way as the American. It is only necessary to refer to the high levels of party cohesion in the UK to illustrate the point. A system with a separation of powers in which an executive whose party controlled the legislature through strong party cohesion would probably operate very differently from the American system. However, there are other possibilities. For instance, since 1958 France has had a hybrid presidential-parliamentary system, with a separately elected executive president, combined with a prime minister and government dependent on majority support in the legislature. This has, from time to time, produced a president from one party and a prime minister from another, not in the form of a coalition but sometimes uncomfortable co-existence. Israel has produced yet another variation, not so much a separation of powers, but electing the prime minister and the members of the legislature simultaneously but separately, allowing the electorate to choose the 'best' person as prime minister and vote for a different party for legislative representation. It has proved a recipe for choice, though not necessarily for stability.

Devolution and federalism

Devolution in Scotland and Wales is one of the most important constitutional changes introduced by the Labour government since 1997. Substantial responsibility and political power has been passed to the Scottish Parliament and Executive, rather less to the National Assembly for Wales and the Welsh Executive. In Scotland, devolution has created a separate parliamentary system, operating in many respects in much the same way as Westminster but with distinctive features of its own. In Wales, what was intended to be more akin to a super-local government system has in practice evolved more on parliamentary lines. This has, of course, developed alongside the longer-standing arrangements in Northern Ireland, the post-1998 Good Friday Agreement version of which involves a power-sharing executive emphasising the distinctiveness of Northern Ireland politics. In the meantime, regional government in England has developed in the form of Regional Development Agencies and non-elective regional assemblies, but more extensive regional government has yet to emerge. Nonetheless, legislation has been passed allowing those regions that wish to move towards an elective form of regional devolution to do so, although there are no plans to extend this process other than by consent. What has in effect been established is a form of quasi-federalism, a set of arrangements well short of full federalism, which normally involves equal or largely similar arrangements in all component parts of the federal system. Of course, in theory parliamentary sovereignty remains intact. What Westminster has given, it can take away, but, with the possible exception of Northern Ireland (where it has happened before), politically the initiative for any reversal of devolution would have to come from Scotland or Wales, not Westminster.

In theory, the step from devolution to federalism is a short one; in practice it is a long one. The Liberal Democrats and their Liberal predecessors have long favoured fully fledged federalism, but it has yet to find its way on to the agenda of political reality. Federalism would certainly require a written constitution, not least because means of modifying the division of policy responsibilities and settling disputes over them are necessary. More importantly, opinion in England, neither generally nor regionally seems inclined to press for federalism. Regions such as the North East, North West, Yorkshire and possibly the South West may press for regional assemblies, but there seems to be little support for greater regional devolution, let alone federalism. It is sometimes argued that a federal system in which England were the largest unit would be so unbalanced in socio-economic terms as not to be feasible. Certainly, there is no federal system in which one unit is so much larger in population and economic significance, but the present devolution arrangements leave England in a position somewhat akin to that situation. However, federalism is barely, if at all, on the political horizon.

Nonetheless, devolution may have an impact on the UK's parliamentary system in two ways. First, a UK government has yet to experience governments of totally different political complexions at Westminster, on the one hand, and Edinburgh and Cardiff, on the other. If and when that happens, the course of devolution may run less smoothly. Second, those involved in the development of devolution in Scotland and Wales consciously sought to avoid being Westminster clones and both the Scottish Parliament and the National Assembly for Wales have developed procedures and practices from which Westminster could learn and possibly adopt. What devolution has not done is reduced the burden on Westminster: there has been no reduction in Westminster's number of sitting days, nor in the volume of primary or secondary legislation. A lessening of the constituency role for MPs from Scotland and Wales has occurred, but that is of little help to Parliament as a whole. The government has quietly filled the space created by devolution.

Electoral reform

Probably the most frequent call for external change has been that of electoral reform, either by modifying the existing simple plurality or first-past-the-post (FPTP) system or by adopting some form of proportional representation (PR). All parties have their electoral reform advocates, but it is parties that suffer under FPTP which are usually most in favour of change, and those that benefit from FPTP which are usually against. Labour actually came to power in 1997 with a pledged to review the electoral system: 'We are committed to a referendum on the voting system for the House of Commons. An independent commission on voting systems will be appointed early to recommend a proportional alternative to the first past the post system.'[8] Headed by the former Leader of the Social Democratic Party, Lord Jenkins, a commission was duly appointed and reported in October 1998,[9] recommending a mixed PR system involving a modified form of FPTP and the introduction of a significant number of 'top-up' seats to make the overall outcome more proportional. The proposal involved the use of the alternative vote, designed to eliminate the election of candidates in single-member constituencies on the minority of the votes cast by redistributing second preferences, with the 'top-up' seats being distributed according to each party's overall vote. In spite of a further but less firm pledge in 2001, involving reviewing the experience of electoral systems used for the devolved legislatures, the London Assembly and European Parliament elections, the Jenkins Report has remained on the shelf gathering dust, and the prospects for changing the electoral system have receded, with the possible exception of introducing the supplementary vote system, which would almost certainly favour Labour. There was also talk of introducing PR for local elections, but that too has faded away, with the important exception of Scotland, where, following a 2003 post-election deal between Labour and its Liberal Democrat coalition partners, PR will be introduced for local government elections in Scotland in 2007. The UK therefore retains its mix of electoral systems, some FPTP, some PR (with different types being used in

Scotland, Wales and for the Greater London Assembly, Northern Ireland, and for the European Parliament), and the supplementary vote for electing the London mayor.

There is compelling evidence that had the alternative vote been used in 1997 or 2001, Labour's majority would have been larger that that achieved by FPTP,[10] hardly a recommendation for either, if greater proportionality or reducing the distorted relationship between votes and seats were the objective. Adopting some form of PR would make coalition government more likely at Westminster, possibly making it the norm. Parties only want to share power when there is no alternative, so the reluctance of most members of the Conservative and Labour Parties to favour PR is understandable and electoral reform is likely only if the existing system consistently fails to produce single-party majorities, especially in two or more successive elections. Were coalition governments to become the norm, a crucial question is what sort of coalition would likely emerge. If the experience of Scotland and Wales were to apply to the UK as a whole, then it would be a Labour–Liberal Democrat coalition. Such a coalition might well put the Conservative Party in a position of more or less permanent opposition and, if that were to happen, it could have a profound effect on parliamentary attitudes, particularly in the Commons. Labour and the Liberal Democrats might become essentially government minded, the Conservatives opposition minded, seeing little point in co-operating through the usual channels if their prospects of winning power were significantly diminished. This pattern emerged in Canada after the First World War, when the Liberals became the principal party of government and the Conservatives the principal party of opposition.

Adopting PR would also have an impact on the constituency role of MPs, since all PR systems require either multi-member constituencies in whole or part, or, in a few cases treat the whole country as a single constituency, as in Israel and the Netherlands. The constituency role is much valued by MPs and it is likely that, were PR introduced, it would take the form of either the single transferable vote (STV), which uses constituencies of five to seven members, or the added-member system, which combines single-member constituencies with regional or lower level multi-member ones to achieve proportionality. Northern Ireland uses the STV for Assembly and European Parliament elections and it is also used in the Republic of Ireland. The AMS is used for elections to the Scottish Parliament, the National Assembly for Wales and the Greater London Assembly and is the system that would most likely be used for Westminster elections. However, the single-member constituencies involved would inevitably have larger electorates, thus increasing the burden on the MPs concerned. In addition, conflicts could emerge over the constituency role between single-member constituency MPs and multi-member constituency MPs. Multi-member constituencies would also almost certainly increase central party control over the selection of candidates, since party lists would have to be used.

Referendums

Table 12.4   *Public support for the use of referendums, 1995*

Question: Should the government decide all important issues, or would you like Britain to adopt a referendum system whereby certain issues are put to the people to decide by popular vote?

Decision	%*
The government	19
Referendums	77
Don't know	5

Source: Dunleavy *et al.*, *Voices of the People*, London, Politico's, 2001, Table 46.

Note: * Totals more than 100 per cent because of rounding.

   The UK has only limited experience of referendums, although popular support has long been considerable when elicited via opinion polls and surveys, as Table 12.4 illustrates; a similar poll in 1991 produced an almost identical result. Moreover, the same poll also found that 77 per cent thought it 'a good idea' that if a petition were signed by 'say a million people', the government should be required to hold a referendum. However, the UK has no provision for regular referendums or for the use of the initiative to trigger them. Referendums have therefore come about in two ways: first, when used by governments to deal with a particular issue and, second, when forced upon governments by factors beyond their control. The 1975 referendum on the UK's continued membership of the EEC (EU) illustrates the first type. The Labour government elected in 1974 was seriously divided over EEC membership (as was the Conservative opposition) and a referendum offered a way out of the dilemma. It also seemed to offer a way of settling the European issue once and for all, but that view subsequently proved both naïve and inaccurate. Similarly, the referendums held in 1973 to test opinion in Northern Ireland over continuing to be part of the UK and in 1998 to approve the Good Friday Agreement and those seeking endorsement for devolution to in Scotland and Wales, also in 1998, are further examples of government-initiated referendums. The Labour government elected in 1997 initiated another referendum in 1998 to seek approval for an elected mayor and assembly for London, and established procedures for local referendums on proposals for elected mayors in other parts of England. These referendums only took place if demanded by 1 in 20 electors and, in 2001 and 2002, 29 mayoral referendums were held, resulting in approval of having an elected mayor in 11 cases. Referendums were also promised on changing the electoral system, adopting the euro, and proposals for regional assemblies, the latter to be triggered by local demand. In contrast, the referendums held in 1979 on devolution to Scotland and

Wales were forced on the then Labour government by a combination of its own backbenchers and opposition parties and, arguably, the referendum on the draft EU Constitution, promised by Tony Blair in 2004, represented a similar retreat, faced with increasingly vociferous demands for a popular vote.

Not surprisingly, opposition parties have also proposed referendums on various issues, as did the Conservatives over reform of the House of Lords and over Irish Home Rule between 1910 and 1914, over protection and imperial preference in 1930, and Labour did over Europe while in opposition between 1970 and 1974. And in 1945, while still Prime Minister, Winston Churchill proposed a referendum on the continuation of the wartime coalition until after the defeat of Japan, but this was rejected by Labour's Leader, Clement Attlee: 'I could not consent to the introduction into our national life of a device so alien to all our traditions as the referendum.'[11] This is the common response from British politicians – Britain is a parliamentary democracy in which decisions are taken by a government responsible to Parliament and accountable to the electorate at general elections. Thus Edward Heath rejected a referendum on the UK's entry to the EEC, Harold Wilson initially resisted but later conceded a referendum on continued membership, John Major refused one on the Maastricht Treaty in 1992, and Tony Blair adopted the same argument over the draft EU Constitution until reversing his stance in 2004.

All this illustrates one of the major problems with the referendum: on what matters should it be used? For most countries that use referendums to approve constitutional amendments, the answer is clear, but beyond that it is difficult to define issues that should be subject to a referendum. The simplest answer is to combine the referendum with the initiative, which is the practice in nearly half the states in the United States, and nationally and in the cantons in Switzerland. It is sometimes argued that the referendum is an innately conservative device, that electorates are more likely to opt for the status quo, especially when linked to the initiative. Referendums in Switzerland, for example, rejected votes for women until 1971, but this needs to be set against the fact that between 1848 and 1978 government legislation was challenged on 95 occasions but overturned only 34 times.[12] The cynical view of the referendum is that ad hoc calls for its use are only made by those who believe the outcome will favour their point of view, the periodic demands for referendums on the EU being a case in point, but experience does not always bear this out: at the outset of the referendum campaign in 1975 polls showed a clear majority against continued membership of the EU; by the end the campaign a two to one majority in favour had emerged. One thing is clear, the use of the referendum is not something that should be left simply to the politicians; either its use should be formally limited to clearly designated issues, constitutional or otherwise, or triggered by an initiative.

There are other problems, however, which need to be acknowledged. Constitutional amendments determined by referendums are commonly subject to threshold provisions. In Australia, for example, constitutional amendments must be approved by Parliament and then by a majority of those voting and by voters in a majority of the states. The 1979 devolution proposals in Scotland and Wales required the approval of 40 per cent of the electorate, not just those voting. In short, should a referendum be subject to a minimum electoral turnout and to a specified proportion of votes in favour, such as half or two-thirds? A further matter is the wording of the question put in a referendum. In some cases this is straightforward, but in others there is a danger that the form of words is biased towards one view or another and consequently affects the outcome. It is therefore important that an appropriate mechanism for determining the question is available. Even where the question is straightforward, the arguments for and against are often complex. Thus adequate resources for running the referendum campaign need to be available. In the British case these matters are covered by the Political Parties, Elections and Referendums Act 2000, which requires the government to consult the Electoral Commission established by the Act on the wording of the question and sets limits on who may campaign and what they may spend. However, the decision whether or not to hold a referendum remains with the government. Finally, the status of the referendum result also needs to be established. Referendums in the UK have been advisory rather than mandatory, but in practice it is difficult to envisage a government repudiating a referendum result unless there were no threshold provisions and turnout was low. Even so, this did not stop the Scottish National Party and some others in favour of devolution to Scotland from arguing that the 1979 referendum should be ignored because a small majority of those voting had actually voted in favour. Nonetheless, regardless of these problems, the referendum has become a more familiar device in the UK, particularly since 1997 and this is likely to feed demands for it use – 'We had a referendum on this, so why not on that? – and such demands will become more difficult for governments to resist. However, any move towards their more frequent use should be accompanied by a more systematic approach involving clearly defined parameters and rules.

Fixed-term Parliaments

Since the Parliament Act 1911 the maximum life of a Parliament has been five years (before then it was seven), but in practice elections are mostly held every four years. Short of losing a vote of confidence in the Commons, the decision on when to dissolve Parliament and hold a general election lies essentially with the Prime Minister, who, understandably, tries to choose a time propitious for his or her party. Parliaments only serve their full term when the governing party finds itself behind in the opinion polls as the time for an election draws closer, as happened in the 1959–64 and 1992–97 Parliaments, for example. On the other hand, the elections of 1983, 1987 and 2001 were all held four years after the previous election, when the polls were favourable to the government. Of course, it is a matter of judgement and occasionally the

Prime Minister gets it wrong, as happened in 1923 and 1970. Similarly, and occasionally Prime Ministers miss their chance, as did James Callaghan in 1978, when he decided to postpone a dissolution, even though Labour led in the polls at the time. Occasionally, elections are held close together, either in times of crisis, such as the constitutional conflict between Commons and Lords, resulting in the two elections of 1910, or when the government has only a small majority, as in 1964–66, or no majority at all, as in February–October 1974, and seeks a working majority.

The ability to call an election to the government's advantage is an immense power in the hands of the Prime Minister, especially with modern polling techniques, even if the polls are sometimes wrong or there is a late change in electoral opinion. It is, however, a common practice in Westminster-style systems, such as those in Australia, Canada, India and New Zealand, but the United States has fixed-term elections and the German Bundestag may only be prematurely dissolved in limited circumstances. More pertinently, the Scottish Parliament, the National Assembly for Wales, and the Northern Ireland Assembly all have fixed-term elections. And, in 1992, the Labour manifesto clearly stated: 'Although an early election will sometimes be necessary, we will introduce as a general rule a fixed parliamentary term.' Had Labour won the 1992 general election, it would have been interesting to see whether that pledge would have been fulfilled; it did not feature in the 1997 manifesto. The dissolution of Parliament is a throwback to medieval and later times, when monarchs summoned Parliaments when necessary and dissolved them once their task was complete. Prime Ministers have been called 'elected monarchs', having acquired most of the powers once exercised by the crown. Whether they should retain the power to 'advise' a dissolution is a moot point. Clearly, it would be fairer to opposition parties, though it would not remove the government's ability to endeavour to manipulate public opinion by making decisions likely to attract electoral support and postponing those that might alienate it. Apart from the political advantage it confers, it also means that parliamentary time and effort are wasted, as bills that have not completed all their stages have to be reintroduced in the new Parliament (assuming the government wins the election) and committee inquiries are aborted. There would still be some problems were fixed terms adopted, with the last months of a Parliament inevitably affected by the looming election, but legislative planning could take this into account and seek to use the time available as productively as possible.

Parliament, reform and the people

Politicians are not held in high esteem by most people in the UK, although surveys have found that electors invariably value their own MP above Parliament generally. A 2003 poll found that 36 per cent of the respondents were 'satisfied with Parliament', but there was, as other surveys have found, a marked difference in trust in politicians generally – 27 per cent; and the proportion satisfied with their own MP – 41 per cent.[13] The days of mass public meetings addressed by MPs are a thing of the past, though mass marches and demonstrations are a different matter. The membership of political parties has declined sharply since its zenith in the 1950s, but more people are engaged in pressure politics than ever before. At the same time the whole process of government has become more accessible, especially with the development of modern technology. Parliament, government departments, the Cabinet Office and No. 10 all have their own websites, as do many MPs and some peers. Lords, Commons, Westminster Hall debates and many select committees are now televised and there is a dedicated Parliamentary Channel. Quite apart from publishing their proceedings, both Houses have information offices that provide the public with considerable amounts of data directly through a wide range of publications and by responding to telephone and e-mail inquiries and indirectly via the Parliament website. The services provided by the Commons' Information Office are much more extensive – dealing with 80,000 inquiries in 2002–03, but the Lords' Information Office dealt with over 21,000 inquiries in 2002–03. The Parliamentary Education Unit provides support for teachers and students and arranges educational visits, while tours of the Palace of Westminster have been made more user friendly.

Yet, like politicians, Parliament is not held in high esteem. This may be partly to do with its image as an old-fashioned, not particularly effective talking-shop, characterised by arcane procedures and outmoded ceremonies, suffocated by tradition, and the repository of childish 'yah-boo' politics. Few familiar with Parliament would see this description as other than a caricature; but, like all caricatures, it has an important element of truth in it. Ministers damage Parliament by too often stating, 'This is a matter for Parliament' or 'Parliament will decide', when the reality of party cohesion means that only rarely does Parliament actually decide. The media damage Parliament by focusing too much on personalities and not enough on the issues, emphasising the confrontational far more than the consensual aspects of Parliament, and, on television in particular, by using parliamentary proceedings as televisual wallpaper. And MPs damage Parliament, a few by personal misconduct so that all are tarred by the same brush, sometimes by exaggerating what they as individual MPs can do, and sometimes by too readily accepting the party line. Parliamentary procedure is necessarily complex and in that respect arcane, but the simple rules of a debating society are totally inadequate for securing a balance between the government's need to secure its business and Parliament's need to render the government accountable. The idea that procedure is still locked in nineteenth-century obscurity is a nonsense; the real question is whether the procedural balance between government and Parliament is about right or needs shifting in one direction or the other. Ceremonies or practices which clearly bring Parliament into ridicule should be reconsidered, but it is noticeable that one of few changes made since 1997 is the abolition of the wearing of a folding opera hat in the Commons to indicate that a Member wishes to raise a point of order during a division. Betty Boothroyd abandoned the wearing of the Speaker's wig (although the Lord Chancellor still wears his) and her successor as Speaker has followed her lead, but the Clerks at the Table of the House still wear wigs and gowns and the 'doorkeepers' or attendants uniforms and chains of office. The Speaker still processes into the Commons' Chamber before each sitting and MPs process to the bar of the House of Lords to hear the Queen's Speech, after being ceremonially summoned by the Gentleman Usher of the Black Rod, the marks of whose staff on the doors of the House of Commons, which are ceremonially slammed in his face, would be seen as evidence of vandalism in a different context. Yet, the Speaker could just as easily enter the Chamber informally, without wigs and gowns the Clerks would not be no more or less efficient (although their uniforms do mark the doorkeepers out as officials), and the Queen's Speech does not have to be read to MPs in the presence of the Lords Spiritual and Temporal in the their ceremonial robes. Changing or abolishing some practices might enhance the image of Parliament, but would have little or no impact on its prime task of calling the government to account. Confrontation, both inside and outside Parliament, nationally and locally, is part and parcel of politics, but it is not the whole of politics and greater access to Parliament (and to government generally) may help the more co-operative aspects of politics to come to the fore. Not only do fewer people belong to political parties but fewer allow their electoral behaviour to be driven by simple party identification; politics has become more like the supermarket and less like the boxing ring. Politics, however, is a minority interest; most are interested only when something affects them or is likely to affect them, more at general elections than local elections, more when it matters to them. The opportunities for political participation have increased and opportunity and access are probably at least as important as participation, possibly more so.

Labour came to power in 1997 with a pledge to 'modernise' Parliament and, in the Commons, set up a Select Committee on Modernisation. 'Modernisation', however, is an ambiguous term, clear enough when it refers to, say, using more efficient technology but less so in reference to making Parliament 'more efficient': more efficient for whom? – the government in implementing its policies or Parliament in calling the government to account? If Parliament, especially the House of Commons, is to become more effective in this latter role, the solution lies in the hands of MPs and peers, on the one hand, and governments, on the other. Arguably, the means already exist and it is up to MPs and peers to use them and governments to allow them to do so, but it can also be argued that one or more of the internal or external reforms already discussed would strengthen the hand of Parliament or people, or both, vis-à-vis the government, but governments must be prepared to listen and respond if Crick's paradigm of influence, advice, criticism, scrutiny and publicity is to be fully realised.

Notes

1 Labour Party Manifesto, 1997.
2 *Ibid.*
3 Alpheus Todd, *On Parliamentary Government in England: Its Origins, Development and Operation*, London, Longman, 2nd edn (ed. A. H. Todd), 1887, Vol. I, p. xii (originally pub. 1867).
4 Third Earl Grey, *Parliamentary Government* (originally pub. 1858) cited in Todd, *On Parliamentary Government*, Vol. I, p. 32.
5 Cited in Todd, *On Parliamentary Government*, Vol. I, p. 478.
6 See Peter Riddell, *Parliament Under Blair*, London, Politico's, 1998, pp. 225–6 and 251.
7 Royal Commission on the Reform of the House of Lords, *Report: A House for the Future*, Cm. 4534, January 2000, paras. 17.9, 10 and 12.
8 Labour Party Manifesto, 1997.
9 *Report of the Independent Commission on the Voting System*, Cm. 4090-I, October 1998.
10 David Butler and Dennis Kavanagh, *The British General Election of 1997*, London, Macmillan, 1997, Table A2.11.
11 Cited in Bogdanor, *The People and the Party System: The Referendum and Electoral Reform in British Politics*, Cambridge, Cambridge University Press, 1981, p. 35.
12 *Ibid.*, p. 86.
13 The Electoral Commission and the Hansard Society, *An Audit of Political Engagement*, London, 2003. See also Philip Norton, 'The United Kingdom: Building the Link between Constituent and MP', in Philip Norton (ed.), *Parliaments and Citizens in Western Europe*, London, Frank Cass, 2002, Table 2.6.

Sources and further reading

General

There is no shortage of information and analysis on Parliament, although some aspects are better covered than others and some need more up-to-date studies than are currently available. Nonetheless, there has been an immense burgeoning of the literature on Parliament in the last forty or so years, while the development of the Internet has made a great deal of primary and secondary material easily accessible. What follows is intended to enable readers to explore further what is covered in this book, both generally and specifically.

Parliamentary publications

Parliament itself has long published a great deal of information about its proceedings, but each of the two Houses is responsible for its own output, most of which is available on the Parliament website (www.parliament.uk). Thus, both Commons and Lords separately publish their debates (formally known as the Official Report but commonly known as *Hansard*), committee proceedings and reports, and bills at various stages of their passage through Parliament. In addition, a considerable range of reports and other documents are presented to Parliament by government departments and other bodies. *Hansard*, which records debates (including the Westminster Hall debates), all parliamentary Questions given oral or written answers, and division lists, is available on the Parliament website, but the printed volumes can be found in most university and many public libraries in the UK. Committee proceedings and reports and some other parliamentary publications (such as reports of the Parliamentary Ombudsman and the Health Service Ombudsman) are published as House of Commons (HC) or House of Lords (HL) paper with numbers starting at 1 each parliamentary session or year. Similarly, each House publishes bills, including proposed amendments, starting anew each session, with Commons' stage designated Bill 1, Bill 2, etc. and Lords' stages HL Bill 1, HL Bill 2, etc. However, many other reports and documents presented to Parliament, including government White Papers and consultation papers, and reports of royal commissions, are known as command papers and designated Cm. 1, Cm. 2, etc., but, unlike HC or HL papers, are not numbered by the session, running instead from 1 to 9,999, at which point a new series is started. The present series began in October 1986, before which the prefix was Cmnd. and earlier series used Cmd., Cd. and C.

One of the most useful parliamentary publications is the House of Commons' yearly *Sessional Information Digest*, which contains detailed statistical information on a wide range of activities and is particularly useful when used in conjunction with the yearly *Sessional Return*, which provides data on the number parliamentary Questions asked and answered, the number of early day motions (EDMs), the use of closure and allocation of time, list all private and public bills, and details standing and select committee activity. There is also a *Weekly Information Bulletin*. The House of Commons Library published a range of *Factsheets*, of which 65 were available in 2004, covering procedure, elections, a number of historical matters, MPs' and ministers' pay and allowances, and so on – all available on the Parliament website or free within the UK from the House of Commons Information Office. The Library also publishes research and other briefing material, which is also available on the Parliament website. The House of Lords Information Office similarly publishes *Briefing Papers* on matters such as the role, functions and powers of the upper house, its membership, delegated legislation, the work of the European Union Committee, and actual and proposed reform of the House of Lords since 1900. Particular committees of both Houses also publish reports relevant to the working of Parliament. These include the Procedure Committees of each House, Constitutional Affairs, Public Administration and the Select Committee on the Modernisation of the House in the Commons, and the Constitution Committee in the Lords, which also reviews its operation through ad hoc working groups.

The House of Commons Information Office (tel.: 020-7219-4272; e-mail: hcinfo@parliament.uk) and the House of Lords Information Office (tel.: 020-7219-3107; e-mail: hlinfo@parliament.uk) answer inquiries from the general public and are particularly useful for checking facts and getting up-to-date information and advice. There are also a number of other official websites that can provide relevant information, either about government activity or for comparative purposes. These include the Cabinet Office (www.cabinet-office.gov.uk), No. 10 Downing Street (www.number-10.gov.uk), the open government site (www.opengov.uk), the Scottish Parliament (www.scottish.parliament.gov.uk), the National Assembly for Wales (www.wales.gov.uk), and the Northern Ireland Assembly (www.ni-assmbly.gov.uk). In addition, the Inter-Parliamentary Union (www.ipu.org) and the Commonwealth Parliamentary Association (www.cpahq.org) are useful sources of comparative information outside the UK. Several organisations outside Parliament are valuable sources of information and comment, including the Hansard Society for Parliamentary Government (www.hansardsociety.org.uk), the Policy Studies Institute (www.psi.ork.uk), the Constitution Unit (www.ucl.ac.uk/constitution-unit), and the Study of Parliament Group (www.spg.org.uk), all of which conduct research and publish reports, pamphlets and books on Parliament. Pressure groups like Charter 88 (www.charter88.org.uk) and the Fabian Society (www.fabian-society.org.uk), and 'think tanks such as the Centre for Policy Studies (www.cps.org.uk), Demos (www.demos.co.uk), the Institute for Public Policy Research (www.ipr.org.uk), the Institute of Economic Affairs (www.iea.org.uk), and the Social Market Foundation (www.smf.co.uk) produce proposals for parliamentary reform.

Books

The number and variety of books on the nature of politics and different approaches to the study of politics is enormous and much depends on the interests and tastes of readers. The following provide a cross-section of different style and approaches, including examples of standard texts on British politics: Harold Lasswell, *Who Gets What, When, How*, Chicago, McGraw-Hill, 1936; W. G. Runciman, *Social Science and Political Theory*, Cambridge, Cambridge University Press, 1963; David Easton, *A Framework for Political Analysis*, Englewood Cliffs, NJ, Prentice-Hall, 1965: W. J. M. Mackenzie, *Politics and Social Science*, London, Penguin, 1967; Robert A. Dahl, *Dilemmas of Pluralist Democracy*, New Haven, Conn., Yale University Press, 1982, and *A Preface to Economic Democracy*, New York, Polity Press, 1985; Patrick Dunleavy, *Democracy, Bureaucracy and Public Choice*, London, Harvester Wheatsheaf, 1991; Jan-Erik Lane and Svante Ersson, *The New Institutional Politics*, London, Routledge, 2000; Bernard Crick, *In Defence of Politics*, London, Centaur, 5th edn 2000 (first pub. 1964); Bill Jones, Dennis Kavanagh, Michael Moran and Philip Norton, *Politics UK*, London, Pearson Longman, 5th edn, 2003; Ian Budge, Ivor Crewe, David McKay and Ken Newton, *The New British Politics*, London, Pearson Longman, 3rd edn, 2004.

Similarly, there are a large number of books on Parliament, although understandably in many cases they concentrate far more on the House of Commons than the House of Lords, often devoting no more than a separate chapter to the latter. Robert Blackburn and Andrew Kennon, *Griffith and Ryle on Parliament: Functions, Practice and Procedure*, London, Sweet and Maxwell, 2003, provides the most comprehensive coverage, but earlier literature, including some classic works, is well worth reading or consulting – Walter Bagehot, *The English Constitution: Collected Works*, ed. Norman St John Stevas, London, *The Economist*, 1974 (originally published 1865–67); Sidney Low, *The Governance of England*, London, Fisher Unwin, 1904; A Laurence Lowell,

The Government of England, New York, Macmillan, new edn 1920 (origin-
ally published 1908); Harold Laski, *Parliamentary Government in England*,
London, Allen & Unwin, 1938; and Sir Ivor Jennings, *Parliament*, Cambridge,
Cambridge University Press, 1939, 2nd edn, 1957. Later works also worth
consulting are Lord Campion (ed.), *Parliament: A Survey*, London, Allen &
Unwin, 1952; Peter G. Richards, *Honourable Members: A Study of the British
Backbencher*, London, Faber, 1st edn, 1959, 2nd edn, 1964, later updated
as *The Backbenchers*, London, Faber, 1971; Ralph Miliband, *Parliamentary
Socialism*, London, Merlin Press, 2nd edn, 1973; Anthony King, *British Mem-
bers of Parliament: A Self-Portrait*, London, Macmillan, 1974; Philip Norton,
The Commons in Perspective, London, Martin Robertson, 1981; Philip Norton
(ed.), *Parliament in the 1980s*, Oxford, Blackwell, 1985; and Philip Norton,
Does Parliament Matter?, London, Hemel Hampstead, Harvester Wheatsheaf,
1993.

   Works on the House of Lords are much fewer in number. There was little
before P. A. Bromhead, *The House of Lords and Contemporary Politics*, London,
Routledge & Kegan Paul, 1958, which was rapidly overtaken by the impact of
the Life Peerages Act 1958 and no other broader works until the excellent
Donald Shell, *The House of Lords*, Hemel Hampstead, Harvester Wheatsheaf,
2nd edn, 1992 and Donald Shell and David Beamish (eds), *The House of Lords
at Work: A Study of the 1988–89 Session*, Oxford, Clarendon Press, 1993,
although Janet Morgan, *The House of Lords and the Labour Government, 1964–
70*, Oxford, Oxford University Press, 1975 is a valuable study. A recent overall
look at the upper house is Michael Wheeler-Booth, 'The House of Lords', in
Blackburn and Kennon, *Griffith and Ryle on Parliament*, pp. 637–737.

   The political memoirs and diaries of politicians and journalists often provide valuable contemporary pictures of Parliament, but are too numerous to
list here. However, a number of very readable 'insider' views of Parliament,
usually focusing exclusively or largely on the Commons, have been published,
for example, Austin Mitchell, *Westminster Man: A Tribal Anthropology of the
Commons People*, London, Thames Methuen, 1982; John Biffen, *Inside Westminster: Behind the Scenes at the House of Commons*, London, Andre Deutsch,
1996; and Paul Flynn, *Commons Knowledge: How to Be a Backbencher*, Bridgend,
Seren Press, 1997. A historical and often entertaining perspective can be found
in Christopher Sylvester (ed.), *The Literary Companion to Parliament*, London,
Sinclair Stevens, 1996.

Journals

The most relevant and useful journals are *Parliamentary Affairs*, *The Journal
of Legislative Studies*, and *Parliamentary History*, but articles on or related to
Parliament can be found in *The British Journal of Political Science*, *The British
Journal of Politics and International Relations*, *The Political Quarterly*, *Political
Studies*, *Public Administration*, and *Public Law*.

Chapter 1: Parliament in context

For a brief discussion of the concepts of power, authority and legitimacy see Michael Rush, *Politics and Society: An Introduction to Political Sociology*, Hemel Hampstead, Harvester Wheatsheaf, 1992, Chapter 3. Kenneth Wheare, *Modern Constitutions*, Oxford, Oxford University Press, 1951, and S. E. Finer, *Five Constitutions: Contrasts and Comparisons*, London, Pelican, 1979, are excellent introductions to the role and nature of constitutions, and R. L. Maddox, *Constitutions of the World*, London, Routledge, 1996, provides more recent information. Constitutional law textbooks, like Peter Jackson and Patricia Leopold, *Hood Phillips' Constitutional and Administrative Law*, London, Sweet and Maxwell, 8th edn, 2001, and A. W. Bradley and K. D. Ewing, *Constitutional and Administrative Law*, London, Harlow, Longman, 13th edn, 2003, are invaluable aids to understanding the UK's constitutional arrangements. Classic works, such as Bagehot's *The English Constitution* (1865–67), A. V. Dicey, *The Law of the Constitution*, London, Macmillan, 10th edn, 1959 (originally published 1885); and L. S. Amery, *Thoughts on the Constitution*, Oxford, Oxford University Press, 1st edn, 1953, new edn with an introduction by Geoffrey Marshall, 1964; A. H. Birch, *Representative and Responsible Government*, London, Allen & Unwin, 1964; and Nevil Johnson, *In Search of the Constitution*, London, Pergamon, 1977, all have important things to say and the are a number of good, recent commentaries: Peter Hennessy, *The Hidden Wiring: Unearthing the British Constitution*, London, Gollancz, 1995; Rodney Brazier, *Constitutional Practice: The Foundations of British Government*, Oxford, Oxford University Press, 3rd edn, 1999; Jeffrey Jowell and Dawn Oliver (eds), *The Changing Constitution*, Oxford, Oxford University Press, 4th edn, 2000; and Vernon Bogdanor (ed.), *The British Constitution in the Twentieth Century*, Oxford, Oxford University Press, 2003. More specialised works on particular aspects of the constitution included Jeffrey Goldsworthy, *The Sovereignty of Parliament: History and Philosophy*, Oxford, Oxford University Press, 1999; M. J. C. Vile, *Constitutionalism and the Separation of Powers*, Oxford, Oxford University Press, 1967; and Geoffrey Marshall, *Constitutional Conventions*, Oxford, Oxford University Press, 1984.

W. H. Greenleaf, *The British Political Tradition: I The Rise of Collectivism; II The Ideological Heritage; III A Much-Governed Nation; IV The World Outside*, London, Routledge/Methuen, 1983–87, is an excellent source on the ideological underpinning of British politics; Geoffrey K. Fry, *The Growth of Government: The Development of Ideas About the Role of the State and the Machinery of Government Since 1780*, London, Cass, 1979, focuses the development of the governmental machine; and David Judge, *The Parliamentary State*, London, Sage, 1983, places Parliament clearly in its social and political context.

Comparative perspectives are provided by Kenneth Bradshaw and David Pring, *Parliament and Congress*, London, Constable, 1977; Philip Norton (ed.), *Parliaments and Government in Western Europe*, London, Cass, 1998; and N. D. J. Baldwin and Donald Shell (eds), *Second Chambers*, London, Cass, 2001.

Chapter 2: Origins and development

Broader histories, such as Philip Edwards, *The Making of the Modern English State, 1460–1660*, Basingstoke, Palgrave, 2001; Jeremy Black (ed.), *British Politics and Society: From Walpole to Pitt*, Basingstoke, Macmillan, 1990; Eric J. Evans, *The Forging of the Modern State, 1783–1870*, Harlow, Longman, 2001; Robert Rhodes James, *The British Revolution: British Politics 1880–1939*, Oxford, Blackwell, 2 vols, 1976 and 1977, and Martin Pugh, *The Making of Modern British Politics, 1867–1939*, Oxford, Blackwell, 2nd edn, 1993 are important to an understanding of the origins and development of Parliament, while the series English/British Historical/Political Facts, (Ken Powell and Chris Cook, *English Historical Facts, 1485–1603*, London, Macmillan, 1977; Chris Cook and John Wroughton, *English Historical Facts, 1603–1688*, London, Macmillan, 1980; Chris Cook and John Stevenson, *British Historical Facts, 1688–1760*, London, Macmillan, 1988, Chris Cook and John Stevenson, *British Historical Facts, 1760–1830*, London, Macmillan, 1980; Chris Cook and Brendan Keith, *British Historical Facts, 1830–1900*, London, Macmillan, 1975; and David Butler and Gareth Butler, *Twentieth Century British Political Facts, 1900–2000*, Basingstoke, Macmillan, 8th edn, 2000) are invaluable sources of factual information, as are the introductory surveys in the History of Parliament Trust series on the House of Commons (Romney Sedgwick, *History of Parliament: The House of Commons 1715–54*, London, HMSO, 1970; Sir Lewis Namier and John Brooke, *History of Parliament: The House of Commons 1754–90*, London, HMSO, 1964; and R. G. Thorne, *History of Parliament: The House of Commons 1790–1820*, London, Secker & Warburg, 1980). The best account of the origins and early development of Parliament remains A. F. Pollard, *The Evolution of Parliament*, London, Longman, 2nd edn, 1926, and K. R. Mackenzie, *The English Parliament*, London, Penguin, 1951, is a good short historical account. Similarly, Josef Redlich, *The Procedures of the House of Commons* (trans. A. Ernest Steinthal), London, Constable, 1908 (originally published 1905) and Edward Porritt, *The Unreformed House of Commons: Parliamentary Representation Before 1832*, Cambridge, Cambridge University Press, 2 vols, 1909, remain standard works. T. A. Jenkins, *Parliament, Party and Politics in Victorian Britain*, Manchester, Manchester University Press, 1996 covers the nineteenth century, while Ronald Butt, *The Power of Parliament*, London, Constable, 2nd edn, 1969; S. A. Walkland (ed.), *The House of Commons in the Twentieth Century*, Oxford, Clarendon Press, 1979; and Michael Rush, *The Role of the Member of Parliament Since 1868: From Gentlemen to Players*, Oxford, Oxford University Press, 2001, carry the story to the end of the twentieth century. Brief accounts of the development of the House of Lords can be found in Donald Shell, *The House of Lords*, Chapter 1, and Michael Wheeler-Booth, 'The House of Lords', in Blackburn and Kennon, *Griffith and Ryle on Parliament*, Chapter 12, sections 12-001–12-046.

Chapter 3: The functions of Parliament

Philip Norton (ed.), *Legislatures*, Oxford, Oxford University Press, 1990, provides an excellent framework for considering the functions of Parliament and
Chapter 4, 'The Functions of the House of Commons in the Twentieth Century', in his *The Commons in Perspective* is a valuable summary. Functions are
dealt with in more depth in Birch's *Representative and Responsible Government*,
Chapters 1–9, Crick's *The Reform of Parliament*, Chapters 3–5, and Blackburn
and Kennon, *Griffith and Ryle on Parliament*, Chapter 1. The functions of the
House of Lords are covered in Shell, 'The House of Lords in Context', in Shell
and Beamish, *The House of Lords at Work*, and Michael Wheeler-Booth, 'The
House of Lords', in Blackburn and Kennon, *Griffith and Ryle on Parliament*,
Chapter 12, sections 12-118–12-163, while the *Report of the Royal Commission
on the Reform of the House of Lords: A House for the Future*, Cm. 4534, January
2000, sets out the royal commission's views of the functions of the second
chamber in Chapters 4–5.

The role of the Member of Parliament is discussed in Donald Searing,
Westminster's World: Understanding Political Roles, Cambridge, Mass., Harvard
University Press, 1994, Rush, *The Role of the Member of Parliament Since 1868*,
particularly Chapter 1, and Lisanne Radice, Elizabeth Vallance and Virginia
Willis, *The Member of Parliament: The Job of the Backbencher*, London, Macmillan,
2nd edn, 1990.

Chapter 4: Parliament and democracy

Democracy as a concept is defined and discussed in David Held, *Models
of Democracy*, Cambridge, Polity Press, 2nd edn, 1996. The nature and operation of electoral systems are discussed in Douglas Rae, *The Political Consequences of Electoral Laws*, New Haven, Conn., Yale University Press, 1967, and
David Farrell, *Comparing Electoral Systems*, London, Macmillan, 1999, with
a focus on the British case in David Butler, *The Electoral System in Britain Since
1918*, Oxford, Oxford University Press, 2nd edn, 1963, and Robert Blackburn,
The Electoral System in Britain, London, Macmillan, 1995. There are many
studies of elections and electoral behaviour in the UK, notably the Nuffield
series on British general elections since 1945, of which the two latest are
David Butler and Dennis Kavanagh, *The British General Election of 1997*,
London, Macmillan, 1997, and *The British General Election of 2001*, London,
Palgrave, 2002, but these should be read in conjunction with Paul Webb, *The
Modern British Party System*, London, Sage, 2000, and more specialised works
on electoral behaviour such as Anthony Heath, Roger Jowell and John Curtice,
How Britain Votes, Oxford, Oxford University Press, 1985; Mark Franklin, *The
Decline of Class Voting in Britain: Changes in the Basis Electoral Choice, 1964–
83*, Oxford, Oxford University Press, 1985; Richard Rose and Ian McAllister,

Voters Begin to Choose: From Closed Class Voting to Open Elections in Britain, London, Sage, 1986; Anthony Heath, John Curtice, Roger Jowell, Geoff Evans, Julia Field and Sharon Witherspoon, *Understanding Political Change: The British Voter, 1964–87*, London, Pergamon, 1991; and David Denver, *Elections and Voters in Britain*, London, Palgrave, 2002.

On referendums, David Butler and Austin Ranney (eds), *Referendums Around the World: The Growing Use of Direct Democracy*, Basingstoke, Macmillan, 1974, and Vernon Bogdanor, *The People and the Party System: The Referendum and Electoral Reform in Britain*, Cambridge, Cambridge University Press, 1981, provide excellent coverage.

Chapter 5: The personnel of Parliament

Though dated, W. L. Guttsman, *The British Political Elite*, London, MacGibbon and Kee, 1963, provides an excellent overview; see also David Cannadine, *The Decline and Fall of the British Aristocracy*, London, Macmillan, 1992, especially Chapters 4 and 5. The selection of candidates is described and analysed in Austin Ranney, *Pathways to Parliament*, London, Macmillan, 1965, Michael Rush, *The Selection of Parliamentary Candidates*, London, Nelson, 1969, and Pippa Norris and Joni Lovenduski, *Political Recruitment: Gender, Race and Class in the British Parliament*, Cambridge, Cambridge University Press, 1995, and Alison Young, *The Reselection of MPs*, London, Heinemann, 1983, covers an important aspect of parliamentary recruitment. A comparative perspective is provided by Michael Gallagher and Michael Marsh (eds), *Candidate Selection in Perspective: The Secret Garden of Politics*, London, Sage, 1988, and a historical view by Heinrich Best and Maurizio Cotta (eds), *Parliamentary Representatives in Europe, 1848–2000*, Oxford, Oxford University Press, 2000. Data on the socio-economic backgrounds of British MPs can be found in the relevant chapters of the Nuffield election series, in Colin Mellors, *The British MP: A Socio-Economic Study of the House of Commons*, Farnborough, Hants, 1978; and Rush, *The Role of the Member of Parliament Since 1868*, Chapter 4.

Chapter 6: The professionalisation of Parliament

Peter Riddell, *Honest Opportunism: The Rise of the Career Politician*, London, Hamish Hamilton, 1993, is an excellent relatively recent treatment of the subject and Anthony King, 'The Rise of the Career Politician in Britain – and Its Consequences', *The British Journal of Political Science*, 2, 1981, pp. 249–85, provides a valuable conceptual analysis. The professionalisation of Parliament as an institution and of the role of the MP is discussed in Rush, *The Role of the Member of Parliament Since 1868*, Chapters 3 and 5, with particular aspects being covered in Anthony Barker and Michael Rush, *The Member of Parliament and His Information*, London, Allen & Unwin, 1970; Michael Rush and Malcolm Shaw (eds), *The House of Commons: Services and Facilities*, Allen & Unwin, 1974; and Michael Rush (ed.), *The House of Commons: Services and Facilities, 1972–1982*, London, Policy Studies Institute, 1983. Up-to-date information on the pay and resources of MPs and on ministers' salaries is available in House of Commons *Factsheets M5* and M6 and on 'Short Money' for the Commons and 'Cranborne Money' for the Lords in House of Commons Library, *Standard Note SN/PC/1663* (all available on the Parliament website). The annual reports of the House of Commons Commission and the Annual Reports and Accounts of the House of Lords also provide information on parliamentary resources and finances.

Chapter 7: The organisation of business

Blackburn and Kennon, *Griffith and Ryle on Parliament*, Chapters 5, 6 and 7 contain detailed information on the organisation of the House of Commons and on parliamentary procedure, although much of this is also relevant to Chapters 8 and 9 of this book, with similar information on the House of Lords in the Wheeler-Booth chapter on the upper house, particularly sections 12-064–12-100, and a brief description of the organisation and procedure in the Lords can be found in Shell's *The House of Lords*, Chapter 4. Much more detailed information is available in the parliamentary 'bible', Erskine May, latest edition: *Erskine May's Treatise on the Law, Privileges, Proceedings and Usage of Parliament*, 23rd edn, edited by Sir William McKay, London, Lexis Nexus, 2004. However, a particularly user-friendly book on Commons' procedure is Paul Evans, *Handbook of House of Commons Procedure*, London, Vacher Dod, 2003.

Most textbooks on Parliament devote some space to the role of the whips, but a more substantial account is found in Robert J. Jackson, *Rebels and Whips: Dissension, Discipline and Cohesion in British Political Parties Since 1945*, London, Macmillan, 1968, and, apart from brief references in many books, a description of the operation of 'the usual channels' can be found in Donald Wade, *Behind the Speaker's Chair*, Austick Publishers, Leeds, 1978, Chapters 2 and 3, but the most recent and fullest account is Michael Rush and Clare Ettinghausen, *Opening up the Usual Channels*, London, Hansard Society, 2002.

Chapter 8: The legislative role

The literature on the legislative role is limited, with more devoted to backbench than government legislation, and less to delegated legislation. More broadly, Nelson Polsby, 'Legislatures', in F. I. Greenstein and N. W. Polsby, *Handbook of Political Science*, Reading, Mass., Addison-Wesley, 1975, vol. 5, pp. 277–96, and Michael Mezey, 'Classifying Legislatures', in M. Mezey (ed.), *Comparative Legislatures*, Durham, N.C., Duke University Press, 1979, pp. 21–44, offer useful ways of categorising legislatures. Both are reproduced in Philip Norton (ed.), *Legislatures*, Oxford, Oxford University Press, 1990, which also provides an excellent overview. S. A. Walkland, *The Legislative Process in Great Britain*, London, Allen & Unwin, 1968, remains a useful short analysis of the legislative role and David Miers and Alan Page, *Legislation*, London, Sweet and Maxwell, 2nd edn, 1990 and, *Making the Law: The Report of the Hansard Society Commission and the Legislative Process*, London, 1993 provide more up-to-date surveys. However, J. A. G. Griffith, *The Parliamentary Scrutiny of Government Bills*, London, Allen & Unwin, 1974, is still the most comprehensive study. Peter Richards, *Parliament and Conscience*, London, Allen & Unwin, 1970 and Philip Cowley (ed.), *Conscience and Parliament*, London, Cass, 1998, examine legislation on moral issues, mostly dealt with by Private Members' bills, and P. A. Bromhead, *Private Members' Bills in the British Parliament*, Routledge and Kegan Paul, 1956 and David Marsh and Melvyn Reade, *Private Members' Bills*, Cambridge, Cambridge University Press, 1988, deal comprehensively with backbench legislation. Edward C. Page, *Governing by Numbers: Delegated Legislation and Everyday Policymaking*, is an excellent study of secondary legislation and Priscilla Baines, 'Parliamentary Scrutiny of Policy and Legislation: Procedures of the Lords and Commons', in Philip Giddings and Gavin Drewry (eds), *Britain in the European Union: Law, Policy and Parliament*, similarly deals with European secondary legislation.

Chapter 9: The scrutiny role

Here the literature is considerably more extensive, both over time and in range, although more has been written about investigatory committees than any other means of scrutiny, while parliamentary Questions have been the subject of two major studies: D. N. Chester and Nona Bowring, *Questions in Parliament*, Oxford, Clarendon Press, 1962, and Mark Franklin and Philip Norton (eds), *Parliamentary Questions*, Oxford, Clarendon Press, 1993, the latter including a chapter by Donald Shell on Questions in the House of Lords, and Patrick Howarth, *Questions in the House: The History of a Unique British Institution*, London, The Bodley Head, 1956, provides an historical perspective.

Two books in the 1960s focused on contemporary investigatory committees: Nevil Johnson, *Parliament and Administration: The Estimates Committee 1945–65*, London, Allen & Unwin, 1966, and David Coombes, *The Member of Parliament and the Administration: The Case of the Select Committee on Nationalised Industries*, London, Allen & Unwin, 1966. These were followed by Ann Robinson, *Parliament and Public Spending: The Expenditure Committee of the House of Commons, 1970–76*, London, Heinemann, 1978, the comprehensive Gavin Drewry (ed.), *The New Select Committees: A Study of the 1979 Reforms,*

Oxford, Clarendon Press, 2nd edn, 1989, and Alex Brazier, *Systematic Scrutiny: Reforming the Select Committee System*, Hansard Society Commission on Parliamentary Scrutiny, Discussion Paper 1, London, 2000. The Commission's Report, *The Challenge for Parliament: Making Government Accountable*, London, Hansard Society, 2001, provides an excellent overview of parliamentary scrutiny, as well as making a wide range of recommendations. David Judge, *Backbench Specialisation in the House of Commons*, London, Heinemann, 1981, looks at scrutiny from the individual MP's point of view.

Studies of financial scrutiny are less common: in addition to Ann Robinson's *Parliament and Public Spending*, London, Heinemann, 1978, Gordon Reid, *The Politics of Financial Control: The Role of the House of Commons*, London, Hutchinson, 1966, though dated, is a good introduction and Andrew Likierman, *Public Expenditure: The Public Spending Process*, London, Penguin, 1988, is a comprehensive view of the supply side of the equation, while Alex Brazier, *Parliament and the Public Purse: Improving Financial Scrutiny*, Hansard Society Commission on Parliamentary Scrutiny, Discussion Paper 3, London, 2000, is an up-to-date and valuable contribution. Finally, Peter Richards, *Parliament and Foreign Affairs*, London, Allen & Unwin, 1967, and Philip Giddings (ed.), *Parliamentary Accountability: A Study of Parliament and the Executive Agencies*, London, Macmillan, 1995, cover particular aspects of scrutiny.

Chapter 10: Parliament and the people

C. S. Emden, *The People and Parliament*, Oxford, Oxford University Press, 2nd edn, 1956, is a historical study of Parliament and public opinion, with Birch's *Representative and responsible Government*, Chapters 14–16, providing a more conceptual approach. An up-to-date picture is provided by Stuart Weir and David Beetham, *Political Power and Democratic Control in Britain*, London, Routledge, 1999, and Patrick Dunleavy, Helen Margetts, Trevor Smith and Stuart Weir, *Voices of the People: Popular Attitudes to Democratic Renewal in Britain*, London, Politico's, 2001.

Parliament and the media is dealt with in David McKie, *Media Coverage of Parliament*, London, Hansard Society, 1999; Stephen Coleman, *Electronic Media, Parliament and the People*, London, Hansard Society, 1999, with a comparative perspective provided by Ralph Negrine, *Parliament and the Media: A Study of Germany, Britain and France*, Royal Institute of International Affairs, 1998.

The constituency role of MPs is excellently covered by Philip Norton and David Wood, *Back From Westminster: British Members of Parliament and their Constituents*, Lexington, Ky., University of Kentucky Press, 1993, by Greg Power, *Representatives of the People: The Constituency Role of MPs*, London, Fabian Society, 1998, and Greg Power (ed.), *Under Pressure: Are We Getting the Most from Our MPs*, London, Hansard Society, 2000. Philip Norton (ed.),

Parliaments and Citizens in Western Europe, London, Cass, 2002, provides an excellent comparative view. Roy Gregory, Philip Giddings, Victor Moore, and J. Pearson, *Practice and Prospects of the Ombudsmen in the UK*, London, Edwin Mellen Press, 1995; M. Senivirante, *Ombudsmen in the Public Sector*, Milton Keynes, Open University Press, 1994; and Philip Giddings, 'The Parliament Ombudsman: A Successful Alternative?', in Dawn Oliver and Gavin Drewry (eds), *The Law and Parliament*, London, Butterworths, 1998, pp. 125–38, provide a good coverage of the ombudsman system.

Wyn Grant, *Pressure Groups and British Politics*, London, Macmillan, 2000, is an excellent overview of pressure politics and Michael Rush (ed.), *Parliament and Pressure Politics*, Oxford, Clarendon Press, 1990, is a major study of the lobbying of Parliament.

Sleaze and the personal conduct of MPs are comprehensively dealt with in David Leigh and Ed Valliamy, *Sleaze: The Corruption of Parliament*, London, Fourth Estate, 1997; Maureen Mancuso, *The Ethical World of British MPs*, Montreal/Kingston, Ontario, McGill/Queen's University Press, 1995; and Oonagh Gay and Patricia Leopold (eds), *Conduct Unbecoming: The Regulation of Parliamentary Behaviour*, London, Politico's, 2004.

Chapter 11: Parliament and the government

The roles of the Cabinet and the Prime Minister have been the subject of numerous studies going back many years, including Sir Ivor Jennings, *Cabinet Government*, Cambridge, Cambridge University Press, 3rd edn, 1959; John P. Mackintosh, *The British Cabinet*, London, Stevens, 3rd edn, 1977; Peter Hennessy, *Cabinet*, Oxford, Blackwell, 1985; Simon James, *British Cabinet Government*, London, Routledge, 1997; Dennis Kavanagh and Anthony Seldon, *The Powers Behind the Prime Minister*, London, Collins, 1999; and Peter Hennessy, *The Prime Minister: The Office and Its Holders Since 1945*, London, Allen Lane, 2000, while Herbert Morrison, *Government and Parliament: A Survey from the Inside*, Oxford, Oxford University Press, 3rd edn, 1964, still provides a useful overview.

Ministerial responsibility is excellently dealt with in several books: Birch, *Representative and Responsible Government*, Chapters, 10–13; Geoffrey Marshall (ed.), *Ministerial Responsibility*, Oxford, Oxford University Press, 1989; and Diana Woodhouse, *Ministers and Parliamentary Accountability in Theory and Practice*, Oxford, Clarendon Press, 1994.

Backbench dissent is similarly covered in a number of excellent studies: Robert J. Jackson, *Rebels and Whips: Dissension, Discipline and Cohesion in British Political Parties Since 1945*, London, Macmillan, 1968; Philip Norton, *Dissension in the House of Commons, 1945–74*, London, Macmillan, 1975; *Conservative Dissidents: Dissent within the Parliamentary Conservative Party, 1970–74*, London, Temple Smith, 1978; *Dissension in the House of Commons,*

1974–79, Oxford, Clarendon Press, 1980; and Philip Cowley, *Revolts and Rebellions: Parliamentary Voting Under Blair*, London, Politico's, 2002.

Chapter 12: Reforming Parliament

More has probably been written on the reform of Parliament than any other parliamentary topic, so that what follows is inevitably a selection, but it includes three older publications, partly because they still have highly pertinent things to say and partly to illustrate that a number of ideas for reform have a long pedigree. Bernard Crick's *The Reform of Parliament*, first published in 1963 is a touchstone, not because his proposals were unique but because his book played such a seminal part in subsequent developments. Much of the literature focuses exclusively on the House of Commons, but proposals for the reform of the House of Lords has resulted in much more attention being paid to the second chamber: The Hansard Society, *Parliamentary Reform: A Survey of Recent Proposals for the Commons*, London, Cassell, 3rd edn, 1967 (originally published 1961); David Judge, *The Politics of Parliamentary Reform*, London, Heinemann, 1983; John Garrett, *Westminster: Does Parliament Work?*, London, Gollancz, 1992; Stuart Weir and Tony Wright, *Power to the Backbenches: Restoring the Balance Between Parliament and Government*, London, Democratic Audit, 1996; Rodney Brazier, *Constitutional Reform: Reshaping the British Political System*, Oxford, Oxford University Press, 2nd edn, 1998; and Peter Riddell, *Parliament Under Blair*, London, Politico's, 2000. Robert Blackburn and Raymond Plant (eds), *Constitutional Reform: The Labour Government's Constitutional Reform Agenda*, London, Longman, 1999, usefully covers the post-1997 developments.

Charter 88, the Hansard Society and the Conservative Party have also produced significant reform proposals: Greg Power, *Reinventing Westminster: The MPs' Role and Reform of the House of Commons*, London, Charter 88, 1996; the Hansard Society, *Report of the Commission on Legislative Process: Making the Law*, London, 1992; Greg Power, *Creating a Working Parliament: Reform of the House of Commons*, London, Hansard Society, 2000; and the Conservative Party, *Report of the Commission to Strengthen Parliament: Strengthening Parliament*, London, 2000.

On the House of Lords, the *Report of the Royal Commission of the reform of the House of Lords: A House for the Future*, Cm. 4534, January 2000, may be seen as redundant, but it focuses clearly on the issues of second chamber reform, and Meg Russell, *Reforming the House of Lords: Lessons from Overseas*, Oxford, Oxford University Press, 2000, provides an excellent comparative perspective. However, as Ivor Richard and Damien Welfare point out Lords' reform is *Unfinished Business: Reforming the House of Lords*, London, Vintage, 1999, a view equally applicable to parliamentary reform in general and, indeed, to the study of Parliament.

Index

Note: 'n' after a page reference indicates the number of a note on that page

Abortion Law Reform Association 173, 259
Act of Settlement (1701) 3, 14, 38, 39
Acts of Parliament 13, 14, 18, 51, 60, 62, 67
Adonis, Andrew 231
Adoption and Children Bill 179–80
adversary system 22–4, 137–44, 180
Anne, Queen 39, 171
Anti-Corn Law League 255
Appropriations Bill 205
Aristotle 3, 71
Armed Forces Bill 181
Atkins, Humphrey 279
Attlee, Clement 50, 52, 191, 270, 309
Australia 3, 12, 15, 23, 82, 115, 134, 295, 311
Austria 115
authoritative texts, constitutional 20
authority 2–3, 24

Bagehot, Walter 18, 43, 45, 46
Baker, Kenneth 276, 278
Balfour, Arthur 41, 47, 152, 290
Ballot Act (1870) 41, 94
Barlow Clowes, collapse of (1988) 275
Beer, Samuel 284
Belgium 115
Bell, Martin 98, 101

Benn, Tony xiv, 125–6, 276, 279
Bill of Rights (1689) 21, 37
bills
  amendments 182, 183–5
  ballot 188
  carry-over of 182–3
  consolidation 68, 69, 173
  draft 175, 176
  government 171–87
  presentation 188
  private 161, 163, 167–9
  Private Members' (PMBs) 63, 159–73 *passim*, 180, 187–91, 192, 200, 247, 257
  public 161, 163, 169–91
  ten-minute rule 188
  timetabling of 54, 164, 185–6, 200
Blair, Tony 32, 53, 55, 75, 98, 106, 145, 210, 213, 261, 262, 263, 282, 283, 309
Blair government 53, 64, 172, 173, 174, 175, 197, 280, 301, 302
Bloodhound missile (1964) 276, 277
Blue Streak missile (1960) 276, 277
British Legion, Royal 255, 257
Brittan, Leon 274
Brown, Gordon 210
Brown, Nick 276, 277
BSE 276–7

Buckingham Palace intruder 275, 276
Budget, the 158, 159, 203, 204, 208–10, 239
Burke, Edmund 61, 95, 110, 244
Burt, Thomas 261
by-elections 73–4, 242
Byers, Stephen 274–5

Cabinet, the 36–7, 39, 43–6, 127, 175, 270, 271, 296
Callaghan, James 58, 278, 311
Campaign for Nuclear Disarmament (CND) 173, 256, 259
Campbell, Alastair 231
Canada 3, 12, 15, 23, 82, 106, 115, 134, 295, 303, 307, 311
candidates, selection of 96–100, 307
Carrington, Lord 274, 279–80
Catholic Association 255
Catholic Emancipation 255
Chancellor of the Exchequer 15, 28, 64, 126, 158, 203–10 *passim*, 239
Channon, Paul 277
Charles I 26, 34–5, 204, 270
Charles II 35–7
Chartists, the 41, 42, 114, 255
Child Support Agency 194, 235, 250
China, People's Republic of 8–12 *passim*
Churchill, Sir Winston 17, 32, 309
Clark, Alan 276
Clerk of the House of Commons 19, 20, 128
Clerk of the Parliaments 128, 129
collectivism 8–10
Committee of Supply 204
committee of the whole House 178–80, 204
Committee of Ways and Means 204
committees
    chairs, payment of 115
    critical reports by 235, 236
    grand (Commons) 170, 178
        see also Grand Committee (Lords); Northern Ireland Grand Committee; Scottish Grand Committee; Welsh Grand Committee

investigatory 225–37, 239–40, 281, 295, 300–1
legislative 178, 179–81, 191–9 *passim*, 295
second reading 170, 177, 179
select 150, 170, 175, 181, 230–7, 281
special standing 180–1
standing 141–2, 150, 170, 178, 179–81
Commons, House of *see* House of Commons
Companion to the Standing Orders (House of Lords) 20, 164
Comptroller and Auditor-General (C&AG) 207, 208
Confederation of British Industry 255
    see also employers' associations
Conservative MPs
    career patterns 119–25
    selection of 96–100
    socio-economic background of 101–6
Conservative Party 44, 45, 49, 51, 79–95 *passim*, 100–10 *passim*, 307
Consolidated Fund Bills 205, 223
consolidation bills *see* bills
constitutions 4–12, 309–10
    see also UK, constitution the
Convention Parliament (1689) 37
    see also Scottish Constitutional Convention
conventions, constitutional 13, 15–18, 268–9, 303
Cook, Robin 51, 276, 283
Co-operative Party 261, 262
Corn Laws 52, 255
Corrupt and Illegal Practices Act (1883) 41, 94, 114
Counsel to the Lord Chairman of Committees 194
Countryside Alliance 173, 266
Court Line case (1974) 276, 279
'Cranborne money' 133
Crichel Down Affair (1954) 274
Crick, Bernard 53, 59, 286, 291, 313
Criminal Justice and Public Order Bill 184

Criminal Law Review Committee 173
Cromwell, Oliver 35
crossbench peers *see* peers, crossbench
Crossman, Richard 45, 152
Crown Agents (1960s/1970s) 276, 277
Curia Regis 28, 29
Currie, Edwina 274
custom, constitutional 18–20

Dalton, Hugh 273
Dangerous Dogs Act (1991) 173
Davies, Ron 273–4
Declaration of Independence, American
      6–7
Declaration of Right (1689) 37, 38
Declaration of the Rights of Man (1789)
      7, 8
debates
   adjournment 161
   on the Budget 209, 210
   Commons 161, 162
   emergency 223–4
   initiation of 216–18, 221–3
   on legislation 169
   Lords 162
   ministerial responsibility 281
   nature of 143, 224, 239
   on Queen's Speech 158
   time spent on 159, 216
   unstarred Questions 163
   see also Opposition Days; Westminster
      Hall sittings
Delegated Powers and Regulatory
      Reform Committee (Lords) 70,
      115, 198
   see also Regulatory Reform Committee
      (Commons)
democracy
   definition of 71–9
   elections 79–95
   growth of 40–3
   Parliament 94–5, 110–12
De Montfort, Simon 28, 32
Deregulation and Regulatory Reform
      Committee (Commons) *see*
      Regulatory Reform Committee
      (Commons)
de Tocqueville, Alexis 71–2

devolution 14, 15, 21, 27, 74, 77, 172,
      175, 288, 294, 296, 305–6,
      308–9
   see also National Assembly for Wales;
      Northern Ireland Assembly;
      Scottish Parliament
Disraeli, Benjamin 32, 45, 47, 54
dissolution of Parliament 16, 82, 156,
      241, 301–11
Douglas-Home, Sir Alec 17, 126, 145
Dowse, Robert 246
Dugdale, Sir Thomas 274
Duncan Smith, Iain 145, 150

early day motions (EDMs) 224–5, 239,
      247
ECHR *see* European Convention on
      Human Rights (ECHR)
Economic Affairs Committee (Lords)
      203, 210
e-democracy 76, 246
Eden, Sir Anthony 17
Edward I 32–3
Edward II 33
elections 41–3, 72–4, 79–95, 241–2,
      310–11
electoral behaviour 88–95
electoral reform 79–81, 294, 306–7
Electoral Reform Society 255
electoral systems 73, 79–88
Elizabeth I 34
emergency debates *see* debates
employers' associations 254
Environmental Audit Committee 115,
      227, 301
Environmental Pollution, Royal
      Commission on 172
Erskine May, Sir Thomas 19, 20
estimates 204–7
Estimates Committee 206, 226
Estimates Days 234
European Convention on Human Rights
      (ECHR) 8, 9, 21, 172, 175, 187,
      289, 304
European Elections Act (1999) 14, 55,
      182
European Parliament 74, 81, 87, 98,
      121, 242, 299–300

European Scrutiny Committee
(Commons) 115, 198–9
European Union (EU) 21, 52, 53, 172,
198–9, 200, 226, 308–9
European Union Committee (Lords)
198–9, 227
European Union legislation 168, 198–9,
299–300
excess votes 205, 206
Exchange Rate Mechanism (ERM),
Britain's withdrawal from (1992)
53, 276, 278
executive dominance 40–56 *passim*
expenditure, scrutiny of 204–8
Expenditure, Select Committee on 206,
226
ex-servicemen's associations 255

Falconer, Lord 276
Falklands, invasion of (1982) 274, 276,
279–80
federalism 11, 22, 27, 305–6
Finance Bill 161n, 181, 184, 203, 209,
210, 211, 229, 239
Firearms (Amendment) Act (1997)
174
First Lord of the Treasury *see* Prime
Minister
fixed-term elections 82, 310–11
Foot, Michael 53
foot-and-mouth disease (2001) 276,
277
France 4, 6–12 *passim*, 82, 115, 134,
164, 295, 304
Freedom of Information Act (2000) 14,
289–90
fuel crisis (1947) 276, 277

George I 26, 39
George II 26, 39
George III 4, 39–40
Germany 8–12 *passim*, 31, 82, 83, 106,
116, 166, 295, 298, 303
Gladstone, W. E. 32, 47, 54, 58, 145,
203, 207, 290
Glorious Revolution (1688–89) 37,
270
'golden age of Parliament' 43–6

government
composition of 63–4
control of the House of Commons
43–8, 137–8, 200, 265, 286,
290
defeats in House of Commons 283,
284–5
growth of 51–2, 113
relationship with Parliament 268–9
Government Chief Whip (Commons)
(Parliamentary Secretary to the
Treasury) 117, 149, 152–3,
165n
Government Chief Whip (Lords) 117,
149, 154–5
Grand Committee (Lords) 168, 178,
179
Greater London Assembly 80, 81, 306,
307
Green Papers 168, 174
Griffith, John 183, 186
groundnuts scheme (1949) 276, 277

Habeas Corpus Act (1679) 14, 35
Hague, William 145
Halifax, Lord 17
Hamilton, Alexander 4
Hansard (Official Report) 65, 122, 215,
245, 247
Hansard reporters 140, 142, 143
Hansard Society 51
Hansard Society survey of MPs 65, 119,
124–5, 237, 245, 250, 253
Hansard Society Commission on the
Legislative Process 197
Heath, Edward 15, 17, 53, 150, 309
Heffer, Eric 281
Henry I 28, 29
Henry II 28
Henry V 31
Henry VII 34
Henry VIII 26, 31, 34
'Henry VIII clauses' 198
Heseltine, Michael 283
Hobbes, Thomas 2
Hola Camp (1959) 276, 277
Hoon, Geoff 276, 280
House Committee (Lords) 129

House of Commons
  business, distribution of 159–60
  Chamber 138, 139, 141, 143, 159
  control of 43–8, 137–8, 200, 265,
    286, 290
  financial supremacy of 33, 157
  financing of 134–5, 298
  functions of 59–65
  House of Lords 21, 24, 28, 33,
    49–50, 173, 177, 181–5, 200
  Leader of 51, 152, 153, 165n
  legislative scrutiny 62–3, 167–200
    passim, 299–300
  meeting place 31, 128
  ministers in 124–5
  organisation of 137–8, 152–62,
    297–8
  origins and early development 28–34
  party organisation in 144–52
  privileges 19–20
  procedure 162–5
  redress of grievances 28, 35, 62
  scrutiny role 64–5, 203–40 *passim*
  sittings of 51, 156–62, 297–8
  staff 131
  standing orders 51, 164
  taxation 28, 35
  time, allocation of 137–8
  timetable
    daily 160–2
    weekly 160–2
    yearly 156–60
  see also committees; debates
House of Commons Commission 129
House of Commons Library 131, 133
House of Fraser takeover bid (1987–90)
    276, 277
House of Lords
  abolition and restoration 35–6
  activity of 69–70
  business, distribution of 159–60
  Chamber 140, 141, 158
  composition of 54–5, 106–10,
    110–12
  control of 49–50, 55, 138, 200
  financial scrutiny 203, 210, 300
  financing of 134–5
  functions of 59–70 *passim*, 165

House of Commons 21, 24, 28, 33,
    49–50, 173, 177, 181–5, 200
  Leader of 64, 126, 153, 154
  legislative scrutiny 62–3, 167–200
    passim
  ministers in 63–4, 126–7
  organisation of 137–8, 152–62, 163,
    297–8
  origins and early development 28–34
  Prime Minister 17, 64, 126
  procedure 162–5
  reform of 49–50, 54–5, 111, 289, 302
  scrutiny role 54–6, 64–5, 203–40
    passim
  second chambers, compared with
    other 106, 115–16, 128, 134–5,
    297
  staff 133
  standing orders 164
  time, allocation of 138
  timetable
    daily 162, 163
    weekly 162, 163
    yearly 156–60
  see also committees; debates; Parliament
    Acts (1911 and 1949)
House of Lords Act (1999) 14, 55, 126
House of Lords Library 133
House of Lords, Royal Commission on
    Reform of (Wakeham
    Commission) 55, 172, 297
House of Lords, Working Group on the
    Practices of 165, 197
Howard, Michael 145, 276, 278
Howarth, Alan 98
Hughes, Beverley 274–5, 278
Human Rights Act (1998) 14, 21, 175,
    227, 268
Human Rights, Joint Committee on 115,
    227

impeachment 5, 19, 28, 34, 270
initiative, the 72, 74–6, 308
IRA prisoners, escape of (1982 and
    1991) 276, 277–8
Iraq
  arms to (1988–90) 276, 280
  dossier on (2003–04) 280

Ireland 38, 41, 83, 115, 116, 307
  see also Northern Ireland
Irish Nationalists 46
Israel 12, 86, 304, 307
Italy 115, 166

James I 34, 204, 270
James II 26, 37
Jamieson, David 187
Japan 115, 295
Jenkins Commission 81, 306
John, King 28, 30, 32
judicial review 20–1, 77–8

Kelly, Dr David (2003–4) 172, 276,
    280–1
Kinnock, Neil 53

Labour MPs
  career patterns 119–25
  selection 96–100
  socio-economic background of 101–6
Labour Party 46, 50, 79–95 *passim*,
    100–10 *passim*, 114, 289, 307
Labour Representation Committee 27,
    97, 260
Liaison Committee (Commons) 50–1,
    235, 291–2
Liaison Committee (Lords) 227
Lamont, Norman 276, 278
Lasswell, Harold 1–2
Law Commission 172–3
Law Lords 59, 125
League Against Cruel Sports 173, 259
Legalise Cannabis Alliance 253
legislation
  delegated *see* legislation, secondary
  Parliament 62–3, 166, 199–200,
    299–300
  primary 63, 167, 168, 202, 299
  private 46, 51–2, 62–3, 161, 163,
    167, 168
  public 46, 62–3, 167
  secondary 63, 159, 191, 193–9, 202,
    295, 299
  timetabling 54, 164, 185–6, 200,
    218, 290, 291, 292
  types of 62–3, 167, 168

legislatures, types of 168
legitimacy 2, 31–2, 34, 60, 111, 182
Lennox-Boyd, Alan 276, 277
Lever, Harold 231
Liberal Democratic Party 83–95 *passim*,
    100–10 *passim*, 153–4, 155,
    307
Liberal/Liberal Democrat MPs
  career patterns 119–25
  selection of 96–100
  socio-economic background of
    96–100
Liberal Party 44, 45, 49, 52, 81, 83,
    114, 154, 307
libertarianism 8–10
Life Peerages Act (1958) 14, 68, 69,
    107, 125, 126, 132, 290
Lloyd, Tony 276, 278
Lloyd George, David 32, 49
lobbyists, professional *see* political
    consultants
Locke, John 2, 3, 6, 71
Lord Chancellor 64, 116, 117, 126,
    128, 164, 313
Lord Great Chamberlain 128–9
Lords, House of *see* House of Lords
Luce, Richard 279
Lyell, Sir Nicholas 276, 280

Macdonald, Alexander 261
Macmillan, Harold 17, 52, 126, 242, 283
Madison, James 4
Magna Carta 30–1
Major, John 53, 74, 84–5, 150, 173,
    175, 221, 241, 278, 280, 309
Mandelson, Peter 273, 276
Maudling, Reginald 263
May, Sir Thomas Erskine *see* Erskine
    May, Sir Thomas
Melbourne, Lord 281
Members' Interests, Register of 262,
    263–4
Members of Parliament
  age 105–6
  allowances 129–30
  backbench 118–19, 122–3, 187–91,
    192, 215–16, 216–17, 221–5,
    247, 262, 284–6, 296–7

backbench dissent 284–6
career patterns 119–25
class background 105–6, 260–2
Code of Conduct 263, 270, 292
constituency role 243–53, 307
educational background 102–3
ethnic minority 106
frontbench 118–19, 122–5, 215–16
full-time 118–19, 160
ministerial office 124–5
number 294–6
occupational background 103–5
office accommodation 130–1
parliamentary activity 122–4,
     215–17, 223–4, 246–8
payment of 114–16, 129, 293,
     297
pressure politics 243–64
professionalisation of 114–25,
     129–30, 132
role of 53–4, 65–7, 293–5
sponsored 260–2
staff 129–30
views on Parliament 65–7, 237–8
women 41, 100
Miliband, David 98
Miliband, Ed 231
Mill, John Stuart 42, 57–8, 71–2, 79
Millennium Dome (1997–2001) 236,
     276, 277
Ministerial Code 270, 271
ministerial responsibility
   collective 15, 46, 278, 281–6
   definition 269–71, 272
   development of 46
   individual 15, 46, 271–81
ministerial statements 161, 163,
     218–19, 239
ministers
   correspondence with MPs 248
   number 124–5
   parliamentary activity 123
   payment of 115, 116–18
   recruitment of 63–4, 151
   resignation 273–5, 282–3
   special advisers 231–2
   see also ministerial responsibility
'Model Parliament' (1295) 28, 32

Modernisation, Select Committee on
     165, 186, 207, 313
monarchy, role of 26–40 *passim*
   see also Queen, the
Montesquieu, Baron de 3–4
Moore, Jo 275
Morris, Estelle 274

NAO see National Audit Office (NAO)
National Assembly for Wales 27, 74,
     80, 84, 99, 121, 122, 135, 156,
     191, 201n, 242, 294, 295, 298,
     302, 305–6, 307, 311
National Audit Office (NAO) 207–8,
     233, 300
National Farmers' Union (NFU) 255,
     262
Nationalised Industries, Select
     Committee on 226
National Union of Teachers (NUT) 262
Netherlands, the 39, 83, 86, 166, 307
New Zealand 3, 12, 15, 23, 82, 87,
     295, 311
Nolan Committee see Standards in
     Public Life, Committee on (Nolan
     Committee)
non-departmental bodies (NDPBs) 208
North, Lord 40, 244
Northern Ireland 21, 27, 39, 305, 306,
     307, 308
   see also devolution
Northern Ireland Act (1998) 14
Northern Ireland Assembly 39, 80, 81,
     121, 135, 311
Northern Ireland Grand Committee 177,
     222
Norton, Philip 251–2
Nott, John 276, 279, 280

O'Connell, Daniel 255
ombudsman systems 72, 78
   see also Parliamentary Ombudsman
opinion polls 72, 76, 311
Opposition Chief Whip (Commons) 115,
     117, 152–3
Opposition Chief Whip (Lords) 117, 155
Opposition Days 204, 219–21, 224
   see also Supply Days

Opposition, Leader of (Commons) 17, 115, 116, 117, 128, 131–2
Opposition, Leader of (Lords) 117, 152
opposition, official 17, 23–4, 47–9
Orders in Council 63, 168

Page, Edward C. 195, 197
Palmerston, Lord 44
Parkhurst prison escapes (1995) 276, 278
Parliament Acts (1911 and 1949) 14, 21, 41, 49–50, 54, 55, 68–9, 182, 241
Parliamentary Commissioner for Standards (PCS) 263, 292
parliamentary control, concept of 57–9, 286
parliamentary government
    concept of 2–3, 268–9
    development of 26–8
    devolution 305–6
    in eighteenth century 39–42, 160
    in nineteenth century 42–6, 157, 290–2
    under Tudors and Stuarts 34–9, 160
    in twentieth century 46–56, 157, 290–2
    in UK 12–24
Parliamentary Ombudsman 78, 226, 248, 249–50, 275, 279
    see also ombudsman systems
Parliamentary Private Secretaries (PPSs) 124, 151, 281, 296
parliamentary Questions
    cross-cutting 301
    government refusal to answer 215
    'inspired' 213, 219
    ministerial responsibility 281
    MPs' use of 213, 214, 215–16, 247
    number of 211, 213, 214–15
    for oral answer 211–12, 213, 214, 292
    Private Notice 163, 213, 214, 239
    purpose of 238–9, 240
    starred (Lords) 213, 214
    supplementary 213
    unstarred (Lords) *see* debates
    Urgent (Commons) 161, 213, 214

for written answer 211–12, 213, 214–15, 216
Parliamentary Secretary to the Treasury *see* Government Chief Whip (Commons)
parliamentary supremacy 21–2
Parliament, Scottish *see* Scottish Parliament
parties, political
    pressure groups 253–4
    see also party cohesion; party system; *individual names*
party cohesion 44–6, 149–52, 269, 284–6
party system 22–4, 36, 40–6, 53, 84–9, 253–4, 269
passport delays (1999) 236, 275
Peel, Sir Robert 58, 255
Peerages Act (1963) 14, 125–6
peers
    allowances 132–3
    attendance 127, 132
    career patterns 125–8
    crossbench 55, 107, 149
    educational background 108
    hereditary 55, 106–7
    life 55, 106–9
    ministerial office 126–7
    occupational background 108–9
    office accommodation 133
    party affiliation 55, 106–8
    pressure politics 258, 259–60, 264
    role of 293–5
    unpaid 115–16, 134–5, 297
Peers' Interests, Register of 264
petitions 33, 161, 242–3
Pitt the Younger, William 32, 40
Plant Commission on the electoral system 81
Plato 71
policy, Parliament 202–3, 286
political consultants 256, 262–4
Political Parties and Referendums Act (2000) 14, 94, 181, 310
politics
    defining 1–6
    theory and practice 6–10, 24
Poulson, John 263

Powell, Jonathan 231
power 2–6, 24, 71
PRC *see* China, People's Republic of
Pre-Budget Report 158, 205, 206,
    208–9, 210, 239
pressure groups
    early 254–5
    growth of 256–7
    number of 257
    see also employers' associations;
        ex-servicemen's associations;
        pressure politics; trade unions;
        individual names
pressure politics 72, 77, 173,
    253–64
primary legislation *see* legislation
Prime Minister
    appointment of 15, 16, 17, 47
    in House of Lords 17, 126
    as Leader of the House of Commons
        165n
    ministerial responsibility 270, 278,
        282–3
    origins and development of office 40,
        46
    power of 22, 241, 310–11
    resignation of 15, 17, 269
    role of 15
    salary 116, 117
Prime Minister's Questions (PMQs)
        138–9, 143, 211–13, 237, 238,
        291, 292
Prior, James 276, 277
Private Members' bills (PMBs) *see*
    bills
Private Notice Questions (PNQs) *see*
    parliamentary Questions
procedure, significance of 162–5
Procedure Committee, Select Committee
    on (Commons) 164, 197, 226
Procedure Committee, Select Committee
    on (Lords) 226
Profumo, John 273
proportional representation (PR) *see*
    electoral systems
Provisional Collection of Taxes Act
    (1968) 209, 210
Public Accounts Commission 207–8

Public Accounts Committee (PAC) 115,
    131, 207–8, 211, 225, 227,
    232, 239, 300
Public Administration Committee 115,
    227, 232, 301
Public Expenditure, White Paper on
    205, 206
public opinion
    elections 241–2
    legislation 173–4
    on MPs 311–12
    on Parliament 264–6
Public Service Agreements (PSAs)
    204–5

Queen, the 15–16 *passim*, 158
Queen's Speech (Speech from the
    Throne) 158, 171, 175
Questions *see* parliamentary Questions
Question Time (Commons) 159, 161,
    162, 164, 211–13, 214, 238–9,
    301
Question Time (Lords) 159, 162, 163,
    164, 214, 235

recall 72, 74–6
Referendum Party 253
referendums 72, 74–6, 308–10
reform, parliamentary
    context of 290–2
    external 302–11
    internal 293–302
    and the political system 288–90
    post-1997 291–311
Reform Act (1832) 41, 42–3, 44, 51,
    97, 290
Reform Act (1867) 41, 44, 290
Reform Act (1884) 41, 45, 290
Reformation, the 34, 35
Regulatory Reform Committee
    (Commons) 115, 197
    see also Delegated Powers and
        Regulatory Reform Committee
        (Lords)
representation 40–3, 60–1, 110–12,
    294–6
Resource Accounting and Budgeting
    206–7

Rhodesia, sanctions against (1965–70) 279
Richard III 26
rights 6–10, 78–9
  see also European Convention on Human Rights (ECHR)
Rousseau, Jean-Jacques 2, 7, 241
Rover car company, sale of (1989) 276
royal assent 18, 38, 126, 169, 170, 171, 174, 178
royal commissions 172–3
royal prerogative 13, 18, 47, 60, 63
Royal Society for the Prevention of Cruelty to Animals (RSCPA) 254, 255
rule of law 29, 72, 77

Salisbury, Lord 17, 47
'Salisbury doctrine' (Salisbury Convention) 50, 182
Scotland 38, 39, 111, 305–6
  see also devolution
Scotland Act (1998) 14
Scott, Sir Nicholas 189, 278
Scottish Constitutional Convention 288
Scottish Grand Committee 177, 222
Scottish Parliament 27, 38, 39, 74, 80, 84, 99, 121, 122, 135, 156, 177, 201n, 242, 234, 295, 298, 302, 305–6, 307, 311
secondary legislation *see* legislation
second chambers *see* House of Lords
Senior Salaries Review Body (SSRB) 114–15, 116, 118, 129
separation of powers 3–6, 43, 304
Sexual Offences (Amendment) Act (2000) 55, 182
Shadow Cabinet 145, 146
Shinwell, Emmanuel 276
Short, Clare 283
'Short money' 131
Sierra Leone, arms to (1998) 235, 276, 278
Smith, Chris 276
Smith, John 53
Social Democratic Party 91–2

Society for the Protection of Unborn Children 173, 256
South Africa 3
Soviet Union (USSR) 8–12 *passim*
Spain 8–12 *passim*, 31, 115
Speaker 16, 115, 116, 117, 164, 204, 213, 215, 313
Speaker, Deputy 115, 116, 117, 128, 129
Speaker's Counsel 194
Speech from the Throne *see* Queen's Speech (Speech from the Throne)
Speed, Keith 281
Standards in Public Life, Committee on (Nolan Committee) 260, 261, 262, 263, 264
standing committees *see* committees
standing orders *see* House of Commons; House of Lords
  see also Companion to the Standing Orders (House of Lords)
State Earnings-Related Pension Scheme (SERPS) 236, 276, 277
statements, ministerial *see* ministerial statements
statutes, constitutional 13–15
Statutory Instruments, Joint Committee on 115, 194–8, 210
statutory instruments (SIs) 63, 163, 167, 168, 191, 193–8, 201n
Strachey, John 276
Straw, Jack 276
Study of Parliament Group 53, 125, 256
Supply Days 204, 219
  see also Opposition Days
Sweden 78, 86
Switzerland 115, 309

taxation, scrutiny of 208–10
Tax Law Rewrite, Joint Committee on 180, 210
Taylor, Richard 101
Thatcher, Margaret 32, 53, 91, 150, 173, 253, 279
Thorpe, Jeremy 17
Top Salaries Review Body (TSRB) *see* Senior Salaries Review Body
Tories 36, 37, 44
Trades Union Congress (TUC) 254, 262

trade unions 104–5, 114, 154, 173,
  254, 256–7, 260–2
Triennial Acts 34, 37–8, 82

UK constitution, the 12–24, 268–9,
  303–4
  see also constitutions
United Kingdom Independence Party
  (UKIP) 253–4
United States 4–12 *passim*, 15, 22, 43,
  72–3, 115, 134, 268, 270, 295,
  304, 309
Urgent Questions *see* parliamentary
  Questions
USSR *see* Soviet Union
'usual channels, the' 16, 23, 48, 144,
  149, 151, 152–6, 179, 185,
  217, 218, 219, 221, 227

Vehicle and General Insurance (1971)
  276, 277
'votes' 206
votes on account 205, 206
  see also excess votes

Wakeham Commission *see* House of
  Lords, Royal Commission on the
  Reform of the

Waldegrave, William 276, 280
Wales 35, 111, 305–6
  see also devolution
Wales, National Assembly for *see*
  National Assembly for Wales
Wales Act (1998) 14
Walpole, Sir Robert 38, 39, 40
War Crimes Bill (1990) 54
Washington, George 7, 15
Weber, Max 2, 31
Welsh Grand Committee 177, 222
Westminster, Palace of 128–9, 130–1
Westminster Hall sittings 64, 138,
  142–4, 160, 162, 221, 222–3,
  234–5, 291, 295–6, 301
Whigs 36, 37, 44
'whip, the' 146–7
whips 146–52
Whitelaw, William 275, 276
White Papers 170, 174–5, 218–19
William I 29, 31
William II 37
Wilson, Harold 17, 53, 186, 231, 278,
  279, 291, 309
Witanagemot 28, 29
Woodward, Shaun 98

Young, Lord 276